Paragons of Virtue: Women and Domesticity in Seventeenth-Century Dutch Art is the first systematic analysis of paintings of domestic themes, which were among the most popular and endearing images produced by Dutch artists during the Golden Age. Focusing on their broader function and significance within Dutch culture, this study has made extensive use of sixteenth- and seventeenth-century family treatises that are important sources for understanding these paintings. These hortatory texts are significant because they reflect contemporary attitudes toward women as they are paradigmatically presented as maidens, as housewives skilled in the administration of household affairs, as attentive mothers, and as pious widows. In short, family literature corroborates the existence of general ideals as well as specific ideas about women and domesticity as expressed through art. Through its rich source material and the paintings themselves, *Paragons of Virtue* sheds further light on the position of women in seventeenth-century Dutch society and on the critical role that art played in early modern Europe in espousing and maintaining the patriarchal status quo.

Paragons of Virtue

Paragons of Virtue

Women and Domesticity in Seventeenth-Century Dutch Art

Wayne E. Franits
Syracuse University

CAMBRIDGE
UNIVERSITY PRESS

Published by the Press Syndicate of the University of Cambridge
The Pitt Building, Trumpington Street, Cambridge CB2 1RP
40 West 20th Street, New York, NY 10011-4211, USA
10 Stamford Road, Oakleigh, Melbourne 3166, Australia

First published 1993

First paperback edition 1995

Printed in the United States of America

Publication of this book has been aided by a grant from
The Millard Meiss Publication Fund of the College Art Association of America.

Library of Congress Cataloging-in-Publication Data

Franits, Wayne E.
Paragons of virtue : women and domesticity in seventeenth-century
Dutch art / Wayne E. Franits.
p. cm.
ISBN 0-521-43129-8 (hbk.) ISBN 0-521-49875-9 (pbk.)
1. Women in art. 2. Genre painting, Dutch. 3. Genre
painting – 17th century – Netherlands. I. Title.
ND1452.3.N4F73 1993
754'.09492'09032 – dc20 92-23436

A catalog record for this book is available from the British Library.

ISBN 0-521-43129-8 hardback
ISBN 0-521-49875-9 paperback

This book is lovingly
dedicated to
Linnéa
who, with much forbearance,
has taught me the true meaning
of domestic bliss

CONTENTS

ILLUSTRATIONS

ACKNOWLEDGMENTS

This book began as a doctoral dissertation that was submitted to the faculty of the Institute of Fine Arts, New York University, in February 1987. Since the early 1980s, when I first began my research, the fields to which it is germane, namely, Dutch seventeenth-century art, women's studies, and social history, have undergone sweeping changes. Therefore, my initial intention to make only a few, minor changes in the dissertation manuscript before submitting it for publication had to be abandoned. Changes in these disciplines made it incumbent upon me to conduct further research and to expand and revise the original dissertation completely.

Both the dissertation and the present book owe an enormous debt to many individuals and institutions who gave generously of their time and resources. First and foremost I wish to thank my friend and mentor Egbert Haverkamp-Begemann. It was he who first suggested that I investigate the topic of domesticity in Dutch art and, over the years, has continued to provide advice, encouragement, and support on a scale that he cannot possibly realize. My heartfelt thanks are also extended to Dr. and Mrs. Alfred Bader, whose generous financial assistance enabled me to conduct research in the Netherlands from 1984 to 1986 and to finish the dissertation project in New York. In the intervening years, when it became apparent that further research abroad was needed, the National Endowment for the Humanities provided a summer stipend (1988) for this purpose. The Syracuse University Senate Committee on Research also contributed funds for one final research trip to the Netherlands for this project during the summer of 1990.

I am also grateful for the assistance of staff members from a large number of libraries, museums, and related institutions. In particular, I would like to thank the staff members of the Rijksbureau voor Kunsthistorisch Documentatie (The Hague), Witt Library of the Courtauld Institute of Art (London), The Frick Art Reference Library (New York), Rijksprentenkabinet (Amsterdam), Albertina (Vienna), and Gemeentelijk Archief (Amsterdam), and those of the libraries of the University of Amsterdam, University of Utrecht, University of Leiden, Institute of Fine Arts, Cornell University, Harvard University, New Brunswick Theological Seminary, New York University, Princeton University, Syracuse University, Yale University, and finally, those of the Koninklijke Bibliotheek (The Hague), Herzog-August-Bibliothek (Wolfenbüttel), New York Public Library, and the Library of The Metropolitan Museum of Art.

The contributions of many friends and colleagues must not go unnoticed. Among those who have provided valuable advice and insights were Jan Baptist Bedaux, Marten Jan Bok, Josua Bruyn, Rudolf Dekker, Stephanie Dickey, Thomas Döring, Jeroen Giltay, Peter Hecht, Elizabeth Honig, Michael Hoyle, Guido Jansen, Eddy de Jongh, Alison Kettering, Jennifer Kilian, Kitty Kilian, Katy Kist, Gerbrand Kotting, Maria Leuker, Machteld Löwensteyn, Dietmar Lüdke, Volker Manuth, J. A. L. de Meijere, Hessel Miedema, Sir Oliver Millar, Lawrence W. Nichols, Rob Ruurs, Robert Scheller, Larry Silver, Leonard J. Slatkes, Eric Jan Sluijter, David Smith, P. J. J. van Thiel, and John Wilson. Special thanks are owed to H. Perry Chapman, Laurinda Dixon, Egbert Haverkamp-Begemann, Alison Kettering, and Herman Roodenburg for patiently reading earlier mutations of the revised text. I have also benefited enormously in this regard from the assistance of Elizabeth Allen. The English translations of the seventeenth-century Dutch texts that I quote were ably provided by Hans Luitjen, Johanna Prins, Yopie Prins, and Herman Roodenburg. I also wish to thank the editors of *Simiolus* and the *Leids Kunsthistorisch Jaarboek* for permission to reproduce material first published in their journals. I must also acknowledge Beatrice Rehl of Cambridge University Press whose timely and infectious enthusiasm for this project sustained me when my own patience and zeal to guide it to fruition had waned considerably.

Finally, for their unflinching moral support, I wish to thank my parents, Edward and Theresa Franits; my wife, Linnéa Franits; Herbert H. Westphalen III; and several colleagues at Syracuse University: Laurinda Dixon, Amanda Porterfield, Gary Radke, and Dennis Romano.

Cazenovia, New York
December 1991

INTRODUCTION

The Lace-Maker by Caspar Netscher is one of the most endearing images of seventeenth-century Dutch life (Fig. 1). Netscher's picture is small but nonetheless charming; a modestly dressed young woman makes lace within a spartan interior whose only adornment is a print crudely nailed to the cracked plaster wall. She is diligently absorbed in her task, as her intently focused gaze suggests. She is also turned at a slight angle toward the wall, a position that effectively eliminates any interaction between subject and viewer. Pose, expression, and attire combine here to offer a compelling construction of ideal femininity and domesticity. The reasons for this picture's popularity today, and that of dozens of similar paintings of domestic subjects, undoubtedly reside in what we perceive as their typical "Dutch" characteristics: they have a peculiar charm and modesty as they provide a vision of the centrality of domestic life in a long-vanished, democratic society.

The book before you examines representations like Netscher's, namely, images of domestic virtue in Dutch seventeenth-century genre painting. By "images of domestic virtue," I mean works of art that represent women in a variety of wholesome situations, most of which pertain to the home and the family.[1] Such paintings were equally popular in the seventeenth-century Dutch Republic; therefore, my interest is in how they functioned within that culture. I do not regard these representations of domesticity as neutral reportage, for my study is grounded in the assumption that the paintings were carriers of cultural significance, that they shaped and in turn were shaped by a firmly established system of beliefs and values about women that were endorsed within the patriarchal social order of the day.

In the past twenty-five years, art historians have made enormous strides in the interpretation of seventeenth-century Dutch art, but too often their efforts have been restricted to works that are thought to depict vice.[2] Representations of virtuous subjects have been neglected by comparison. This is

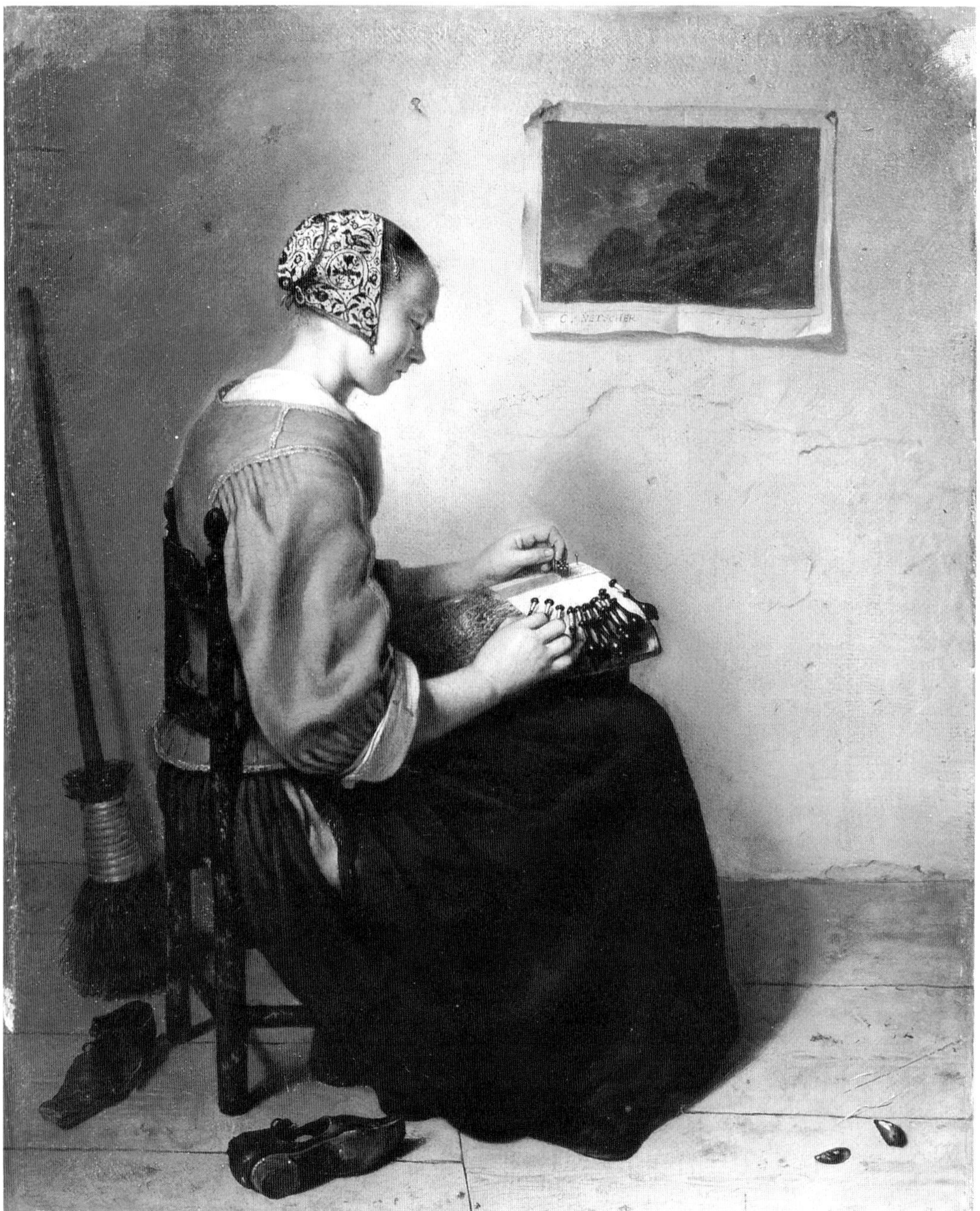

Figure 1. Caspar Netşcher, *The Lace-Maker*, 1662 (oil on canvas, 34 × 28 cm). London, Wallace Collection. Photo: Wallace Collection.

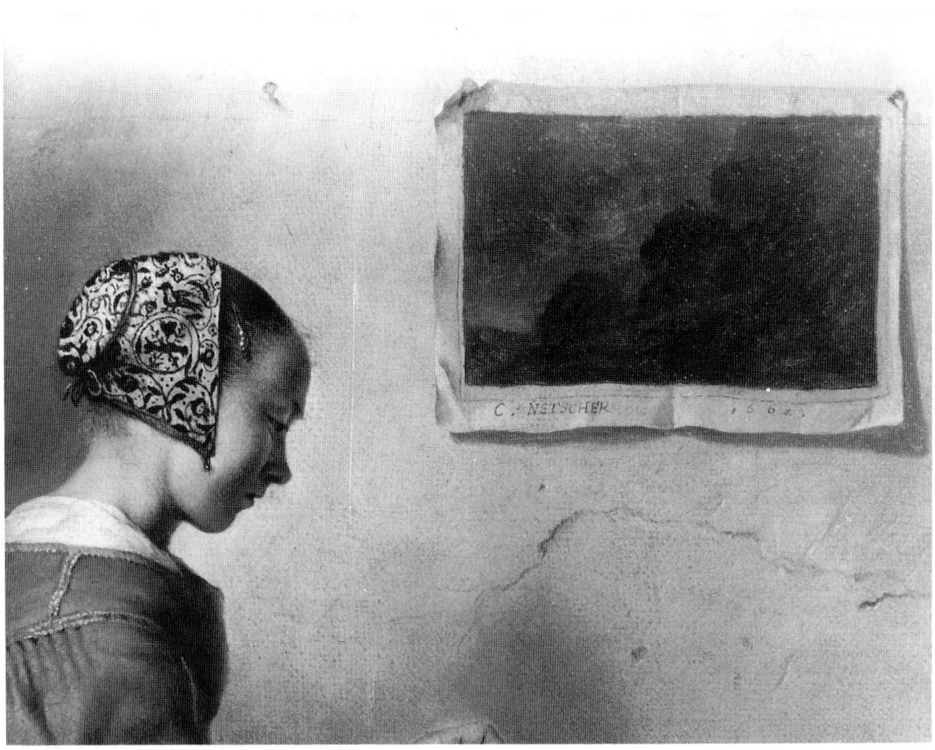

Figure 1a. Detail of Figure 1.

especially true of domestic imagery; indeed, the only scholar to address this subject in any detail was not an art historian but a historian, namely, Simon Schama in his ambitious book *The Embarrassment of Riches* (1987).[3] Schama's lucid, anthropologically informed study is no mere survey of epic events that occurred during the seventeenth century in the Dutch Republic. To the contrary, the author attempts to define and explore the Dutch *mentalité* of the period, which, he argues, revolved around the dialectical play of inherent tensions between piety and morality, on the one hand, and unprecedented prosperity and materialism, on the other.[4] The Dutch celebration of domesticity and "obsession" with cleanliness is placed squarely within this construct: " 'Home' existed in the Dutch mentality in a kind of dialectical polarity with 'world,' and in particular the street, which brought the mire of the world, literally, to its doorstep. . . . The struggle between worldliness and homeliness was but another variation on the classic Dutch counterpoint between materialism and morality."[5]

In his chapters on women and children, Schama examines a limited number of paintings of domestic virtue as documents of contemporary Dutch culture. His analyses, skillfully interwoven with interpretations of domestic literature, are sensitive and, indeed, remarkably refreshing, particularly when compared to those by other historians who have treated art as documentary evidence. Moreover, his approach of relating depictions of virtuous women with those representing their antipode, vice, is intriguing.[6] Nevertheless, just as in other chapters in his book, Schama's focus here on polarities that purportedly reflect greater tensions within Dutch culture is not always convincing. At times his theses even appear somewhat forced, particularly his argument that the concepts of virtue and vice existed in some sort of symbiotic relationship, where contemporaries adjudged, inter alia, brothels as "anti-homes" whose squalor and general immorality inverted the domestic norms of cleanliness, sobriety, and moderation.[7]

Despite the importance and value of Schama's study, to date a systematic study of domestic subjects within Dutch art as a whole is still lacking.[8] Deeper insights into these works can only be gained by examining a significant number of thematically related groups of pictures. This approach is valuable, yet it is important to note its inherent, if not inevitable, pitfalls. Any attempt to define seventeenth-century attitudes toward women and domesticity that are mirrored in contemporary art is hazardous, if only for the passage of three centuries' time. This is compounded by an unavoidable element of subjectivity that affects both the selection of themes and the interpretation of individual paintings. Despite these drawbacks, the themes considered here do facilitate our understanding of domestic subjects in Dutch art and of the culture that created them.

Any study of domestic virtue, particularly one devoted to its expression in Dutch seventeenth-century genre painting, is a study about women. The principal occupations for females at this time – at least for women belonging to the elite – the ones for which they were ordained at birth, were housewifery and motherhood. Therefore, it is no mere coincidence that so many paintings show women engaged in a variety of tasks that were intrinsic to these offices, among them sewing and spinning, the supervision of servants, the care of their children, and the like. Such paintings are best understood in connection with other, related forms of art that also provide access to widespread beliefs concerning women and domesticity.

Among these related forms of art are prints and portraits. Prints, especially those with inscriptions, are particularly revealing; owing to their relatively low price and wide availability, they serve as an accurate barometer of the outlook of a considerable segment of society at that time. However, they must be examined with caution because their inscriptions sometimes stray from the artists' original intentions.[9] Nevertheless, they can provide insights into the types of associations that viewers attached to domestic imagery.

Contemporary portraiture is also illuminating as it frequently includes motifs that refer to the sitter and to her station and role in life.[10] In no other genre do we find such a quintessential expression of the ideals and aspirations of the upper strata of society who could afford to have themselves portrayed. Prints and portraits, highly traditional tools of interpretation, thus furnish ample information from both ends of the social spectrum about seventeenth-century concepts of womanhood and domesticity.

I have also utilized another rich body of source material, one largely neglected by art historians. It is axiomatic that depictions of domestic themes must also be perceived in relation to contemporary familial ideals. Since these were largely fostered by and reflected in contemporary literature, sixteenth- and seventeenth-century books pertaining to women and the family are especially enlightening. Yet it would be misleading to posit one-to-one correspondences between motifs in paintings and particular texts; their relationship is not the same as one finds, for example, between a narrative text from the Bible and the iconography of a painting depicting that specific episode. Paintings and treatises both present an ideal, yet theoretically imitable female, well trained to administer the household and to care for children. The relationship between family literature and domestic themes in art may even extend to the shared use of metaphors that refer to ideal feminine virtues and domesticity. However, it is most accurate to view domestic imagery in art as visually analogous to the prescriptions of contemporary authors and their elucidation of the roles and duties of women (and other family members as well).

In fact, the importance for Dutch art of one particular seventeenth-century family book has long been known: Jacob Cats's *Houwelyck* (Marriage), first published in 1625.[11] Anyone who still doubts its relevance to the study of Dutch art need only look at the *Portrait of a Family* by an anonymous artist active within the circle of Thomas de Keyser (Fig. 2). Seldom have the links between art and literature been more decisively demonstrated than in this portrait in which the *materfamilias* holds a copy of the first edition of *Houwelyck,* opened to page seventy-two of the chapter entitled "Vrouwe" (Housewife; Fig. 2a).

Cats may not have been the most gifted poet of his day, but to cite Eddy de Jongh's witty and perceptive observation, "if there were a muse of the history of morals, she would never be without a copy of his complete works."[12] One might add that if this muse were permitted to have only one of Cats's many books, it would be *Houwelyck. Houwelyck* is a comprehensive treatise on marriage and family life, complete with an alphabetic index for easy reference. Although this treatise was, arguably, among the most popular of its kind at the time, it was far from unique. The tendency among art historians to regard it as the sole seventeenth-century book about marriage and the family overlooks equally exhaustive works published in the Netherlands and in England – the latter, as we shall see, exerted an enormous influence on Dutch thought about family life.[13] (Cats's work is therefore only one of many sixteenth- and seventeenth-century domestic treatises that I will cite.) However, what distinguishes *Houwelyck* from other books of this genre is that it was not addressed primarily to men but to women. Furthermore, its focus is the stages of a woman's life (discussed ahead) rather than a systematic male-oriented presentation of all aspects of household relations and work.

The 1625 edition was richly illustrated with fine engravings after designs by Adriaen van de Venne, an indication that it was originally intended for an elite audience. Some later editions – twenty-one in all appeared during the seventeenth century – substituted crude woodcuts for the engravings and were published in quarto rather than duodecimo in an effort to make the book affordable for less affluent readers. Judging from the fact that there were at least fifty thousand copies of *Houwelyck* in circulation by midcentury, its contents and format – well illustrated and written almost entirely in alexandrines – must have been immensely appealing.[14]

Houwelyck is divided into six sections or chapters, each devoted to a specific stage in the life of a woman: "Maeght" (Maiden), "Vryster" (Sweetheart), "Bruyt" (Bride), "Vrouwe" (Housewife), "Moeder" (Mother), and "Weduwe" (Widow).[15] Cats's comprehensive approach afforded him innumerable pretexts to deliver homilies on the virtues, tasks, and obligations of women in every phase of their lives. The contents of the six chapters are adumbrated in the book's frontispiece, which illustrates (with the aid of visual metaphors) the transition of a woman's life from childhood to the grave (Fig. 3). The dramatis personae of the frontispiece act on a space that is tilted, thereby creating the impression that they are ascending and descending a miniature hill whose sloping contours emphasize their advancing ages as they pass from childhood to the grave.[16] In fact, their placement is reminiscent of that of contemporary prints illustrating the steps of life (Fig. 4).[17] The same didactic intention governs these illustrations of figures posed on steps as they ineluctably reach their final destination: death.

The organization of Cats's *Houwelyck* provided the model – and the justification – for the chapter titles and divisions employed in this book. It is arranged primarily according to the age or approximate life phase of the figures depicted in the paintings, conforming to contemporary habits of thought (expounded, e.g., by Cats and numerous other authors) that divided a woman's life into specific stages, each of which warranted specific virtues and obligations. Chapter 1, corresponding to the first two chapters of *Houwelyck,* "Maeght" (Maiden) and "Vryster" (Sweetheart), examines paintings of young, unmarried women. I discuss images of the Dutch housewife in Chapter 2, in correlation with Cats's chapters "Bruyt" (Bride) and "Vrouwe" (Housewife). Chapter 3 is devoted to the representation of the

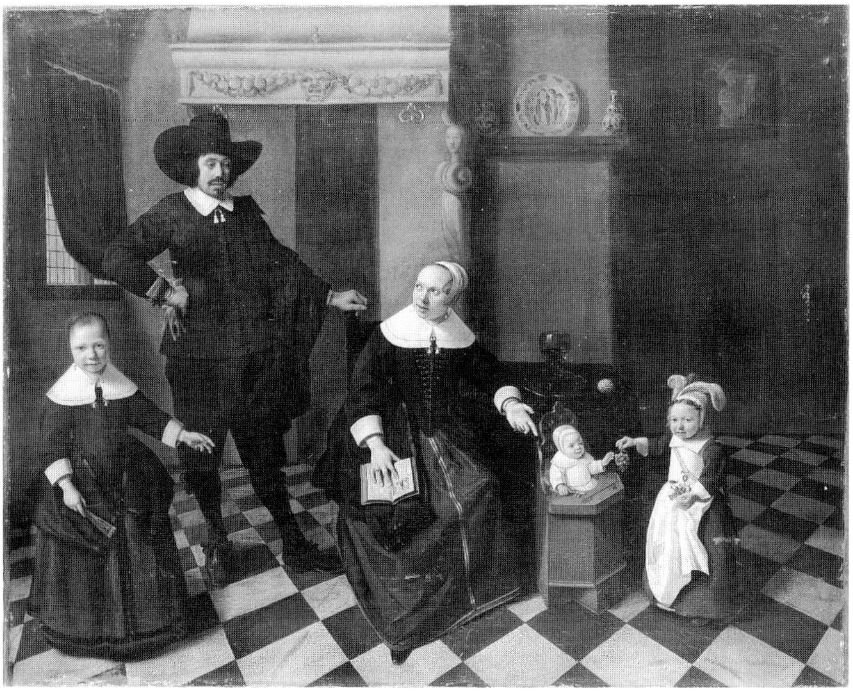

Figure 2 (above). School of Thomas de Keyser, *Portrait of a Family* (oil on canvas, 85.5 × 107.5 cm). Budapest, Museum of Fine Arts. Photo: museum.

Figure 2a (right). Detail of Figure 2.

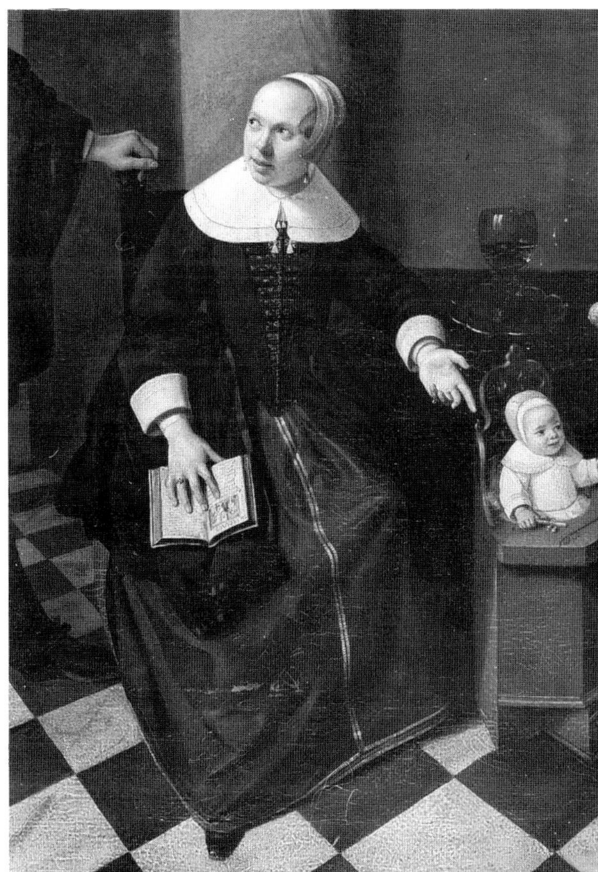

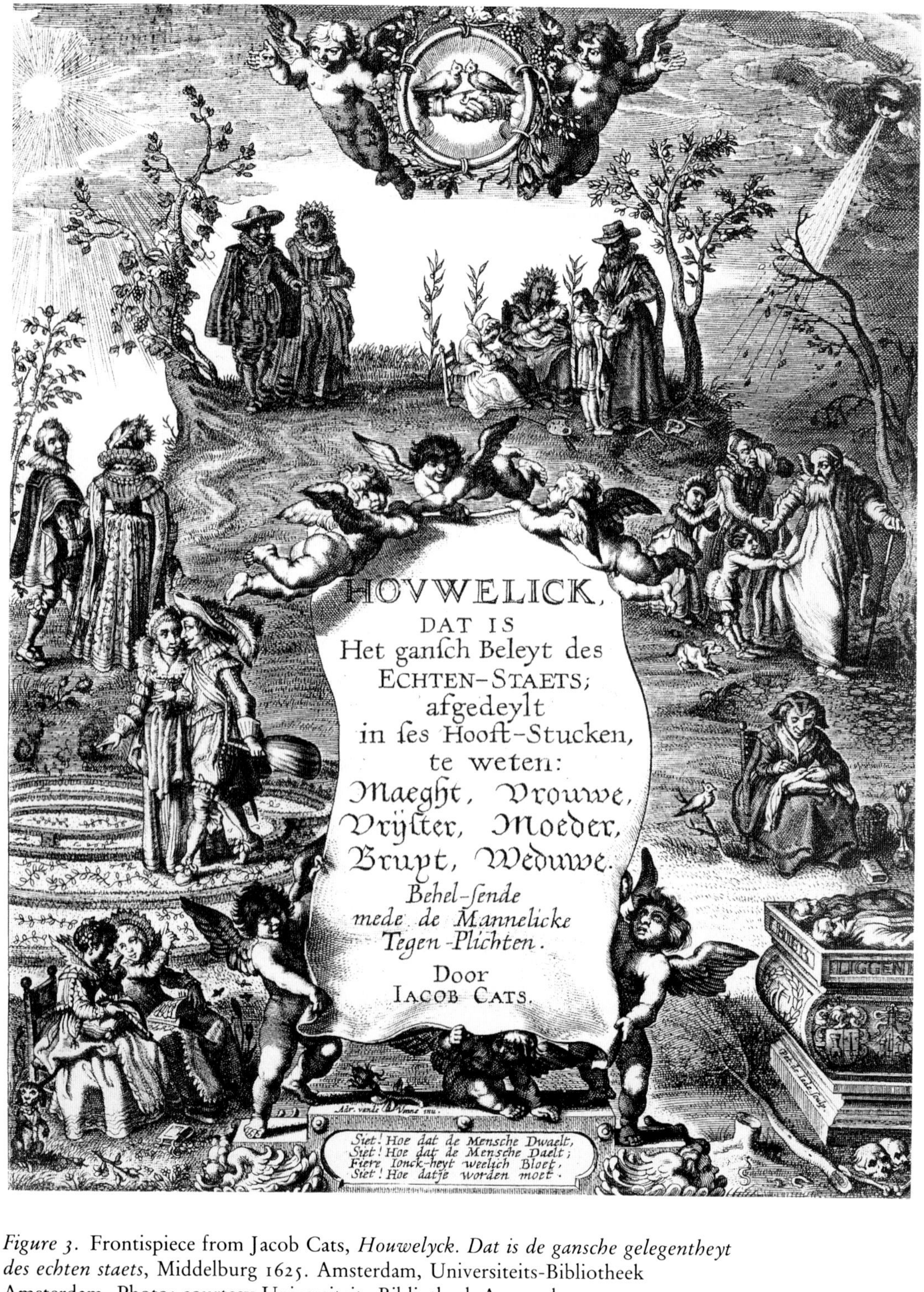

Figure 3. Frontispiece from Jacob Cats, *Houwelyck. Dat is de gansche gelegentheyt des echten staets*, Middelburg 1625. Amsterdam, Universiteits-Bibliotheek Amsterdam. Photo: courtesy Universiteits-Bibliotheek Amsterdam.

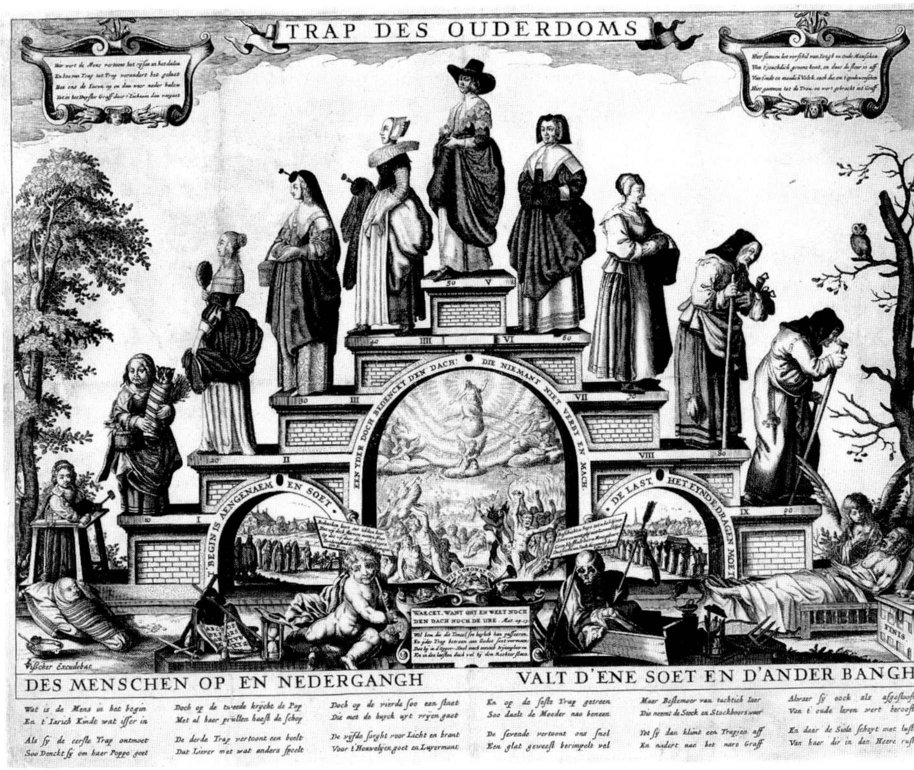

Figure 4. Claes Jansz. Visscher, *Trap des ouderdoms* (engraving). Amsterdam, Rijksprentenkabinet. Photo: Rijksmuseum-Stichting.

all-important office of motherhood, in association with the observations and advice offered in the chapter "Moeder" (Mother) in *Houwelyck.* In connection with Cats's final chapter, "Weduwe" (Widow), Chapter 4 of this book focuses on works of art depicting the final stages of a woman's life: old age and widowhood.

Domestic themes in art may exhibit distinct connections with books like *Houwelyck,* but it would be reductive to regard them as illustrations of literary ideals. Yet it would be equally reductive to deem them value-free slices of life. In their ostensibly faithful rendition of the surrounding world, and in their painstaking attention to detail, paintings of domestic themes can rightly be called realistic.[18] Nevertheless, their realism is merely plausible because they do not simply transcribe daily life in the Netherlands during the seventeenth century. It is now common knowledge that the verisimilitude of paintings, their presentation of a plausible reality that was so esteemed, served as a conduit for ideas and associations.

This aspect of Dutch art has been explored only in recent decades. After several pioneering studies by earlier scholars, Eddy de Jongh developed a new, decisive approach to the study of the iconology of Dutch art.[19] De Jongh maintains that the purpose of Dutch seventeenth-century art – particularly genre paintings – was to instruct and delight the viewer. The sheer visual beauty of these paintings engaged the viewer, who was consequently stimulated to uncover the concealed meaning of the work, one that was largely didactic or moral in nature. Evidently influenced by Erwin Panofsky's term "disguised symbolism," De Jongh contends that the didactic meanings of paintings are conveyed by symbolism that is not immediately apparent but lies beneath the ostensibly "realistic" representation of itself.[20] He adduces an impressive variety of contemporary sources as evidence for this hypothesis. For example, the authors of some of the most popular emblem books of the period repeatedly expounded on the concept of concealed meanings – their methodological explanations of how emblems communicate meaning are said to be applicable to paintings on the basis of Horace's celebrated doctrine *ut pictura poesis* (as is painting, so is poetry), which established the close relationship between art and literature, or the "sister arts" as they were known in the seventeenth century.[21] Moreover, the art theorists Karel van Mander and Samuel van Hoogstraten discuss the hidden symbolism of paintings.[22] De Jongh further argues that the veiled symbols intrinsic to Dutch seventeenth-century paintings can be deciphered with the assistance of sources such as prints with inscriptions, popular literature, and emblem books.

As sound as this reasoning seems, and as fruitful as it has proved for the interpretation of Dutch art, it is not without pitfalls. First and foremost is: how do we detect veiled symbols in numerous, meticulously wrought Dutch paintings that so convincingly present a coherent impression of reality? In other words, if this symbolism was so well concealed, how did seventeenth-century viewers – let alone modern day ones – recognize it?[23] It would seem that the presumed presence of hidden symbols is difficult to reconcile with the exquisitely crafted surfaces of Dutch paintings and with the contemporary appreciation of and delight in their naturalism.[24]

Undoubtedly, some paintings contain hidden symbolism, but one nevertheless wonders to what extent this can be considered a general characteristic of Dutch seventeenth-century art. If we believe this to be true on the basis of contemporary emblematic theory, we overlook the fact that an emblem is in essence a literary conceit – distinct even within literature – with entirely different traditions and purposes than painting, the realistic appearance of Dutch emblematic *picturae* and the doctrine of *ut pictura poesis* notwithstanding.[25]

If, on the other hand, we accept this notion on the basis of contemporary art theory, then we fail to acknowledge that the theorists' comments about hidden symbols actually pertain to history paintings (representing episodes from the Bible, mythology, classical and medieval history), the loftiest category in the thematic hierarchy of art because they ostensibly best demonstrated the artist's erudition and creativity.[26] For example, in Samuel van Hoogstraten's scheme, history painting receives the highest ranking, followed by genre painting (itself ill-defined among "cabinet pieces of every sort"), which in turn is positioned above the lowest stratum of art, a wide range of still-life subjects.[27] In Van Hoogstraten's view, it is noble history painting that is "door Zinnebeelden verrijkt" (enriched by emblems) because, theoretically, the sophisticated literary conceit of the emblem is most germane to this elevated form of art.[28]

In light of these considerations, it should perhaps come as no surprise that De Jongh's method, though at first widely accepted, slowly began to draw criticism, interestingly enough, at approximately the same time that Panofsky's venerable theory of disguised symbolism was challenged.[29] Svetlana Alpers has emerged as one of the most intriguing – and controversial – critics of De Jongh's methods and views of Dutch seventeenth-century art. In her book *The Art of Describing* (1983), Alpers argues that historians of art have erroneously entangled Dutch art within the theoretical framework of Italian Renaissance art with its predominantly narrative and literary nature. In contrast to Italian art, the sine qua non of Dutch art is its "description" of the surrounding world. For Alpers, meaning is not hidden beneath the surface but is directly visible as an attestation of the empirical knowledge gained by the Dutch in the seventeenth century, an era of great scientific discovery. As controversial as these hypotheses are – indeed the book has been bitterly attacked by some scholars, including De Jongh – and as overstated as Alpers's criticisms are of De Jongh's method, which she misleadingly terms "emblematic interpretation," she nonetheless rightly observes that efforts to uncover the purportedly concealed meanings of paintings compromise their visually stunning surface features – hence the need to emphasize the realistic aspects of Dutch art more strongly.[30]

The most recent studies have tended to address precisely these issues. In an important article published in 1988, Eric Jan Sluijter decried the overemphasis in professional art history – which has even spread to the general public – on hidden meanings, sophisticated literary allusions, and didacticism in Dutch art. His sobering analysis of a number of seventeenth-century theoretical works written between 1620 and 1670 suggests that these were not necessarily paramount concerns.[31] Although Sluijter does not deny that some paintings have concealed symbols and moralizing meanings, he notes the general lack of interest among seventeenth-century Dutch art theorists in these aspects of art. On the contrary, they appear more often to be preoccupied with aesthetic questions. Their enthusiasm for the visual qualities of paintings was shared by many contemporary collectors and connoisseurs.[32]

To Sluijter's arguments can be added the observation that the visual qualities of paintings also attracted seventeenth-century poets. As several studies have shown, they sometimes wrote in a "pictorial style" characterized by implicit as well as explicit references to painting, a literal application of *ut pictura poesis*.[33] In some instances, their choice and use of language, particularly when describing landscapes, edifices, crowds, and even the human face, was conditioned by their response to contemporary painting (though mostly to history painting). At times authors even deliberately employed words that properly belonged to the terminology of painting.[34] Joost van den Vondel was one of the leading practitioners of this literary "pictorialism." As Karel Porteman has observed:

> For Vondel, pictorialism became an artistic, even a programmatic premise, as can be seen in the prefaces of many of his tragedies. The pictorial element of his writing, his emphatic visual style, and his sense of painterly order and movement, correspond primarily (and consciously) with the international history painting so admired in higher social circles. However, in general, many traces of the very intense national artistic tradition are unmistakably present in his work.[35]

The adaptation of the pictorial style was not restricted to more elevated forms of literature, like Vondel's tragedies, nor was it developed only in response to history painting, the most exalted level of art in the theoretical hierarchy of types. The comments of Gerbrandt Adriaensz. Bredero are especially instructive in this regard. In the much-quoted preface to his *Great Songbook* of 1622, Bredero defends his "realistic style," that is, his decision to reproduce the peasant vernacular in his text. Realism in this context denotes the author's decision to use a vernacular that is true and apposite to the peasant caste of his characters. Bredero's defense of his style is actually couched and justified in terms that reveal his interest in painting:

> As for me, I have learned from one book only, the book of practice; if I have made some mistakes because of my insufficient knowledge of foreign languages, sciences, and arts, I, unscholarly layman, beg your pardon; be a little tolerant of this Dutchman, because as a painter, I have followed the saying, common among painters: Those who come closest to real life are the best painters . . . as much as possible I have expressed the pleasantries in the most appealing peasant vernacular.[36]

This passage, and several others in the text itself, clearly reveal Bredero's pictorial interests, which must have been at least partly grounded in his appreciation of the realistic qualities of painting.[37]

Encomiastic poetry written for specific pictures also provides revealing accounts of the contemporary estimation of art, as, among others, Jan Emmens and, more recently, Lawrence Goedde have pointed out.[38] Such poetry was governed by the rhetorical tradition of *ekphrasis*, a form of description, descended from antiquity, that attempted to evoke vivid images of subjects ranging from people and places to works of art (both real and imaginary).[39] By actively engaging the reader in highly charged, empathic readings of art works, ekphrastic poems (and ekphrastic descriptions) not only demonstrate the superiority of the written word over the painted image – a standard preoccupation of this literary topos – but also, and for our purposes most importantly, afford insights into how pictures were viewed in the seventeenth century.

Ekphraseis may be grounded in literary convention, but their emphasis on the vivid lifelikeness of paintings must reflect, at least to some degree, their authors' actual response to the engaging naturalism of art, a quality that could be exploited to elicit the reader's empathy. In fact, in their efforts to draw the reader empathically into the subjects of the paintings, the authors deliberately present them as objects for sensual contemplation. Yet they simultaneously present paintings as objects for emotional and intellectual engagement. Thus, ekphrastic descriptions of paintings also address their content.

Although most *ekphraseis* were written about portraits and history paintings, the insights they provide into how contemporaries viewed pictures are applicable to other genres since, by analogy, all Dutch paintings of the period had the capacity, through their mimetic naturalism and dramatized compositions, to induce empathic and intellectual responses from the viewer.[40] This is especially true of genre painting for its potential rhetorical capacities, its staging of narrative to elicit the viewer's response can approximate that of history painting. Ekphrastic poetry therefore offers one methodological model for our investigation of seventeenth-century images of domesticity.[41] It admonishes us that we must pay heightened attention to the realistic qualities of these paintings, because it was precisely their visual properties – versus an elaborate program of concealed symbols – that communicated meaning for contemporaries.

Another important aspect of seventeenth-century Dutch art that has long been recognized but not given sufficient emphasis is the conventional nature of its imagery.[42] Owing to the extremely limited number of subjects depicted and the repetition of specific formulations, the much-vaunted "reality" represented in these paintings can only be described as a selective, fictitious construct.[43] Thus, images of domestic virtue, and for that matter most Dutch seventeenth-century art, are meticulous re-creations of reality that are fictitious because they synthesize observed fact and invention. Moreover, they were forged by artists in response to pictorial traditions, to personal aesthetic interests, and even to the demands of the market – some domestic subjects were frequently painted while others never took root within the limited artistic repertoire.

The selectivity of domestic imagery, or more precisely, the conventions by which it is governed, bespeaks an intrinsic level of significance within the individual themes themselves. For not only artistic concerns, but more importantly, popular attitudes and ideas dictate the existence and production of conventional imagery.[44] Thus, meaning in Dutch paintings is not necessarily concealed from the viewer but is an essential constituent, intimately bound up with their mimetic qualities.

This leads to the important question of how paintings communicate meaning or, phrased in another manner, how they mirror yet contribute to the value system of which they are part.[45] In my opinion, they do so in two interdependent ways – first, through pictorial style, an aspect of Dutch seventeenth-century art that is only infrequently thought of as a carrier of meaning. Works of art are always related to, if not imprinted with, the ideals and mores of the culture in which they were produced; in this sense pictorial style can be defined as the aesthetic form that these ideals and mores adopt.[46] This is especially true of domestic imagery created in the Netherlands in the seventeenth century, with its male-oriented society. When painting domestic subjects, Dutch artists (who were mostly male) invariably represented women as types. Very often they are generalized and objectified, their individuality and psychic dimension minimized, in the interests of having them embody an idea or, more accurately, an appropriate feminine virtue.[47] Moreover, in contemporary group portraits and in pendant pairs, a different aesthetic governs the representation of women. They are subject to the well-known heraldic convention of being placed to the left of their husbands, but the differences even extend to such stylistic characteristics as depicting females in passive poses and rendering their features in a comparatively flat, superficial manner.[48] Furthermore, as we shall see, in portraits and in genre paintings, artists repeatedly surround these women with the same, surprisingly limited number of meticulously painted objects that could only have been meant to connote virtue.

Second, paintings also impart meaning through objects or motifs replete with significance.[49] This is axiomatic, so much so that I hardly need to comment on it further. I will simply add here that, in light of the preceding discussion, we can assume that, in most cases, the significance of such motifs could not have been hidden or recondite, given – at least in the case of domestic representations – the widespread beliefs about the role of women in Dutch society, a role experienced or understood by the population at large. In other words, the expression in these paintings of universally held ideals about women and domesticity guaranteed that access to their meanings

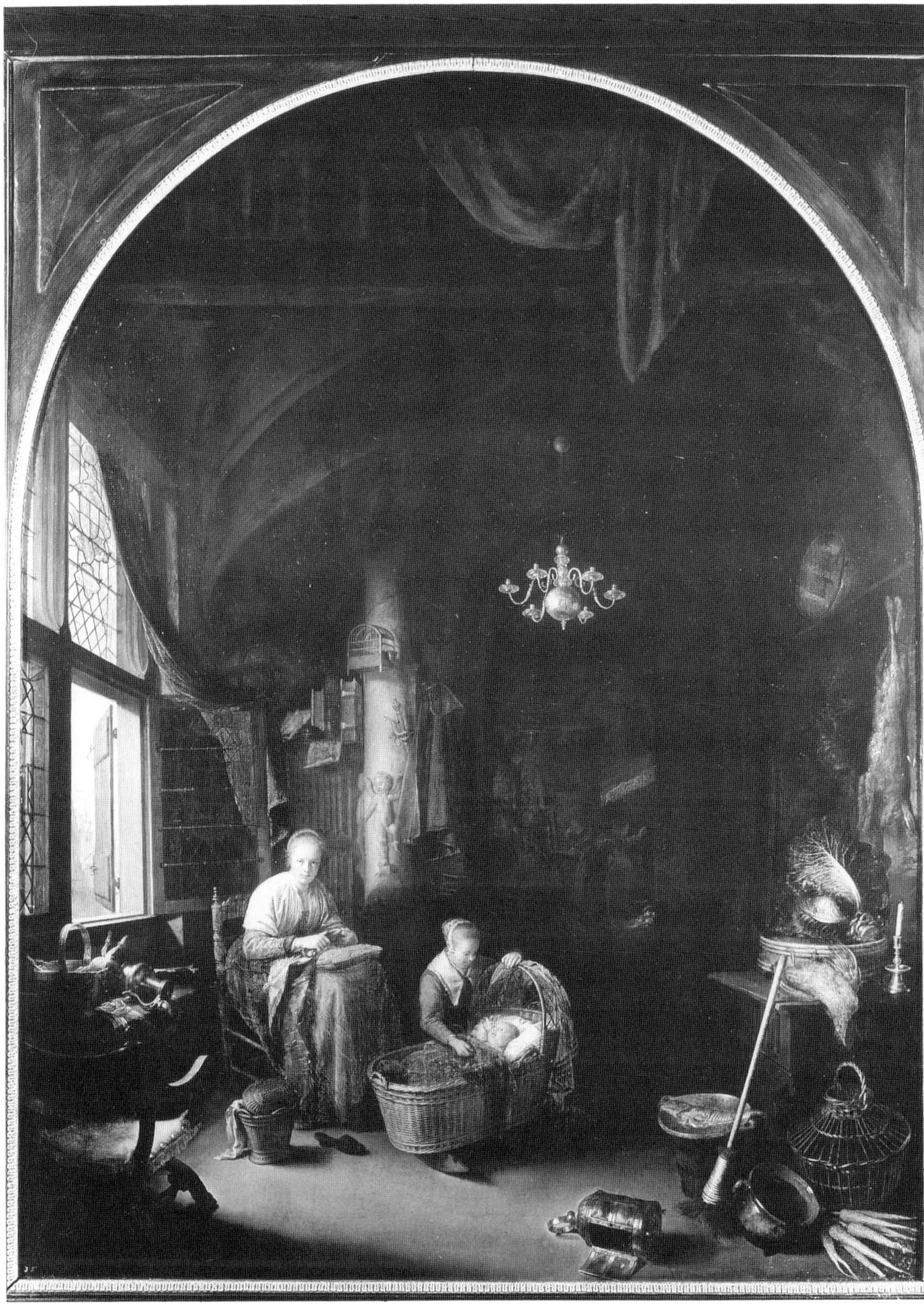

Figure 5. Gerard Dou, *The Young Mother* (oil on panel, 73.5 × 55.5 cm). The Hague, Mauritshuis. Photo: A. Dingjan, The Hague.

was not normally dependent on the viewer's capacity to uncover veiled symbols. Although symbolic motifs are at times difficult for the modern viewer to detect, let alone understand, they must have been readily apparent to the seventeenth-century viewer because they were immediately perceived on the surface of the painting as they were intrinsic to its skillful and engaging presentation of a plausible reality. Therefore, it is misleading – and anachronistic – to divorce form, that is, pictorial style, from content, for both were inextricably bound together.

We must also allow for the possibility that some paintings reflect the shared values and assumptions of both artist and viewer while others do not. What I am suggesting is that, in interpreting Dutch art, it is sometimes necessary to make a distinction between an artist's intentions with respect to meaning (or the lack of it) in a work of art and the types of associations that it evoked for the viewer. Perhaps more light can be shed on this premise with an example. Peter Hecht's thought-provoking suggestion that Dou intended his slickly painted, subtly lit *Young Mother* (Fig. 5) primarily as a "staalkaart van zijn schilderkunstige mogelijkheden" (sample card of his painterly possibilities) may well be correct.[50] However, it does not satisfactorily answer the questions of why the artist chose to represent this subject, a domestic interior; why, more importantly, it was composed in the manner that it was, that is, with a woman rather than a man sewing beside her children; and why he has included particular motifs – ones that are found in innumerable images of domestic virtue during this period – to the exclusion of others. The point is that Dou, despite his consummate artistic abilities and prominence as one of the leading artists of his generation, is a historically located personality and, as such, was consciously or subconsciously influenced by the value system of his day, an influence that most assuredly extended to his choice of subjects and – though this is difficult to demonstrate – even to the style in which they were painted.[51] Ultimately, the domestic subjects that Dou and other artists chose to depict and the aesthetic forms in which they were presented served to endorse and perpetuate the order of seventeenth-century Dutch society, and in this respect, they have the potential to furnish just as much information about that society as any lengthy family treatise.

If Hecht's suggestion is correct – that Dou's principal reasons for painting this picture were indeed lavish pictorial display and self-promotion – it does not preclude an intention on his part to convey particular ideas as well, neither does it exclude the possibility that those who saw the painting attached particular associations to it, all the more so because of its stunning visual effects.[52] For it has long been known that there is no such thing as an innocent eye as all viewers are conditioned by culturally shaped habits of "seeing." Therefore, the meaning of these images was rooted in the culturally defined experience of the seventeenth century. While paintings may not always contain hidden symbols, they nevertheless mirror and contribute to the value system of the culture in which they were produced. While these pictures do represent plausible realities, we must make "some attempt to clarify *whose* reality we are talking about," as Linda Nochlin has said in another context.[53] In this case, the reality we are talking about is very definitely that of a patriarchal social order.[54] Weighty, abstruse messages may not lurk behind every representation of domestic virtue, but these pictures nonetheless reverberate with an entire system of values, ideals, and even prejudices, all of which reflect men's attitudes toward women that were commonplace in seventeenth-century culture.

Contemporary viewers must have "read" domestic imagery on various, related levels that were contingent on a number of governing factors, among others their level of education, the degree to which they conformed to the value system, and the popularity and conventionality of the subjects portrayed. If we seek to uncover the multiplicity of meanings that contemporary viewers attached to domestic imagery in art – as much as this is possible given the distance in time that separates us – we must investigate the broadest possible cultural factors that would have been germane in the seventeenth century. It is to these cultural factors and, more importantly, to the images themselves, that we now turn.

"MAEGHT" AND "VRYSTER"

A surprising number of Dutch seventeenth-century paintings depict female adolescents and those of marriageable age. Portraits of demure maidens posed passively yet resolutely with their books or needlework undoubtedly mirror the interests of their commissioners, the parents of these women. Genre paintings of young women absorbed in domestic tasks often emphasize the conscientious performance of work. Perhaps the most popular theme in art involving young women was that of courtship. Fashionably dressed young people dally in love gardens or in lavish interiors in pictures that celebrate love while illustrating the requisite behavior of maidens participating in this important ritual. Considered in their entirety, these paintings testify to the keen interest in the premarital stages of female life at this time.

Contemporary literature likewise affirms this preoccupation with maidenhood. For example, in Jacob Cats's *Houwelyck* (Marriage), two chapters, "Maeght" (Maiden) and "Vryster" (Sweetheart), examine the difficulties and uncertainties faced by young, unmarried women.[1] The first chapter consists of a dialogue between Phyllis, a maiden who has only recently become attracted to the opposite sex, and the older, more experienced Anna, who offers wise counsel. The second chapter expands on the first as the newlywed Sibille advises Rosette, a young lady who is courting. Through the rhymed dialogues of these four interlocutors, Cats sermonizes on the "rules" and dangers of courtship and the virtues most befitting women of marriageable age.[2]

Cats's attention to the problems of young women in *Houwelyck* was not unique. He had already discussed this topic at length some seven years earlier in his *Maechden-plicht* (Maiden's Obligation, 1618), a work written for maidens approaching marriage.[3] Several other seventeenth-century books addressed the same audience, among them Zacharias Heyns's *Deuchden-schole ofte spieghel der jonghe-dochteren* (School of Virtues or Mirror of

Young Daughters, 1625a) and Jan Soet's *Maagden-baak* (Maiden's Beacon, 1641). Many other works dealt in part with the subject of maidenhood while still others were intended for young people of both sexes.[4]

Seventeenth-century authors considered youth a distinctive period in life, fraught with dangers, temptations, and uncertainties about the future.[5] In fact, their observations correspond in many respects to modern-day ones.[6] Contrary to the theories of some social historians, our ancestors were indeed conscious of adolescence as a separate stage in human development.[7] Cats and his contemporaries believed that certain emotional and physical characteristics were peculiar to this life phase between childhood and adulthood and, therefore, that specific admonitions were needed to ensure safe passage to the latter.[8]

Admonitory literature was merely one source of guidance for adolescents; the brunt of responsibility naturally fell on their parents, who were enjoined to act as proper role models, to discipline their children, and to provide them with practical training that was, naturally, differentiated according to sex.[9] For girls and young, unmarried women, its purpose was to instill sound moral habits and to develop domestic skills that would enable them to perform those tasks intrinsic to the offices to which they were destined: housewifery and motherhood.[10] Cats, for example, exhorts young women to be chaste, diligent, silent, and obedient to their parents and to remain in the home – "het maegden-hof" (the maiden's court) – honing their domestic skills while trusting God to furnish them with suitable spouses.[11]

The contemporary vision of the virtuous, well-trained young woman, expounded relentlessly in literature, clearly informs portraiture. Portraits always express the ideals of the sitters – in this case, those of the probable patrons, the parents of the woman represented – ideals inextricably linked to their age or approximate stage in life. For example, in an early portrait by Gerard Dou, style and motifs combine to offer a compelling ideological construction of femininity (Fig. 6).[12] A young woman sits rigidly within a spacious interior; Dou minimizes her interaction with the viewer by placing her in a passive, self-contained pose, a highly conventional one often adopted for females in portraiture.[13] Her pose effectively communicates her dignity, humility, and sobriety.

The young sitter holds an open songbook in her lap, and two more books, one a tightly clasped Bible, lie on the table beside her.[14] It is unlikely that her books refer primarily to intellectual accomplishment, for this was considered, with a few notable exceptions, an exclusively male pursuit.[15] For women, the ability to read had a largely practical value for it assisted them in managing a household efficiently. It also had didactic purposes; hence the moralists' repeated exhortations that women read about the lives of their virtuous sisters and similar edifying stories, not to mention the Bible.[16]

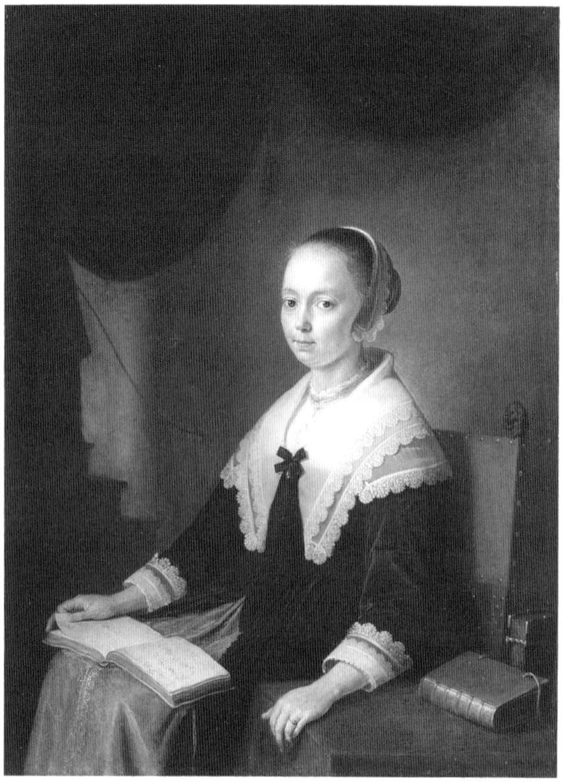

Figure 6. Gerard Dou, *Portrait of a Young Woman* (oil on panel, 26.6 × 19 cm). Private collection. Photo: B. Jones, Rocky Point.

Many seventeenth-century Dutch songbooks, especially those primarily composed of sacred music, had an edifying purpose as well.[17] In this regard it is no mere coincidence that the book in the sitter's lap is a songbook. Songbooks appear on the ground in the *Maeghde-Wapen* (Maiden's Coat of Arms), a captivating print that, with its accompanying explanatory poem, prefaces the first chapter of Cats's *Houwelyck* (Fig. 7).[18] Here, one of the young female personifications holds a parrot and an embroidery sampler on a stretcher. The songbooks, more needlework, and sewing paraphernalia lie strewn on the ground while a dog squats on its hind legs beside her. The inscription below, "Leer-sucht" (literally, Willingness to Learn) clarifies the meaning of these seemingly disparate motifs: they function as attributes of docility, the virtue that the maiden herself personifies.[19] If anything, the books in Dou's portrait complement the sitter's modest dress and passive pose as all convey her rectitude. The portrait therefore reflects behavioral desiderata for young women at this time, yet simultaneously constructs them as it renders abstract virtues in a visually recognizable form.[20]

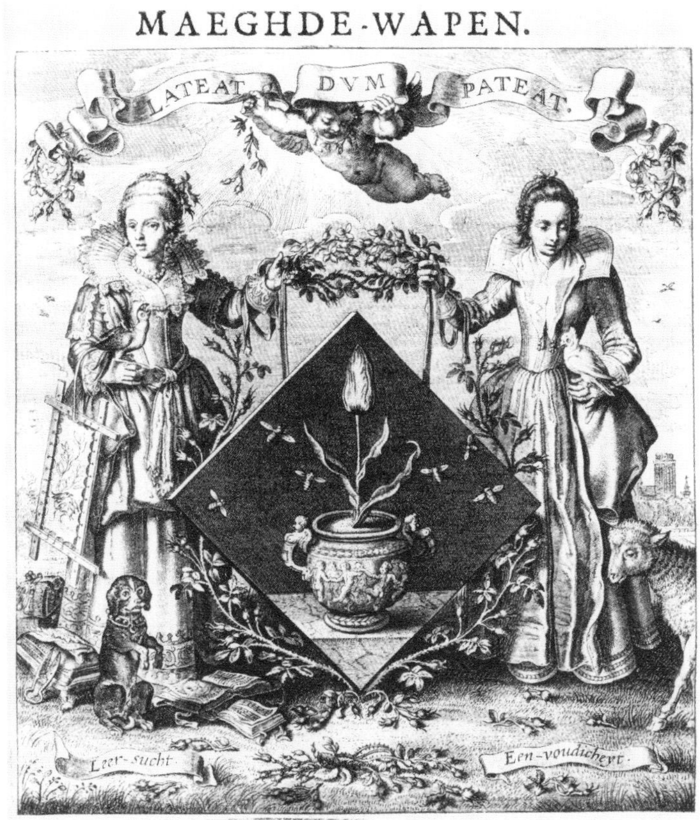

Figure 7. Illustration, *Maeghde-Wapen*, from Jacob Cats, *Houwelyck. Dat is de gansche gelegentheyt des echten staets*, Middelburg 1625. Amsterdam, Universiteits-Bibliotheek Amsterdam. Photo: courtesy Universiteits-Bibliotheek, Amsterdam.

Needlework is another motif that frequently appears in portraits of young women. Joachim Wtewael depicts his twenty-one-year-old daughter Eva, holding her shears and lacework, with an expensive sewing cushion in her lap (Fig. 8).[21] A sewing basket filled with more lacework lies on the floor beside her. The thick book on the table, presumably a Bible, refers, like the one in Dou's portrait, to the sitter's virtue, piety, and good training. Her needlework conveys analogous ideas; we need only recall that the *Maeghde-Wapen* contains various needlework implements that are actually metaphors of docility (Fig. 7). The needlework and book do more than merely testify to Eva's tractability; they also signify a host of feminine virtues like domesticity and diligence, associations present in other portraits of the period (see, e.g., Fig. 9).[22]

Once again, pictorial style functions as an expression of these values. It is instructive to compare Wtewael's portrait of Eva with that of her brother,

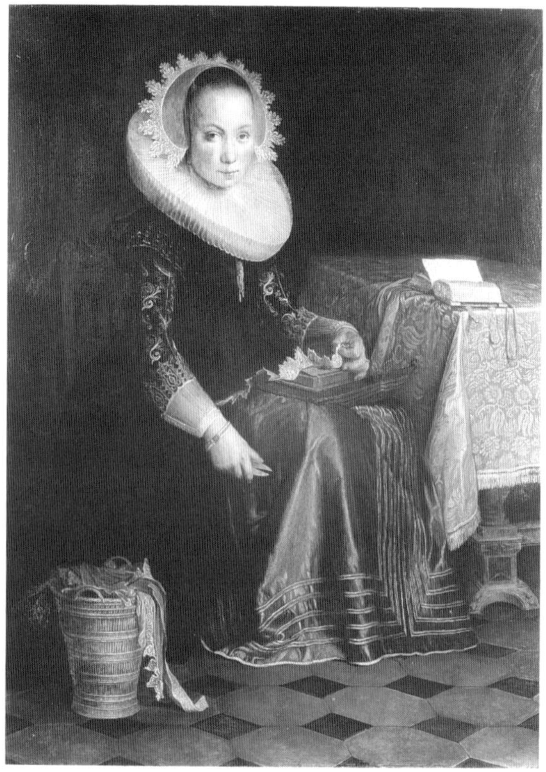

Figure 8. Joachim Wtewael, *Portrait of Eva Wtewael*, 1628 (oil on panel, 55.5 × 40.5 cm). Utrecht, Centraal Museum. Photo: museum.

the painter Peter Wtewael (Fig. 10).[23] Both figures are illuminated from the right. However, the resultant pictorial effects are quite different. In the portrait of Peter, light models his face and articulates its plasticity, investing it with a psychic dimension. The light in Eva's portrait flattens her countenance, thereby minimizing the potential to communicate with the viewer. Although Peter's portrait is not even half-length, it is – in comparison to the full-length but dry, descriptive image of Eva – undeniably more dynamic and psychologically interactive.[24] Like her book and needlework, Eva's closed, rigid pose, augmented by the artist's lighting technique, conveys her modesty and rectitude.

Genre paintings of maidens occupied with needlework likewise convey virtuous associations revolving around probity and proper training. In a painting by Nicolaes Maes, a well-dressed adolescent girl studiously attempts to thread a needle (Fig. 11). Through such pictorial devices as the even illumination and the tight, almost claustrophobic space, Maes focuses our attention on this young lady's total absorption in her task. No mere servant

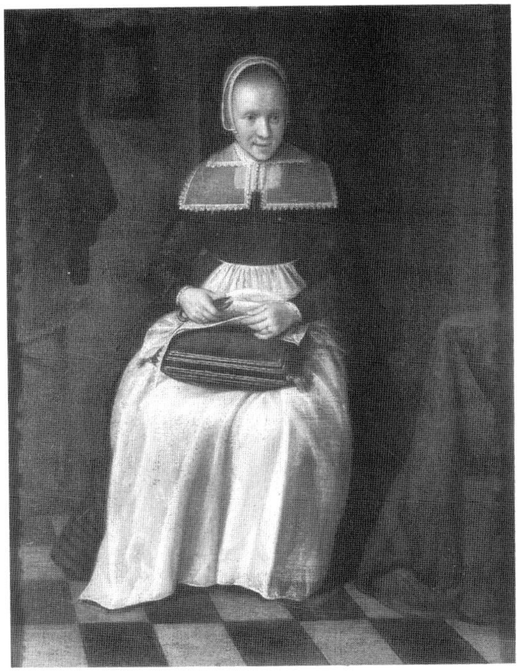

Figure 9 (left). Jan Albertsz. Rotius (attributed to), *Portrait of a Young Girl.* Antwerp, Museum van de Commissie van Openbare Onderstand, Maagdenhuis. Photo: copyright A.C.L.-Brussels.

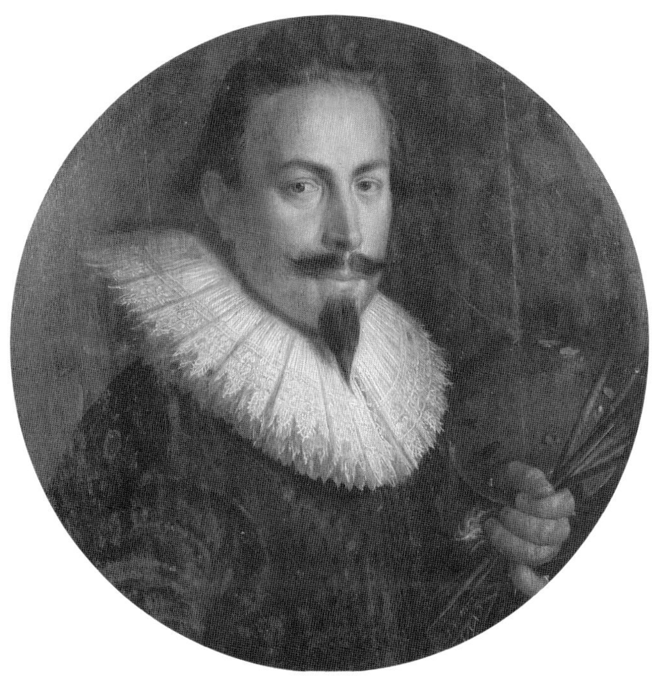

Figure 10 (right). Joachim Wtewael, *Portrait of Peter Wtewael,* 1628 (oil on circular panel, 56.8 cm in diameter). Utrecht, Centraal Museum. Photo: museum.

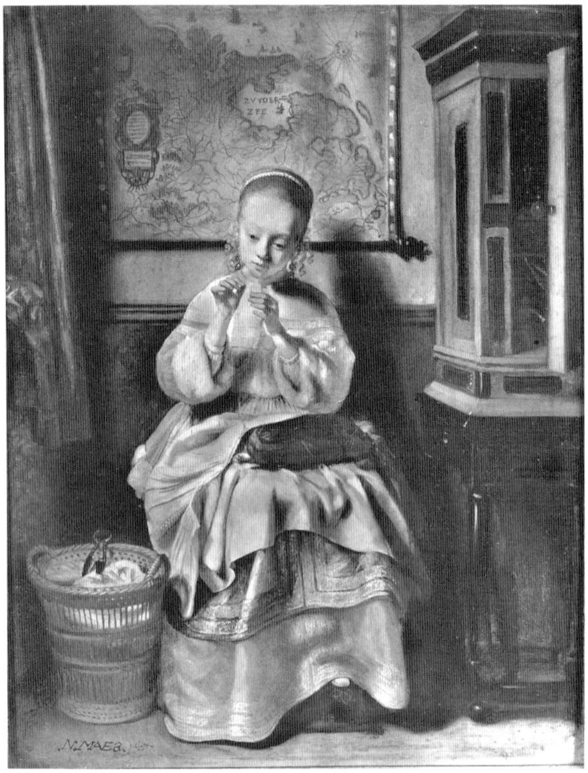

Figure 11. Nicolaes Maes, *Young Girl Sewing*, 1657 (oil on panel, 40 × 31 cm). Private collection. Photo: A. Reeve.

– her expensive clothing indicates otherwise – she is a model of diligence and proper training.

Several unusual variations on this theme show young women sewing in the presence of parrots. In Gabriel Metsu's *Young Lady with a Parrot,* a parrot perched near the top of its cage watches a young woman sewing (Fig. 12). In a painting by Frans van Mieris the Elder, a maiden has interrupted her work – her thimble remains on her finger – to feed a parrot (Fig. 13).[25] In the *Maeghde-Wapen* a screeching parrot perches on the hand of the personification of docility beside her embroidery. This bird can likely be equated with docility because the breed is easily tamed and taught to "speak."[26] The presence of parrots in the paintings by Metsu and Van Mieris signifies the proper training of their mistresses.[27]

These diligent young needleworkers wear luxurious garments whose sheen is deftly captured by the artists' meticulous technique. Equally modish is the beautifully braided hair, adorned with brightly colored ribbons, of the maiden in Van Mieris's painting. The women's porcelainlike skin as well as

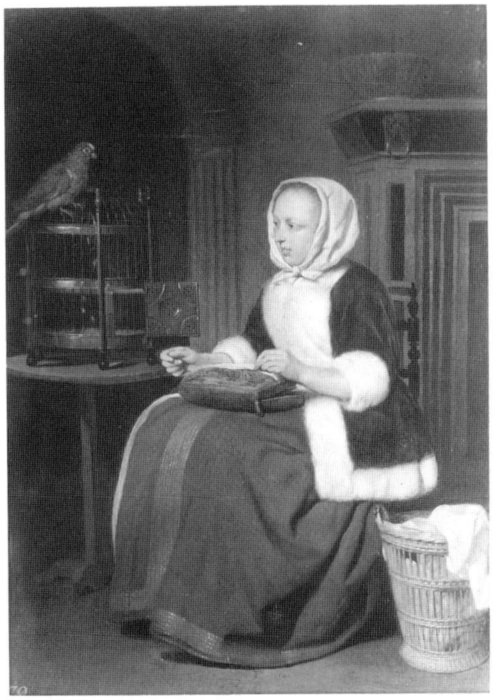

Figure 12. Gabriel Metsu, *Young Lady with a Parrot* (oil on panel, 34 × 26 cm). Moscow, Pushkin Museum. Photo: museum.

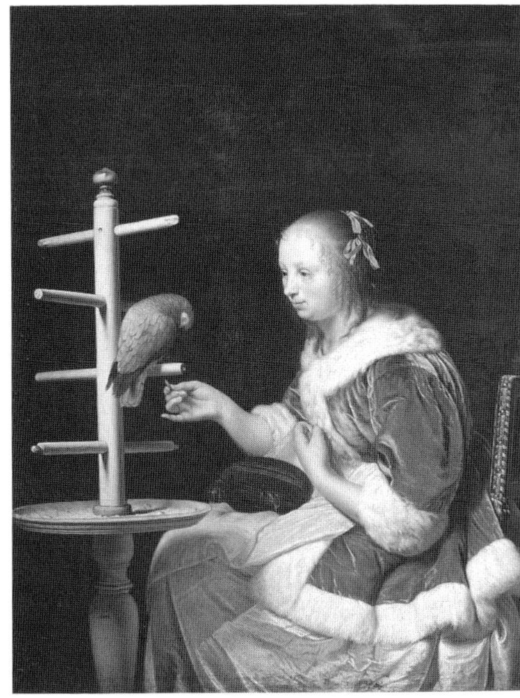

Figure 13. Frans van Mieris the Elder, *Young Lady with a Parrot* (oil on copper, 22.5 × 17.3 cm). London, The National Gallery. Reproduced by courtesy of the Trustees, The National Gallery, London.

the sinuous outlines of their forms heighten the impression of elegance. Van Mieris and Metsu emphasized the grace of these women and, in connection with their needlework, created an urbane image of paradigmatic femininity. As paragons of elegance and diligence, these comely figures function as ideological constructs in a manner homologous to their "living" counterparts in contemporary portraiture. Consequently, both genre paintings and portraits offer a visual analogue to the premium that contemporary writers attached to the moral and domestic training of young women. In this sense, both art and literature present an exemplary image, a topos that does not necessarily reflect the actual situation of young women in seventeenth-century Dutch culture.

Many sixteenth- and seventeenth-century texts contain exhortations to parents to train their daughters to perform needlework. Besides thwarting slothfulness, the daily practice of this and other domestic tasks was crucial for their future offices as housewives, for maidens

> must learn what belong to housewifery / how they should be humbly submissive and loving to their husbands (if God calls them to marriage) / how they should raise their children / how they should run their household / how to make purchases / how to sew / spin / be neat and diligent / and similar things which are part of women's callings.[28]

This quotation, from a pedagogical treatise by the Middelburg schoolmaster Johannes de Swaef, equates sewing and other domestic tasks with the virtue of diligence. Many of De Swaef's contemporaries made this very same connection, and it is found in the visual arts as well, as, for example, in a print representing the age of twenty by Conrad Meyer from his series of the ten ages of man (Fig. 14).[29] Meyer depicts two youths: a boy resisting the onslaughts of debauchery, and a girl sewing. The assiduous activity of the girl is, as the inscription implies, requisite for foiling innumerable vices.

A late-sixteenth-century print from a series illustrating the traditional association of the phases of life with the planets conveys similar ideas (Fig. 15).[30] The print depicts adolescence under the auspices of Venus. In the presence of Spring/Youth, personified by a young man holding a falcon, maidens practice their needlework while several others read and play music. The inscription below the one who is embroidering, "Diligentia," confirms that she is a personification of diligence. Consequently, in this context, her needlework functions as an attribute of this virtue.

Young, unmarried women were enjoined to be diligent as were women of all ages – and men as well.[31] However, contemporaries were acutely aware that sedulous habits needed to be implanted in their children, beginning at the earliest feasible age. They considered childhood and adolescence highly impressionable developmental stages in which acquired habits (both good and bad) became permanently ingrained – hence the repeated exhortations to promote industriousness in children, which would ultimately benefit society at large because, as a consequence, there would be few indolent, "evil" adults.[32]

An illustration from Johan van Nyenborgh's *Toonneel [sic] der ambachten* (Theatre of Trades) depicts this pedagogical desideratum (Fig. 16).[33] Two girls practice their needlework in the presence of their parents and siblings. The inscription "Van de goede opvoedinge der Kinderen" (On the Good Training of Children) clarifies the pedagogical import of the girls' activity and also, as the accompanying poem states, refers to their diligence:

> If one accustoms them to working
> they will stay industrious.
> But if one permits them to remain lazy and indolent,
> They will take root in it and cherish idleness.[34]

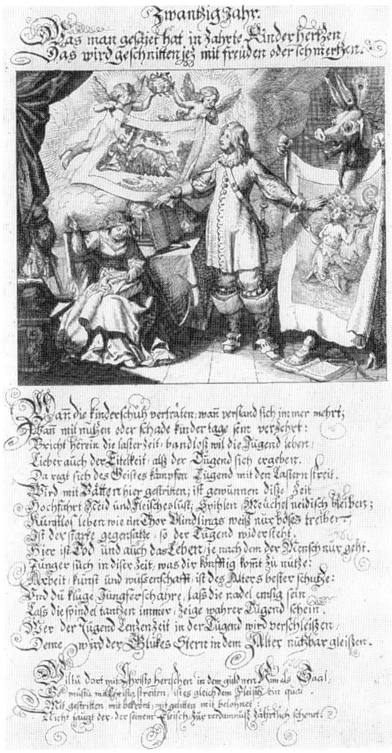

Figure 14. Conrad Meyer, *Age Twenty* (engraving from the series *The Ten Ages of Man*), 1675. Amsterdam, Rijksprentenkabinet. Photo: Rijksmuseum-Stichting.

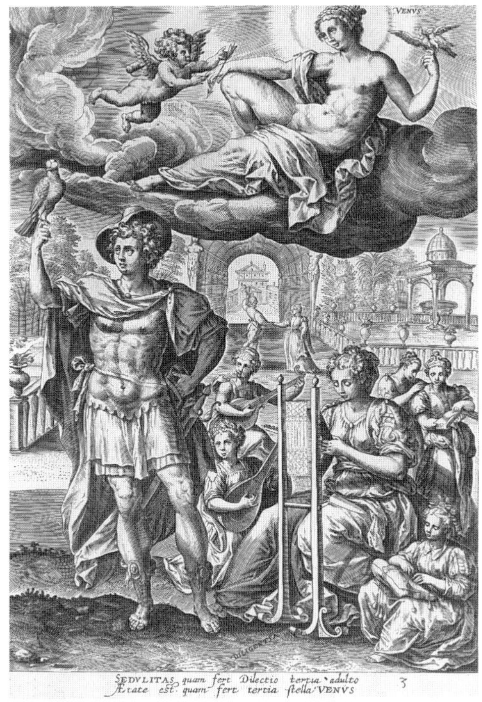

Figure 15. Adriaen Collaert after Maarten de Vos, *Venus-Adolescence* (engraving from the series *The Seven Planets and Ages of Man*), 1581. Amsterdam, Rijksprentenkabinet. Photo: Rijksmuseum-Stichting.

The illustration closely corresponds to an anonymous family portrait painted around 1640 (Fig. 17). Here there is no question of direct influence – indeed the book was published about nineteen years after the painting. Instead, both may be viewed as analogous expressions of important familial and pedagogical ideals endemic to seventeenth-century Dutch culture. The unknown portraitist has arranged the family group according to gender. Performing the skills and arts intrinsic to their sex, the boys concentrate on intellectual pursuits in preparation for their future professional careers while the girls are busy with housework and needlework.[35] Although the visual effects created by the awkward, frozen poses of the girls are almost humorous, the demonstration of their diligence and training for their future office as housewives is totally in earnest.

The connection between needlework and the virtue of diligence was stressed at every possible occasion, perhaps most appropriately in pattern books, which consisted of collections of prints illustrating embroidery pat-

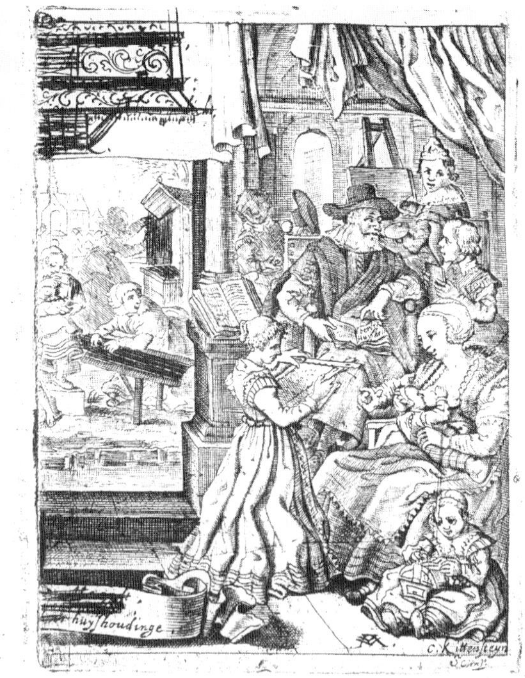

Van de goede opvoedinge der Kinderen.

Figure 16 (left). Emblem from Johan van Nyenborgh, *Toonneel [sic] der ambachten: of den winckel der handt-wercken en konsten*, 2d ed., Groningen 1659. Amsterdam, Universiteits-Bibliotheek Amsterdam. Photo: courtesy Universiteits-Bibliotheek Amsterdam.

Figure 17 (below). Anonymous, *Portrait of a Family* (canvas, 64 × 88 cm). Present location unknown.

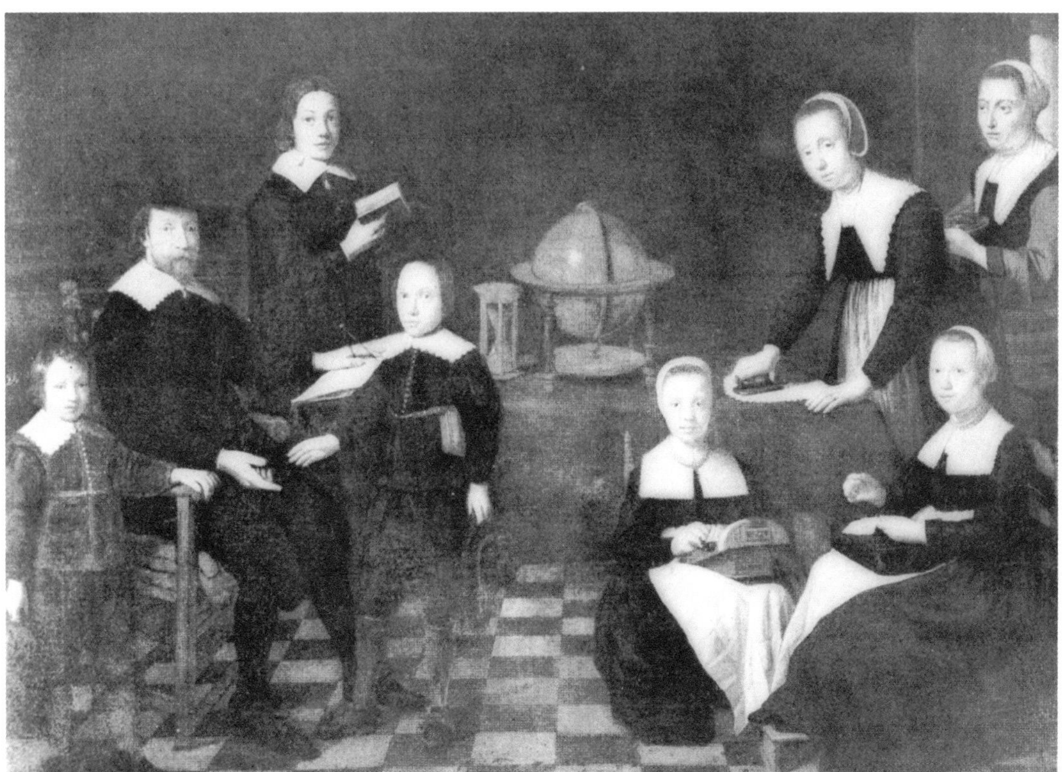

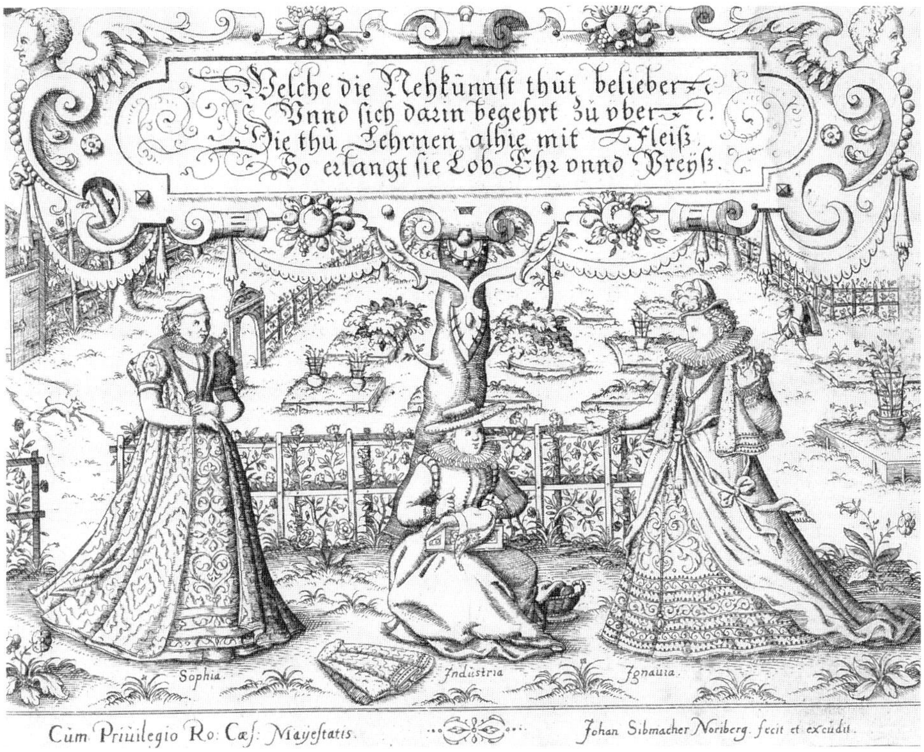

Figure 18. Frontispiece from Johan Sibmacher, *Newes Modelbüch in Küpffer gemacht*, 2d ed., Nuremberg 1604. Amsterdam, Rijksprentenkabinet. Photo: Rijksmuseum-Stichting.

terns that the user could copy when decorating clothing, drapery, or other textiles.[36] The frontispiece to one of the most popular pattern books of the period, Johan Sibmacher's *Newes Modelbüch . . .* (New Book of Patterns), shows three women engaged in a spirited conversation (Fig. 18).[37] The one seated in the middle is sewing and is appropriately inscribed "Industria" (Industry). In the accompanying poem, she defends herself against "Ignavia" (Idleness; depicted to her left) with the aid of "Sophia" (Wisdom; depicted to her right). In this winsome scene, in some respects reminiscent of that of Hercules at the Crossroads, Industria, flanked by virtue and vice, wins her argument with Ignavia by cleverly equating needlework with diligence, demonstrating once again that contemporaries associated the performance of feminine tasks with probity.[38] That this association could even serve to introduce a popular pattern book demonstrates just how important it was to seventeenth-century society.

Representations of the theme of young women who are spinning are replete with similar connotations. A number of sixteenth-century portraits of women in the act of spinning survive, the most famous being that by Maarten van Heemskerck in the Rijksmuseum.[39] Seventeenth-century portraits of women of any age spinning, however, are practically nonexistent, but the task frequently appears in genre painting. The absence of portraits of spinners indicates that sitters, if they desired to be portrayed working, preferred that it be with needlework.[40] Perhaps they considered needlework a more refined domestic occupation than spinning, one more reflective of status and therefore more appropriate for a portrait.[41] Yet changes in taste can only partly account for this phenomenon. The presence of flourishing commercial textile industries in Haarlem and Leiden and the importation from Silesia of enormous quantities of spun flax virtually eliminated the need for women to spin as they had done in previous centuries.[42] Archival evidence corroborates this: a random survey of 300 seventeenth-century *boedels* (official inventories of the possessions of the deceased drawn up at the time of their death) revealed that spinning wheels were present in only about one in five homes.[43] Even this statistic somewhat inflates the amount of spinners since not everyone who owned a spinning wheel necessarily used it.

Thus, the negligible number of women who actually spun suggests that, in contemporary paintings, the motif functioned as a pure topos of domestic virtue, especially since the spinning wheel was a time-honored symbol of domesticity.[44] One perplexing question remains: Why did some moralists encourage parents to teach their daughters to spin as part of their domestic training?[45] Perhaps they were motivated by disappointment as the number of women still adept at spinning decreased. It is more likely that their prescriptions should be construed as literary topoi because, in order to justify their advice, they frequently cite passages from the Bible and other ancient texts that laud the merits of spinning. Therefore, in paintings that depict women spinning, and in the literature they mirror, it is necessary to make a distinction between their function as exempla and the reflection of actual historical reality.

A work by Caspar Netscher is among the most beautiful genre paintings exemplifying the theme of young women spinning (Fig. 19). Like the paintings of women sewing, the artist lavishes attention on such stunning pictorial effects as the young woman's luminous, enamellike skin and the light dancing on her silk dress and fur-lined jacket. The maiden's physical beauty and her meticulously rendered garments – a hallmark of the *fijnschilder* (fine painter) style – convey an aura of fashionable opulence that seems incongruous with the simple spinning wheel beside her. The spinning wheel functions as a pure symbol of domesticity. It confirms that Netscher's painting represents a sophisticated topos, which, with its smooth, refined style, celebrates feminine virtue.[46]

Even more modest representations of the theme, like that by Matthias

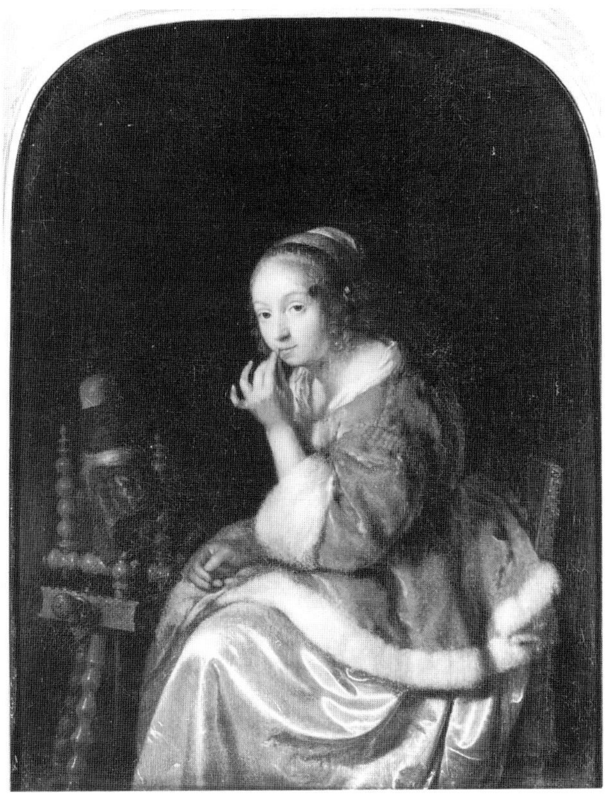

Figure 19. Caspar Netscher, *A Lady at a Spinning-Wheel*, 1665 (oil on panel, 22.5 × 17.7 cm). London, The National Gallery. Reproduced by courtesy of the Trustees, The National Gallery, London.

Naiveau (Fig. 20), employ subtle pictorial devices that signal virtue. In this solemn picture, a maiden actively spins. Naiveau convincingly captures the whirring movement of the wheel controlled by the treadle below. Within the dark, still interior, bright rays of sunlight stream through the window illuminating this young woman at work. Her rapt gaze underscores the direction of the light as well as its intensity, which is offset by the dim interior and the subtle penumbra that envelops other objects, namely the baby's high chair and the lantern in the lower right corner.[47] In a peculiarly evocative manner, the light adopts a preternatural dimension; it focuses our attention on the maiden as it bathes her features, mysteriously purifying them and transforming her radiant image into an icon of moral perfection.[48]

The works hitherto examined are paradigmatic, portraying ideal maidenly virtues such as docility, purity, industriousness, and domesticity. By cultivating such virtues in their daughters, parents could prepare them for their future roles in marriage. Moreover, properly armed with these virtues, maid-

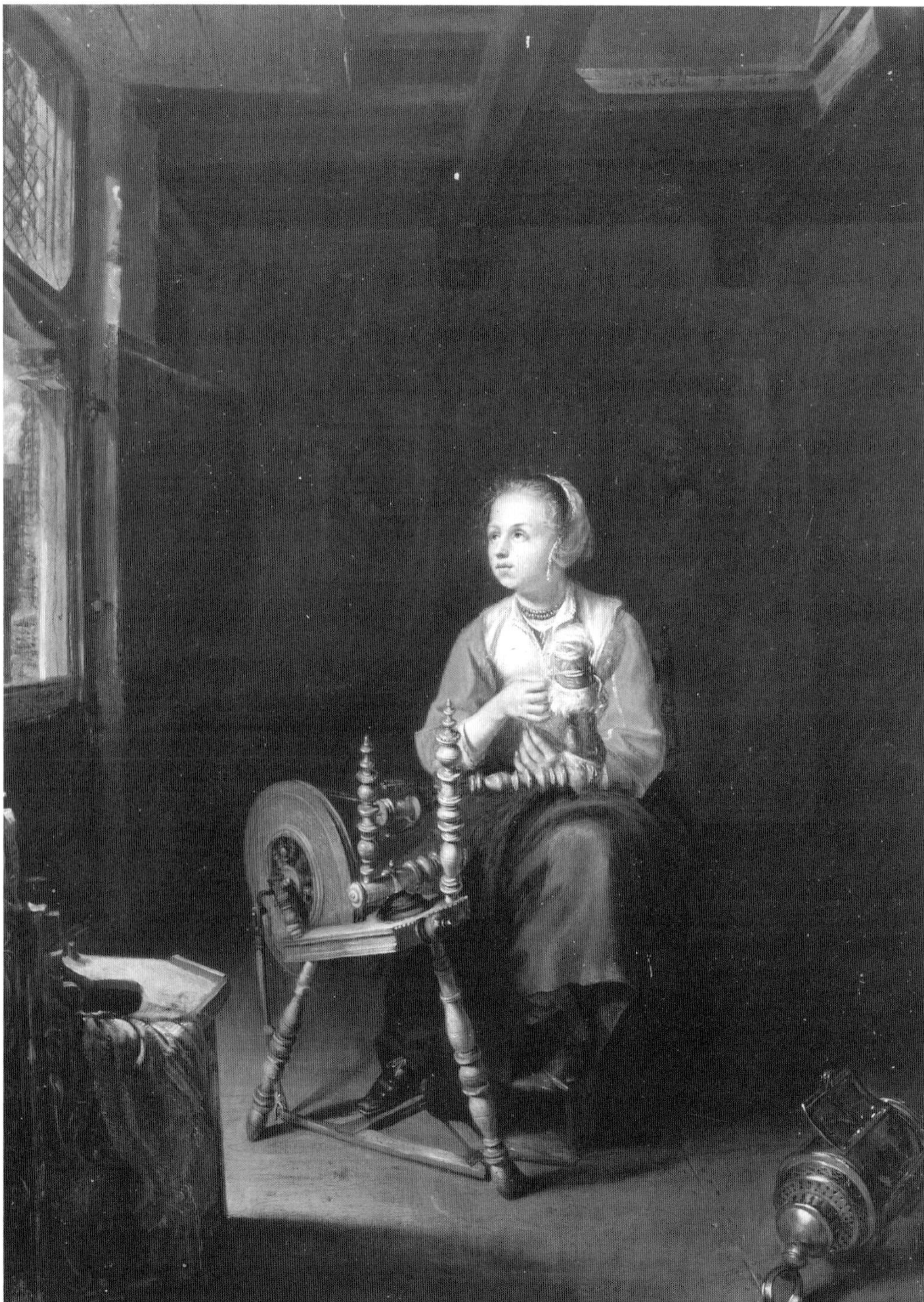

Figure 20. Matthias Naiveau, *Interior with Young Woman Spinning.* Present location unknown. Photo: courtesy Sotheby's, London.

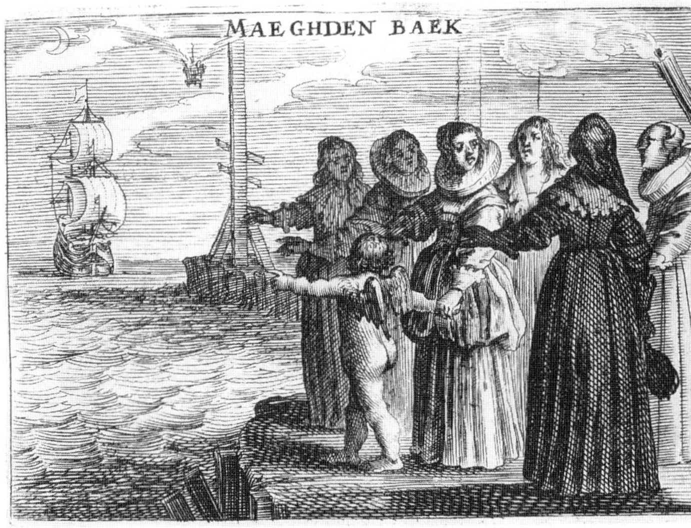

Figure 21. Frontispiece from Jan Soet, *Maagden-baak* . . . , Amsterdam 1641. The Hague, Koninklijke Bibliotheek. Photo: Koninklijke Bibliotheek.

ens could safely participate in the critical ritual of courtship in which they would attract and scrutinize potential spouses. Seventeenth-century authors devoted their full attention to the problems of courtship, explicating its "rules" and dangers. We have already noted Cats's discourse on this subject in the first two chapters of *Houwelyck* and in his *Maechden-plicht.* The latter consists of a rhymed dialogue between two young women skillfully interwoven with forty-four emblems, all offering counsel about courtship and its pitfalls.[49] Jan Soet, in his *Maagden-baak* (Maiden's Beacon) of 1641, treats the subject of courting even more comprehensively than Cats. The charming frontispiece to Soet's book (Fig. 21) shows Cupid trying to encourage some maidens to watch an approaching ship that has been guided into a harbor by the fiery beacon behind them, but they have all turned to a mysterious woman wearing a veil. This veiled figure likely personifies Pudicitia (Chastity),[50] a fitting virtue in this context, for, as the author explains, maidens are like ships because they must weather the storms and perils of courting in order to enter the harbor of marriage unharmed. However, maidens, like ships, must have guidance in order to reach their desired goal; hence the beacon, Soet's book, which the author proudly proclaims as a "leersame light" (light of instruction). With the assistance of some "aerdige Leer-beeltjens" (pleasant images of instruction), Soet promises to escort young women through the perils of courting, on into the tranquil haven of matrimony.[51]

What counsel did Cats, Soet, and other writers offer or, more accurately,

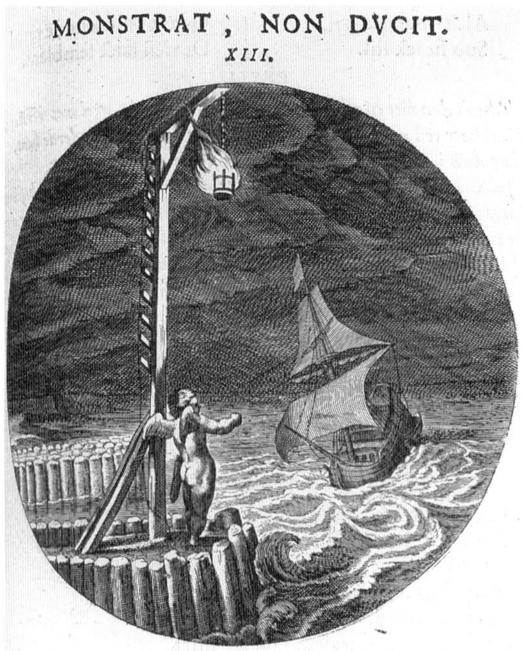

Figure 22. Emblem from Jacob Cats, *Maechden-plicht ofte ampt der ionck-vrouwen in eerbaer liefde, aen-ghewesen door sinne-beelden*, Middelburg 1618. Amsterdam, Universiteits-Bibliotheek Amsterdam. Photo: courtesy Universiteits-Bibliotheek Amsterdam.

what "rules" did they prescribe? First and foremost, that young ladies be permitted only a limited degree of initiative in courting. An emblem from Cats's *Maechden-plicht* elucidates this; its *pictura* shows Cupid standing beside a fiery beacon as he points to an incoming vessel – another example of the ship and harbor as a metaphor of courtship and marriage (Fig. 22).[52] The *subscriptio* likens the beacon, which is only capable of guiding a ship into the harbor, to courtship and the limitations placed on the maiden in promoting it. Young ladies were encouraged to meet suitors within the protective confines of their own homes, under parental supervision. Moreover, they were to avoid the display of excessively swank clothing and jewelry to attract men. On the contrary, they were to ornament themselves with the "jewels" that would most appeal to men, namely the virtues apposite to their sex: humility, modesty, piety, tractability, steadfastness, industriousness, and so forth. Frivolous courtship was discouraged. In fact, no respectable youth would come wooing without ultimately intending to propose marriage. The final decision, namely, the choice of a spouse, depended on parental approval.[53]

The torrent of strictures about courting unleashed by Cats, Soet, and other authors would lead us to believe that they were a stodgy lot of spoilsports. Yet their stern admonitions often seem at odds with the sheer sentimentality

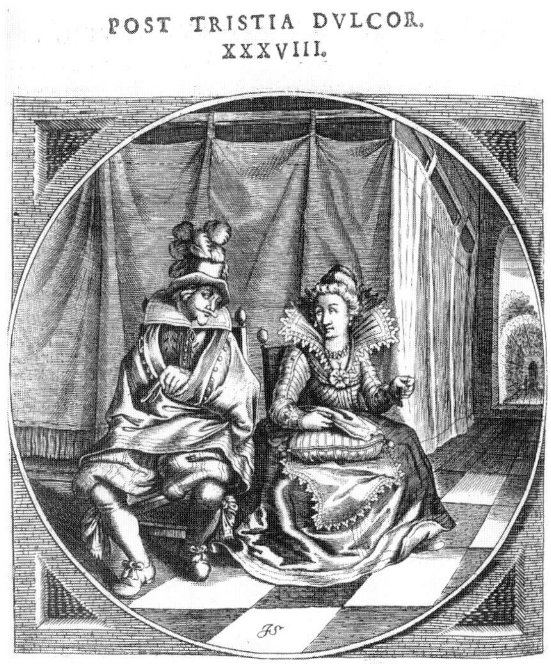

Figure 23. Emblem from Jacob Cats, *Proteus ofte minne-beelden verandert in sinnebeelden*, Rotterdam 1627. Amsterdam, Universiteits-Bibliotheek Amsterdam. Photo: courtesy Universiteits-Bibliotheek Amsterdam.

of the delightful imagery that they employ to convey them. In short, many moralists were acutely aware of the dizzying vicissitudes of love, with its pleasures and pain, and strove to communicate this to their readers in the gentlest possible manner. At times, their sensitive observations even take a curious domestic turn. This is true of an emblem by Cats whose *pictura* shows a man, undoubtedly a suitor, watching a woman sew (Fig. 23). In the *subscriptio,* we learn that this scene and its thought-provoking inscription, "Post Tristia Dulcor" (Sweeter after Sadness) carry amatory overtones:

> Late with my love I did discourse, where as shee
> soweinge sate,
> My grieffes I did complaine, (but marke) shee
> paide mee with her prate.
> Regard, quoth shee, what here I doe, unto it grue good
> heede;
> With needle first a hoole I make, then stopp it
> with the threede.
> Hee that a smale wounde getts, then streight his
> Armes doth cast away
> And calls for plaisters, hee's un fit for Venus
> fielde, I say.
> For love and war therein agree, each hath a
> prosperouse howre.

No sweetnesse can be counted sweete, but first it
hath bene sowre.[54]

Cats's use of sewing as a metaphor for wounding a lover, of military terminology to describe courting, and his dialectical play on the opposites sweet and sour demonstrate the extent to which Petrarchan conceits saturate this emblem.[55]

The rich imagery of Petrarch's sonnets to his beloved Laura (which eventually became known as the *Canzoniere*) exerted a tremendous impact on Dutch seventeenth-century culture, as well it had all over Western Europe since the fourteenth century.[56] Important authors like Huygens, Hooft, and Heinsius, as well as moralists (and oddly, authors of travel books) adapted aspects of Petrarch's style, especially his conceits, which were reworked like formulae in an ever-changing variety of contexts.[57] At this time, the use of Petrarchan imagery had become highly fashionable in a society preoccupied, if not obsessed, with love as a subject of conversation, poetry, and song. As we shall see, such thought also informs, at least on one level, paintings of courtship.[58]

Dutch verse inspired by the works of Petrarch and his followers share common conceits, oxymora, antitheses, and the like. The conventionality of their style and imagery is matched by the conventionality of their subject matter as they invariably focus on two constants: the lady, who is the object of the lover's affection, and the nature of love itself. The lady embodies physical and spiritual perfection; even nature pales by comparison. The typical Petrarchan poem first inventories her external features with characteristic hyberbole. This leads to the revelation that the lady's stellar qualities are only surpassed by her numerous inner virtues, chief among them, her chastity. She is a continual object of adoration, but the poet simultaneously laments her deleterious effect on her love-struck admirers. The classic dilemma, echoed with endless variation, is that of the poet violently seized by love that unfortunately eludes the insouciant object of his affections. The languishing victim desperately hopes that amorous feelings overtake this lady, his *dolce nemica*, the source of his painful, unrequited love.[59]

The visual character of Petrarchan imagery was well suited to amorous emblem books, a genre that flourished during the first two decades of the seventeenth century. We have already quoted an example from the work of Jacob Cats. Some authors were fond of actually lifting lines from Petrarch's sonnets for their *inscriptios,* among them, Heinsius, who does this several times in his *Emblemata amatoria.*[60] Emblem books of the period compare distraught suitors, overpowered by love, to mice caught in traps or ominously threatened by cats, to squirrels running futilely on caged wheels, to stags shot by arrows, to insects attracted to burning candles, while the objects of their undying affection are likened to stars in the firmament, to the sun, to the power of the wind, and even to cold-hearted executioners.[61]

Petrarchan conceits also infuse amorous songbooks, a popular genre consisting of various combinations of songs, poems, and beautiful engravings, often emblematic in nature.[62] In these works we once again encounter lamenting lovers and unattainable paradigms of female beauty and virtue. Like emblem books, the production of songbooks flourished in the first two decades of the seventeenth century with the publication of relatively expensive, lavishly illustrated, elegant tomes with songs and poems penned by some of the best young writers of the period (including Hooft, Vondel, and Bredero).[63] In fact, the distinction between amorous songbooks and emblem books was not always apparent (which probably explains why their owners sometimes had them bound together). Both were published in the same oblong format, often using *caractères de civilité;* both contained similar illustrations and verses that explore love's vicissitudes; and both were targeted for the same rather sizeable audience of affluent young people.[64]

The owners of such emblem books and songbooks did not simply collect them as *objets de luxe;* their use was more practical as young people toted them on excursions (particularly in the country, as such locales were best thought to hasten courtship), to weddings, and other festive gatherings, where they facilitated singing and polite discourse about love.[65] Lovers even exchanged them as presents – in some books, the buyer could insert the coat of arms of his beloved in a space provided therein.[66]

Other types of amatory literature introduced seventeenth-century readers to the pains and pleasures of courtship.[67] Practical guidebooks on the subject were perhaps the most popular, especially the loose translations of one of the most renowned books of antiquity, Ovid's *Art of Love.*[68] All of these works had an important, practical function; although they were objects of leisure, their contents – which frequently employed conventional Petrarchan conceits – provided a framework for the institutionalized conduct of serious courtship leading to marriage.[69] These very same conceits may have been pure literary topoi, but whether contemporary readers recognized them as such is moot because young people likely employed them in their courting strategies. In this sense the literature of love, however conventional, played a dynamic role in shaping seventeenth-century culture.

Representations of courtship in art, although dependent on long-standing pictorial traditions, clearly reflect the aims and content of contemporary amatory literature. It would be reductive, however, to regard these art works as passive receptors of literary influence as both literature and art made decisive contributions to the complicated courting rituals of the day. As we shall see, the sophisticated renderings in art of well-heeled young people were

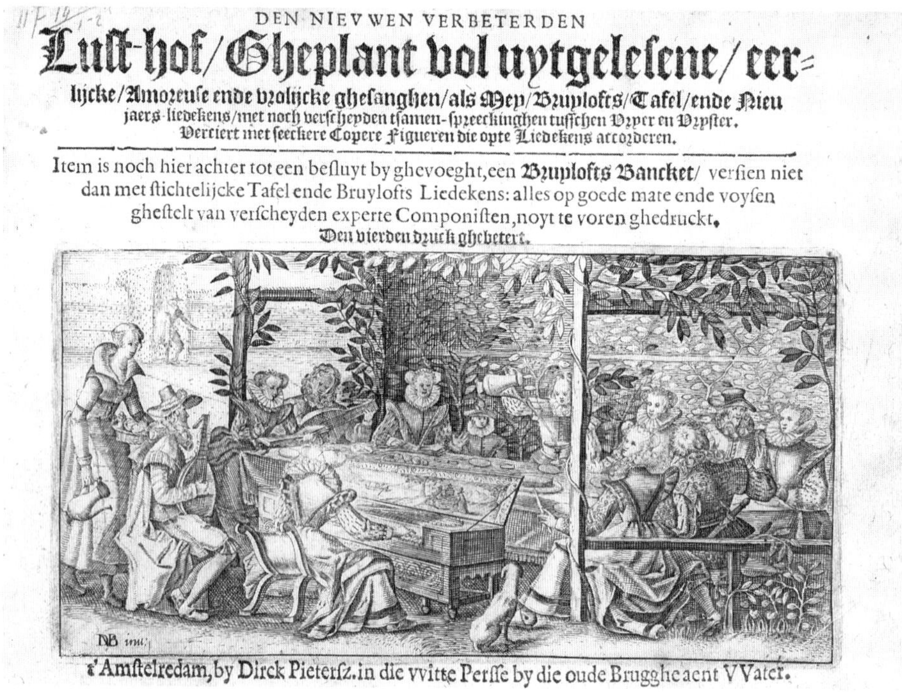

Figure 24. Title page from Anon., *Den nieuwen verbeterden lust-hof*, Amsterdam 1607. The Hague, Koninklijke Bibliotheek. Photo: Koninklijke Bibliotheek.

cleverly calculated to appeal to the very same elite groups who were avid purchasers of songbooks, *emblemata amatoria,* and the like.

An illustration by David Vinckboons, which appeared on the title page of several early seventeenth-century songbooks, demonstrates just how closely contemporaries perceived the links between courtship in art and amatory literature (Fig. 24). The illustration in question depicts music making and merriment within the refreshing confines of a leafy arbor.[70] The pleasant, open-air surroundings, the poses of the couples, their fancy costumes and actions, and the presence of lutes and a spinet recall a number of paintings by the artist of *buitenpartijen* (outdoor garden parties). Vinckboons played a crucial role in the development of this voguish theme in the early seventeenth century, one that flourished precisely at the same time that lavishly produced emblem books and songbooks began to saturate the market.[71]

Vinckboons's painting *Outdoor Merry Company* typifies his approach to this theme (Fig. 25).[72] Within a lush, sylvan setting, splendidly attired youths enjoy one another's company as they play music, dance, and engage in polite conversation. The delicate treatment of the foliage that forms coulisses into the verdant distance offers a botanical parallel to the elegant affectations of

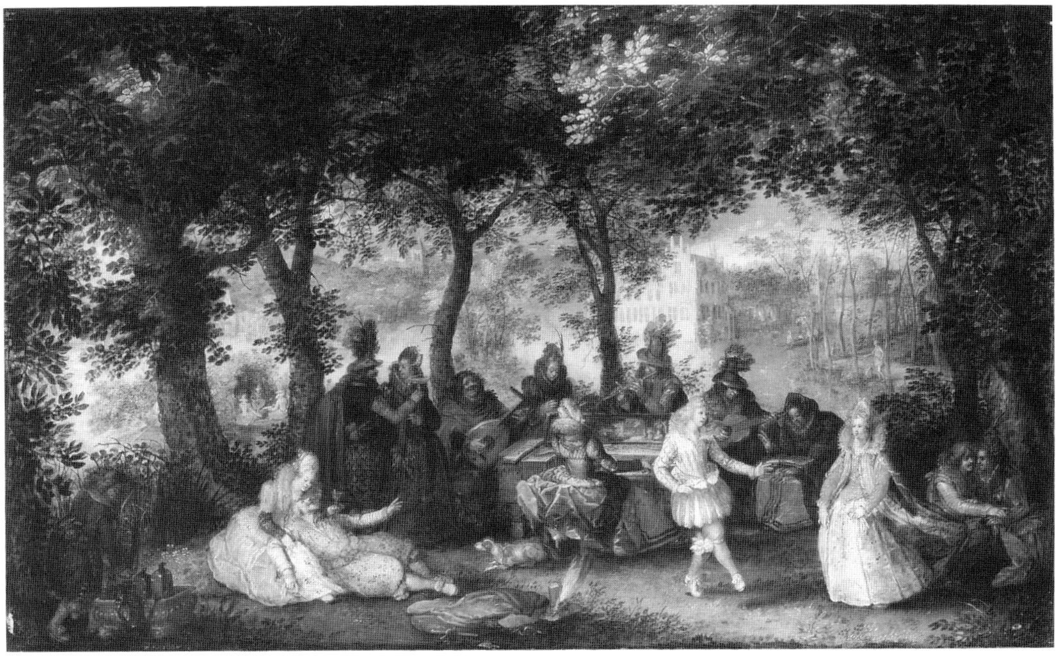

Figure 25. David Vinckboons, *Outdoor Merry Company*, 1610 (oil and tempera on panel, 41 × 68.3 cm). Vienna, Gemäldegalerie der Akademie der bildenden Künste. Photo: Gemäldegalerie.

the revelers. The artist has grouped musicians and singers around a large spinet. Songbooks are present, of the same oblong type for which the artist provided illustrations. Young people also cavort and drink; in the foreground, a young man reclines in the lap of his beloved.

Scholars usually deduce the argument that paintings of *buitenpartijen* carry weighty, didactic content from the observation that they are to some extent pictorially dependent on the tradition of representing mythological and religious themes in garden settings, most notably that of the Prodigal Son squandering his inheritance on prostitutes and drink, a theme of obvious moral condemnation.[73] Yet the insistence on linking garden party images by Vinckboons and other artists to moralizing themes of the sixteenth century, like the parable of the Prodigal Son, is misleading primarily because the visual evidence summoned to establish this link is insufficient.[74] In fact, it has led to the rather awkward argument that it was no longer necessary for artists to include explanatory details in images of garden parties that refer back to these earlier moralizing themes since these very same references were implicitly understood as present. Context determines whether a work represents a garden party, the Prodigal Son, or Mankind before the Last Judgment. It therefore seems fallacious to postulate that *buitenpartijen* carry the same admonitory content as Prodigal Son scenes or those of Mankind before the Last Judgment on the basis of compositional similarities alone or minor, somewhat ambiguous iconographic details (like wine and peacock pies, a seventeenth-century pie made with peacock meat and dressed with the creature's feathers) especially in light of the virtual absence of major ones (like the Prodigal Son himself or episodes from the parable depicted in the background) that would support such a reading.

To be sure, the conduct of young people portrayed in other paintings of this theme invites moral condemnation as the revelers vomit and generally dissipate themselves. Furthermore, there can be no doubt that some contemporaries disapproved of such scenes, but we must not underestimate the complexity of seventeenth-century culture by reading admonitory content into every image of youths indulging themselves in pleasurable activities.[75] In fact, the propensity to view such pictures as morally suspect and predominantly didactic probably stems from our all too homogeneous view of seventeenth-century Dutch culture as dogmatically Calvinist. While it is true that some overzealous clergymen wrote vehement tracts denouncing the evils of drink, it would be reductive to assume that the entire population endorsed their objections.[76]

This view also overlooks the evidence of other sources, like songbooks, that imply that drinking and the pleasure-seeking activities depicted in Vinckboons's painting and other representations of this theme were not always construed negatively. For example, the motif of a suitor in his beloved's lap appears in songbook illustrations where its Petrarchan import is anything but censored (Fig. 26).[77] The professed intention of many of the songbooks themselves, and much of the amatory literature in general, is edification.[78] The ideology that imbues this literature advocated caution, self-control, moderation, and reliance on God's sovereignty.[79] Even the loose translations of Ovid's popular *Art of Love* alter the text of the very bawdy original in the interests of morality and decorum.[80] Such texts must have struck a sympathetic chord with the parents of their young audiences.

I would conclude that the behavior of the figures in Vinckboons's painting should not necessarily be considered excessive. They simply pursue innocuous pleasures that center around the promotion of courtship. This picture, and others like it, celebrate love and must therefore be tied to the contemporary fashion for amatory imagery in all its manifold visual, textual, and even audible forms.

Although the theme of the *buitenpartij* remained highly conventional, it underwent further transformation in the hands of a slightly younger generation, most notably in the works of Esaias van de Velde, who was probably Vinckboons's pupil.[81] Neatly cultivated formal gardens and garden terraces

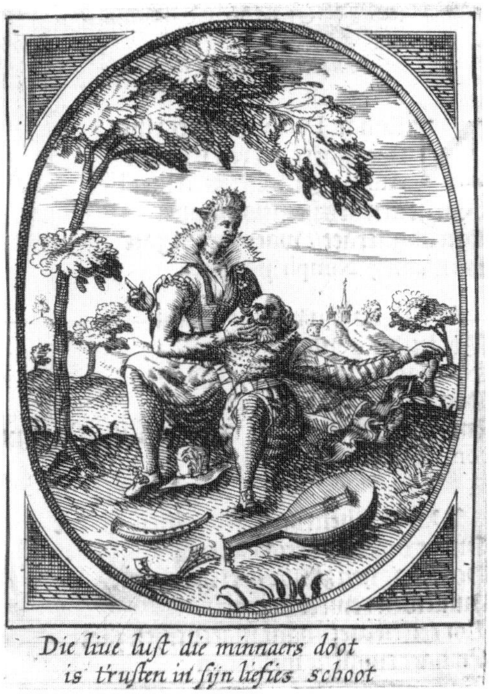

Figure 26. Illustration from W. I. Stam, *Cupido's lusthof*, Amsterdam 1613. The Hague, Koninklijke Bibliotheek. Photo: Koninklijke Bibliotheek.

replace the bosky settings, and the figures themselves shed their anonymity, metamorphosing into stocky, somewhat more individualized young citizens of the Dutch Republic. Van de Velde's *Banquet in a Garden before an Arbour* illustrates these changes (Fig. 27).[82] As in Vinckboons's painting, elegantly clad youths gather outdoors, but in this case in a well-groomed pleasance with a large fountain. They are seated around a table laden with a sumptuous feast, attended by servants.

I contend that this painting too should not be interpreted primarily as a moral lesson just because of its ostensible resemblance to portrayals of the parable of the Prodigal Son. While there is little doubt that some contemporaries viewed these paintings as images of idleness and reckless dissolution – indeed, inscriptions on some prints after such images confirm this – others probably recognized them as scenes of innocuous, youthful merriment with the garden an appropriate place, as so much of the amatory literature suggests, to congregate.[83]

The theme of the *buitenpartij* flourished well into the middle of the century and beyond. In keeping with overall developments within Dutch genre painting, works from this latter period characteristically emphasize elegance and gentility. A good example is Gerbrand van den Eeckhout's *Party on a Terrace* of 1652, which shows young people congregating on a classical portico before a parklike setting containing a statue of Cupid (Fig. 28).[84] This setting,

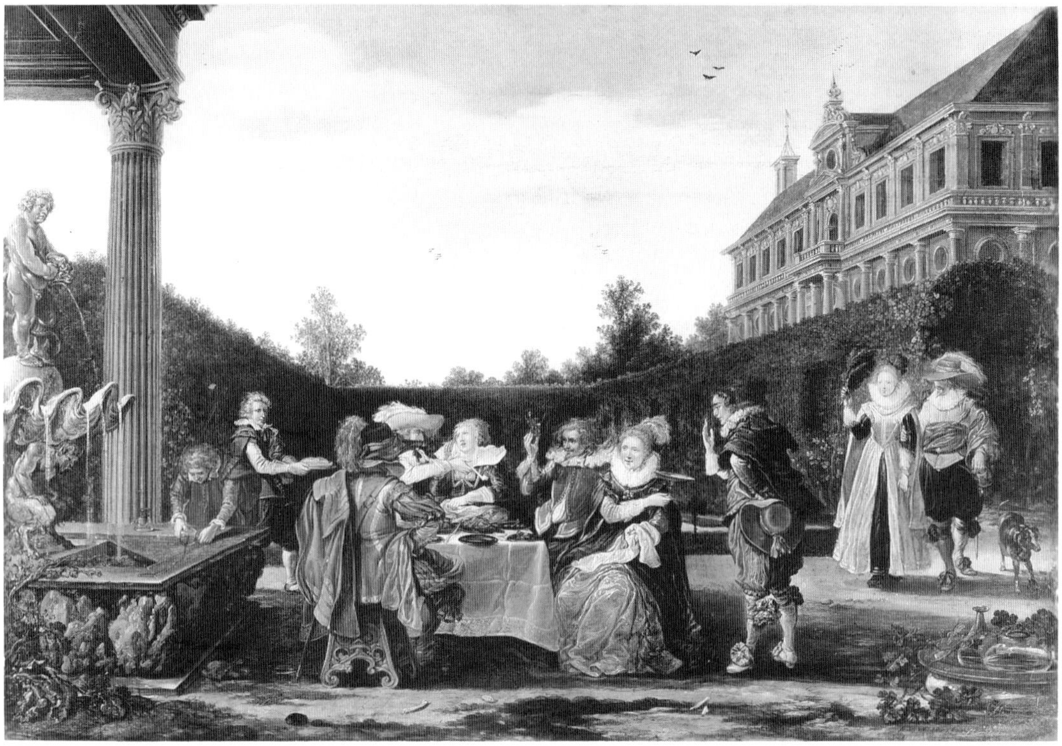

Figure 27. Esaias van de Velde, *Banquet in a Garden before an Arbour*, 1624 (oil on panel, 47 × 67 cm). Vienna, Kunsthistorisches Museum. Photo: museum.

the relaxed poses of the figures, their sartorial splendor, and even Van den Eeckhout's palette, doubtlessly inspired by Flemish art, all convey an atmosphere of affluence and nonchalance.

However elegant, the painting essentially constitutes an updating of the *buitenpartij* theme as the now-familiar motifs are once again present: a lute, songbooks, wine, a servant, and naturally, courting couples, though the latter now proportionally occupy much more space within the canvas. The women in this picture have nearly identical hairdos, garments, and facial features. They are especially beautiful and chic; their silky dresses, crowned by exceptionally wide, layered lace collars, complement their idealized features. These women are quintessential beauties who have become the objects of their ardent suitors' attentions. Their beauty and refinement echo that of the garden setting behind them – no mere coincidence since it was a common literary conceit of the period to compare feminine beauty with nature.[85] The principal identifying feature of their male companions is their modish hats. The individuality of all of these figures is subordinated to the overall courtship

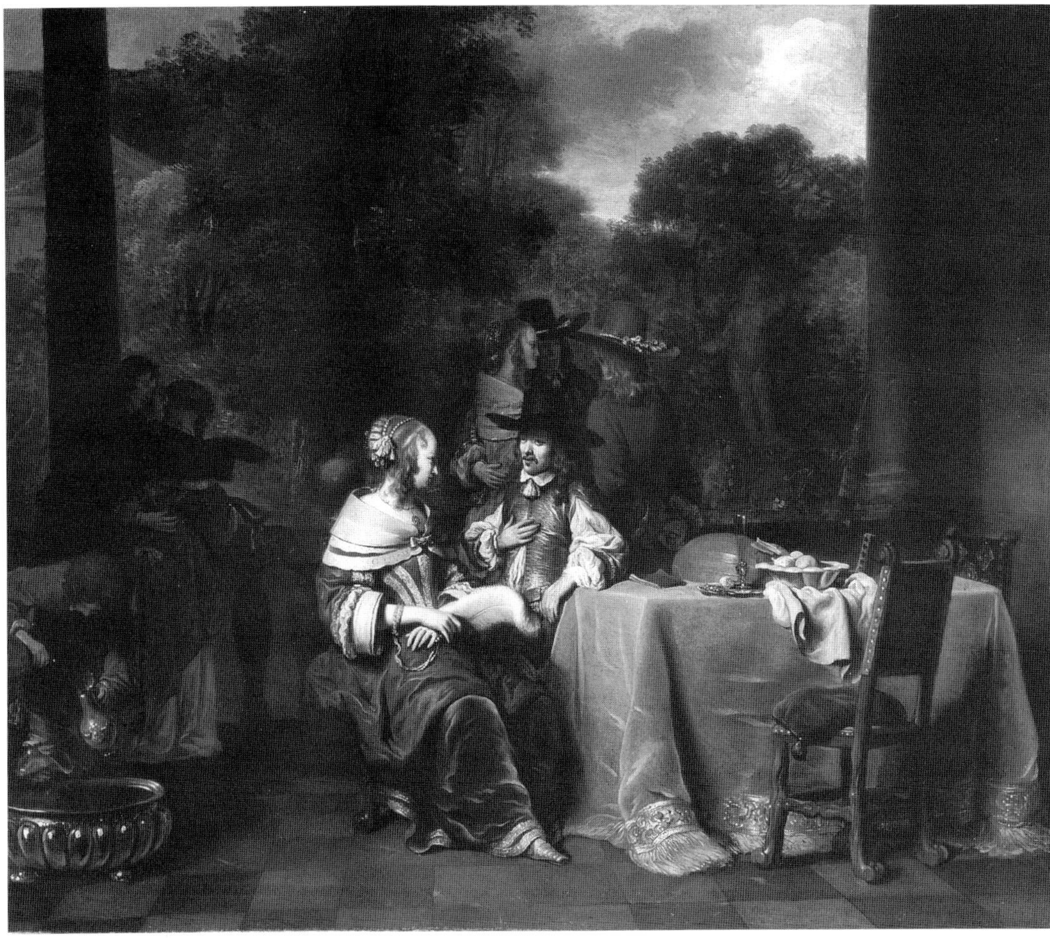

Figure 28. Gerbrand van den Eeckhout, *Party on a Terrace*, 1652 (oil on canvas, 53.5 × 64 cm). Worcester, Worcester Art Museum. Photo: museum.

ritual in which they are engaged, one in which pose, attire, and setting smack of gallantry, polite conversation, and haute couture.

Much more so than other images discussed in this book, paintings of courtship easily lend themselves to narrative readings. A closer examination of Van den Eeckhout's composition confirms this; although the mood of this scene is somewhat restrained, the couples are actively involved in the courting process. In the foreground a man importunes his beloved, the sincerity and urgency of his overtures underscored by his hand held over his heart. She holds a fan, a motif that must have been replete with associations for contemporaries given its frequent appearance in scenes of courtship.[86] It is impossible to determine its precise significance here, but it is clear that her suitor's companions have been more fortunate, especially the one to the left with his arm around the waist of a maiden holding a songbook.

I base my discussion of the narrative dimension of this painting (and, as we shall see, other images of this type) on the wide-ranging associations that one encounters in contemporary ekphrastic descriptions of paintings. As stated in the introduction, the authors of *ekphraseis* attempted to induce empathic responses from their readers by presenting paintings as objects for sensual contemplation and emotional and intellectual engagement.[87] Popular conceits that involve languishing lovers and insouciant ladies would have stimulated contemporary viewers to project their own feelings and experiences into the narratives of many scenes of courtship.

Van den Eeckhout produced several paintings of elegant courtship in the early 1650s. In fact, the Worcester painting closely resembles one of the same subject now in The Metropolitan Museum of Art in New York (Fig. 29). Once again, the artist has depicted a party of well-dressed youths gathered on a columned terrace before a wooded grove. In the background, a man gestures to his heart as he woos a fashionably dressed young woman holding a fan.[88] In front of this couple is a man with his arm around the chair of his lady; he gently touches her shoulder as they sing from an oblong songbook.[89]

The man in the foreground is clearly the focus of attention in this painting by virtue of his position within the composition and the light that softly illuminates his resplendent form. He sits in a chair beside a large hunting dog, in front of a servant and a table with music books on it. This young man stares wistfully at the couple singing the duet, his distress indicated by his head resting on his hand, the time-honored gesture of melancholia.[90] In this context, his melancholy ensues from unrequited love – in fact, his gesture appears in other paintings with amatory themes where the plaintive suitor is likewise set apart from a couple to underscore his despondency and rejection.[91] This man, along with his counterparts in other pictures, represents the classic spurned suitor whose laments are commonplace in amatory poetry and songs of the period.[92]

The focus in paintings of *buitenpartijen* on the ritual of courtship, fashion, and gentility leads to the question of who constituted the audience for such images. These canvases were likely aimed at the same elite public who, motivated by shared values and sizeable disposable incomes, purchased large quantities of amatory songbooks and emblem books.[93] Many members of the leisure class actually owned country properties (particularly after mid-century) and, if they did not, would nonetheless retire regularly to formal gardens or more bucolic locales for parties – the woods surrounding Haarlem were praised as an ideal gathering place.[94] Artists did not rely on actual *buitenpartijen* for inspiration – in other words, these works do not document

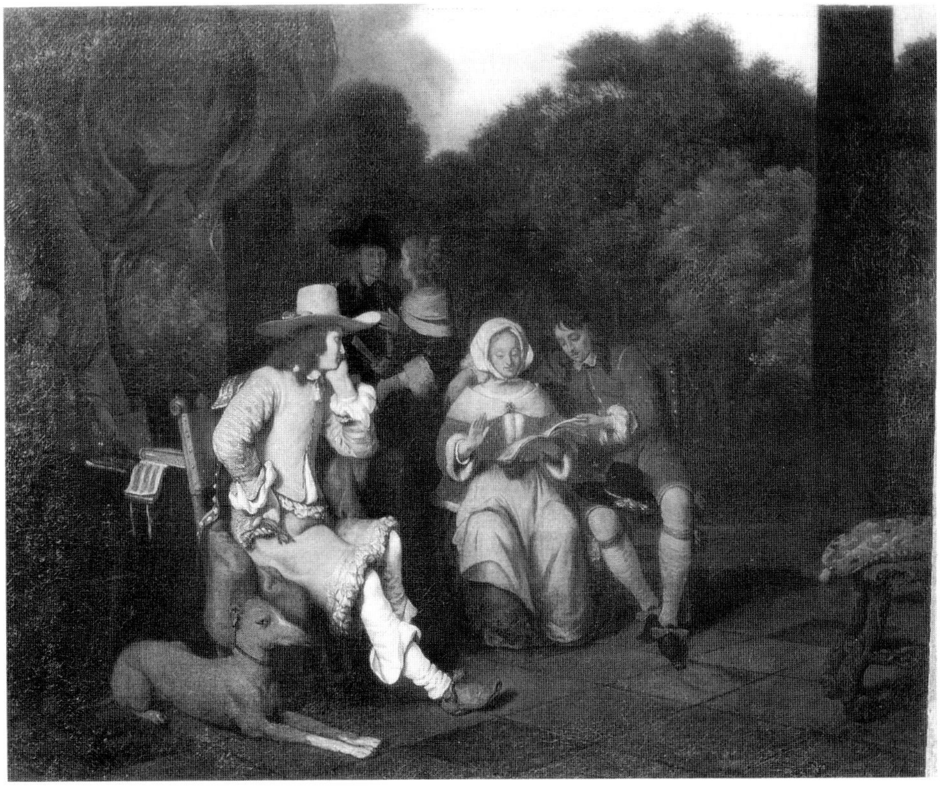

Figure 29. Gerbrand van den Eeckhout, *Party on a Terrace* (oil on canvas, 50.5 × 62.5 cm). New York, The Metropolitan Museum of Art, Bequest of Annie C. Kane 1926 (26.260.8). Photo: museum.

social realities of the day; indeed their close adherence to long-standing pictorial traditions is obvious. Nevertheless, prospective purchasers must have recognized the sophisticated revelry depicted in these paintings as an imaginative artistic equivalent to actual festivities.[95]

The conventionality of the *buitenpartij* imagery attests to its popularity and provides evidence of widely shared attitudes and expectations among contemporaries. On the basis of the types of associations that contemporary *ekphraseis* evoked, we can assume that some viewers, enticed by the mimetic naturalism of such paintings with their idyllic settings inhabited by sleekly dressed youths with whom they were able – or wished – to identify, vicariously projected themselves into the courting rituals depicted therein – in much the same manner that popular songbooks invited those who sang their tunes to empathize with the emotions explored in the songs.[96] (This likely explains, in works by Van den Eeckhout and others, the presence of empty chairs that seem to draw the viewer into the scene.) Thus, these paintings functioned as objects for contemplation and empathic response and, like the vast body of amatory literature they mirror, served to stimulate witty, cultured conversation about the vicissitudes of love. Far from passively reflecting contemporary preoccupations with love, these paintings actively articulated them.

Young people also court in interiors in seventeenth-century Dutch paintings, which were classified at that time as *gezelschapjes* (usually translated as "merry companies").[97] These pictures likewise stem from critical developments in early seventeenth-century genre painting, which crystallized in the slick, evocative works produced during the second half of the century, a period in which the repertoire of themes pertaining to courtship expanded.[98] It is probably no accident that along with the development of new themes came a number of stylistic innovations that ultimately proved well suited to the imagery of elegant love. Artists such as Gerard ter Borch, Jacob van Loo, and Frans van Mieris the Elder remained sensitive to the renderings of materials and stuffs, but now produced these with unprecedented refinement. They also focused on the subtle, natural evocations of light and shadow on figures and objects that occupy carefully constructed spaces, often vertical in format. The evenly lit, monochromatic interiors of their predecessors seem archaic in comparison to these delicately illuminated, exquisitely crafted works of great narrative subtlety. Yet despite the technical mastery of these paintings, they too are striking for the conventionality of their imagery, for the incessant repetition of a limited number of stock motifs and types.

Jacob van Loo was an important member of this younger generation of artists who helped transform genre painting. Like the paintings of his Amsterdam colleague Gerbrand van den Eeckhout, Van Loo's work is pivotal to the development of courtship imagery around midcentury.[99] His representations of this theme generally vary in the degree to which decorum prevails, ranging from downright bawdy to completely innocuous. Given the scope of this book, however, it is most profitable to focus on the latter. One example shows a youth watching a maiden make lace in a room with other busy young women (Fig. 30). It seems unnecessary to read weighty, censorious overtones into this work; in fact, it is difficult not to accept this picture at face value, as a representation of courting among adolescents. It actually resembles a detail from an eighteenth-century catchpenny print that, as the costumes of the figures suggest, was printed from a seventeenth-century woodblock (Fig. 31).[100] This print, its crude lines indicating that it was intended for mass distribution, illustrates the transition of life from the cradle to matrimony. Like Van Loo's painting, the detail in question (Fig. 31a) includes a man beside a maiden making lace in a room with other young people. It is simply but aptly inscribed "hier vryen de Jongmans" (Here the Young Men Court).

Young people are portrayed courting in another, well-known painting by Van Loo (Fig. 32). Its psychological subtlety surpasses the picture just discussed as does its overall pictorial refinement. It has been suggested that this painting represents an elegant updating of the earlier, more bawdy portrayals of brothels because of the presence of the canopied bed in the room, the large glass on the table, and the shell – an attribute of Venus – in the pediment above the door.[101] This interpretation is somewhat problematic. To begin with, the presence of a canopied bed does not necessarily mean that a room in a brothel or even a bedroom is being represented. During much of the seventeenth century, beds could be found in any number of rooms, including the kitchen.[102] While the shell is unquestionably an attribute of Venus, it must not necessarily be interpreted as a symbol of sexual impropriety. After all, Venus herself sometimes appears on the title pages of songbooks devoid of prurient content.[103] Therefore, contemporaries did not always construe the presence of Venus or her attributes among courting young people negatively.

Van Loo focuses on the gentle entreaties of the elegant young man, which probably explains why this work has long carried the title *Wooing*. Judging from his attentive gaze and gesture, the youth seems to entreat his beloved. The nuances of his posture, gesture, and facial expression, along with those of his lady, match the soft luminous style of the painting. The evocation of emotion, specifically that of longing on the part of the young man confronted with the ostensibly inattentive object of his supplications is thoroughly Petrarchan.

Other details in the painting confirm this reading. A basket filled with fabric and a sewing cushion to the side of the maiden are motifs that may convey particular associations in this context. A common conceit in amatory texts of this period is that of the enervated lover who is so overwhelmed with affection that he or she can no longer perform daily tasks effectively. An emblem by Jan Harmensz. Krul depicts this conceit. I do not cite this emblem as if to posit a one-to-one relationship between it and the motif in the painting for, as I have just stated, the conceit was quite popular. In its *pictura*, a maiden is interrupted while sewing by a cupid bearing a love message (Fig. 33). She is no longer able to concentrate on her work because, as the inscription states, love has caused her to take leave of her senses. Her plight is further expounded in the *subscriptio:*

> My duty requires me to work, but Love will not allow me any rest.
> I do not feel like doing anything;
> My thoughts are nourished by Love, Love nourishes my thoughts,
> And when I fight it, I am powerless.
> Everything I do is against my will and desire,
> Because you, o restless Love, hold me in your power![104]

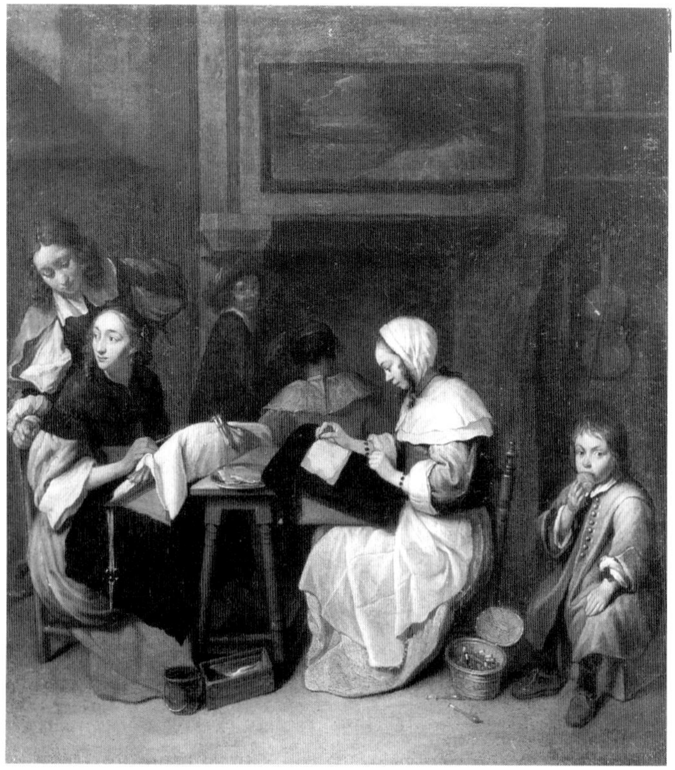

Figure 30. Jacob van Loo, *Interior with Women Making Lace.* Present location unknown. Photo: courtesy Sotheby's, London.

Van Loo's painting may well convey the same idea through the motif of the young lady who has put her sewing aside. This very same motif appears in many other paintings that are replete with amorous associations, among them *The Love Letter* by Johannes Vermeer (Fig. 34). A number of scholars have examined this painting, but the motif of the needlework in the sewing basket beside the lute-playing woman has not been addressed.[105] Given the context, it could very well function in much the same manner as the basket in the picture by Van Loo, that is, as a reference to the maiden's preoccupation with love.

The footwarmer on which the young lady rests her foot is another motif with possible significance in Van Loo's painting (Fig. 32). This motif has been linked to a frequently cited – and often misunderstood – emblem by Roemer Visscher whose *pictura* also shows a footwarmer (Fig. 35).[106] The *inscriptio* calls the warmer a "mignon des dames" (a favorite of women). In the *subscriptio,* Visscher initially notes how women are fond of the object,

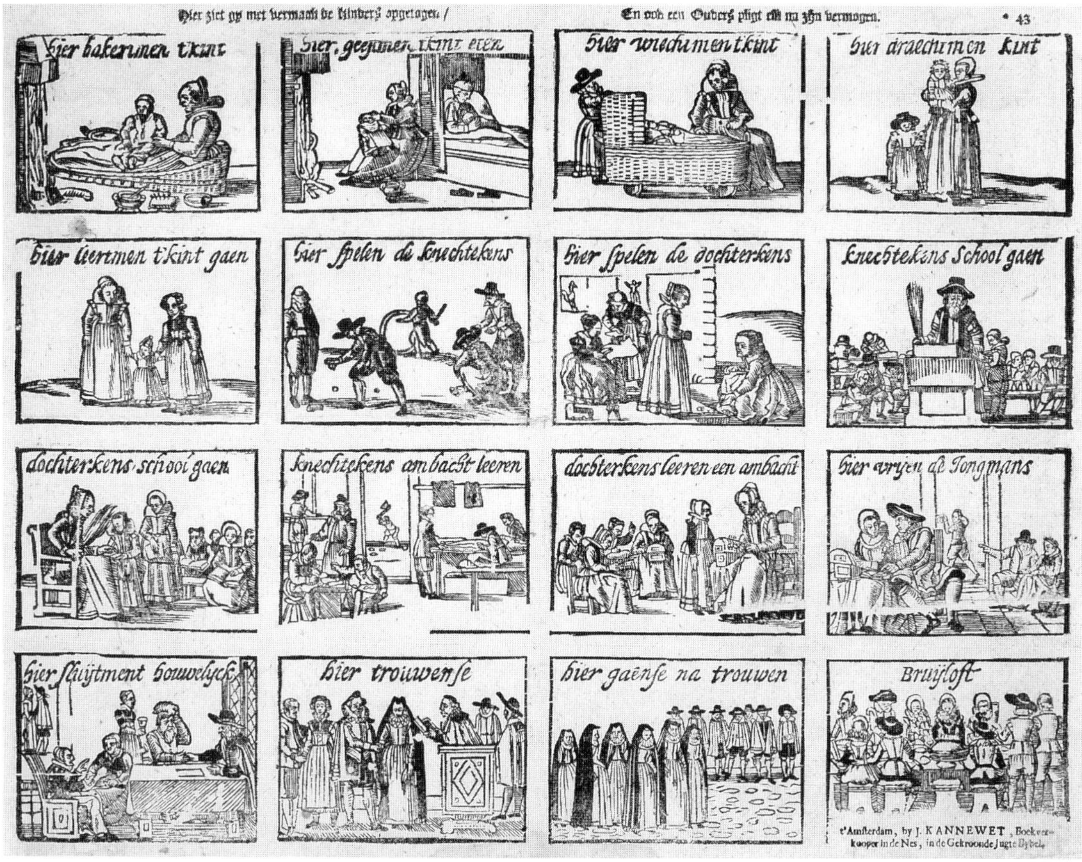

Figure 31. Catchpenny print, published by J. Kannewet. Amsterdam, Rijksprentenkabinet. Photo: Rijksmuseum-Stichting.

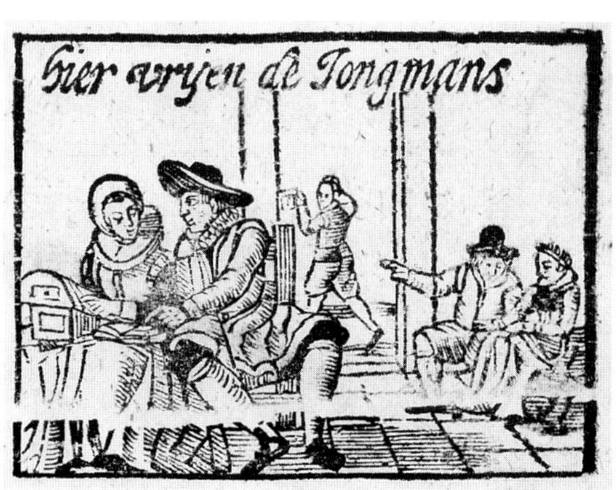

Figure 31a. Detail of Figure 31.

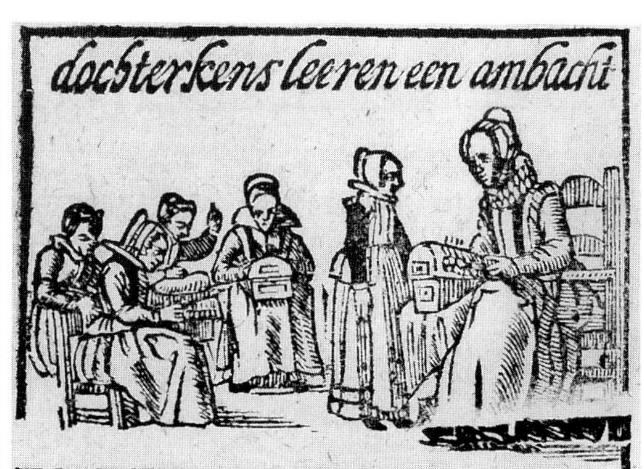

Figure 31b. Detail of Figure 31.

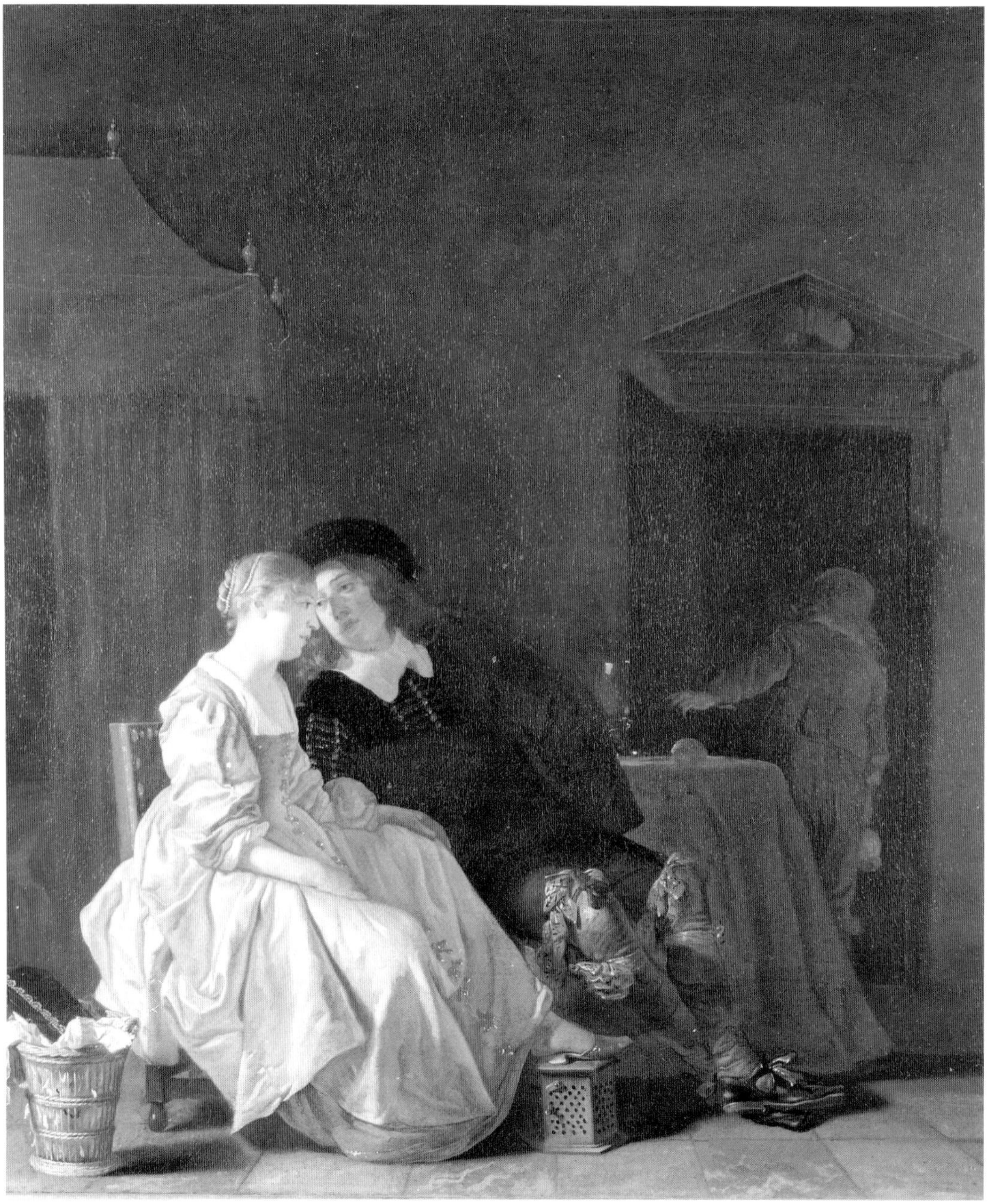

Figure 32. Jacob van Loo, *Wooing* (oil on canvas 73.3 × 66.8 cm). The Hague, Mauritshuis. Photo: A. Dingjan, The Hague.

Vrijsters die minnen,, en hebben geen zinnen.

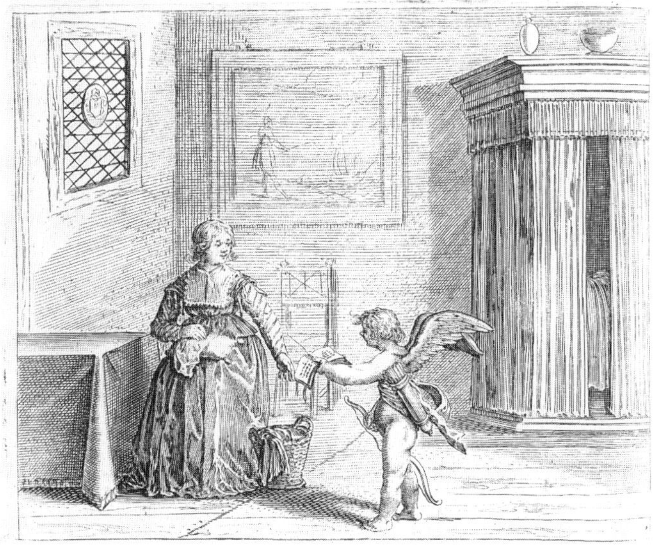

Figure 33. Emblem from Jan Harmensz. Krul, *Pampiere wereld*, Amsterdam 1644. Amsterdam, Universiteits-Bibliotheek Amsterdam. Photo: courtesy Universiteits-Bibliotheek Amsterdam.

particularly in wintry weather, but he quickly arrives at the real subject at hand, to wit, proper courting strategies:

> He who aspires to win second place in [the ladies'] esteem [first place belongs to the footwarmer of course!] must embark upon serving them with sweet, witty and amusing talk, avoiding all boorishness and vulgarity, without reprimanding their cackling and chattering and never mocking their fussy and showy clothes; but praising them for everything they do and propose, then he will be praised in their company as a perfect courtier.[107]

This could be a rare instance in which an emblem functions as a true *clavis interpretandi* for a motif in a painting. The fact that the emblem discusses proper courting tactics supplements our understanding of the painting, especially since other motifs in it – the seashell, the needlework that has been placed aside, and such pictorial factors as the youthfulness of the figures, their silky garments, restrained gestures, and demeanors – all contribute to its display of romance and *civilité.*

The same sentiments that saturate this work are found in other representations of courtship produced during the latter half of the century. In some paintings, zealous suitors sing and play music with their sweethearts. These

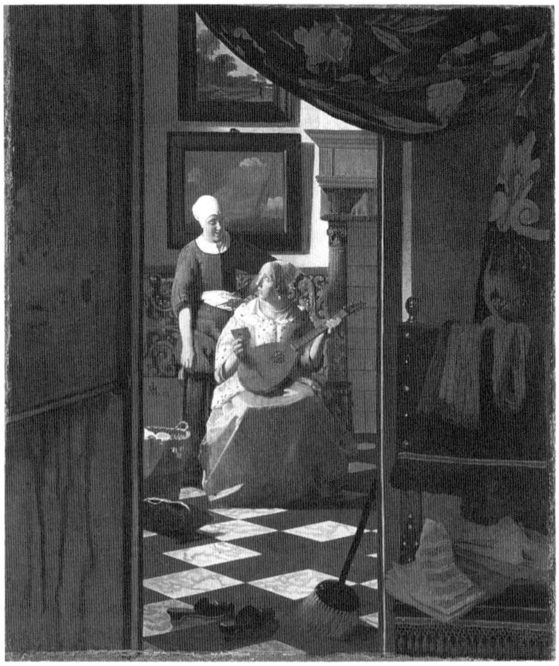

Figure 34. Johannes Vermeer, *The Love Letter* (oil on canvas, 44 × 38.5 cm). Amsterdam, Rijksmuseum. Photo: Rijksmuseum-Stichting.

scenes of young people making music in interiors, among the most popular in Dutch art of the Golden Age, already appear in early seventeenth-century songbook illustrations (see, e.g., Fig. 36). Dirck Hals, Jan Miense Molenaer, Pieter Codde, and other artists of their generation often represented this theme (see, e.g., Fig. 37).[108] Art historians have so frequently discussed images of music making in Dutch art that I will not try the reader's patience here by replicating their findings.[109] I prefer to focus on some of the more unusual ways that artists have treated this theme.

Once again, what is most immediately striking about these paintings is the conventionality of their subject matter. Despite some clear differences in nuance, nearly all consist of swank, youthful figures who sing or play music within well-appointed interiors. Their instruments, often displaying ornately carved necks festooned with brightly colored ribbons, contribute to the general aura of opulence as well, since musical instruments were considered luxury items that connoted status for the owner.[110] The creators of these pictures were clearly responding to a market, that is, to the art-buying public's enthusiasm for such imagery and, by extension, to widely shared ideas and attitudes about love.[111] Nowhere is this more obvious than in paintings with a strong narrative emphasis.

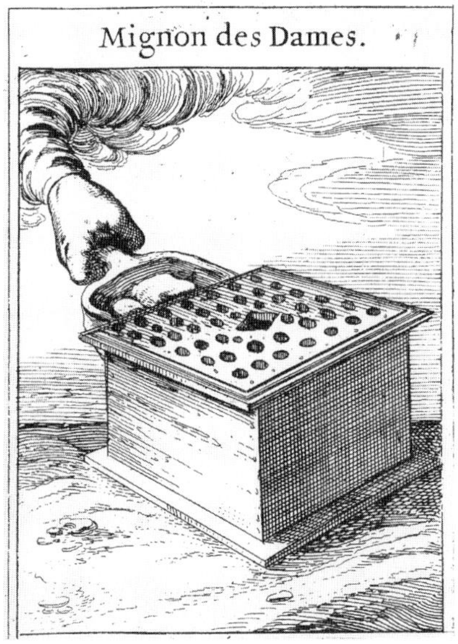

Figure 35. Emblem from Roemer Visscher, *Sinne-poppen*, Amsterdam 1614. Amsterdam, Universiteits-Bibliotheek Amsterdam. Photo: courtesy Universiteits-Bibliotheek Amsterdam.

Gerard ter Borch's *The Music Party* is an outstanding example of this type (Fig. 38).[112] Indeed, one of the most impressive aspects of Ter Borch's art was its uncanny narrative subtlety, its psychic nuance and tension created by scenes and situations left deliberately ambiguous. Moreover, as Alison Kettering has so convincingly demonstrated, Petrarchan notions are often paramount in his paintings of courtship.[113] In *The Music Party,* a woman wearing a silk dress and yellow jacket trimmed with fur has interrupted her performance on the large theorbo held between her knees in order to examine a page of music – among a lady's myriad accomplishments, Petrarchan poetry celebrates her ability to sing and play music.[114] Her equally well-dressed male companion has evidently been singing from the oblong songbook that he holds. He gazes fixedly at the object of his affections, but his desire seems thwarted by her indifference. A third, youthful figure standing behind the couple masterfully underscores the tension created by the suitor's longing and the maiden's insouciance. While they ignore his presence, his rapt attention to their actions emphasizes their somewhat ambiguous relationship. In this painting, music making is the pretext for a subtly articulated yet unresolved narrative revolving around courtship.

Other artists focus on music making as a pretext for courtship themes though their work often lacks the elusive quality of Ter Borch's. A painting by Jacob Ochtervelt entitled *The Music Lesson* is not so much an actual music lesson – a subject that Dutch artists sometimes painted – but a lesson in love (Fig. 39).[115] Elegance and grace abound, as suggested by the richly up-

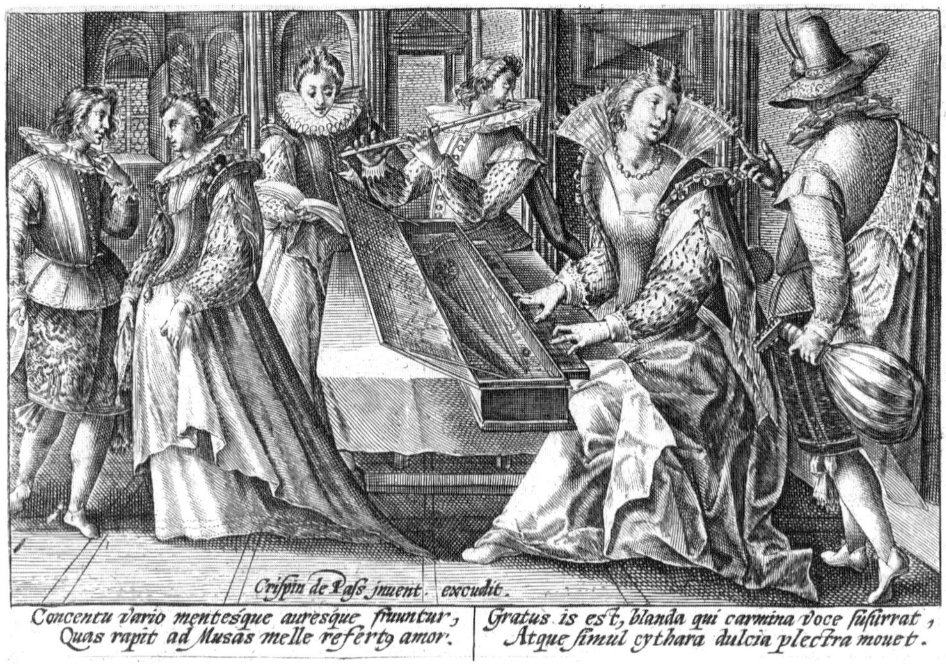

Figure 36. Illustration from Anon., *Nieuwen ieucht spiegel* . . . N.p., n.d. (ca. 1620). The Hague, Koninklijke Bibliotheek. Photo: Koninklijke Bibliotheek.

holstered furniture, the figures' fashionable garments, and especially their slightly oblique poses as they incline toward one another. The young man playing the theorbo gazes rapturously into the eyes of his beloved. However, in classic Petrarchan fashion, she does not return his gaze but looks at the theorbo as she uses her bow to point to a passage in the music book on the table. The inference is that this lady controls not only the music making but the heart of her suitor as well.

Suitors are more successful in other pictures representing this theme. For example, in Jan Verkolje's *Elegant Couple in an Interior* (Fig. 40), the young man grasps the hand of his beloved and beckons her to join him in a duet. She does seem to respond to his overtures, even if her gaze is somewhat ambiguous. Such a richly evocative exchange of glances is often found in other images of music making (see, e.g., Fig. 41). This motif, along with the sumptuous display of exquisitely crafted furnishings and garments, helped to implicate contemporary viewers.

Suitors who long to be the focus of their ladies' affections, a feature of the works just examined, are also central to several rather humorous paintings that show men enviously teasing tiny, playful dogs who have the good fortune

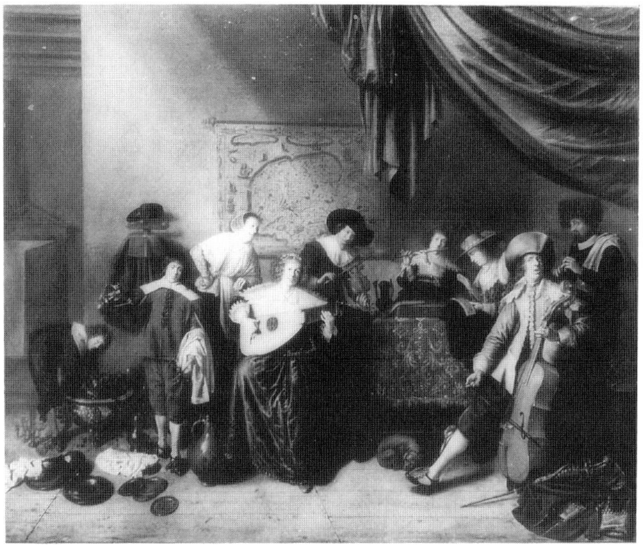

Figure 37. Jan Miense Molenaer, *Interior with Figures Making Music*, 1636 (oil on canvas, 100 × 125 cm). Present location unknown.

to be seated in their mistresses' laps. In one by Frans van Mieris the Elder – in which the artist has used himself and his wife as models – a man pulls on the ear of a puppy in a woman's lap as she simultaneously attempts to push him away (Fig. 42).[116] Some have suggested that this gesture signifies her efforts to preserve her chastity against the onslaughts of a tempter.[117] However, this interpretation seems inconsistent with the playful appearance of the scene. It is possible that it should be construed in Petrarchan terms: the suitor's action could be one of jealousy as he attempts to displace the animal as the principal object of this aloof beauty's affection. The conceit of the envious suitor who competes with a lap dog for his lady's favor, which Van Mieris illustrates with such tongue-in-cheek humor, is found in several songs and love poems of the period:

> Fortunate little dog, your prosperous lot is envied:
> Fortunate little dog, that so often enjoyed Celestyne's lap,
> And, to my regret, was caressed by her so softly.[118]

Another representation of this theme, by Pieter van Slingelandt (Fig. 43), was likely inspired by Van Mieris's painting.[119] In a dark yet opulent interior (as indicated by the ornate, classical fireplace), a dashing young man

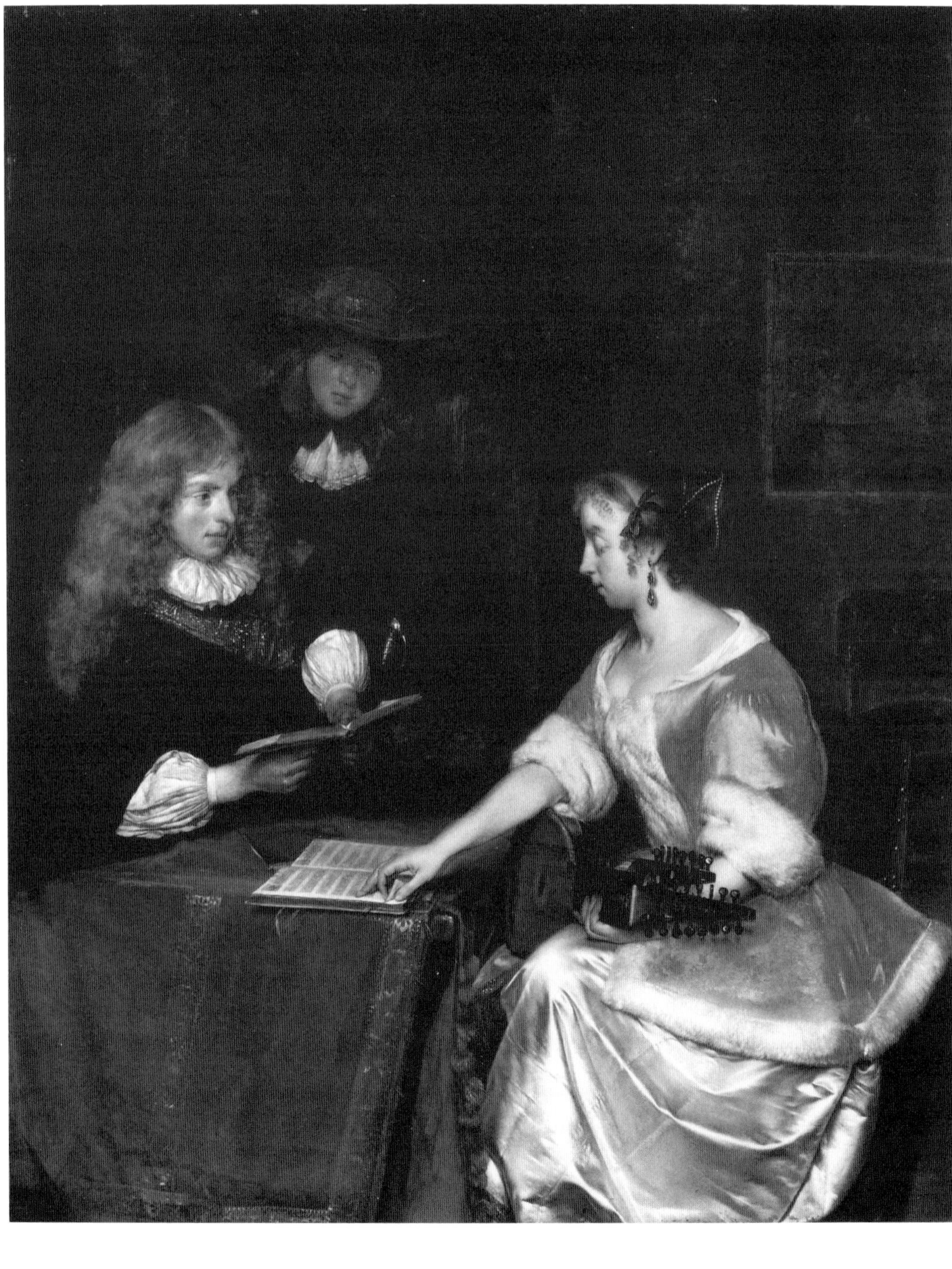

Figure 38. Gerard ter Borch, *The Music Party* (oil on panel, 58.1 × 47.6 cm). Cincinnati, Cincinnati Art Museum, Bequest of Mary M. Emery. Photo: museum.

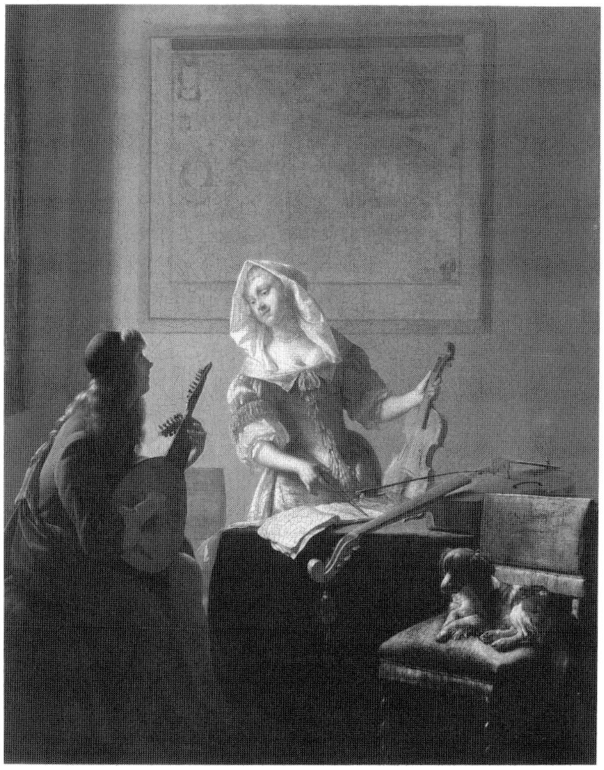

Figure 39. Jacob Ochtervelt, *The Music Lesson*, 1671 (oil on canvas, 80.2 × 65.5 cm). Chicago, The Art Institute of Chicago, Mr. and Mrs. Martin A. Ryerson Collection 1933.1088. Photo: The Art Institute.

uses a recorder to tease the little dog in his lady's lap. She looks at the viewer while halfheartedly pushing her jealous suitor away. This scene may lack the subtle humor of Van Mieris's, but with its prominent display of instruments and songbooks, it is more demonstratively amorous.

Related to these paintings of the young man who vies with a dog for his lady's affection or who gazes longingly at his beloved while singing or playing instruments are those that depict the suitor who gestures obsequiously before the object of his affection (see, e.g., Figs. 44, 45). In each of these works, the youth deferentially removes his hat and bows – in De Hooch's painting, he actually genuflects – before a beautiful woman.[120]

Questions of style aside, the conventionality of this imagery is indeed remarkable. Time and again, we witness the dramatic game of courtship in which the chief participants are resplendent in their sleek, tailored finery. The haute couture of these figures echoes that of the settings that function

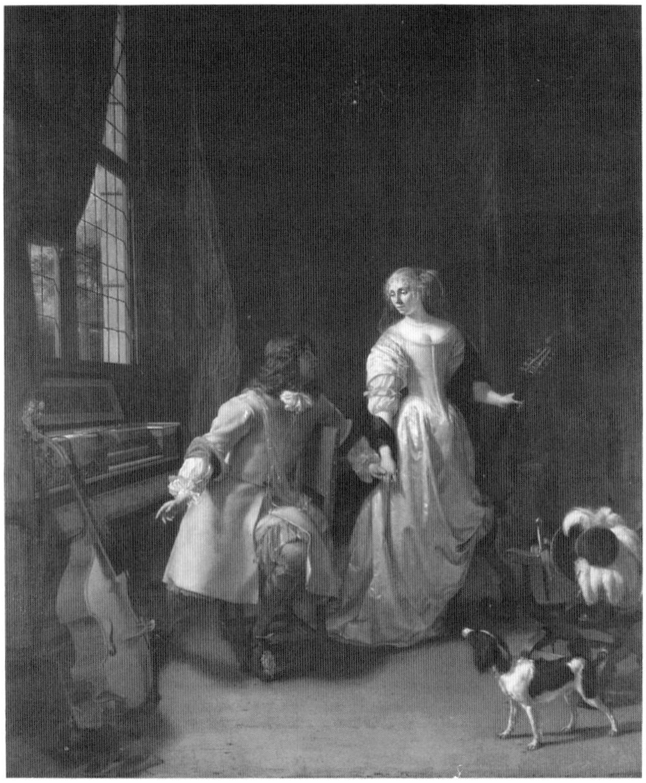

Figure 40. Jan Verkolje, *Elegant Couple in an Interior* (oil on canvas, 96.5 × 57.1 cm). Private collection.

as well-appointed proscenia for the narratives: marble fireplaces of classical design, beautiful chairs, sumptuously draped beds, and tables spread with luxurious carpets abound. These images, and those of music-making couples and men teasing dogs in their mistresses' laps, all display heightened elegance and refinement, sophisticated references to courtship and to Petrarchan notions of love. They thus offered contemporary viewers, already seduced by their stunning visual orchestrations of light and textures, an opportunity to vicariously project themselves into the fictitious love lives of the wealthy *jeunesse dorée* that unfolded before them. In this sense, these works of art, along with amatory literature, contributed to the enormous contemporary appetite for love imagery in all its diverse manifestations.[121]

Again, I would argue that, for contemporaries, paintings of courtship were not always principally moralizing (though for some viewers they undoubtedly were), nor were they mere illustrations of civilized manners and polite con-

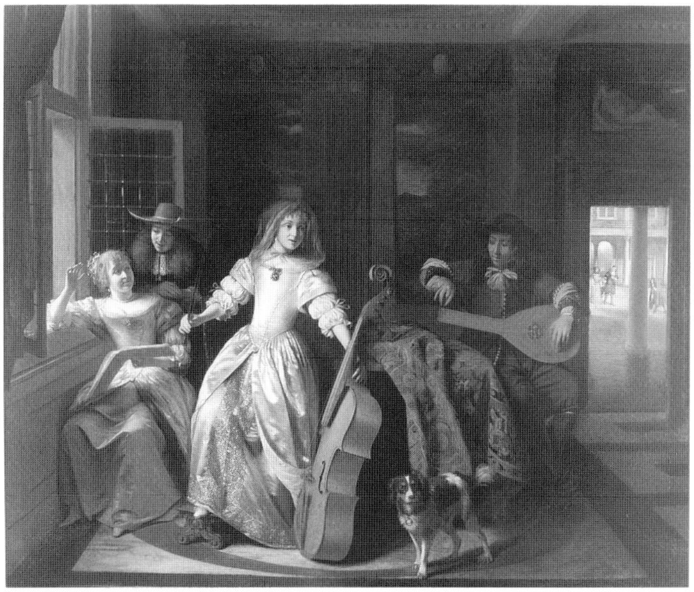

Figure 41. Pieter de Hooch, *A Musical Party with Four Figures,* 1674 (oil on canvas, 98 × 115 cm). Honolulu, Academy of Art, Purchase 1971 (3798.1). Photo: Academy of Art.

versation or demonstrations of national pride in textile production.[122] Far from castigating amorous behavior, these pictures, in their subtlety and restraint, present the young people depicted therein as exemplars of courting etiquette. This is especially true of the maidens; they invariably adopt the same self-contained poses that are seen in contemporary portraits of young women. In their passivity and reserve, often emphasized by the motif of hands folded demurely at the waist, these young women act safely within the parameters of socially and ethically acceptable behavior that Cats, his moralist colleagues, and even the authors of songbooks and related amatory literature, advocated. For them, it was permissible for young women to use their beauty, irreproachable behavior, and fine clothing to attract suitors, but all further initiative in courtship belonged to their admirers.[123] Even the general Petrarchan orientation of these pictures, like that of the songbooks, *emblemata amatoria,* and related works, serves to underscore these values. Despite the power that women exert on submissive men in art and literature saturated with popular amorous conceits, their dominance was pure fiction that paradoxically affirmed and endorsed the existing social order.[124] Women may have subjugated men through their beauty and decorous reserve, but these very qualities consistently championed as quintessentially feminine

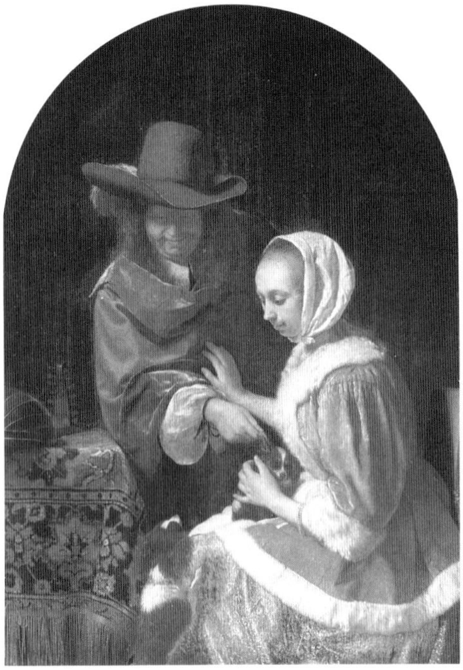

Figure 42. Frans van Mieris the Elder, *Teasing the Pet*, 1660 (oil on panel, 27.5 × 20 cm). The Hague, Mauritshuis. Photo: A. Dingjan, The Hague.

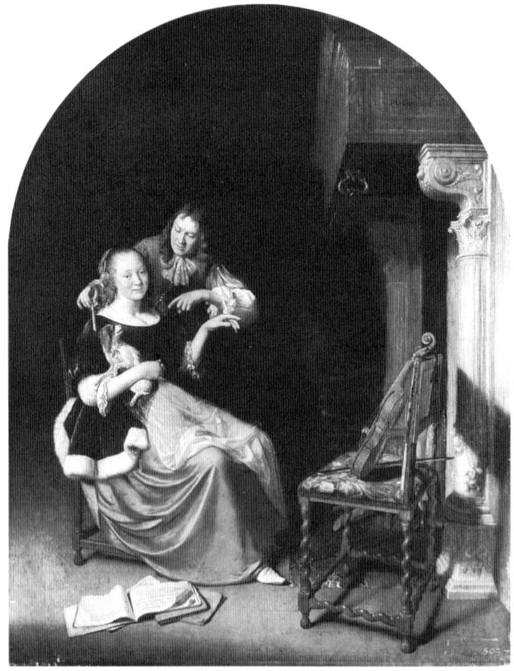

Figure 43. Pieter van Slingelandt, *Teasing the Pet*, 1672 (oil on panel, 39.5 × 30.5 cm). Dresden, Gemäldegalerie Alte Meister. Photo: Sächsische Landesbibliothek, Abteilung Deutsche Fotothek, Dresden.

did not afford them opportunities to exercise direct power in the male-dominated social order of the period.[125] Thus, as we have already seen, art and literature, however elegant and fictitious, nonetheless offered contemporaries a model for the conduct of serious courtship that would lead to marriage.

Cats and other moralists prescribed many rules that contributed to the institutionalized framework for courtship – a framework that underlies many paintings of courtship and much of the amatory literature of the day. These rules are ideal and thus complement the quixotic world of love among comely maidens and gallant youths illustrated in art and described in songbooks and *emblemata amatoria.* Actual courting customs in the seventeenth-century Dutch Republic – so far as they are known – corroborate this. Courting, which must have been conducted over a prolonged period as the Dutch married at comparatively late ages, did not always occur under watchful parental eyes.[126] In fact, the great freedom with which young people were permitted to indulge in it astonished foreigners.[127] Much to the consternation of the clergy, youths would congregate unsupervised at beaches, inns,

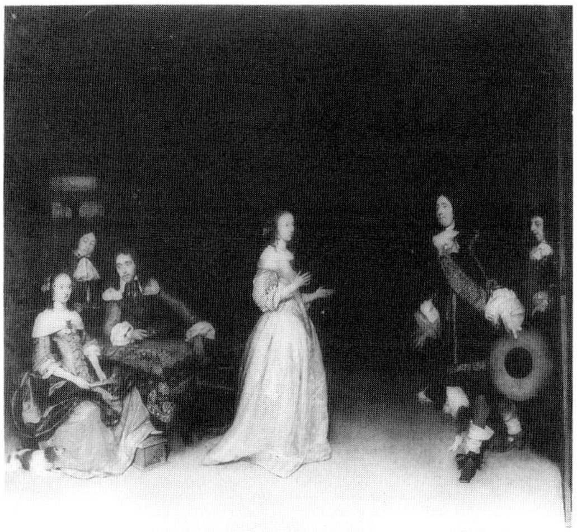

Figure 44. Gerard ter Borch, *The Visit* (oil on canvas, 92 × 104 cm). Present location unknown.

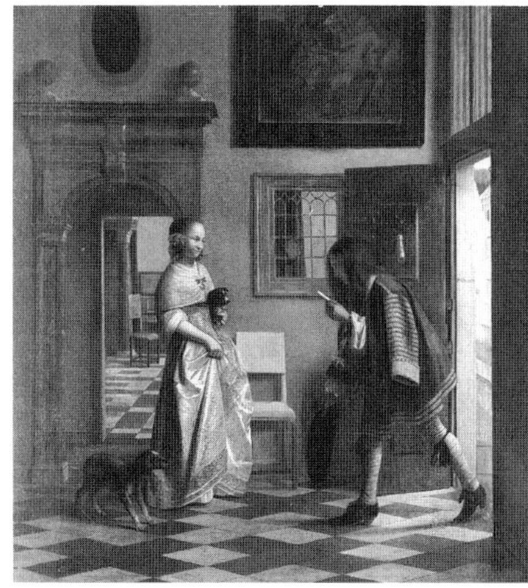

Figure 45. Pieter de Hooch, *A Woman Receiving a Letter from a Man* (oil on canvas, 57 × 53 cm). Hamburg, Kunsthalle. Photo: R. Kleinhempel, Hamburg.

fairs, the theater, and even in churchyards.[128] Several seventeenth-century books actually furnished their readers with lists of some of the most popular locales within cities like Amsterdam and The Hague for meeting members of the opposite sex.[129]

All of the surviving evidence suggests that a distinction must be made between actual courtship in the seventeenth century and the manner in which it is depicted in art and literature. In other words, paintings that treated this theme often adhered to contemporary ideals concerning courtship and the proper virtues most befitting the youths, and especially the maidens, involved. Only when equipped with such virtues would young women theoretically be in a suitable position to court and, ultimately, to marry. It is to marriage, and the roles and responsibilities demanded of them as wives, that we now turn.

Chapter 2

"BRUYT" AND "VROUWE"

The collection of the Rijksmuseum in Amsterdam includes a portrait by Michiel van Musscher representing the artist Michiel Comans II and his third wife Elisabeth van der Meersch (Fig. 46).[1] Michiel stands in a large room with brushes and palette, posed before a large easel that holds his work in progress, a canvas of the Holy Family. Elisabeth, with her sewing basket at her side and an open book in her lap, looks at her husband as he displays an inscribed scroll. Elisabeth's needlework implements and her book function as attributes referring to her role as a housewife, just as her husband's studio props refer to his as an artist.[2]

Besides other contemporary portraits, Van Musscher's painting also recalls earlier representations of artists at work alongside their wives who perform needlework. In several late-sixteenth- and early-seventeenth-century print series illustrating the ages of man, an artist or architect and his wife, mending clothing or making lace, represent age forty (Figs. 47, 48).[3] The figures in these prints function as gender constructs, illustrating the societal and familial roles and duties apposite to each sex at that age. The same is true, mutatis mutandis, of men and women depicted in contemporary portraiture and genre painting, since these works also partake of a visual vocabulary intimately bound to contemporary social conventions.

The depiction in art of masculine and feminine roles could even extend beyond the actual pictorial field. For example, in portrait pendants by Johannes Spruyt of himself and his wife, Judith de Vries, the couple is fashionably dressed *á l'antique* (Figs. 49, 50).[4] Not willing to risk possible incongruencies between their attire and symbolic references, Spruyt cleverly employed carved frames to illustrate the couple's respective roles. Among the motifs are the tools of Johannes's profession as an artist and Judith's sewing box and scrub brush, symbols of her status as a housewife. The woman's role as housewife is the subject of this chapter as we examine

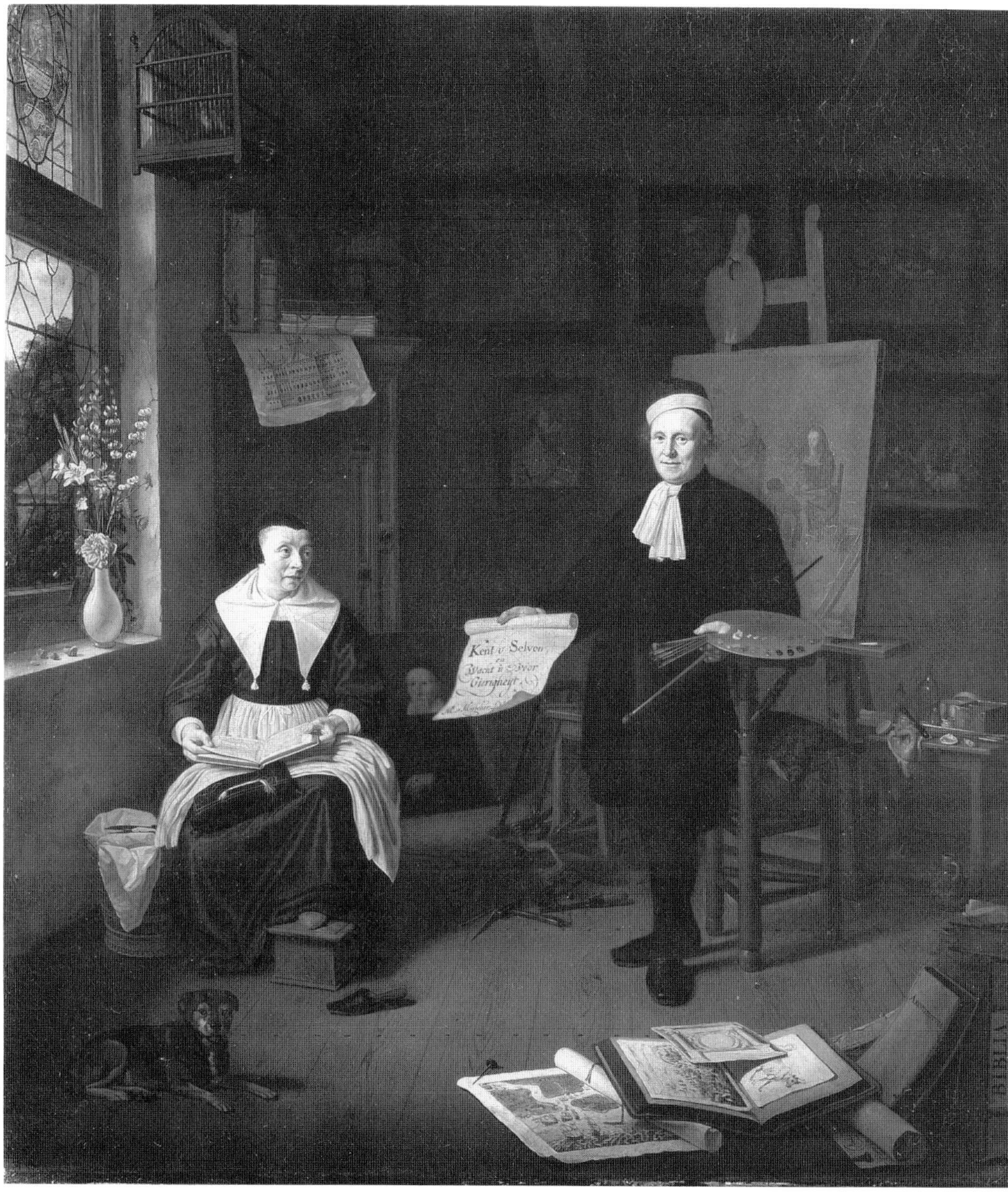

Figure 46. Michiel van Musscher, *Portrait of Michiel Comans II and His Wife, Elisabeth van der Meersch*, 1669 (oil on canvas, 71 × 63 cm). Amsterdam, Rijksmuseum. Photo: Rijksmuseum-Stichting.

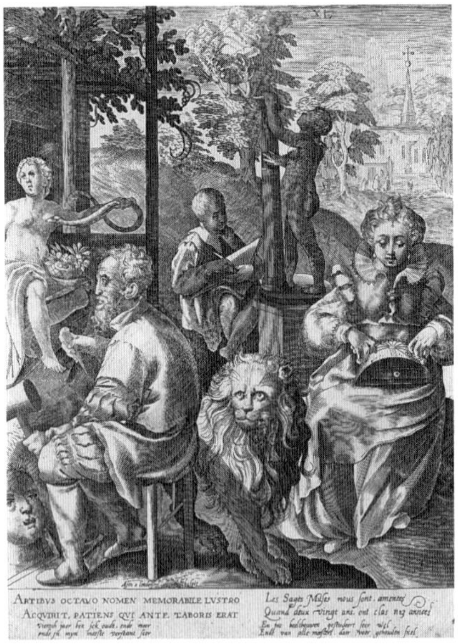

Figure 47. Nicolaes de Bruyn, *Age Forty* (engraving from the series *The Ten Ages of Man*). Amsterdam, Rijksprentenkabinet. Photo: Rijksmuseum-Stichting.

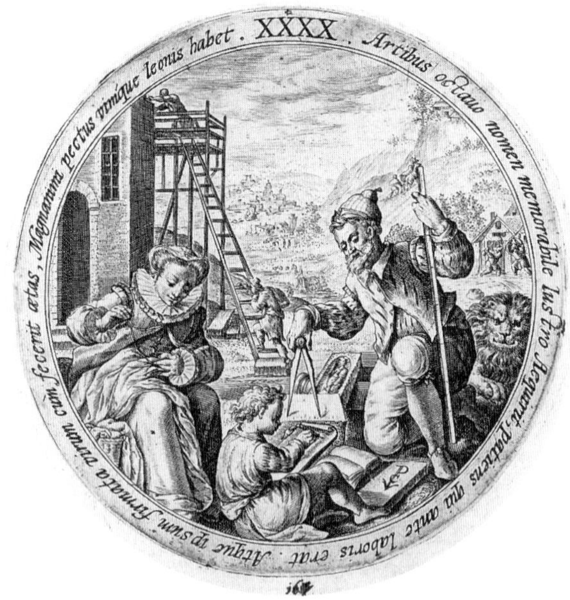

Figure 48. Crispijn van de Passe I, *Age Forty* (engraving from the series *The Ten Ages of Man*). Amsterdam, Rijksprentenkabinet. Photo: Rijksmuseum-Stichting.

representations by Dutch painters of females actively engaged in domestic tasks.

Such highly popular imagery reflected yet simultaneously helped to shape complex and interrelated economic, religious, and social developments. As for economic factors, the gradual rise of capitalism eventually transformed families from the older, feudal type of self-sufficient units of production and consumption in which husbands and wives worked jointly, to units in which production and consumption became separated, the former being identified with men and the latter with women.[5] The workplace – separate from the home (if not physically then at least psychologically) – became the domain of men, particularly for members of the middle and upper classes. Women, on the other hand, found themselves increasingly relegated to the private, domestic sphere.[6] Within the confines of the home, a woman had varied yet circumscribed roles: helpmate to her husband, caregiver to her children, maintainer of the home, and supervisor of servants.[7]

It is doubtful whether citizens of the Dutch Republic would have understood the development of their sex roles in the terms that I have just outlined. For them, theological views of marriage and family life both confirmed and

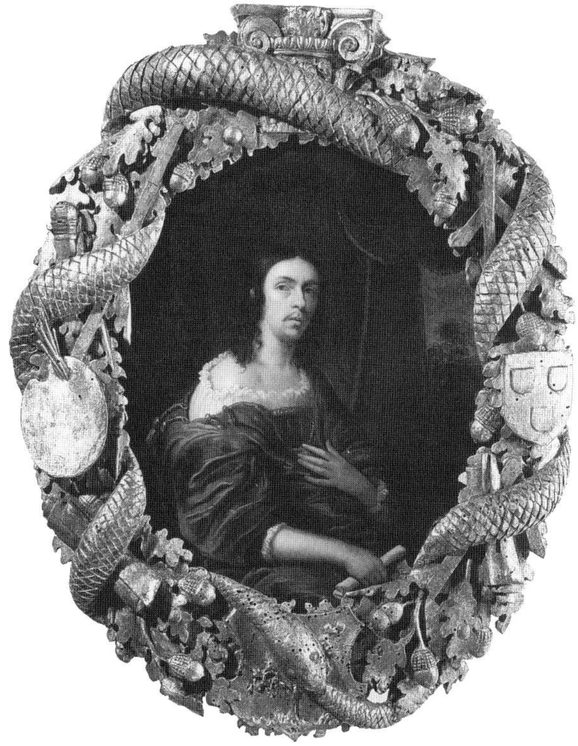

Figure 49 (left). Johannes Spruyt, *Self-Portrait*, 1661 (oil on panel, 29 × 23 cm). Private collection. Photo: Rijksmuseum-Stichting.

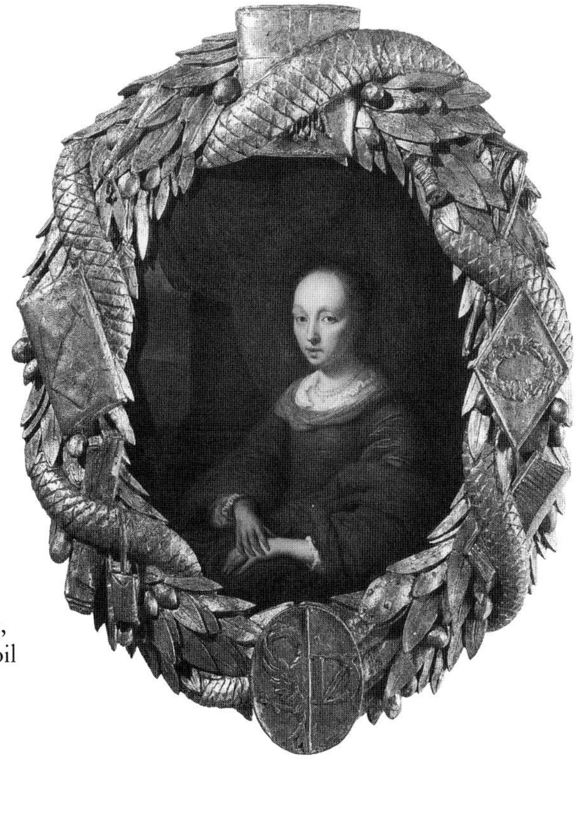

Figure 50 (right). Johannes Spruyt, *Portrait of Judith de Vries*, 1661 (oil on panel, 29 × 23 cm). Private collection. Photo: Rijksmuseum-Stichting.

justified their gender status. Their views were fundamentally endogamous and could in many respects be traced to the ideas of the sixteenth-century reformer Martin Luther and to prominent humanists of that period, namely Erasmus of Rotterdam and Juan Luis Vives.[8] Luther, Erasmus, and other theologians and humanists endeavored to overturn established Catholic doctrines that exalted celibacy by championing matrimony as an honorable state for humankind, ordained by God.[9] Many of them wrote important tracts and books about domestic life, advocating specific roles and responsibilities for individual family members.[10] Thus, literature that focused on the topics of marriage and the family was already in print by the early 1520s, often in the form of published sermons. What began initially as a small trickle of publications would culminate in the exhaustive domestic conduct books that appeared toward the end of the sixteenth and well into the seventeenth century.[11]

Domestic conduct books, remarkable for their nearly uniform outlook, clarified and codified familial duties, providing helpful advice on almost all matrimonial and household matters. These treatises, which appealed to the middle and upper classes, advanced a domestic ethical code based largely on prescriptions gleaned from the writings of classical authors and Christian humanists as well as from the Pauline Epistles and the Ten Commandments.[12] The ideas that they expounded were already familiar to the reader through sermons as well as pastoral visits, catechism lessons, and the like.[13] The conduct book merely recorded what was already being taught, offering a vade mecum for problems concerning domestic life. These hortatory texts contributed in no small measure to the effort of promoting unity and godliness in families, and for this reason, their impact on contemporary society should not be underestimated.[14]

The most detailed domestic conduct books were those published in England around the turn of the seventeenth century.[15] These works were written mostly by English Puritans who were among the founders and earliest disciples of the religious movement known as Pietism.[16] Even if their ideas about marriage and family life were not as innovative as is usually assumed, the Pietists' literary output on these subjects was truly staggering.[17] Their books and tracts were influential in the Netherlands as many of them were translated into Dutch, in some cases almost immediately after their initial publication in English.[18] Moreover, English treatises, even those that escaped translation, often served as sources for similar books by Dutch authors. Cats was familiar with these treatises; his frequent quotation of them reveals his sympathy with the Pietist movement, particularly the flourishing circle in his native Zeeland.[19] The writings of the English and Dutch Pietists thus played an important role in shaping contemporary attitudes toward Dutch domestic life, indirectly influencing the choice and representation of domestic themes in art in the process.

Given the large number of domestic conduct books in circulation, it seems plausible that at least some readers, in varying degrees, followed their prescriptions.[20] Yet we must remember that these books presented an ideal vision of marriage and family life, one that could not possibly reflect reality. Surely, there must have been some variance in the conjugal attitudes and experiences of the populace, which would have been largely determined by upbringing and the depth of religious commitment. Surviving evidence indicates that the courts and consistories – assemblies of deacons and elders who administered church discipline – were continually confronted with a wide range of social problems, including pregnancy among unmarried women, marital disputes and separations (some of which involved wife battering), adultery, and prostitution.[21] Equally telling is the fact that appeals for recantation and reconciliation in these cases would usually be made not on the grounds of a person's guilty conscience or of God's omniscience concerning sin but on that of such secular, socially oriented concepts as honor, shame, and respectability within the overall community.[22] Admittedly, by modern standards, the number of cases – which involved primarily lower-class persons who did not buy the type of paintings discussed in this chapter – was negligible, but their very existence nonetheless speaks volumes about how different actual seventeenth-century Dutch domestic life could be versus the ideal described by countless theologians and moralists. Nevertheless, their vision was fervently desired if not theoretically attainable.

What were the matrimonial convictions of Cats and many of his contemporaries?[23] They considered marriage a natural and honorable state instituted by God, one that descended, in an immutable form, from the Garden of Eden.[24] Since God had decreed it before humankind's fall from grace, they adjudged matrimony to be the oldest "political society" and hence the basis for preserving the divinely ordained cosmos – in other words, the sexual status quo.[25]

Perhaps the idea most zealously argued, one that is often mistakenly seen as a specifically Puritan innovation, was that procreation was not the goal of marriage but rather its consequence.[26] Although they recognized the importance of procreation for the propagation of the church and the state (and for the preservation of the family name), most Protestant theologians believed that the primary objective of marriage was to provide companionship.[27] Genesis 2:18 was invariably cited in order to justify this belief: "It is not good that man should be alone."[28] This same verse was likewise invoked to justify the conviction that God had created Eve to be a helpmate for Adam in a relationship that provided a model for all future marriages.

Matrimony was viewed as a covenantal alliance between spouses who agreed to fulfill particular obligations appropriate to their sex. Marital obligations included the commitment to love and remain faithful to one's spouse and to express mutual concern for his or her spiritual and physical welfare.[29]

Above all, theologians enjoined wives to be subordinate and submissive to their husbands, not as slaves, but as trusted junior partners in the marital enterprise.[30] The fulfillment of these obligations and the diligent performance of practical tasks, inspired by both natural and God-given love, was thought to guarantee the success of marriage, thus promoting stability in society at large.[31]

Protestant writers often described the divinely ordained obligation required of each man and woman, regardless of age, as a "calling" – *beroep*, in Dutch texts of the period – or, as two early seventeenth-century divines defined it, "our appointed charge, and manner of life, in some honest worke, wherin we are daily to labor as we may best profit therein."[32] The man's "calling" or work usually took place in the public sphere, while the woman's was confined to the home, in the service of family and husband: "So a wife likewise, if she also be a mother and a mistris, and faithfully endevour to doe what by vertue of those callings she is bound to doe, shall finde enough to doe."[33] God had called her to become a housewife, her principal office – one commensurate with her character, inclinations, and training.[34]

In theory, a wife's knowledge of the family's needs and of the practical maintenance of the home surpassed her husband's; he was to yield authority to her in such matters, having "greater" concerns himself.[35] The husband's principal duty was to acquire goods for his family, goods that his wife was expected to preserve and administer:

> A housewife needs to take care of what her husband brings home, to put it in its proper place and obediently take only what is needed; but what needs to be saved should be locked up . . . she should not resent being burdened with more chores than other housewives, because she also shares the pleasures of running the whole house, like a ruler and owner.[36]

Socioeconomic factors, namely, burgeoning capitalism and the concomitant privatization of the home, were thus largely understood and justified in theological terms by contemporaries. Authors also justified their conviction that women run the household by what they perceived as disparities in male and female physical traits and capabilities. They argued that God had ordained the husband to provide for his family owing to his superior strength and intellectual abilities, while his wife, given her weaker nature, was to perform household tasks.[37]

Aristotle, whose writings proved so significant for humanist and Protestant theories about marriage and family life, was among the first ancient philosophers to expound this theory of the dichotomous nature of the sexes; he postulated that men, with their robust character, were best suited to work outdoors, while women, because of their natural timidity and weakness, were best suited to work in the home.[38] Sixteenth- and seventeenth-century authors considered Aristotle's theories authoritative along with those set forth by other thinkers from antiquity whose works were known throughout Europe. For example, an English translation of Xenophon's well-known work *Oeconomicus,* entitled *Xenophons Treatise of Housholde* states:

> a woman is borne to take hede of all such thinges as muste be dooen at home. For he hath made men of body, hearte and stomacke, strong and mighty, to suffre and endure hete and cold, to journey and go a warfare. Wherfore God hath in a maner commaunded and charged him with those thinges, that must be done abrode out of house.[39]

Even Johan van Beverwijck accepted these ancient theories despite his reputation as an early advocate for women whose views were sometimes considered too liberal by his countrymen.[40] In order to support his contention that women must remain in the home, Van Beverwijck, in his *Van de wtnementheyt des vrouwelicken geslachts* (On the Excellence of the Female Sex, 1639), cites Aristotle and Xenophon, and also recounts a parable plagiarized from Plutarch's *Conjugalia praecepta* (Laws of Marriage). Van Beverwijck states that Phidias had made a sculpture of Venus standing on a tortoise in order to demonstrate "that the praise of a woman mainly exists in the care she gives to her household. For the turtle is always at home, and carries its house along under all circumstances."[41] An illustration of a woman on a tortoise accompanies this discussion (Fig. 51). In the background, a man digs outdoors and a woman spins inside a home, thus demonstrating the tasks apposite to each sex, as the following verses, which Van Beverwijck appended to the print, make clear: "You, husband, work outside the house / But inside tasks befall your spouse."[42]

The motif of the tortoise appears more frequently in literature than does that of any other creature to convey the idea that a woman's place is in the home.[43] This motif was especially popular in *emblemata,* where it provided the basis for an entire constellation of metaphors, all proclaiming the virtues most esteemed in women. The *pictura* of an emblem by Geoffrey Whitney shows a woman on a tortoise, holding keys in one hand with a finger from the other in her mouth (Fig. 52). The *subscriptio* explains this rather odd, amusing scene:

> This representes the vertues of a wife,
> Her finger, staies her tonge to runne at large.
> The modest lookes, doe shewe her honest life.
> The keys, declare shee hathe a care, and chardge,
> Of husbandes goodes: let him goe where he please,
> The tortoyse warnes, at home to spend her daies.[44]

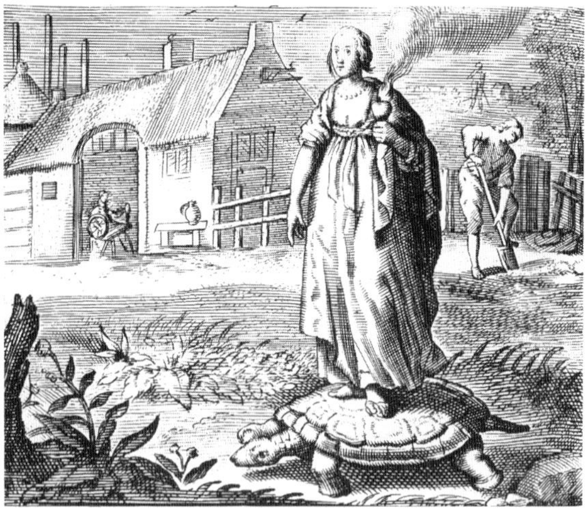

Figure 51. Illustration from Johan van Beverwijck, *Van de wtnementheyt des vrouwelicken geslachts*, Dordrecht 1639. Amsterdam, Universiteits-Bibliotheek Amsterdam. Photo: courtesy Universiteits-Bibliotheek Amsterdam.

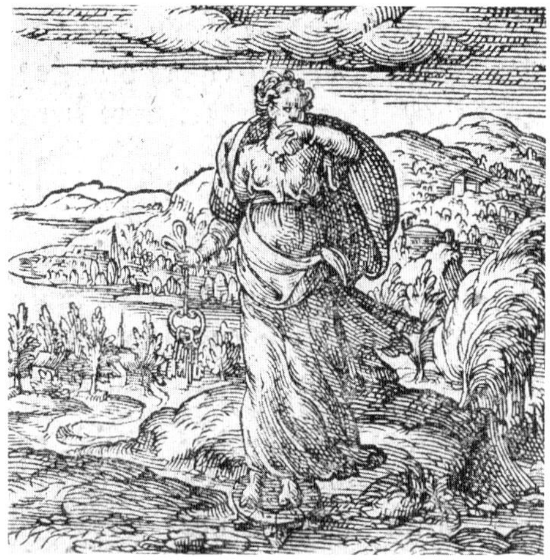

Figure 52. Emblem from Geoffrey Whitney, *A Choice of Emblems*, Leiden 1586. Champaign-Urbana, Rare Book and Special Collections Library, University of Illinois. Photo: University of Illinois.

Whitney's poem succinctly enumerates the virtues and duties that were de rigueur for females at that time. He mentions modesty and silence, traits of a timid disposition continually praised by moralists as most befitting women.[45] The key as a metaphor of domesticity was a common topos during this period. Cats and several of his contemporaries cite the ancient custom of presenting a bride with a key as a symbol of her place in the home and the tasks required of her there.[46] Furthermore, there are a number of seventeenth-century Dutch portraits and genre paintings in which keys clearly refer to domesticity (see, e.g., Fig. 53).[47]

The numerous texts pertaining to issues of marriage and family life are valuable for understanding domestic themes in art for the simple reason that they discuss housewifely duties ad infinitum. However, it would be reductive and misleading to posit a direct influence of literature on art; rather, both independently provide evidence for the existence of particular ideas about domesticity at that time, and both contributed actively to the construction of a normative female type. Moreover, both employ specific metaphors that allude to feminine virtue and domesticity, in effect providing a paradigm by which the reader or viewer could measure her conduct. Far from merely reflecting contemporary ideals of domesticity, art and literature played an active role in shaping them.

In his treatise of household government, William Perkins, the English

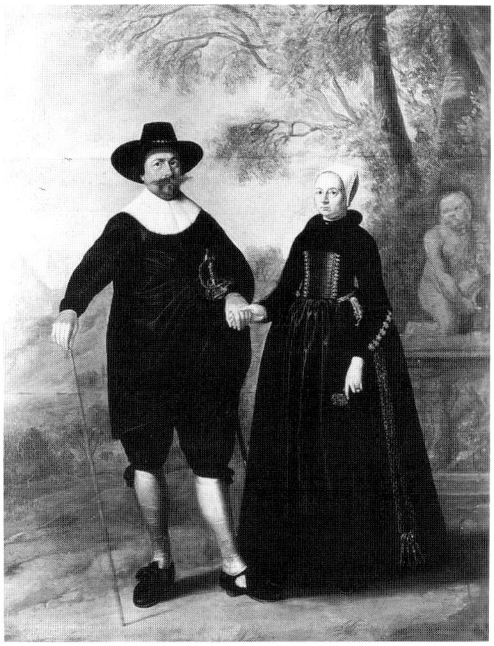

Figure 53. Herman Doncker, *Portrait of a Married Couple in a Landscape* (oil on panel, 67 × 54 cm). Brussels, Musées Royaux des Beaux-Arts de Belgique. Photo: copyright A.C.L.-Brussels.

Puritan divine whose writings were so influential in the Dutch Republic, defines the housewife's duty "to governe the house, as much as concerneth her, in her place" as follows: she must exercise "her selfe in some profitable employments, for the good of her charge" and must appoint "her maids their worke . . . overseeing them therein."[48] First, we will examine paintings that depict women engaged "in some profitable employments," that is, domestic tasks.

Spinning was the one domestic task represented in art that seventeenth-century moralizers unanimously considered the most important for housewives to practice. Cats's comments about spinning typify the contemporary attitude:

> Choose, oh young lady, the spindle over the game.
> Search old times and all past life;
> The richest young lady spun, the mother could weave;
> The princess of the country, the highest in rank,
> Handled pure wool or white flax.
> Consider the esteemed woman described by Solomon,
> She is motivated by the sheer pleasure of spinning;
> She makes her family turn the spindle
> For the good of the house, in the service of her husband.[49]

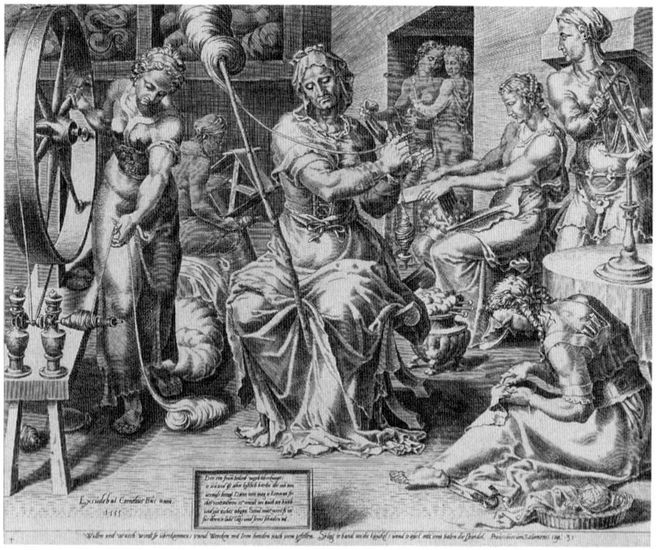

Figure 54. Dirck Volkertsz. Coornhert after Maarten van Heemskerck, *The Virtuous Wife Spinning* (engraving from the series *Praise of the Virtuous Housewife*), 1555. Amsterdam, Rijksprentenkabinet. Photo: Rijksmuseum-Stichting.

In these verses, Cats alludes to the biblical Book of Proverbs written by Solomon, in particular to Proverbs 31, the chapter that praises the virtuous woman. Solomon enumerates her tasks, which range from spinning – as Cats states – to giving succor to the poor. Proverbs 31 not only provided the theological underpinning for many of the discussions of housewifely duties in contemporary literature. To some extent it also influenced the choice of domestic subjects and specific motifs represented in art.[50] It was even illustrated in a print series engraved by Dirck Coornhert after designs by Maarten van Heemskerck (Fig. 54).[51]

In the opinion of Cats and many other moralists, spinning was a necessary occupation for the housewife, one that brought honor to herself and her family. They quoted other texts besides the Bible to support their view, among them several legends of antiquity that offered contemporary readers examples of virtuous women who diligently spun, including Lucretia.[52] Seventeenth-century paintings of the theme of women spinning mirror the virtuous associations evoked by the domesticity of Lucretia and the celebrated housewife of Proverbs 31 (see, e.g., Fig. 55). In the preceding chapter, I noted that although there are numerous seventeenth-century genre paintings of spinners, portraits of women engaged in this task are comparatively rare. I suggested that, at that time, women were no longer spinning for purely domestic needs as they had done in previous centuries.[53] Depictions in art of women spinning,

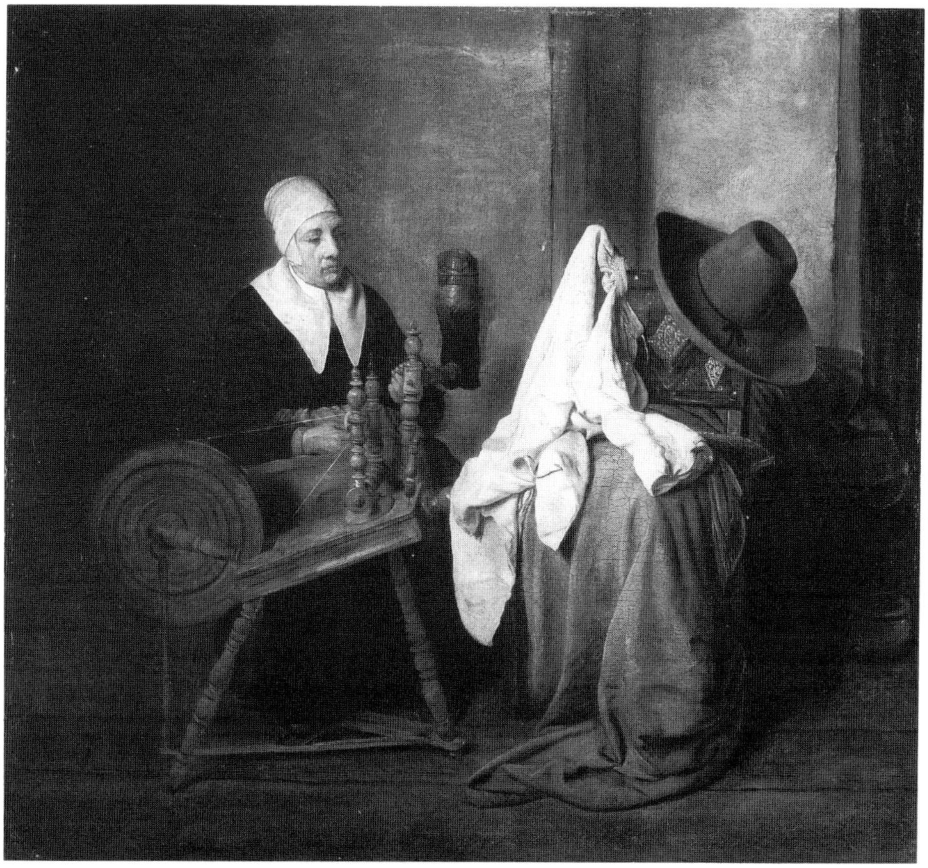

Figure 55. Esaias Boursse, *Woman Spinning.* Present location unknown. Photo: courtesy Christie's, London.

like discussions of spinning in contemporary literature, reflect an ideal vision of the tasks of the housewife, and thus function as topoi of domestic virtue.

Gerard ter Borch's representation of his stepmother Wiesken Matthys at the spinning wheel is, arguably, one of the few seventeenth-century Dutch portraits of a woman spinning (Fig. 56). In fact this odd picture, and its pendant (Fig. 57) of the same woman combing a child's hair, could fall under the category of what Lyckle de Vries has recently termed "genrefied portraits," works in which a sitter participates in a narrative not drawn from literary or historical sources or from pictorial traditions normally associated with portraiture.[54] We have already seen how contemporaries equated the practice of domestic tasks, particularly sewing and spinning, with diligence, purity, and a host of other virtues.[55] Rather than probing the subtle nuances of Wiesken's personality, these two pictures demonstrate the essential tasks

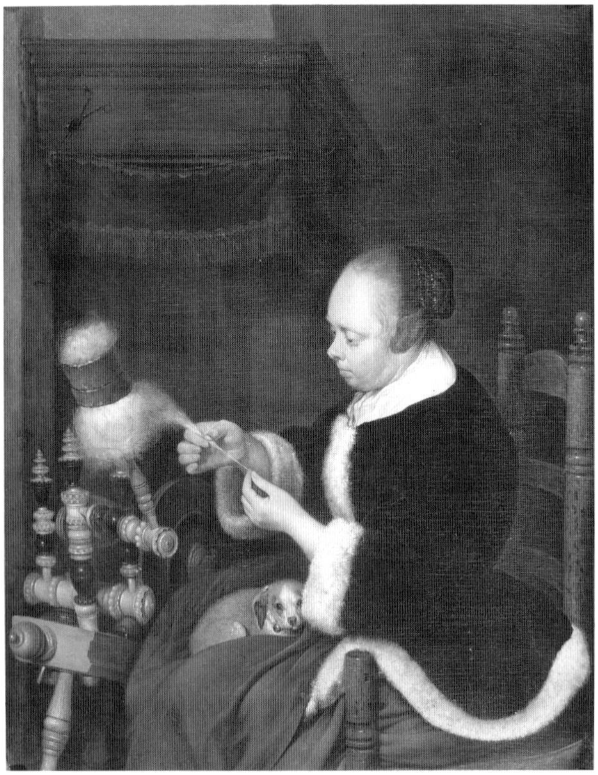

Figure 56 (left). Gerard ter Borch, *Portrait of Wiesken Matthys Spinning* (oil on panel, 34.5 × 29.5 cm). Rotterdam, Stichting Willem van der Vorm, Museum Boymans-Van Beuningen. Photo: copyright Frequin-Photos, The Hague.

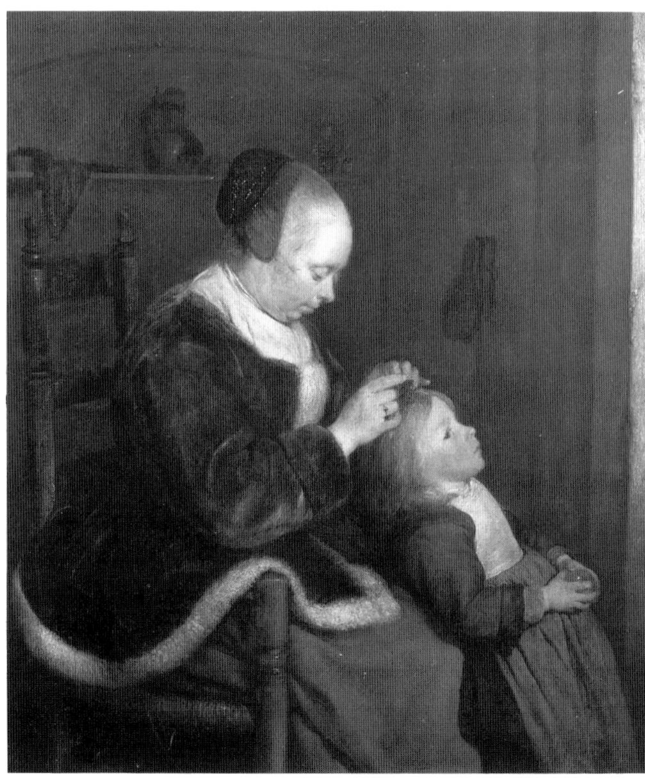

Figure 57 (right). Gerard ter Borch, *Portrait of Wiesken Matthys Combing a Child's Hair* (oil on panel, 33.5 × 29 cm). The Hague, Mauritshuis. Photo: A. Dingjan, The Hague.

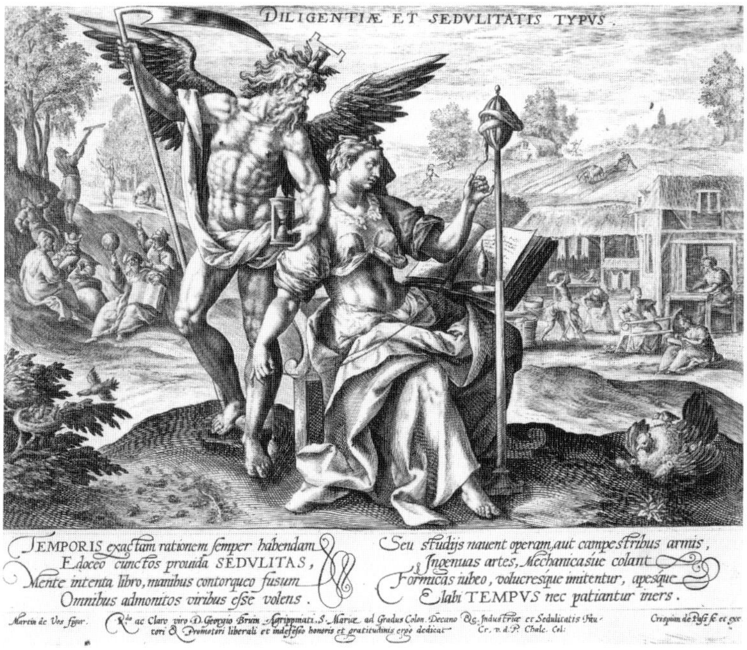

Figure 58. Crispijn van de Passe I after Maarten de Vos, *Diligentiae et sedulitatis typus* (engraving from the series *The Seven Virtues*). Amsterdam, Rijksprentenkabinet. Photo: Rijksmuseum-Stichting.

required of the "weaker sex": housewifely and motherly skills that contributed to moral integrity.[56]

Ter Borch's painting offers a visual parallel to the description of the activities of the virtuous housewife in Proverbs 31 and even to those of Lucretia. However, the artist's contemporaries did not necessarily need to be familiar with these texts in order to understand its significance. The association of spinning with virtue was longstanding and, naturally, was made explicit in prints, including one by Crispijn van de Passe I after Maarten de Vos (Fig. 58).[57] Here, a female personification of diligence manipulates a spindle, her attribute. In the background are other industrious types, each zealously engaged in tasks appropriate to their gender, including a woman making lace.[58]

Ter Borch has depicted his stepmother in the process of plying yarn that will then be fed onto the bobbin of her spinning wheel. The artist has likely represented this specific moment in the process of spinning in order to call attention to the thread. By pulling it taut between her fingers, Wiesken displays the thread to the viewer, an action that could refer to the proverb "Ze spint zuiver garen" (She spins pure thread). Cats' quotation of this proverb in the preface to "Bruyt" in *Houwelyck* clarifies its significance. In outlining the virtues and qualities most desired in a wife, Cats desires that she "spin pure thread," a reference to her domesticity as well as to her unsullied reputation.[59] This passage once again proves how frequently probity was associated with the performance of domestic tasks. In Ter Borch's painting, the motif of his stepmother plying thread demonstrates her skills as a housewife and, by extension, her integrity. A genre painting by Willem van Odekerken of a spinner pointing to her thread conveys a similar idea (Fig. 59).

Like spinning, moralists also praised the housewife's ability to perform needlework.[60] If there is one painting that exemplifies the associations evoked by this theme in art, it is the one that I referred to in the introduction to this book, *The Lace-Maker* by Caspar Netscher (Fig. 1). For this reason, it is worthwhile to examine it in some detail. A young woman makes lace in a spartan interior whose only adornment, a print crudely nailed to the cracked plaster wall, loosely resembles Hendrick Goudt's engraving after Adam Elsheimer's renowned painting *The Flight into Egypt*.[61]

The woman is clearly young but she is already married, as evidenced by the design on her embroidered cap (Fig. 1a). This design includes the motif of clasped hands directly below a bird and what might be a heart.[62] The clasping or joining of right hands, that is, the *dextrarum iunctio,* is a gesture that has been associated with the marriage ceremony since antiquity. Throughout the centuries it has served – and still occasionally serves today – as a sacred and legal sign of a couple's marital agreement, a visible, tangible manifestation of their love and unity. In Dutch seventeenth-century art and literature, the motif of clasped hands commonly functions as a signifier of marital concord just as the gesture did in actual marriage ceremonies of the day.[63] This likely explains its presence as the crowning element (along with doves) in the frontispiece to Cats's *Houwelyck* (Fig. 3).

The young woman in Netscher's painting wears sober, simple clothing of a type that would have met the approval of any moralist.[64] Her activity of lace-making also indicates, if not celebrates, her industriousness and virtue. The woman is completely absorbed in this task, as her intensely focused gaze suggests. She is also turned at a slight angle toward the wall, a position that effectively eliminates any interaction between subject and viewer. Pose, expression, and attire combine here to offer a compelling construction of ideal femininity and domesticity.

Various objects surround this young housewife: a broom, a pair of shoes, and two mussel shells. Their verisimilitude is stunning, particularly that of the mussel shells with their translucent sheen, but this demonstration of the artist's skill cannot alone account for the presence of these particular objects, strategically grouped as they are around her. There can be no question that they form part of a deliberate pictorial construction, that they have been

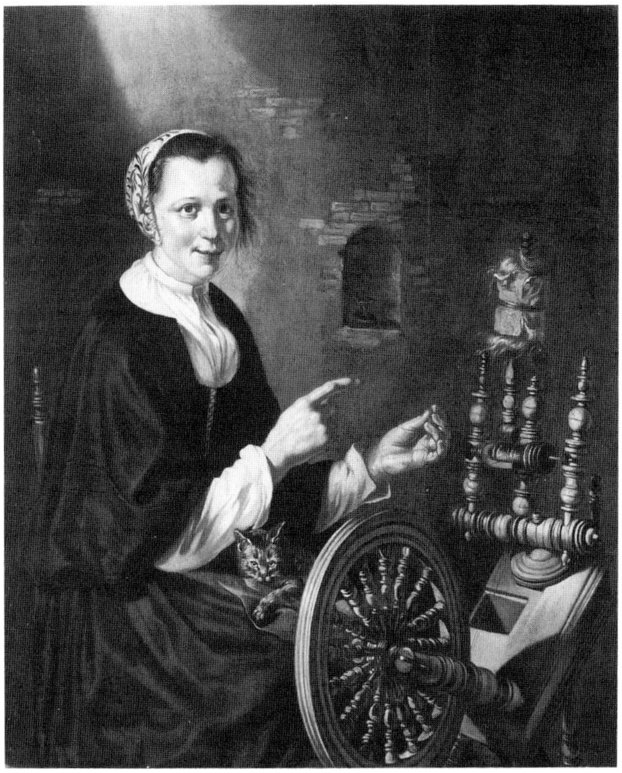

Figure 59. Willem van Odekerken, *Woman Spinning.* Present location unknown. Photo: courtesy Christie's, London.

selected to function as signifiers of appropriate feminine virtues. The broom to her left undoubtedly refers to the housework and cleaning that every good housewife was expected to do.[65]

The pair of shoes on the floor conveys virtuous associations as well. Art historians have written much about the erotic significance of shoes in Dutch seventeenth-century art.[66] However, there is an entirely separate tradition, one that has been hitherto ignored, in which shoes were understood in more wholesome terms. Already in the literature of classical antiquity, specifically in Plutarch's *Conjugalia praecepta,* shoes, when removed, were invoked as reminders to women that they belong in the home.[67] As the title of Plutarch's little book implies, it is a collection of "laws" which in essence contain the author's observations and advice about marriage. Plutarch expounds his opinions with the aid of metaphoric imagery, an approach that was exceptionally appealing to later writers. Judging from the reprints and its frequent quotation by moralists – including Cats – Plutarch's book must have been well known in the Netherlands during the sixteenth and seventeenth centuries.[68]

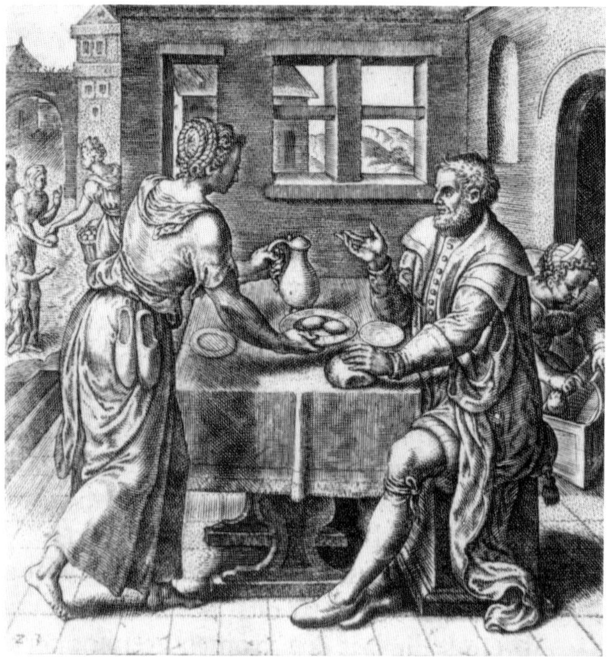

Figure 60. Emblem from Dirck Volkertsz. Coornhert, *Recht ghebruyck ende misbruyck van tijdlicke have*, 2d ed., Amsterdam 1610. Amsterdam, Universiteits-Bibliotheek Amsterdam. Photo: courtesy Universiteits-Bibliotheek Amsterdam.

In one of his laws, Plutarch cites the alleged custom among Egyptian women of not wearing shoes in the home, so that they would learn that they must remain there.[69] Several authors of seventeenth-century treatises on marriage quote this law as they exhort women to oversee the daily affairs of the home.[70] Plutarch's account of the Egyptian custom might have influenced the visual arts, just as several other of his laws of marriage had.[71] The *pictura* to an emblem from Dirck Coornhert's *Recht ghebruyck ende misbruyck* (Right Use and Misuse) represents a virtuous couple who live soberly and piously, providing succor to the needy (Fig. 60).[72] A barefoot woman, her shoes suspended from a belt around her waist, serves a man seated at a table, presumably her husband. The motif of the dangling shoes most likely refers to her virtue and domesticity as a woman who remains in the home. Admittedly, conclusive evidence is lacking concerning whether Plutarch's law was the direct source for this representation. Nevertheless, the very fact that his book was familiar to sixteenth- and seventeenth-century readers confirms that, at this time, the idea existed that a shoe could serve as a metaphor of domesticity. This leads to the question of how to interpret the presence of shoes in the proximity of women not only in Netscher's picture, but in

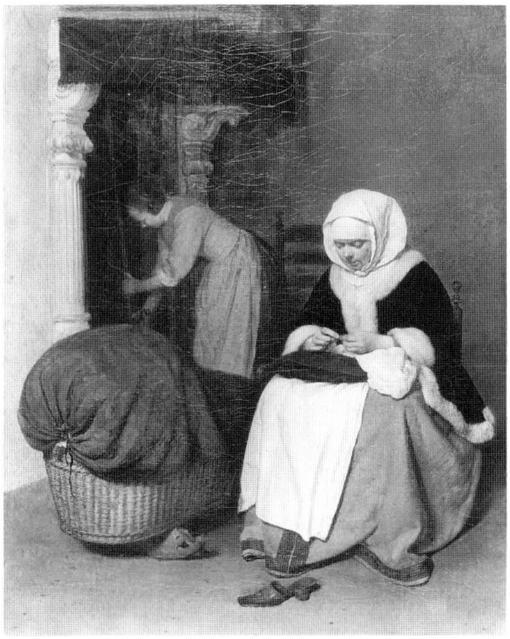

Figure 61. Gerard ter Borch, *Seamstress by a Cradle* (oil on canvas, 46.5 × 38 cm). Private collection.

countless Dutch seventeenth-century paintings of domestic themes (see, e.g., Fig. 61). The conventional placement of shoes in the compositions of so many paintings cannot be mere coincidence. For contemporary viewers, footwear undoubtedly evoked certain associations, ones that must have been wholesome given the virtuous context in which the motif appears. Consequently, shoes in some Dutch paintings probably refer, like the ones in Coornhert's emblem, to domesticity.

Like the shoes, it is difficult to believe that the two mussel shells lying on the floor to the right of the lace-maker could have been placed there arbitrarily. Despite their frequent presence in seventeenth-century Dutch art as erotic symbols,[73] there are several contemporary literary references to mussels and mussel shells as domestic metaphors, metaphors drawn from the observation that the creature continually abides in its shell. In his *Tafereel van sinne-mal* (Tableau of Foolish Senses, 1623), Adriaen van de Venne, the Middelburg artist and publisher, includes the following poem with his delightful illustration of a street vendor of mussels:

> Fresh mussels can be compared to
> The blessed women-folk
> Who speak modestly and virtuously
> And always look after their household;
> All wives must regularly bear
> The burden of their "mussel-house."[74]

Cats resorts to similar imagery when advising wives on how to comport themselves while their husbands travel: "Leeft om desen tijt gelijck een mossel doet" (Live at this time like a mussel does).[75] These literary references demonstrate that mussels were sometimes regarded as metaphors for domesticity, an association that finds analogous visual expression in Netscher's painting.

The conspicuous placement of the broom, shoes, and mussel shells in *The Lace-Maker,* then, is a highly expedient pictorial device that enables the viewer to savor the detailed naturalism of these objects while contemplating their meaning as signs alluding to a host of feminine virtues.[76] This device appears in many other seventeenth-century Dutch genre paintings of domestic subjects, among them Gabriel Metsu's *Woman with Sewing in a Niche,* a picture that also belongs to the theme of women performing needlework (Fig. 62). Metsu depicts a woman with a sewing cushion in her lap who seems to be working on a garment, perhaps a piece of linen. A pair of scissors lie on the ledge of the nichelike enclosure in which she works. Ostensibly, they will be needed to trim the material; however, such a description implies that the artist has momentarily frozen the action. Unlike the paintings of courtship images discussed in Chapter 1, this composition does not contain a strong narrative or anecdotal component. On the contrary, scissors and other objects have been conspicuously arranged like a still life in a stone, architectonic enclosure – a *nisstuk* as it would have been called in the seventeenth century – an enclosure that serves various, interdependent purposes.[77] By creating an interaction between real and fictive space, it calls attention to the artist's cunning illusion of reality. In one sense, the *nisstuk* acts as a visual barrier for the scene within it, though paradoxically, through its very artificiality, it invites the beholder to contemplate the objects meticulously rendered in and around it.[78] The enclosure and the scene enframed by it can rightly be called naturalistic, but at the same time they have the capacity to evoke ideas and associations. Thus, the housewife absorbed in her work here functions as an ideal type, safely enclosed within an architectonic setting, surrounded by objects that, like her very persona, connote virtue.

The woman's specific task is unclear, but the presence of a sewing cushion suggests that it involves needlework. Needlework, as we have seen repeatedly, conveys a gamut of praiseworthy associations, among them virtue, diligence, housewifery. The birdcage on the left jamb signifies domesticity.[79] A bird in its cage is the subject of a well-known emblem by Cats (Fig. 63), which is inscribed "Bly, door slaverny" (Joy through Slavery). In the *subscriptio,* the parrot, who is the "narrator," declares that "the imprisonment of love" has brought it great joy, an allusion to chaste, elevated love, the type required in marriage.[80] However, it was not necessary for contemporary viewers to have been familiar with this emblem in order to recognize and

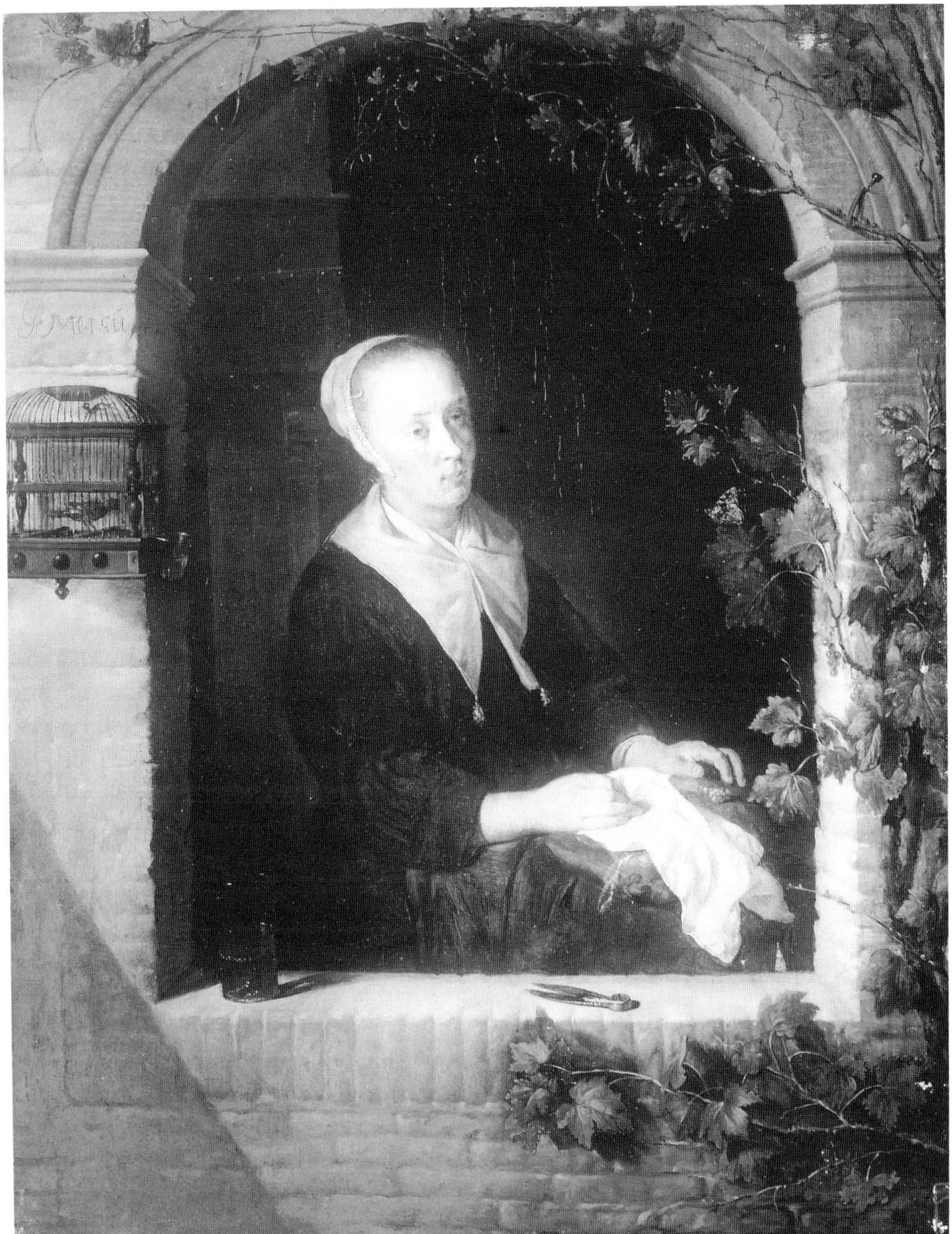

Figure 62. Gabriel Metsu, *Woman with Sewing in a Niche* (oil on panel, 28.5 × 22 cm). Moscow, Pushkin Museum. Photo: museum.

comprehend the motif in the painting, for the associations that birdcages evoked were widely known. For example, elsewhere in Cats's writings, he cites a French proverb that criticizes a woman who wanders about gossiping, remarking that she should be like a bird in its cage, in other words, she should remain at home.[81] Other seventeenth-century writers adopted this metaphor, including Jonker Livinus van der Minnen (pseud.), who used it to make an explicit connection with marriage:

> I saw the green parrot / hanging in the parlor, / Although he was caged, / He spoke beautifully. . . . / And he was so cheerful in his prison / as if in a wedding house. . . . If I may be your slave / Take me, / In slavery, / Tie my hand to your hand, / Let the wedding ring be the band.[82]

Opposite the birdcage, a grapevine creeps along the right jamb of the enclosure, extending over the arch to the other side. Since antiquity, grapevines and similar plants that "climb" by using tendrils have symbolized love, fidelity, and marriage because of their ability to cling firmly to many different surfaces, including walls.[83] A grapevine also appears in Psalm 128, a favorite among seventeenth-century authors and theologians because it employs metaphoric imagery to describe domestic life.[84] Contemporary poets often quoted the third verse of this psalm, "Thy wife shall be as a fruitful vine by the sides of thine house," particularly in wedding poetry, as an allusion to a couple's prospective children.[85] This very same verse, Psalm 128:3, was also understood as a metaphor of domesticity, as the grapevine in Metsu's painting possibly was. In his *Deugden-spoor* (Traces of Virtue), Petrus Baardt interprets the verse as follows: "When the prophet [David] wanted to compare the virtuous and chaste wife to a fruitful vine, he did not want to plant her along the roads outside but guided her inside the walls of her house."[86]

In my opinion, Metsu's *Woman with Sewing in a Niche* can be viewed as a seventeenth-century, secular equivalent of the late medieval *andachtsbild* – a fictive construct that implicates the viewer, inviting close inspection and enjoyment of its mimetic naturalism as well as contemplation of its articulation of implicitly wholesome values, ones universally acknowledged at that time as most befitting women.[87] Countless paintings share these features with Metsu's, not only in terms of a propensity to structure the beholder's viewing experience, but especially in their conventionality with its incessant repetition of specific motifs. The conventionality of these works attests to their popularity, reflecting widespread attitudes and ideas that dictated their production and even their content. Surely the subjectival formulae that constitute these images of domestic virtue evidence what contemporary viewers expected to see, what they enjoyed seeing, and what they deemed significant to see

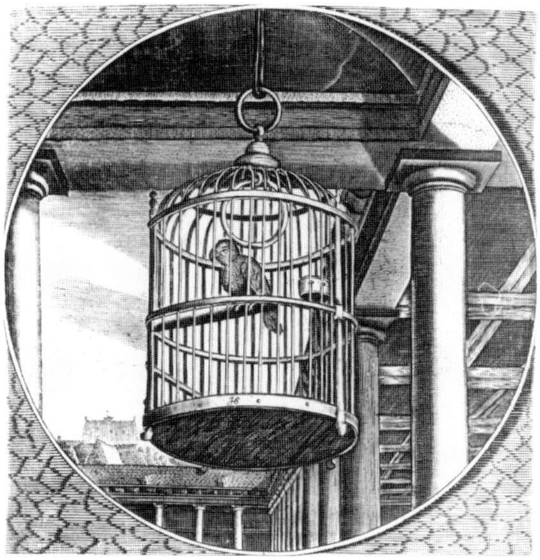

Figure 63. Emblem from Jacob Cats, *Proteus ofte minne-beelden verandert in sinnebeelden*, Rotterdam 1627. Amsterdam, Universiteits-Bibliotheek Amsterdam. Photo: courtesy Universiteits-Bibliotheek Amsterdam.

out of a multitude of representational possibilities. They therefore possess intrinsic levels of meaning that reveal much about the underlying cultural attitudes and interests of the public who purchased them. The presence of many of the same motifs in family literature further confirms the widespread knowledge of particular ideas about domesticity in the Dutch Republic. Although some of the associations that these paintings evoke are difficult for the modern viewer to detect, let alone understand – and therefore it is incumbent upon me to expound them in detail here – they must have been readily apparent to the seventeenth-century viewer, who was so thoroughly conditioned by cultural attitudes toward women and domesticity.

In Adriaen van Gaesbeeck's depiction of a housewife engaged in needlework (Fig. 64), we once again encounter many of the motifs that belong to the standard repertoire of pictures celebrating the virtues of domesticity. A woman sews in an interior as light streams in from an open window. A book lies on the table beside her, and scattered on the floor are a shoe, her sewing basket, and a large, overturned, unlit lantern with its little door open. The virtuous associations of sewing are by now familiar as are those of the shoe. Van Gaesbeeck portrays a furnished room, in contrast to the more abstract setting of Metsu's painting. Yet it is reminiscent of the latter in its careful positioning of motifs about the woman. Therefore it too represents a plausible reality, one composed of elements that signify feminine virtues.[88]

The precise meaning of the lantern in this context is unclear.[89] Lanterns are perhaps second only to shoes as the most frequently recurring motif in images of domestic virtue. In such paintings, this object – primarily intended for outdoor use – invariably appears overturned, unlit, and hence, unused; the implication of its presence in such paintings could be that, like shoes, a lantern simply serves as a reminder that a woman's place is in the home.[90]

An unlit, overturned lantern figures prominently in the foreground of Gerard Dou's celebrated painting *The Young Mother* (Fig. 5).[91] The exquisitely crafted surface of this work, its painstaking depiction of numerous objects scattered about the cavernous room, invites our close examination. Therefore, like so many other images of domestic virtue, the pictorial surface of Dou's painting provides enjoyment of bold, almost palpable mimetic effects as well as intellectual engagement of the motifs depicted therein.[92] In essence, Dou confronts the viewer with a virtual catalogue of motifs, all striking for their conventionality, either illustrating or symbolizing the exemplary woman's tasks and the scope and limitations of her obligations, which, according to contemporary theory, lie exclusively in the home.

The lower right corner of the composition contains several cooking utensils along with a varied assortment of food, including vegetables, poultry, and fish. The presence of a broom and an unlit lantern, along with the shoe and sewing basket on the floor beside the housewife, once again pay testimony to the highly conventional nature of this imagery. The cooking utensils and abundant comestibles advert to the housewife's important duty to prepare food for her family. The shoe and possibly the lantern are, as we have seen, metaphors of domesticity. The woman's needlework and her role as a mother – her eldest daughter tends to the infant in the cradle beside her – evince such unequivocal associations with virtue that they need not be explained. The presence of servants at work in the background probably refers to the housewife's obligation to supervise her maids.

In the left background of this interior are several objects that do not belong to the sphere of the housewife, among them a large bookcase with a globe and large conch on its top shelf. There is also a man's cloak and sword hanging from a peg on the column directly in front of the bookcase. These motifs probably function as attributes of the male realm in contradistinction to those pertaining to the female realm. The books, globe, and seashell most likely connote intellectual attainment, highly esteemed in men, while the cloak and sword evoke the outdoor world that was considered the male domain.[93]

Objects that function as signifiers of spousal roles are fairly common in other genre paintings depicting housewives and servants performing needlework, as in one by Pieter Verelst, monogrammed and dated 1650 (Fig. 65). Here, a young woman – presumably married because of the type of cap that she wears – sews in a darkened interior.[94] A man's cape and sword hang from a hook on the wall behind her, articles of attire that, by extension, are attributes of the masculine, outdoor world. They effectively contrast with

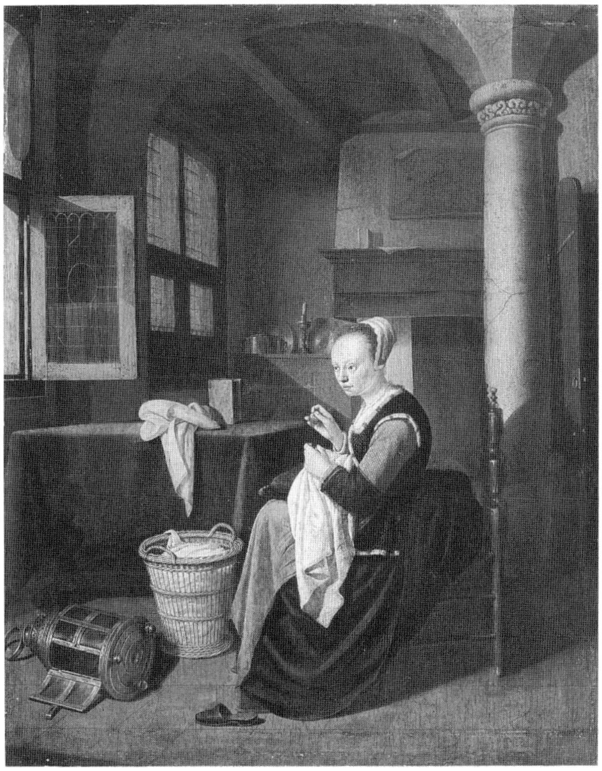

Figure 64. Adriaen van Gaesbeeck, *Woman Sewing* (oil on panel). Berlin, Gemäldegalerie, Staatliche Museen Preussischer Kulturbesitz. Photo: J. P. Anders, Berlin.

the woman's activity of sewing, which undoubtedly refers to the one occupation or office to which all women were called: housewifery.[95]

Still other domestic themes in art besides that of women performing needlework illustrate the "profitable employments" discussed by the English theologian William Perkins. For instance, there are a sizeable number of paintings depicting housewives cooking. The preparation of food was a vital skill for women to develop, presumably after having learned its rudiments from their mothers.[96] Gervase Markham, in his popular book *The English House-Wife,* ranks cooking as the principal skill that a housewife must know. Then, with a typical display of that peculiar logic so characteristic of seventeenth-century male authors writing books addressed to women, he states that cooking

> is a duty rarely belonging to a woman; and shee that is utterly ignorant therein, may not by the Lawes of strict Justice challenge the freedome

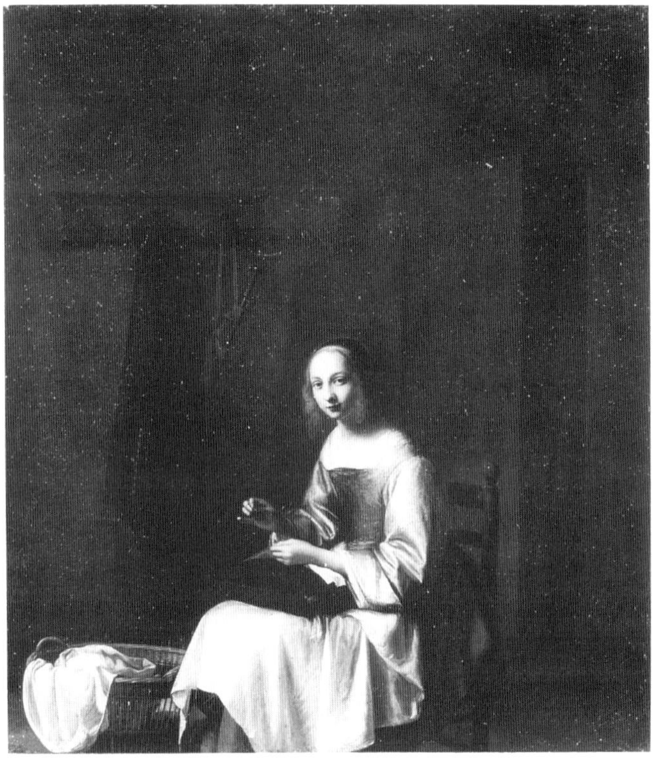

Figure 65. Pieter Verelst, *Woman Sewing*, 1650 (oil on canvas, 33.5 × 29.5 cm). Present location unknown.

> of marriage because indeed shee can then but performe halfe her vow; for shee may love and obey, but shee cannot cherish, serve, and keepe him with that true duty which is ever expected.[97]

This quotation once again demonstrates just how deeply ingrained the conviction was that a woman's ability to perform domestic tasks laid the foundation for a successful marriage. Contemporary authors also liked to justify the housewife's obligation to cook for her family by citing Proverbs 31:15: "She riseth also while it is yet night, and giveth meat to her household, and a portion to her maidens."[98] The sixteenth-century print series after designs by Maarten van Heemskerck illustrating Proverbs 31 (mentioned earlier) represents verse 15 with a housewife feeding her children and servants gathered about a table (Fig. 66).

Recognition of cooking as a fundamental domestic skill probably explains the significance of many Dutch paintings that show women preparing food in one form or another.[99] In the *Portrait of Jacob Bierens and His Family* by Hendrick Sorgh (Fig. 67), the *materfamilias*, Kornelia van Hoeck, peels

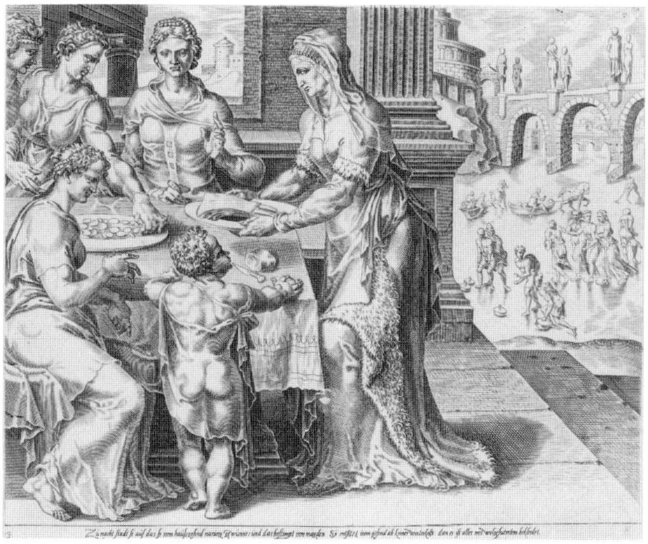

Figure 66. Dirck Volkertsz. Coornhert after Maarten van Heemskerck, *The Woman Serving Food to Her Family* (engraving from the series *Praise of the Virtuous Housewife*), 1555. Amsterdam, Rijksprentenkabinet. Photo: Rijksmuseum-Stichting.

apples.[100] This portrait is unusual because the entire family works in the kitchen (with the exception of the eldest son who plays a *viola da gamba*). In keeping with portrait conventions of the period, Jacob Bierens, the family head, is more dynamically modeled than his wife, whose features, like those of the other females in the room, are flattened by the bright light that illuminates them.[101] As a consequence Jacob is more interactive with the viewer; as he and his youngest son enter the room with a platter of fresh fish, Bierens gazes at the viewer, while holding one of the fish aloft by its gills. His daughter works at a table nearby, plucking a fowl, while a maid washes a jug at the sink in the background.

Various provisions lie strewn on the tile floor in the foreground including still more fish, assorted vegetables, cooking utensils, and a shopping pail. The family members demonstrate their industriousness in prudently gathering and preparing food as they work in this kitchen stocked with abundant provisions. Even the actions of the figures can be linked to the roles assigned to family members in domestic conduct books and related literature. For example, the motif of the elder Bierens holding a platter of fish illustrates the husband's obligation to provide sustenance for his family.[102] His wife, busily peeling fruit, clearly demonstrates her divinely ordained duty to use judiciously what her husband provides. Her daughter, who is plucking the bird, displays her good training in preparation for marriage.

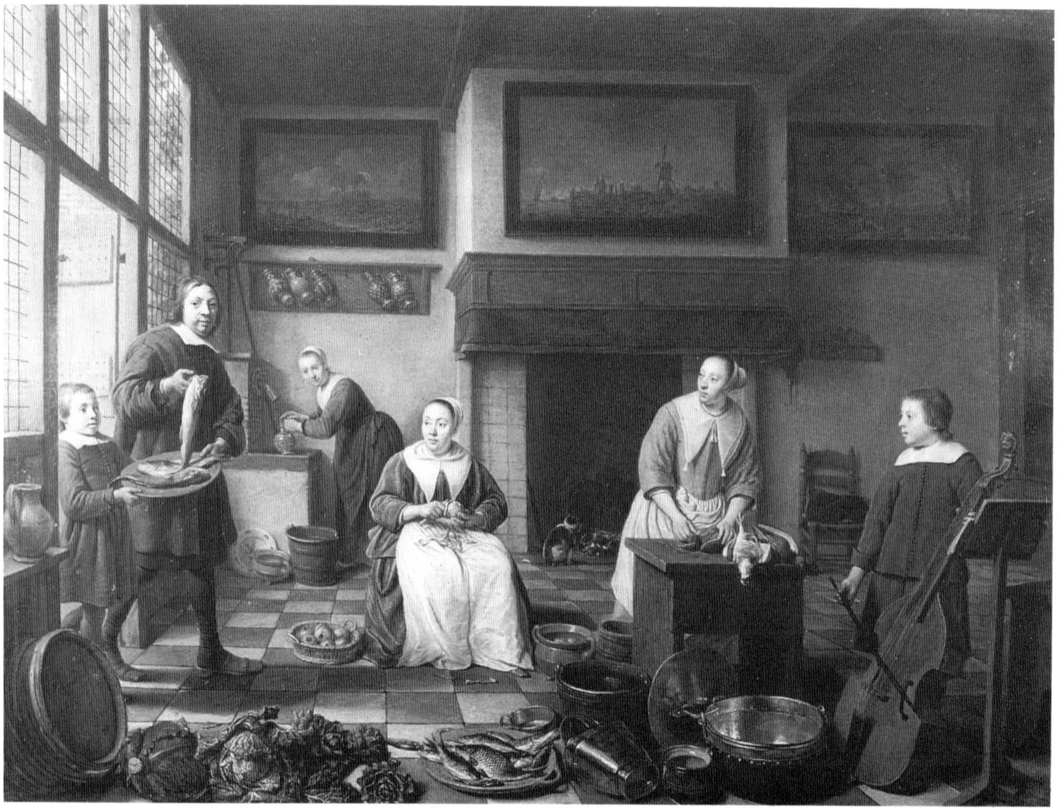

Figure 67. Hendrick Sorgh, *Portrait of Jacob Bierens and His Family*, 1663 (oil on panel, 52 × 71 cm). The Hague, Rijksdienst Beeldende Kunst. Photo: Copyright Rijksdienst Beeldende Kunst.

Given the prominent display in this painting of comestibles and cooking, the inclusion of Bierens's eldest boy playing a *viola da gamba* at first appears quite incongruous. It is by now well known that musical instruments were long-standing metaphors in art and literature for familial harmony. Plutarch's *Conjugalia praecepta* is the likely source behind several sixteenth- and seventeenth-century group portraits in which sitters play musical instruments as a reference to this concept.[103] Undoubtedly, the boy playing the *viola da gamba* in the portrait connotes it as well, yet this motif should not be considered in isolation from the main activity in the portrait, the preparation of food.[104] Actually a strong visual link exists between the motif and the activities of the rest of the family because the boy, his mother, and sister all watch the elder Bierens and his other son enter the kitchen with the platter of fish. As we have seen, the preparation of food is represented here as the woman's task, in fulfillment of her duty to use what her husband provides

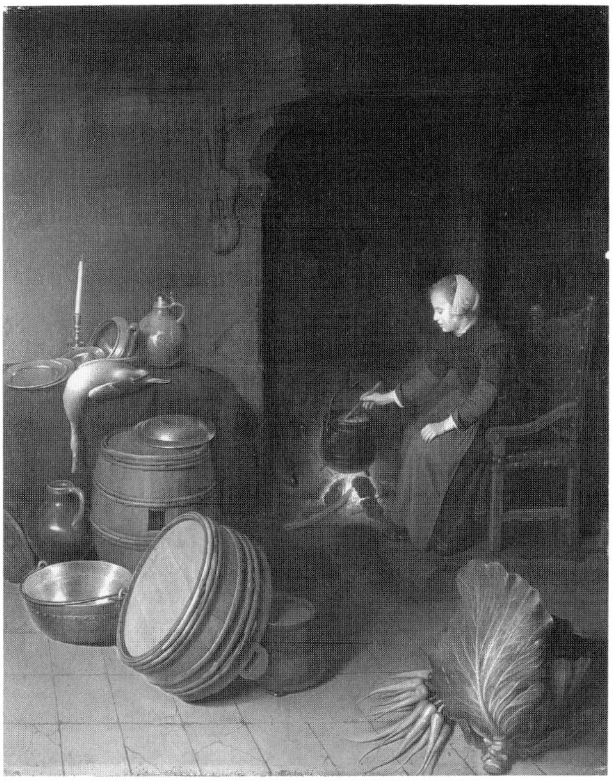

Figure 68. Pieter van den Bos, *The Young Cook* (oil on panel, 57 × 45.5 cm). Basel, Kunstmuseum. Photo: Offentliche Kunstsammlung Basel.

for the family. Contemporary theorists believed that the spouses' successful performance of these and other tasks would ensure harmony and peace within the family. As Robert Cleaver and John Dod state: "Where the husband and wife performeth these duties in their house, we may call it a Colledge of quietnesse: The house wherein these are neglected, we may terme it a hell."[105] Thus, the diligence of the elder Bierens and his wife in discharging their duties as *pater et materfamilias* has resulted in concord within their family, fittingly symbolized by their elder son who plays the *viola da gamba.*

The painting by Sorgh is an exception among those representing the theme of food preparation because it is a family portrait. This theme is far more frequently represented in genre paintings. For instance, in Pieter van den Bos's *The Young Cook,* a young woman – seemingly too young to be a housewife, so likely a servant – in plain clothing stirs a soup or stew in a large kettle hanging in the fireplace (Fig. 68).[106] In the foreground are metal dishes and cooking utensils, as well as a dead, unplucked duck and some vegetables. These objects display exquisite tactile qualities, especially the vegetables in the lower right corner, which seem to protrude into the beholder's space. Such motifs, available for close scrutiny, engage the viewer aesthetically and, at the same time, act as signifiers of domestic virtue. The scene effectively conveys an aura of homeyness and simplicity that was undoubtedly the artist's intention.

Amazingly, some art historians have maintained that paintings of similar subject matter and mood have an erotic content, particularly those that show women plucking ducks or other fowl. For example, it has been stated that Nicolaes Maes's contemporaries would have recognized the veiled erotic message of his *Woman Plucking a Duck* (Fig. 69).[107] In the wake of Eddy de Jongh's influential studies of sexual imagery in Dutch seventeenth-century art,[108] there has been a propensity to interpret motifs like birds – and, for that matter, shoes and other objects – as erotic symbols, regardless of the seemingly "virtuous" contexts in which they appear.

Far from displaying dissolute behavior, a frequent characteristic of paintings where fowls do function as erotic metaphors, Maes's picture, like his other representations of domestic subjects, emanates an aura of wholesome intimacy.[109] By calling attention to this, I am not arguing that this observation can lead to a single, "correct" interpretation of the painting; this would be reductive, and moreover it is inconsistent with how seventeenth-century viewers understood art. Rather, I am suggesting that we attempt to understand it in a manner consistent with its visual qualities, as seventeenth-century viewers likely did; for the painting sympathetically portrays a demure, industrious young woman completely absorbed in her work within a tranquil interior. The game bag and rifle leaning against the back wall of the room undoubtedly belong to the hunter who has shot the duck that she plucks. Given the intimate, peaceful aura of this painting, it seems logical to view the woman's action, along with the other duck, apples, and cooking utensils on the floor, as a reference to the virtuous nature of food preparation and, by extension, to her divinely appointed duty to manage the provisions provided by her husband (or, if she is a servant, by the master of the household).[110] In this picture, the presence of hunting equipment alludes precisely to this husbandly role of providing for the family, just as it does in other genre paintings and even in portraits.[111]

The virtuous associations of the theme of women preparing food can sometimes be quite explicit, as in pendants by Gabriel Metsu. One shows a woman peeling apples in what is likely a kitchen (Fig. 70). A dead rabbit, more fruit, and a shopping pail lie on the table beside her. The sobriety and simplicity of this scene contrasts strongly with that of its pendant (Fig. 71).[112] There a woman has been drinking and smoking; she tips her glass

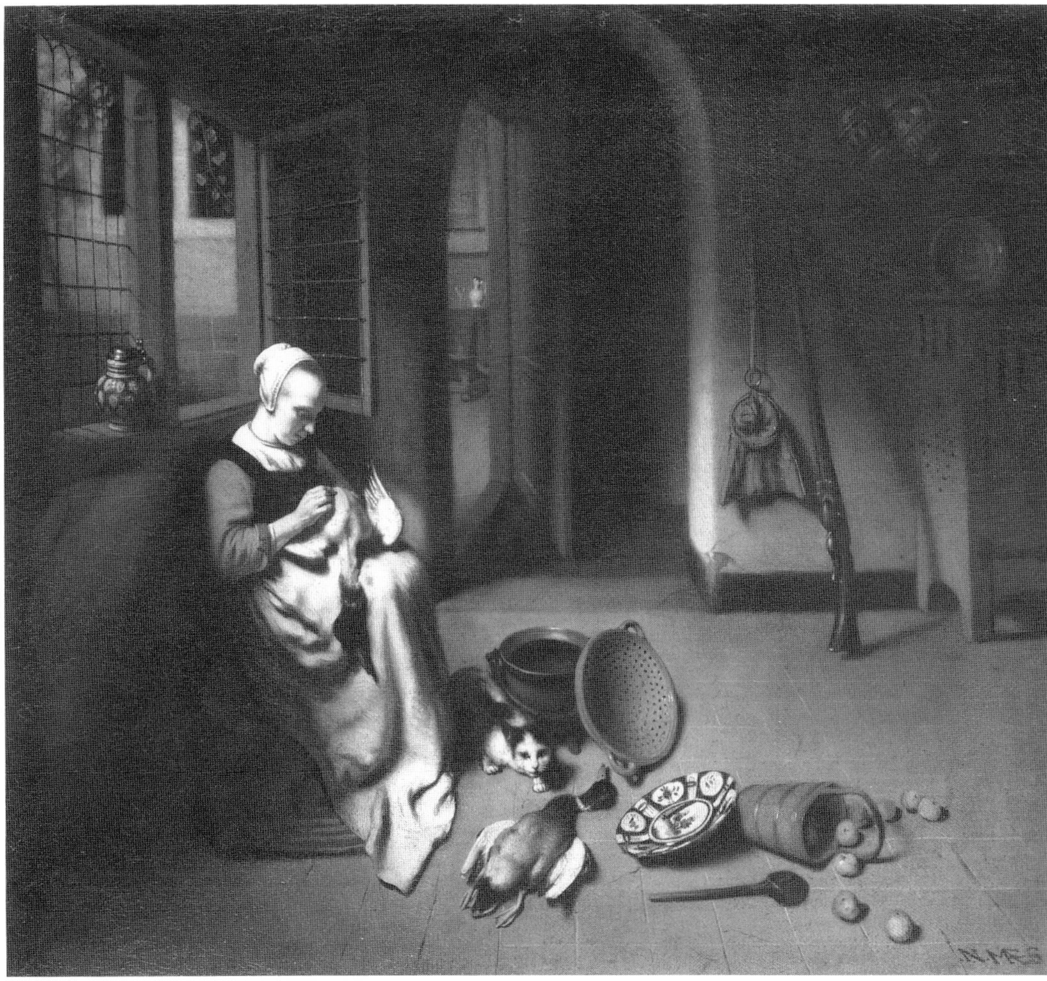

Figure 69. Nicolaes Maes, *Woman Plucking a Duck* (oil on canvas, 58 × 66 cm). Philadelphia, Philadelphia Museum of Art. Given by Mrs. Gordon A. Hardwick and Mrs. W. Newbold Ely in memory of Mr. and Mrs. Roland L. Taylor. Photo: museum.

in the direction of her apple-peeling counterpart as if to toast her. The luxurious carpet on the table contrasts strongly with the plain, unadorned tablecloth in the painting of the apple peeler. The disparities even extend to the background: the painting of the drinker includes a fireplace supported by a classical caryatid, while a more modest fireplace is seen in the kitchen of the apple peeler. In his monograph on Metsu, Franklin Robinson astutely pointed out these differences. He rightly regarded the pendants as illustrations of "two entirely different personalities, even ways of life – the life of pleasure and that of domesticity."[113] However, Robinson's analysis stops short of observing what is fundamentally on display in these pendants: contemporary male convictions about proper and improper female roles and behavior. Their subtle, underlying message is that a woman's only recourse is to domesticity, which theoretically would enable her to resist what were perceived as insidious habits and lifestyles.

A popular theme in Dutch seventeenth-century genre painting related to these scenes of food preparation is that of women purchasing provisions at the marketplace.[114] Cats discusses in detail the practical aspects of the mistress's duty to purchase goods for the household in *Houwelyck*, stating that she should have been taught how to shop by her mother in preparation for marriage.[115] The ability to shop wisely was an important skill since the money her husband provided had to be prudently spent for the good of the family. To Cats, this did not necessarily mean that the cheapest goods should be bought because "the best bargain is never made with the smallest amount of money or with the highest expectations."[116]

The Fishmarket by Jacob Gerritsz. Cuyp, signed and dated 1627, is among the earliest depictions of a housewife shopping (Fig. 72).[117] Here, a mistress accompanied by her maid points to some fish that she has evidently just purchased; the vendor holds several coins in his hand. This scene, which includes a stunning still life of fish, is unusual in its rather individualized rendering of facial features, particularly those of the male.[118] Nevertheless, Cuyp's focus on the transaction and the woman's gesture toward her purchase – located in the center of the composition – illustrates the housewife's virtue as a circumspect shopper. The same idea is also evident in a painting by H. Coveyn in which a vendor gazes at the viewer while pointing to a woman inspecting the fish (Fig. 73). The fact that this woman examines the fish with the aid of pince-nez further emphasizes her discretion.

In addition to genre paintings, there are also several portraits of women purchasing provisions for their households. An unusual portrait by Pieter Codde depicts a family on a beach where fishermen sell their catch (Fig. 74). In the foreground, the mother selects fish from the young fisher boy at her feet, an action stressed by her gesture and glance in our direction. Codde uses this mise-en-scène and the pointing gesture of the daughter in order to call attention to the woman's virtue as a prudent housewife, shopping for her family.

Emanuel de Witte's *Portrait of Adriana van Heusden and Her Daughter at the New Fishmarket in Amsterdam* conveys the same associations (Fig. 75).[119] Mother and daughter stand beside a market stall containing a dazzling assortment of fish. The luminous, wet sheen of the fish is rendered so vividly that it inadvertently detracts from the portrait of the woman and her child. Adriana haggles with the vendor, their gestures alluding to her cautious purchase of fish. De Witte draws on pictorial traditions usually associated with the theme of market shopping in genre painting, thereby creating a

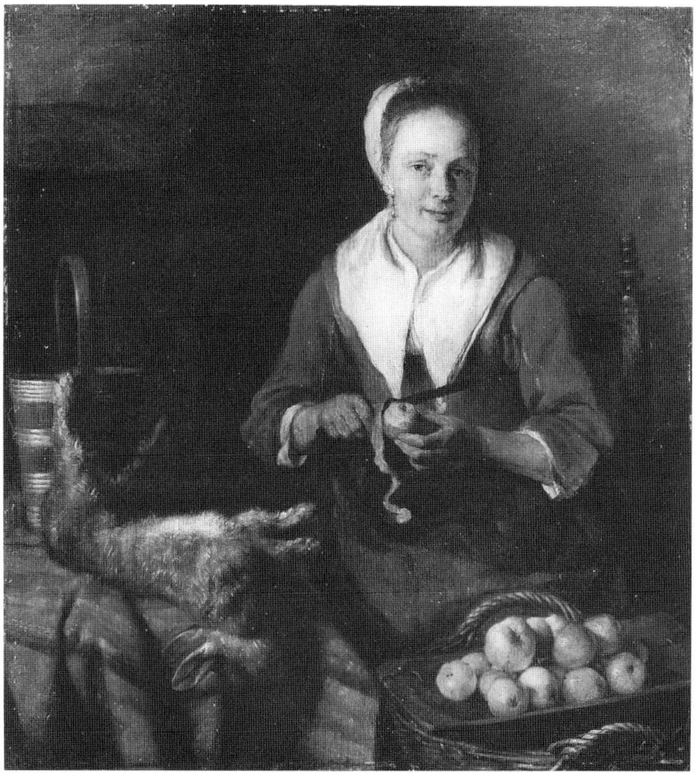

Figure 70 (left). Gabriel Metsu, *Woman Peeling an Apple* (oil on panel, 28 × 26 cm). Paris, Musée du Louvre. Photo: Réunion des musées nationaux, Paris.

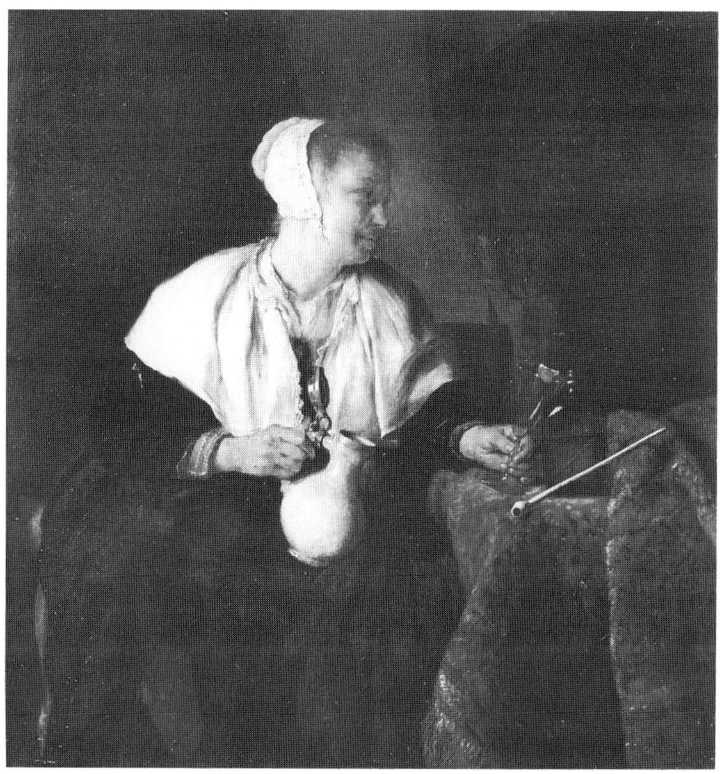

Figure 71 (right). Gabriel Metsu, *Woman with a Glass and Tankard* (oil on panel, 28 × 26 cm). Paris, Musée du Louvre. Photo: Réunion des musées nationaux, Paris.

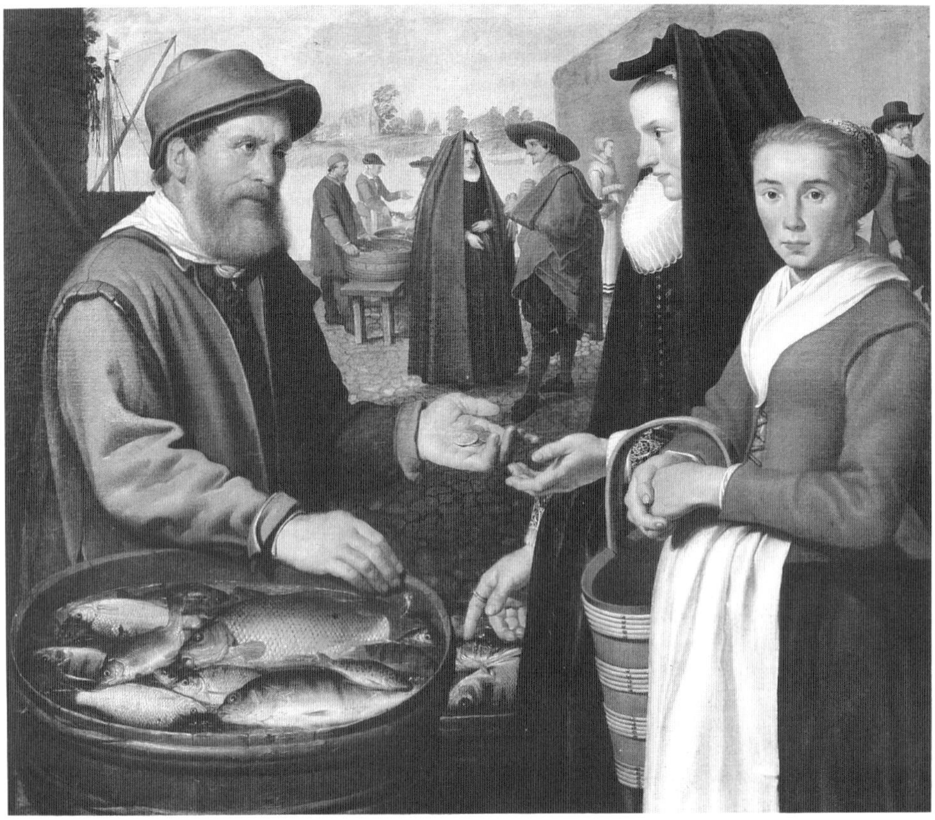

Figure 72 (above). Jacob Gerritsz. Cuyp, *The Fishmarket*, 1627 (oil on canvas, 110.5 × 122.5 cm). Dordrecht, Dordrechts Museum. Photo: Stijns, Dordrecht.

Figure 73 (right). H. Coveyn, *Woman Inspecting Fish*. Present location unknown. Photo: courtesy Christie's, London.

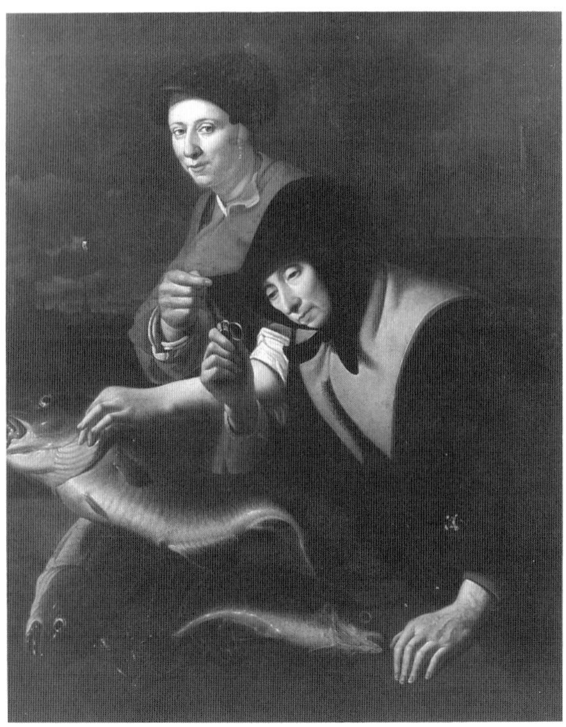

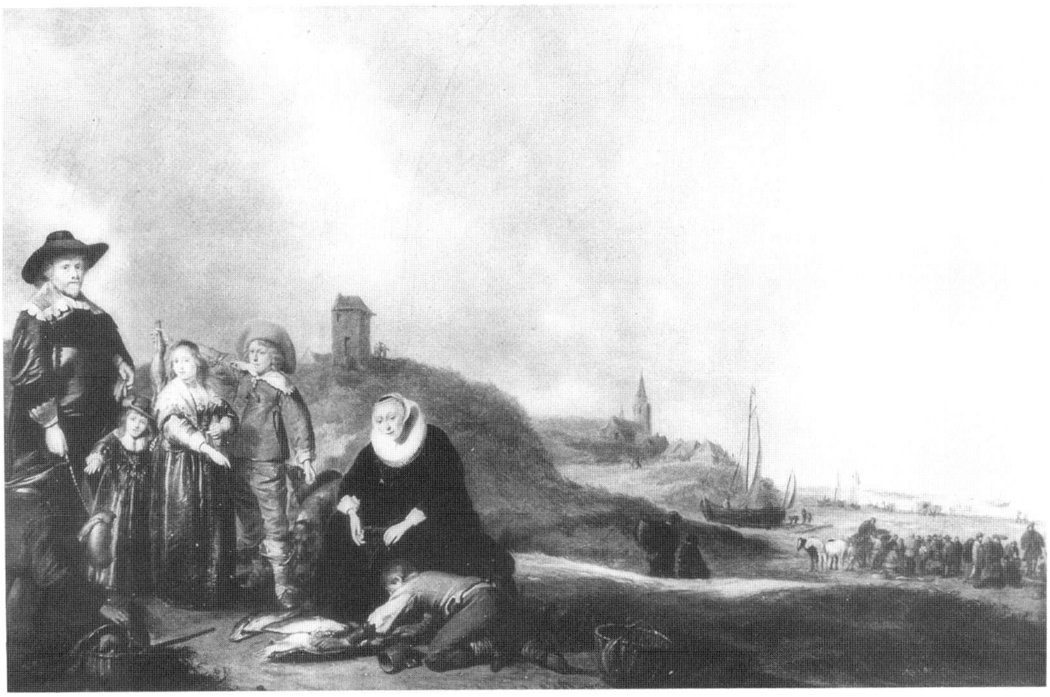

Figure 74. Pieter Codde, *Portrait of Sebastiaen Francken and His Family on the Beach at Scheveningen* (oil on panel, 48.8 × 70.2 cm). Present location unknown.

"genrefied portrait," one that celebrates Adriana's virtue and prudence in her role as housewife.[120]

Thus far, I have restricted my discussion to paintings of women performing needlework and preparing and purchasing food. Dutch painters depicted other themes of housewives performing tasks that William Perkins would call "profitable employment, for the good of her charge."[121] Some of these so-called profitable employments were rarely illustrated in art.[122] For instance, when we consider the near-legendary zeal with which Dutch housewives were said to have kept their dwellings spotless, it is astonishing that genre painters seldom turned their attention to the theme of women cleaning the home.[123] This provides further confirmation that domestic images do not merely record or describe everyday reality but re-create it by representing stock subjects, formulated in response to pictorial traditions, to personal aesthetic interests, and even to market demands. While some subjects were highly popular, others never became firmly established within the limited artistic repertoire.

Surprisingly, the theme of women cleaning and maintaining the home – one with a potentially large variety of subjects – is limited basically to images

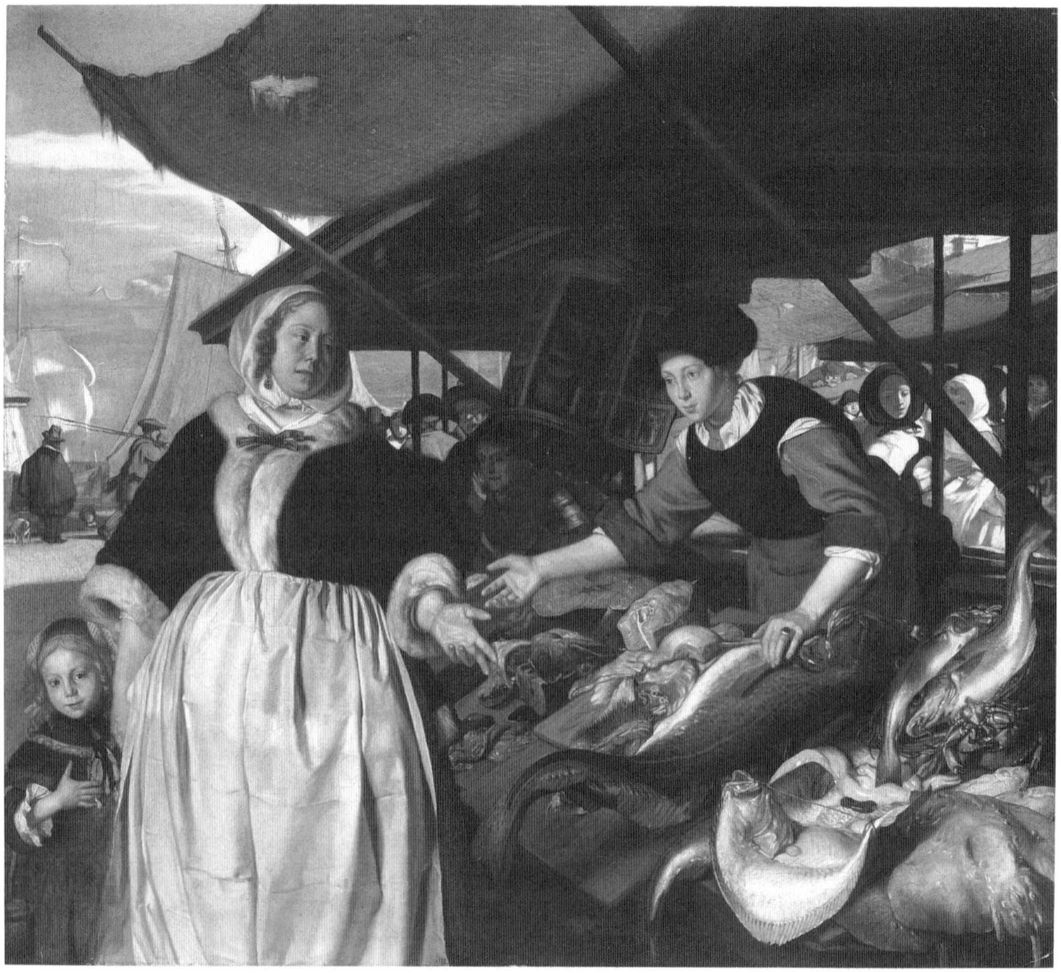

Figure 75. Emanuel de Witte, *Portrait of Adriana van Heusden and Her Daughter at the New Fishmarket in Amsterdam* (oil on canvas, 57.1 × 64.1 cm). London, The National Gallery. Reproduced by courtesy of the Trustees, The National Gallery, London.

of women who clean metal utensils or sweep floors, with the former easily outnumbering the latter. Gerard Dou was one of the first artists to depict women scouring kettles, a subject consequently adopted by many of his pupils (Fig. 76).[124] For example, Metsu's rendition of the subject is strikingly close to Dou's as both show young women – in Dou's case, a servant girl – scouring kettles on the sill of a nichelike enclosure filled with clean, shiny vessels (Fig. 77).[125] As we have already seen, these architectonic enclosures, through their illusionism and play on real and fictive space, simultaneously offer aesthetic enjoyment and intellectual stimulation.

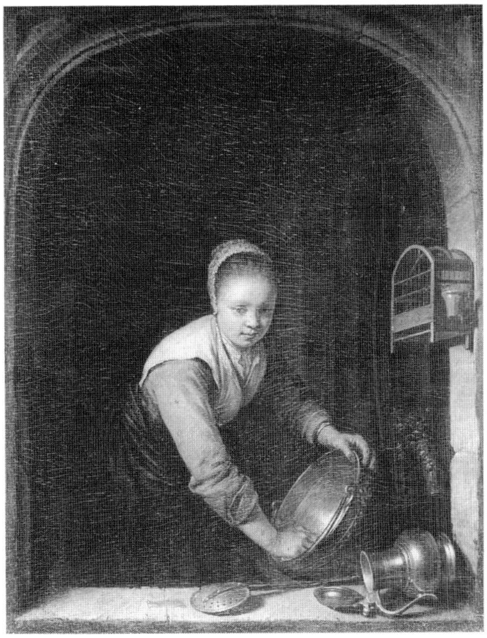

Figure 76. Gerard Dou, *A Maid Servant Scouring a Brass Pan at a Window* (oil on panel, 17.1 × 13.3 cm). London, Collection of Her Majesty the Queen. Copyright reserved; Reproduced by permission of the Lord Chamberlain's Office.

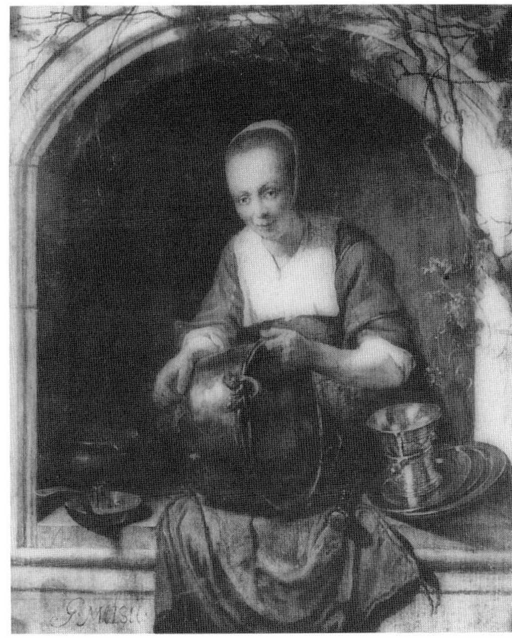

Figure 77. Gabriel Metsu, *Woman Scouring Pots and Pans in a Niche* (oil on panel, 24 × 20 cm). Present location unknown.

In *Young Woman Scouring a Metal Plate* by Pieter van den Bos, a young mother – her child sleeps in a cradle in the background – scours metal plates in a darkened interior (Fig. 78). Domestic implements that are by now familiar lie scattered about the room, among them a spinning wheel and, adjacent to the barrel on which the woman works, the omnipresent lantern, turned on its side with its door wide open. The virtuous connotations of these implements suggest that, in this context, the woman's task of scouring pans conveys analogous ideas. Another motif common to these three paintings also points to the women's virtue: their rolled-up sleeves. This is not a trivial observation; seventeenth-century viewers would have immediately recognized this motif as a sign that these women are assiduous. Contemporary moralists exhorted housewives literally to stick their hands "uyt de mouwen" (out of the sleeves) when working.[126]

Brooms often appear in the immediate vicinity of women at work (e.g., Figs. 1, 5), but the subject of women actually sweeping floors was only infrequently represented. A rarefied atmosphere of intimacy and sanctity

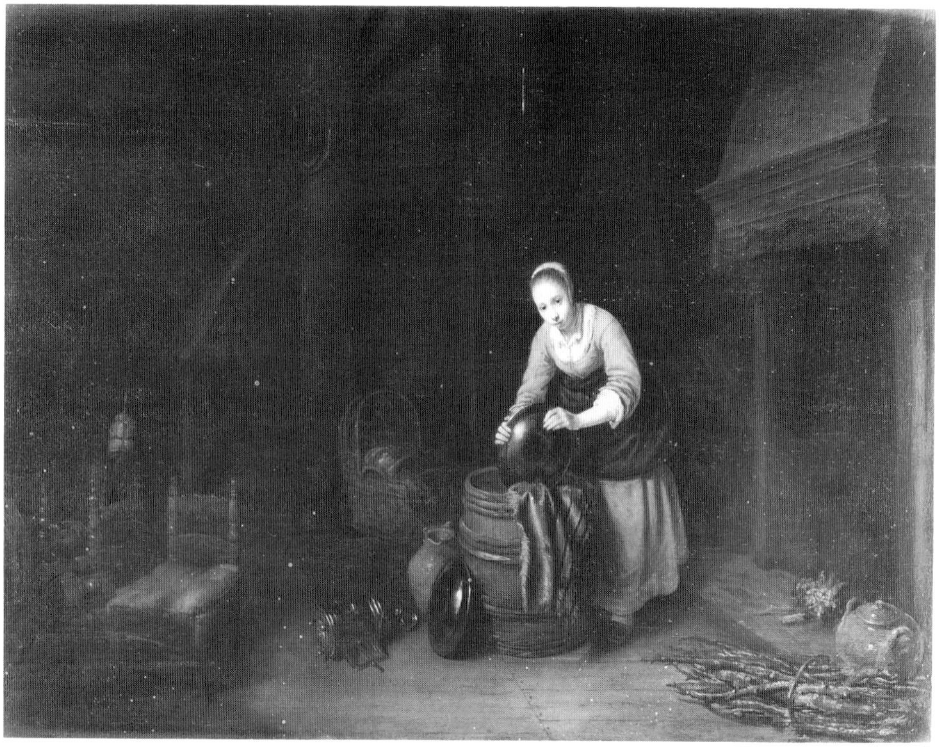

Figure 78. Pieter van den Bos, *Young Woman Scouring a Metal Plate.* York, York City Art Gallery. Photo: art gallery.

pervades images of women sweeping, so much so that it is possible that the activity might convey associations extending well beyond those of mere domestic duty.[127] In one instance, a painting by Pieter de Hooch, a maid carefully sweeps the floor in the foreground of an already immaculate interior (Fig. 79).[128] Behind her, a mother nurses her infant by an open window with brilliant sunlight streaming in. A picture representing the Descent from the Cross hangs on the wall directly above them.[129] Our eye is quickly drawn to this effulgent scene even though the maid with the broom is the principal motif in the painting by virtue of her prominence within the overall composition. The precise significance of the little painting of the Deposition may be unclear, but it undeniably contributes to the almost sacrosanct quality of the portrayal of the mother and child directly below. Perhaps the purity and innocence of the mother and child, heightened by the representation of the Deposition, relates symbolically to the motif of the maid sweeping in the foreground.

Seventeenth-century writers frequently associated the broom with spiritual and moral purity. At times, this association could be quite explicit, as in a

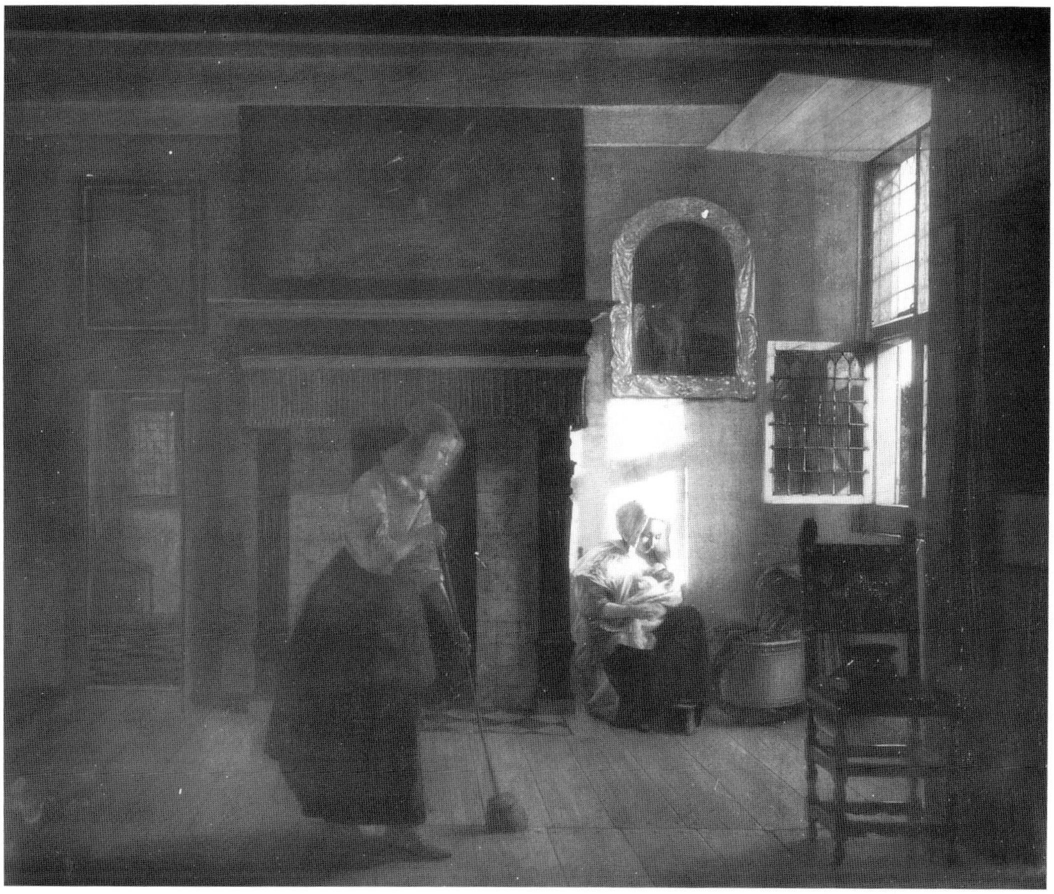

Figure 79. Pieter de Hooch, *Mother and Child by a Window, with a Woman Sweeping* (oil on canvas, 65 × 80 cm). Luton Hoo, Bedfordshire, The Wernher Collection. Photo: The Wernher Collection-Luton Hoo Foundation.

contemporary Jesuit emblem in which the Christ Child sweeps a heart clean of all iniquity.[130] A number of Protestant texts match the unambiguous imagery of the Jesuit emblem. For example, in the frontispiece to Petrus Wittewrongel's influential domestic conduct book *Oeconomia Christiana* (Christian Economy; Fig. 80), a maid sweeps the floor – a purely symbolic activity however, since she vigilantly sweeps away objects of vice, like playing cards, that potentially undermine the spiritual and moral well-being of the family to her right.[131] A passage from a book by one of Wittewrongel's Pietist colleagues, Simon Oomius, provides a literary parallel to this scene. According to Oomius, discipline in the home, that is, spiritual and moral assiduousness, is the broom that cleans it, preparing it to receive God's presence. Oomius uses this metaphor to exhort fathers to care for the souls

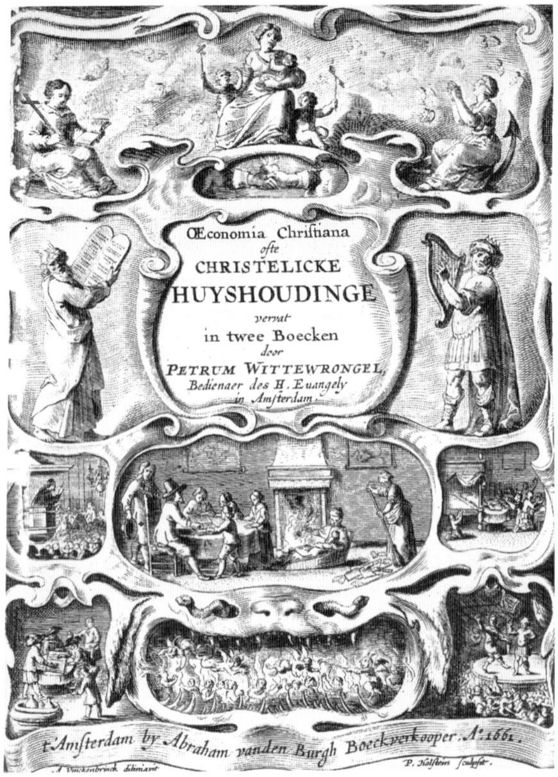

Figure 80. Frontispiece from Petrus Wittewrongel, *Oeconomia Christiana ofte Christelicke huyshoudinghe*, 3d enlarged ed., Amsterdam 1661. Amsterdam, Universiteits-Bibliotheek Amsterdam. Photo: courtesy Universiteits-Bibliotheek Amsterdam.

of their families by being vigilant for transgressions and breaches of conduct.[132] Perhaps similar associations were operative in De Hooch's painting.[133]

By far the most popular domestic theme in Dutch seventeenth-century genre painting is that of the housewife supervising her maids. As with other, related themes, contemporary literature affords insights into the contemporary cultural framework that underlies painted representations of the mistress's supervisory role. I have already cited William Perkins's exhortation that mistresses assign chores to "her maids . . . overseeing them therein."[134] It is important to note once again that the point is not one of the direct influence of literature on art but of an analogous expression of ideals concerning housewifely tasks and obligations. The housewife's duty to oversee her servants was discussed at great length in domestic conduct books of the day and other, related works:

> . . . that she beeyng become a married wife, maie knowe the office and duetie of housholde servauntes, lette her note, and look how aptly and

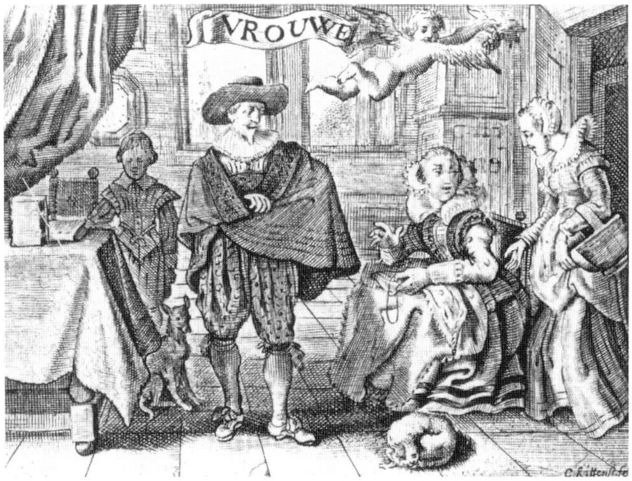

Figure 81. Illustration from Jacob Cats, *Houwelyck. Dat is de gansche gelegentheyt des echten staets*, 4th ed., The Hague 1632. Amsterdam, Universiteits-Bibliotheek Amsterdam. Photo: courtesy Universiteits-Bibliotheek Amsterdam.

> cleanly thei keepe the Chambers, and other like places . . . and lette her be present at every thing that longeth to housholde affaires.[135]

The close parallels between the depiction of housewives supervising their servants in art and the description of this duty in literature are nowhere more evident than in the little frontispiece inserted before the introduction to the chapter "Vrouwe" in the fourth edition of Cats's *Houwelyck* (1632). This illustration, by Cornelis Kittensteyn, represents a virtuous family in an interior (Fig. 81). The housewife has momentarily interrupted her sewing in order to consult with her maid who holds a shopping pail. This scene recalls those portrayed in a number of paintings depicting mistresses about to send their maids off on shopping trips for the family (see, e.g., Fig. 82).[136] All of these postdate the book illustration, and it is possible that they were influenced by it, especially since Cats's book was so popular at that time.

A related group of paintings represent maids who have returned from shopping, displaying purchases to their ever-watchful mistresses (see, e.g., Fig. 83).[137] Related, as well, are the seemingly countless renditions of maids showing housewives food offered for sale by traveling vendors. In Quiringh van Brekelenkam's *Mistress Choosing Fish,* a maid holds a tray of meat for her mistress to inspect while the vendor waits patiently at the door (Fig. 84). The mistress has been sewing and her shoe lies on the floor in front of her, both motifs symbolizing her virtue as a housewife. A large painting of a shepherdess in a landscape hangs on the wall behind her.[138] In view of the

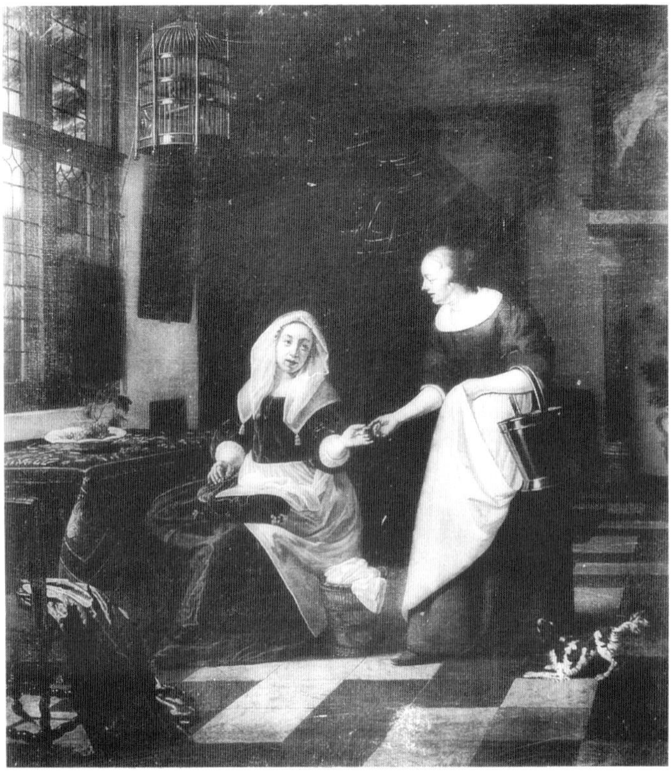

Figure 82. Michael van Musscher, *Marketing Money*, 1669 (oil on canvas, 74 × 65 cm). Present location unknown.

housewife's manifold duties in the home, we can assume that this picture refers to her supervision of the household and its goods: just as the shepherdess must care for her flock, so must the mistress tend to the needs of her family.[139]

Pieter de Hooch depicts a similar scene in a painting in which a mother pauses from feeding her child in order to inspect a large flatfish held by her maid (Fig. 85).[140] The vendor, a fishwife, waits in the background by the entrance to the dwelling. A recent suggestion that the motif of the fish is an erotic metaphor seems dubious; more than likely, it serves to demonstrate the woman's virtue as a circumspect housewife who carefully chooses the "best buys" for her family.[141] Moreover, the fact that the maid shows the fish to her mistress illustrates what contemporary viewers would have perceived as their proper working relationship.

The theme of housewives supervising their servants extended to other subjects besides the inspection of food for purchase. Mistresses and maids often cook together (see, e.g., Fig. 86), and in what is likely a portrait, attributed to Egbert van Heemskerck, a housewife oversees her servants as

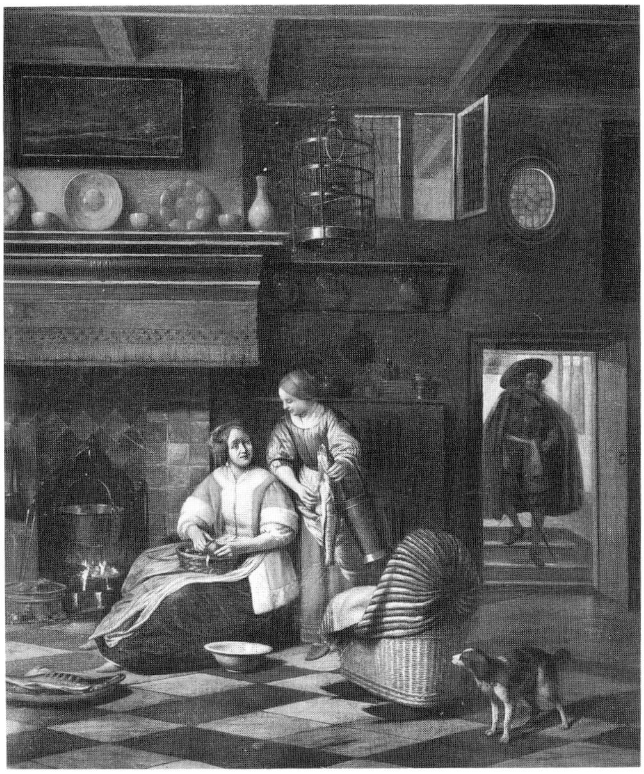

Figure 83 (above). Pieter de Hooch, *A Woman and a Serving Girl with a Fish* (oil on canvas, 83 × 72 cm). Rotterdam, Museum Boymans-Van Beuningen. Photo: Copyright Frequin-Photos, The Hague.

Figure 84 (right). Quiringh van Brekelenkam, *Mistress Choosing Fish*, 1664. Manchester, Assheton Bennett Collection, Manchester City Art Gallery. Photo: gallery.

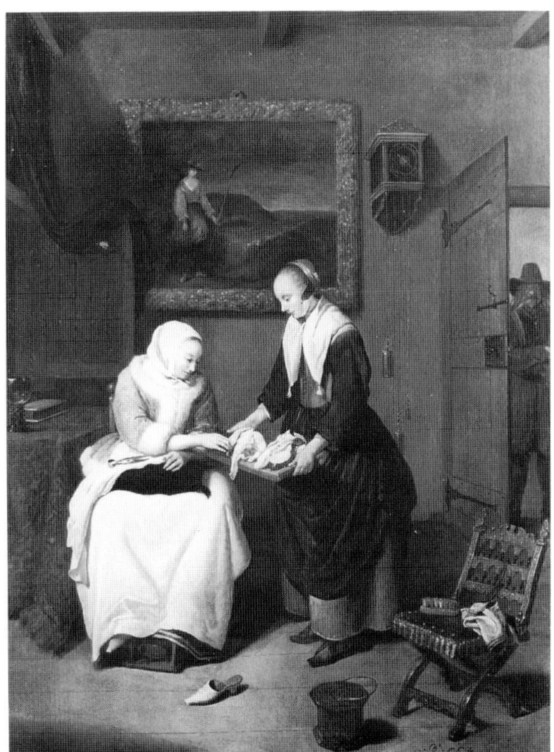

they perform several tasks, among them ironing (Fig. 87). *The Linen Chest* by Pieter de Hooch, signed and dated 1663, shows a housewife helping her maid store linens in a large chest (Fig. 88).[142] Behind these women, to the right, a child plays *colf*, a popular amusement that is the precursor to the modern-day game of golf.[143] The costumes worn by these figures may seem inconsequential to the modern viewer, but to the seventeenth-century one, it served to clarify their identities. The woman to the left, wearing a black jacket and an apron, is a servant. She takes linens from the pile held by her more elegantly attired mistress. De Hooch's use of dress as a signifier of social position would have certainly met with the approval of contemporary moralists for "apparell is one of those outward signes whereby the wisdome of masters and mistresses in well governing their servants is manifested to the world."[144] Moreover, they would have been pleased by the motif of the housewife actively assisting her maid. According to the authors of domestic conduct books, the mistress was not to supervise her servants by delegating every single task; rather, she was to work alongside them.[145] For example, William Gouge interprets Proverbs 31:15, which states that the good housewife "gives a portion" to her maids, as a sign that "shee is with them her selfe; shee worketh willingly with her hands."[146]

According to a recent interpretation of De Hooch's painting, the women's activity of storing linens illustrated the futility of greedy hoarding.[147] In my opinion, this is incorrect because it is deduced from an eighteenth-century emblem by Jan Luiken in which figures depicted performing the very same task symbolize miserliness and vanity. In general, it is dangerous to posit one-to-one relationships between emblems and motifs in paintings; this is especially true of emblems by Luiken since he discusses the symbolic significance of nearly every conceivable object. Many of the subjects of his emblems – and this is especially true of the one cited here – were of his own invention. Since Luiken's works had not been published previously, and since their contents only infrequently reflect literary and pictorial traditions, they could not have been known by artists of an earlier generation.

There is no evidence that the women in De Hooch's painting are hoarding goods. On the contrary, their activity of putting linens into a chest illustrates the housewife's duty to supervise her maids by working alongside them as well as the need to maintain the family's provisions. Not only housewives, but all Christians were charged to be proper caretakers (or stewards) of God's blessings, that is, the material prosperity that He bestows on them. In his *Institutes of Christian Religion,* one of the most influential theological works of the era, John Calvin states:

> It [Scripture] decrees that all those things [earthly possessions] were so given to us by the kindness of God, and so destined for our benefit, that

Figure 85 (right). Pieter de Hooch, *Mother and Child with a Servant Girl* (oil on canvas, 91.5 × 83 cm). Copenhagen, Royal Museum of Fine Arts. Photo: H. Petersen, Copenhagen.

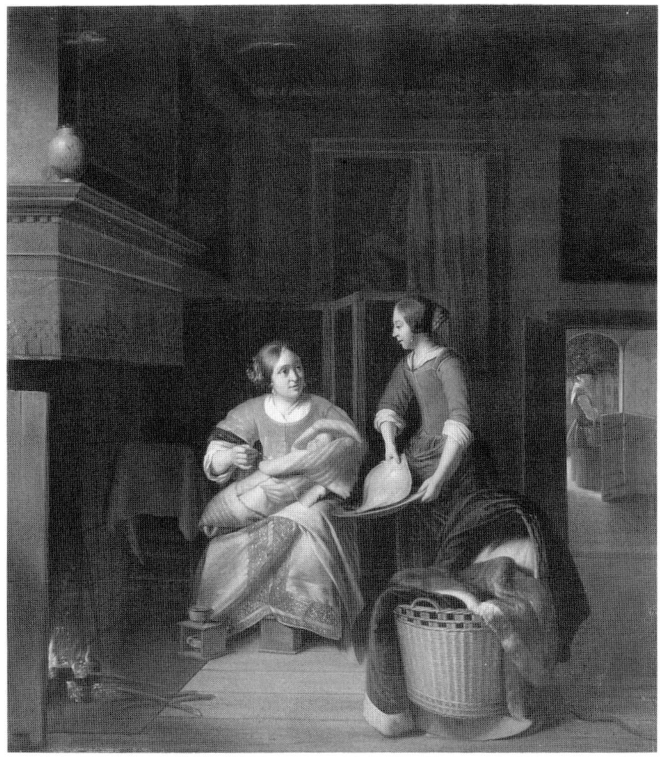

Figure 86 (below). Pieter de Hooch, *Two Women and a Child by a Fireplace* (oil on canvas, 64 × 77 cm). Raleigh, North Carolina Museum of Art, purchased with funds from the State of North Carolina. Photo: museum.

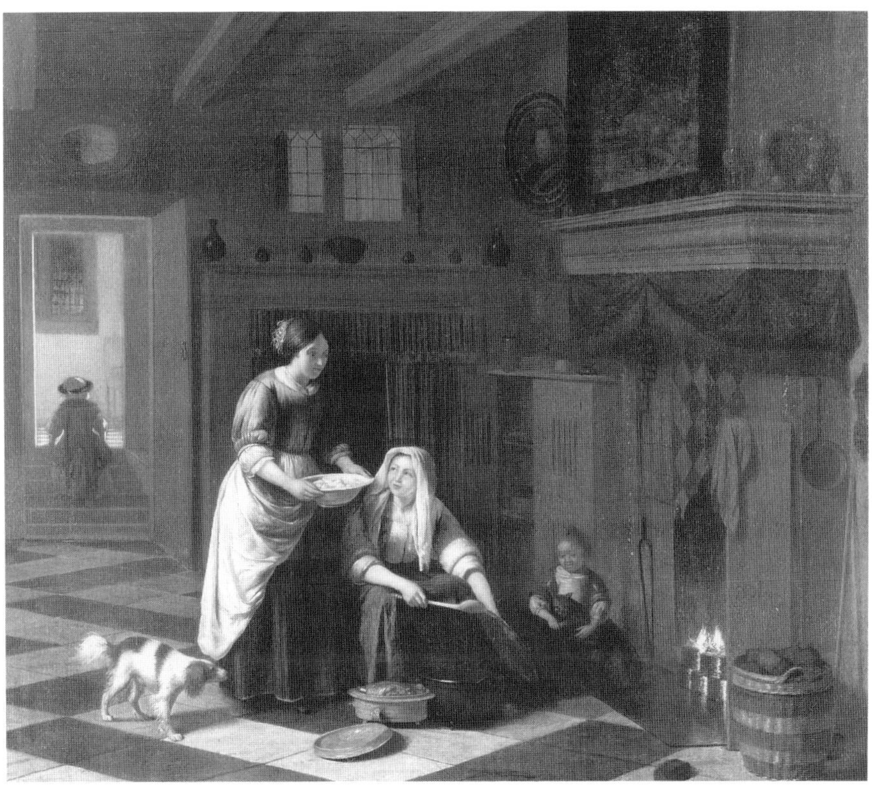

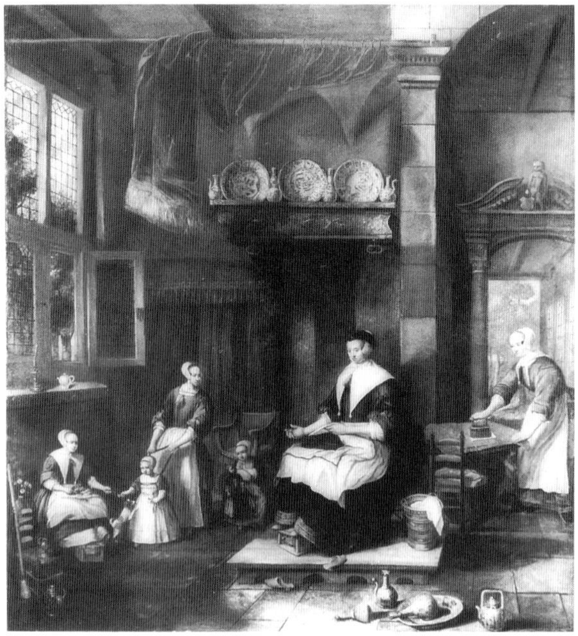

Figure 87. Egbert van Heemskerck (attributed to), *Mistress Supervising Her Maids* (oil on canvas, 155 × 140 cm). Present location unknown.

> they are, as it were, entrusted to us, and we must one day render an account of them. Thus, therefore, we must so arrange it that this saying may continually resound in our ears: "Render an account of your stewardship."[148] (Luke 16:2)

In De Hooch's picture, the fact that these women are storing linen, an expensive commodity in the seventeenth century, likely indicates their good stewardship over material possessions.

The motif of the child playing *colf* is odd in this context, because it is an outdoor game. Dutch artists most often represented the game in paintings of winter landscapes. In contemporary literature, where references are infrequent, the pastime is associated with folly and wasteful pleasure.[149] In De Hooch's painting, the child playing *colf* might convey this association, in symbolic contrast to the women who diligently work.[150] On the other hand, the motif might actually complement and underscore the women's virtuous performance of their tasks. In order to win the game of *colf,* the ball must be struck correctly so that it will travel the greatest possible distance toward the target. An emblematic poem from the anonymous *Kinder-werck* (Children's Work), published in 1626, attaches a metaphoric dimension to this skill. Here, the ability to strike the ball properly in order to win the

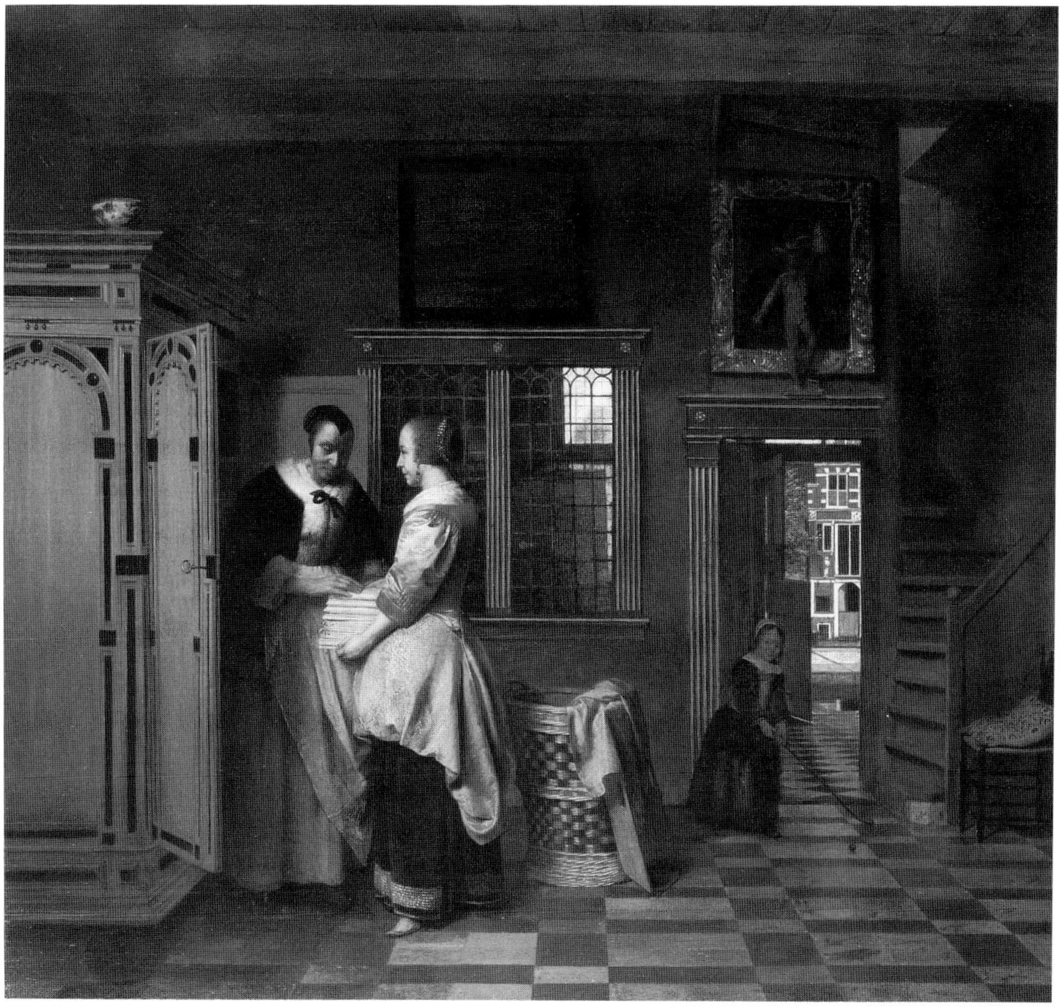

Figure 88. Pieter de Hooch, *The Linen Chest*, 1663 (oil on canvas, 72 × 77.5 cm). Amsterdam, Rijksmuseum. Photo: Rijksmuseum-Stichting.

game symbolizes the need to work toward a clear goal so that one may live profitably.[151] This poem might explain the use of *colf* clubs as attributes in portraits of children – where the motif cannot possibly symbolize folly – as well as the actions of the child in De Hooch's painting vis-à-vis the women.[152] The housewife and maid are working toward a clear goal by working assiduously and by being good stewards over the household possessions. Regardless of whether the motif of the *colf*-playing child symbolically contrasts or underscores the activities of the women, the painting unequivocally celebrates the requisite performance of domestic tasks by exemplary female types.[153]

Housewives were also expected to be vigilant for lapses in their servants' behavior, another important aspect of their supervisory obligations:

> She must have a diligent eye to the behavior of her servants, what meetings and greetings, what tickings and toyings, and what words and countenances there be betweene men and maides, lest such matters being neglected, there follow wantonnesse, yea folly, within their houses, which is a great blemish to the governours.[154]

According to many contemporary moralists, servants were most prone to the vice of idleness. Consequently, mistresses were advised to be watchful for its inevitable appearance among their maids.[155] A painting by Nicolaes Maes, appropriately entitled *The Idle Servant,* illustrates this housewifely duty (Fig. 89). Here, a woman wearing a luxurious jacket with ermine trim – a garment that identifies her as the mistress of the house – gazes at the viewer while gesturing toward her slumbering maid as if to expose her idleness.[156] Various cooking pots and other utensils lie strewn about the floor in this disheveled kitchen. A prowling cat behind the soporific servant steals a plucked chicken; the ultimate consequence of this scene is that the guests gathered around a table in the back room will wait in vain for their meal.

Earlier studies of this painting have rightly linked the maid's somnolent state and pose – her hand supporting her head – to traditional images of sloth.[157] The dishes and utensils strewn about the foreground, some of them overturned, are the reprehensible result of the maid's neglect of duty.[158] The motif of the cat stealing the bird makes the same point. A proverb by Johan de Brune is quite fitting in this context for it states that "a kitchen maid must have one eye on the pan and the other on the cat."[159] De Brune's observation that maids must be vigilant when working in the kitchen is reminiscent of William Gouge's censure of indolent servants who allow food to be stolen by cats and dogs.[160]

Maes's picture is one of several depicting the vices of servants.[161] However, representations of servants who behave poorly are far outnumbered by those in which servants behave virtuously.[162] Their good conduct mirrors descriptions in contemporary literature of the ideal master–servant relationship. With great frequency, moralists exhort masters and mistresses to maintain authority through strict discipline over their hired help. However, they assuage any potential for severity by advising masters and mistresses to treat servants as members of the family, instructing them in the Christian faith, and even caring for them when they become ill.[163] Servants, for their part, are obliged to serve faithfully in their calling "as unto the Lord." Moreover, they are required to pray for their masters' prosperity.[164]

Clearly, the relationship described in contemporary literature is an arche-

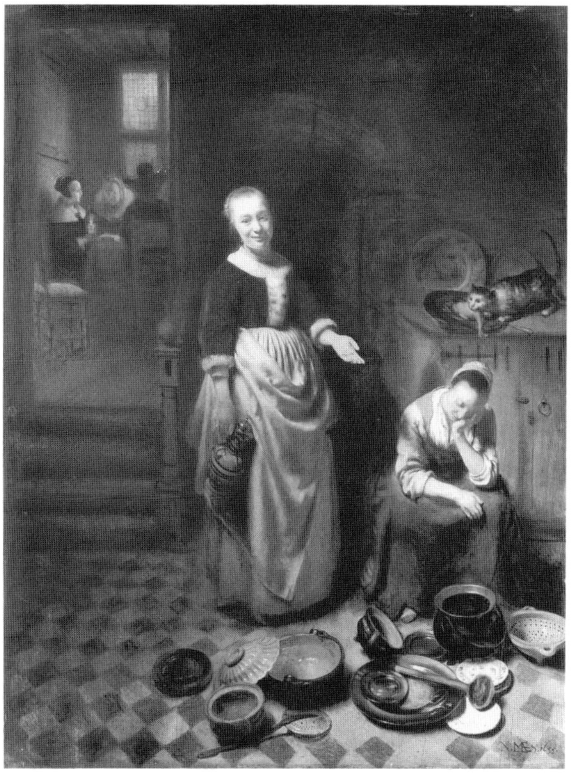

Figure 89. Nicolaes Maes, *The Idle Servant*, 1655 (oil on panel, 70 × 53.3 cm). London, The National Gallery. Reproduced by courtesy of the Trustees, The National Gallery, London.

typal one. The influence of these literary ideals has been so persistent that social historians of the nineteenth century who wrote about Dutch culture during the Golden Age mistook these ideals for the actual situation at that time.[165] For instance, G. D. J. Schotel, in his 1867–8 *Het Oud-Hollandsch huisgezin der zeventiende eeuw* (The Old Dutch Household of the Seventeenth Century), maintained that, during the seventeenth century, maids were treated as full members of the family. Their privileges were said to extend to eating at the same table with the family, even in the presence of guests.[166]

Modern-day social historians have only recently begun to reexamine the nature of master–servant relationships in early modern Europe. Their findings confirm that the writings of Cats, Wittewrongel, and others on this subject present an ideal vision that was anything but universal. Far from being "members of the family" who were loyal and trustworthy, servants, the great majority being women, were hired contractually for only brief periods of time in a rather small percentage of households. Moreover, disputes over wages seem to have been the norm. Female servants, that is, housemaids, were sometimes involved in paternity suits against their employers and in this regard were often accused of ensnaring male members of the household in an effort to attain some sort of financial security. Servants also appear frequently in the criminal records of seventeenth-century cities like Amsterdam.[167] Contemporary servant ordinances further confirm this view. The authorities used these municipal laws governing master–servant hiring procedures and relationships to control the market for servants and, equally importantly, to control their behavior. The ordinances included lengthy enumerations of virtuous and unseemly servant behavior. From her study of such ordinances published during the seventeenth and eighteenth centuries, Marlies Jongejan concluded: "The ideal servant was obedient and served his or her master for many years to come in 'all diligence and faithfulness.' The extensive legislation makes one suspect that practice was not in agreement with this ideal."[168]

These findings offer compelling evidence that the world of the housewife and maid as it appears in Dutch art is pure fiction. Art historians increasingly use social history as a tool in their efforts to uncover the daily reality of life during the seventeenth century that is thought to underlie contemporary paintings. However, this is one instance in which the findings of social historians militate against a view of Dutch art as a reflection of the actual situation at that time. To the contrary, reality has been re-created, for the paintings function as topoi, presenting – like the literature they mirror – an ideal yet theoretically imitable construct of virtuous behavior among housewives and maids. As such, both the art and literature focusing on the housewife and her servants at work played significant roles in espousing and maintaining the patriarchal status quo and thus further elucidate the position of women in seventeenth-century Dutch society.

"MOEDER"

The Utrecht painter Andries van Bockhoven is hardly a household name in the Netherlands today – only three of his paintings have survived. Nevertheless, they reveal an artist of considerable talent. Van Bockhoven's skill is particularly evident in the large portrait (monogrammed and dated 1629) that he made of himself and his family, a work acquired in 1976 by the Centraal Museum in Utrecht (Fig. 90).[1] Van Bockhoven has arranged his parents and siblings in three rows: the artist and his brother above, followed in descending order by his older sisters, the younger children, and his father and mother. The respectful gestures of the children and the religious books held by Van Bockhoven's father and two sisters are given special emphasis in this portrait. These motifs are undoubtedly meant to demonstrate the children's godliness and obedience, in other words, their proper upbringing.

Images of mothers (and, to a lesser extent, fathers) raising children in seventeenth-century Dutch art are the subject of this chapter.[2] Literally hundreds of them are known today. Considered in their entirety, they pay solemn testimony to the ethos of the Dutch home and to the centrality of children in contemporary life. As we shall see, they also offer a convincing, even powerful corrective to some of our enduring misconceptions about the significance of childhood – or more accurately, what is too often perceived as the insignificance of childhood – in earlier times.[3]

If we hope to comprehend seventeenth-century Dutch paintings of child-rearing practices, we must first reconstruct the diffuse cultural factors that contributed to their production. In this regard, the educational theories and prescriptions expounded in contemporary family literature are again, most germane. The paintings mirror the pedagogical aims of these hortatory texts. Moreover, the authors of these texts often employed specific pedagogical metaphors to elucidate their arguments, ones that received analogous visual expression in art. Both literature and art helped to fashion widespread convictions concerning child rearing. It is therefore necessary to begin this discussion by summarizing some of the popular views of parenthood and child rearing articulated in contemporary texts.

A universally held belief during the seventeenth century, which crossed all religious boundaries, was that children were gifts from the Almighty.[4] Parents were therefore enjoined to raise their offspring properly: "Our Lorde God . . . after hee hath created our children, with his owne precious blood hath redeemed them, and committed them to our trust and keeping, to be carefully governed, and diligently instructed."[5] According to authors of all religious persuasions, children were highly impressionable, capable of permanently retaining whatever they were first taught, be it good or evil.[6] Hence, all authors earnestly advocated training as a means to mold good behavior, regardless of whether they considered children innately sinful or innocent.[7] The theory of education's efficacy over natural instinct to foster proper behavior in children was perhaps expressed most compendiously by the English Puritan divines John Dod and Robert Cleaver: "For we are changed and become good, not by birth, but by education."[8]

It is indeed remarkable that all authors, regardless of their religious convictions, considered the primary purpose of child rearing to create pious and virtuous adults who would help to preserve the morality and stability of society.[9] The Dutchman Bartholomew Batty addresses precisely this issue when he reminds his readers: "Thou hast begot children not only for thy selfe, but also for thy countrie. Which should not only bee to thy selfe a joy and pleasure, but also profitable and commodius afterwarde unto the common wealth."[10]

The forums for training children included the church and the school; however, this task was to be conducted principally in the home. Protestants, who wrote exhaustively on this subject, followed classical and humanist thought in considering the home the foundation on which society rests – a true microcosm of the state as a whole – and hence the most effective agent in accomplishing its moral and spiritual transformation.[11] Consequently, they appealed to parents to fashion their families into *kleyne kercken* (little churches), oriented to ethical values based on scripture, characterized by service to its individual members and God, and most importantly, dedicated to raising pious offspring.[12]

The vision of child rearing set forth in contemporary literature and art is unmistakably ideal.[13] It is impossible to determine the extent to which it actually affected domestic life during the seventeenth century. Pedagogical practices likely varied between regions, social groups, and even among individual families.[14] The degree to which parents adhered to the strictures and principles of moralists and divines must have been directly proportional to their own level of religious commitment and devotion.[15] It seems safe

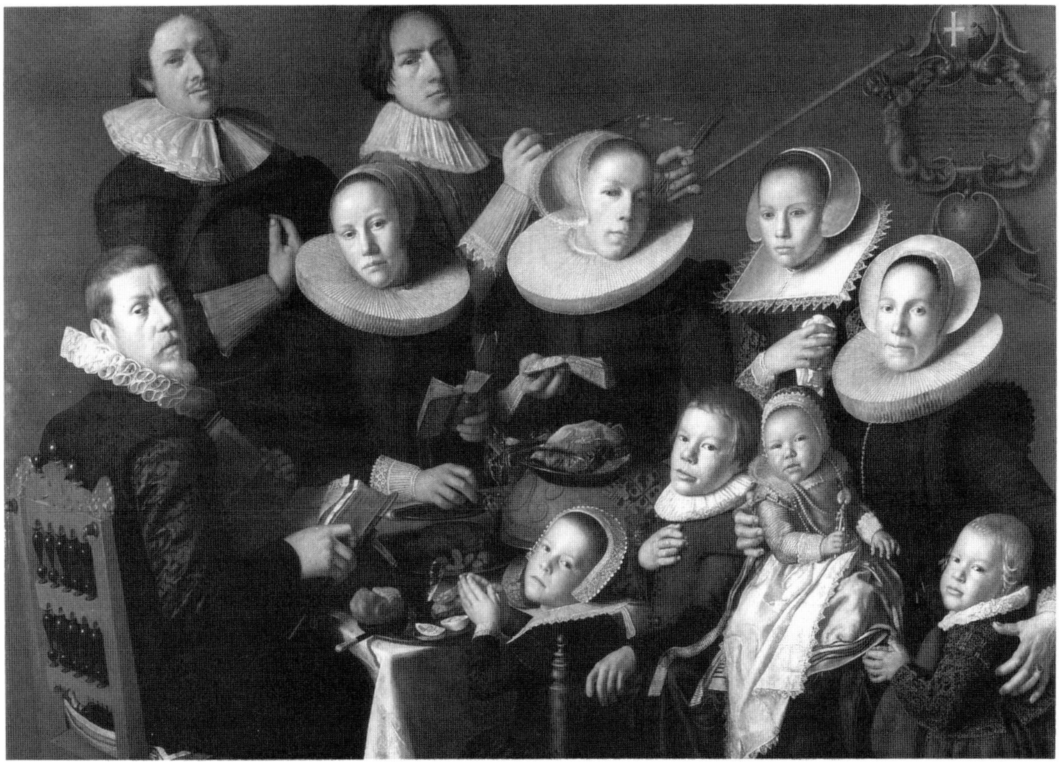

Figure 90. Andries van Bockhoven, *Portrait of the Painter's Family at the Table*, 1629 (oil on canvas, 130.5 × 186.5 cm). Utrecht, Centraal Museum. Photo: museum.

to assume that at least some children were raised in strict accordance with the principles established by Cats and others. Thus, a knowledge of contemporary pedagogical ideals is important for understanding images of mothers and children in art.

The earliest stage of the mother–child relationship represented by Dutch artists is that of women breast-feeding their infants.[16] Humanists, doctors, and theologians discussed the theoretical and practical aspects of breast-feeding ad nauseam.[17] First and foremost, they considered it the most significant of all maternal duties. To them, the practice of hiring wet nurses was repugnant, a serious breach of maternal obligation.[18] God had ordained women to nourish their own children with their breast milk. The Scriptures demonstrated this as did nature, since animals breast-feed their young.[19] The Lord had given females two breasts to be used in His service; the woman who "refuseth this office and duty of mother is declaring herself to be very unthankful to God."[20] Moreover, the act of nursing unquestionably proved a mother's love for her child:

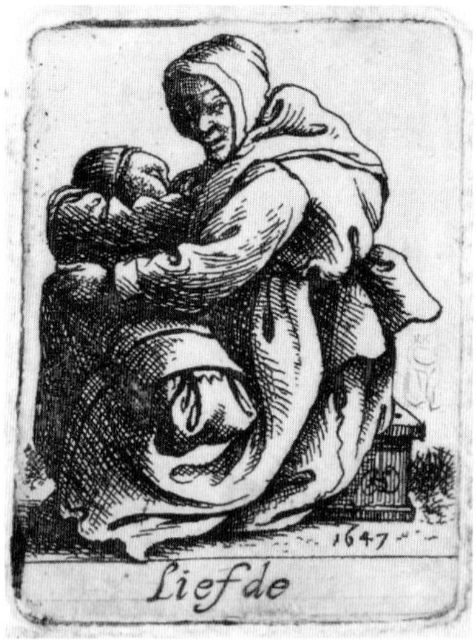

Figure 91. Herman Saftleven, *Woman Nursing a Child*, 1647 (engraving from the series *Nine Figures*). Amsterdam, Rijksmuseum-Stichting. Photo: Rijksmuseum-Stichting.

> How can a mother better expresse her love to her young babe, then by letting it sucke of her owne breasts? As this is a testimony of love, so it is a meanes of preserving and increasing love: for daily experience sheweth that mothers love those children best to whom they themselves give sucke.[21]

The one-word inscription "Liefde" (Love) on Herman Saftleven's tiny print of a nursing mother sums up this belief (Fig. 91). Saftleven's candid, unidealized portrayal of the mother and child matches the simplicity and sincerity of the inscription.

Maternal breast-feeding was thought to offer specific physical and psychological advantages to both mother and child. According to contemporary medical theory, a mother's milk was actually blood that had whitened in the breast, the very same blood that had nourished the infant in the womb and to which it had grown accustomed. The inscription on Hendrick Bary's print of a nursing mother reflects this belief; it states that although the act of breast-feeding is onerous to the mother, the child's ardent desire for her blood consoles her (Fig. 92).[22]

In view of this widely accepted medical theory, it is not difficult to understand why contemporaries thought it harmful for an infant to consume the "blood" of a stranger, that is, the wet nurse's.[23] Perhaps the greatest fear was that the child would imbibe the personality of the woman who nursed it; according to prevailing opinion behavioral traits were passed on to children through breast milk.[24] Thus, if the wet nurse were of questionable character – as many were believed to be – the child would partake of her personality, losing whatever respectable behavioral traits it had at birth. As Jacob Cats

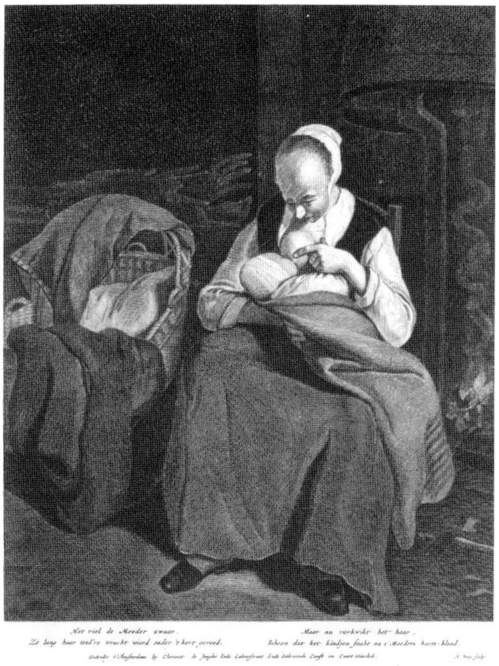

Figure 92. Hendrick Bary (after Quiringh van Brekelenkam?), *Woman Nursing a Child* (engraving). Amsterdam, Rijksprentenkabinet. Photo: Rijksmuseum-Stichting.

remarks, "How many a nice child, healthy and lively, / Has lost its own nature through a wicked wet nurse!"[25] Cats and other authors ominously warned that infants would grow to love whoever nursed them. Consequently, if fed by a wet nurse, a child would prefer her to its natural mother.[26]

Are the contemporary theorists' frequent and vehement objections to wet nurses truly indicative of a widespread practice to hire them?[27] Even if considerable numbers of wet nurses were actually employed, there are insufficient grounds to construe this, as has been done, as evidence of deliberate parental neglect in earlier times.[28] Most seventeenth-century authorities on the subject reluctantly concede that if a mother became ill and physically incapable of feeding her infant – which must have been a comparatively common occurrence at that time given the unsanitary conditions, poor medical care, and frequently difficult deliveries – a wet nurse could be hired, though only after careful consideration of her health and character.[29] Another potentially mitigating factor was the belief that nursing women should not indulge in sexual activity for fear of curdling their milk – hence the need to hire a wet nurse.[30] Lactation also has a contraceptive effect on many women because it induces amenorrhea (an abnormal suppression or absence of menstruation); although they were ignorant of these complex physiological changes, contemporary parents nonetheless recognized the necessity of hiring a wet nurse if they wanted to continue to produce offspring.[31] Regardless of the exact per-

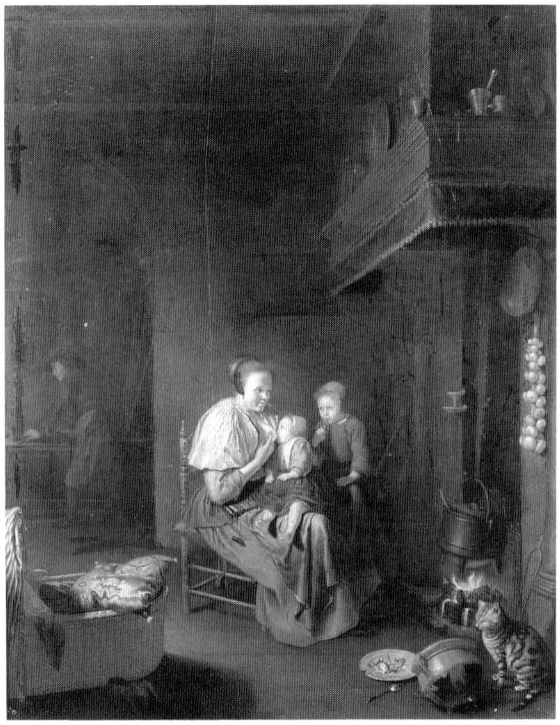

Figure 93. Pieter van Slingelandt, *The Carpenter's Family* (oil on panel, 42.9 × 35.4 cm). London, Collection of Her Majesty the Queen. Copyright reserved; reproduced by permission of the Lord Chamberlain's Office.

centage of wet nurses who suckled other women's children, it is necessary to stress just how significantly the daily realities of seventeenth-century domestic life could differ from the ideals of family literature.

Paintings representing the theme of breast-feeding, like others of women and their children, are visually analogous to specific seventeenth-century prescriptions concerning maternal duties.[32] Bary's print of the breast-feeding mother, whose inscription articulates contemporary notions about nursing, substantiates this because it actually reproduces a now-lost painting, possibly by Quiringh van Brekelenkam. Pieter van Slingelandt's *The Carpenter's Family* also celebrates motherhood and its attendant obligations (Fig. 93). The *paterfamilias,* presumably a carpenter, diligently planes a board in the back room. In other words, he provides for his family by practicing his trade.[33] By contemporary standards, he certainly fulfills his role and calling for, as we have seen in Chapter 2, these were invariably gender specific. His wife fulfills her calling as a mother equally well as she nurses her child.[34] Van Slingelandt's picture exudes an aura of tranquility as it illustrates the con-

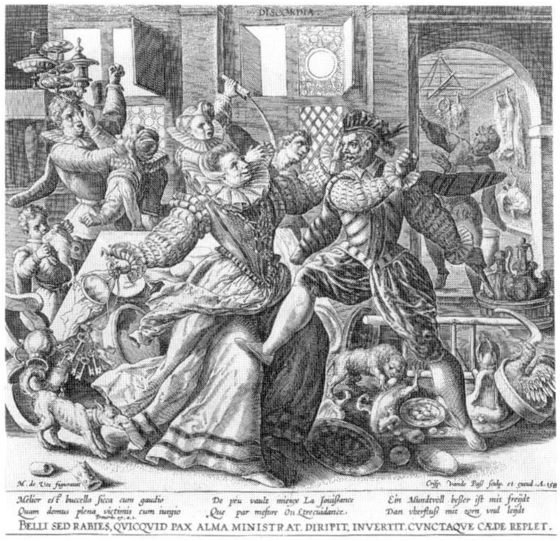

Figure 94. Crispijn van de Passe I, *Discordia* (engraving). Amsterdam, Rijksprentenkabinett. Photo: Rijksmuseum-Stichting.

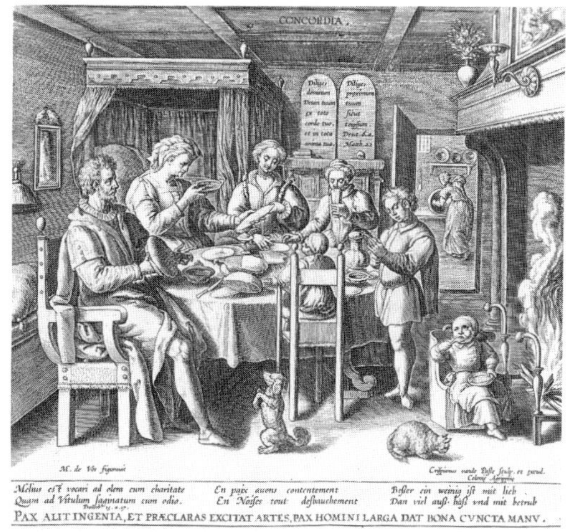

Figure 95. Crispijn van de Passe I, *Concordia* (engraving). Amsterdam, Rijksprentenkabinet. Photo: Rijksmuseum-Stichting.

viction that the diligent performance of spousal and parental duties ensures harmony and peace within the family.[35]

In the lower right corner of the painting, a cat sits beside an overturned cooking pot and a plate of fish. His placidity and restraint in the face of these temptations is diametrically opposed to the actions of his thieving counterparts in other works of art, for example, those depicting vices like sloth or figures engaged in violent arguments (Fig. 94). In those, the unruly cat invariably steals food, a motif meant to underscore the profligate nature of the scene. The presence of this passive, well-behaved feline likely emphasizes the irenic, virtuous qualities of the picture as a whole, as does the appearance of another in a print of a family at the dinner table, appropriately inscribed "Concordia" (Fig. 95).[36]

Conrad Meyer's engraving of a virtuous family provides a graphic equivalent to Van Slingelandt's references to marital duties (Fig. 96).[37] This print includes a number of motifs also found in the painting: a nursing mother and a father engaged in his trade, in this case, as a painter. The artist looks out at the viewer while resting his brush against a maulstick. He works on a painting of Adam and Eve performing tasks apposite to their gender and station – note Eve, her spindle at her side, suckling her child (possibly Cain), while Adam drives a spade into the earth. Their actions unquestionably mirror those of the artist and his nursing wife. The entire scene ingeniously illustrates the belief (discussed in Chapter 2) that marriage and its attendant roles and obligations could be traced back to the Garden of Eden.[38]

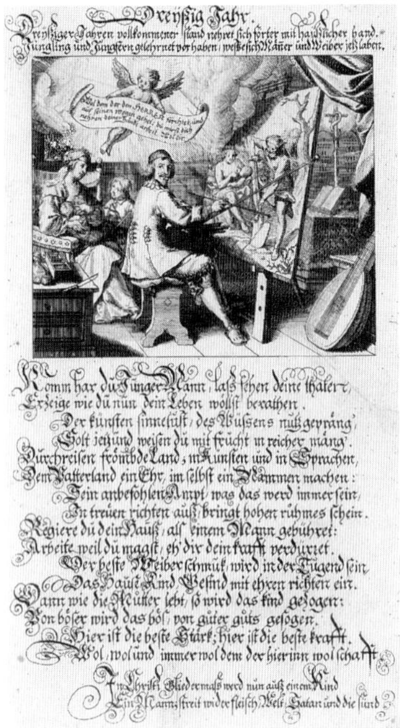

Figure 96. Conrad Meyer, *Age Thirty* (engraving from the series *The Ten Ages of Man*), 1675. Amsterdam, Rijksprentenkabinet. Photo: Rijksmuseum-Stichting.

Other seventeenth-century Dutch paintings adopt a quasi-supernal character as they image women breast-feeding infants with heightened quietude and concentration. In his *Woman Nursing a Child,* Pieter de Hooch has focused on the mother's tender glance at her nursing child by enveloping their forms in soft, gentle light (Fig. 97). The pristine interior space and subtle penumbra of this painting contribute to its aura of love and devotion. The solemnity of De Hooch's scene is only exceeded by that of Nicolaes Maes's *Woman Nursing a Child* (Fig. 98). The artist exalts motherhood with such intensity here that the distinction between religious and domestic subjects becomes blurred. A woman suckles her infant in an apselike space, illuminated by warm light playing upon her breast and the child's face. The sacrosanct aura surrounding this tender mother and her child recalls late medieval images of the *Madonna lactans* with the deferential maid, acolytes, or even a magus kneeling as if in adoration before them.[39] Seemingly countless paintings like Maes's and De Hooch's remind us, as Simon Schama has so astutely observed, that Dutch art offers some of the first sustained images of parental love in European art.[40]

According to most authors, breast-feeding was merely one of a large number of duties that mothers were expected to perform for the benefit of their children. Although both parents were charged with tending to the spiritual and physical needs of their offspring, care for young children in this

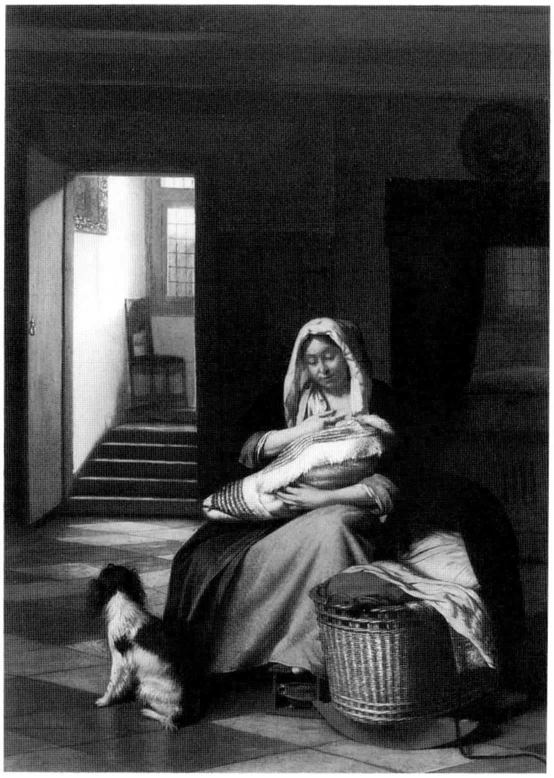

Figure 97. Pieter de Hooch, *Woman Nursing a Child* (oil on canvas, 79.4 × 58.1 cm). Detroit, Detroit Institute of Arts. Photo: Institute of Arts.

patriarchal society in which fathers had more "professional pursuits" was considered an exclusively maternal obligation.[41] A mother's duty to look after her children included feeding, cleaning, and clothing them. She was even responsible for promoting their godliness, "for while children are young, their mother is most in their sight. . . . Her precepts therefore and practise in that respect are best heeded by the children, and she hath the best opportunity to perswade them to what she liketh best."[42]

Artists depicted a variety of maternal tasks, including mothers feeding their children or placing them in cradles (Figs. 99, 100). Gabriel Metsu's *The Sick Child* is perhaps the most renowned representation of motherly care (Fig. 101). Here a mother solemnly tends to her frail child resting feebly in her lap. As has been long noted, their pose evokes images of the *Pietà*;[43] therefore the representation of the Crucifixion on the back wall is probably deliberate. It is difficult to determine why Metsu juxtaposed the *Pietà*-like pose of the mother and child and the picture of the Crucifixion.[44] Nevertheless, an examination of contemporary advice to parents about how

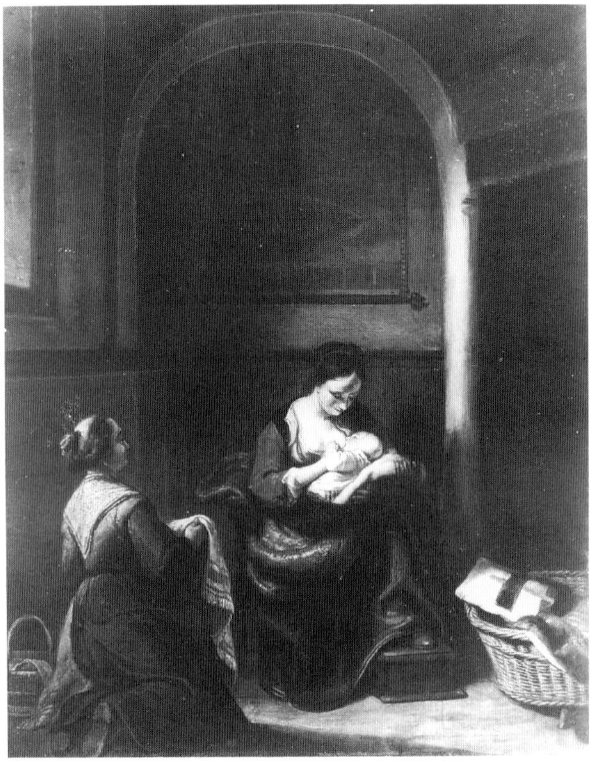

Figure 98. Nicolaes Maes, *Woman Nursing a Child*, 1655 (oil on canvas, 74.5 × 57 cm). Present location unknown.

to care for sick children contributes to our understanding of the painting. Several seventeenth-century pedagogues and doctors offered instructions for parents burdened with sick children, which must have been a common occurrence in those days due to the lack of proper medical care. Joannes de Swaef, a Middelburg schoolmaster who authored an important pedagogical treatise published in 1621, offers the following advice: "Such kindness of the parents pleases the children greatly, so that they think that they are half-recovered when they sit in their mother's lap, nestle against her body, or feel her hand."[45] While it would be ridiculous to posit links between this text and the painting, De Swaef does couch his recommendations in terms reminiscent of the latter, such as his advice to mothers to grant their sick children access to their laps.

Periods of illness were thought to provide excellent opportunities for parents to instruct their children in spiritual matters. In his pedagogical treatise, Jacobus Koelman addresses precisely these issues:

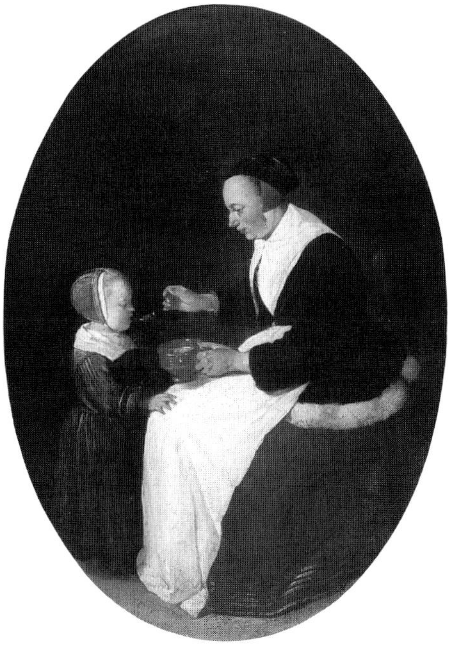

Figure 99. Quiringh van Brekelenkam, *Mother Feeding a Child* (oil on panel, 30.5 × 25.5 cm). Amsterdam, Rijksmuseum. Photo: Rijksmuseum-Stichting.

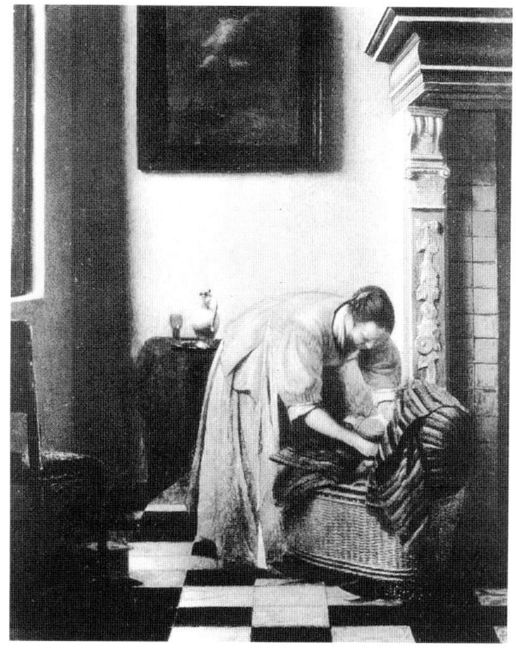

Figure 100. Pieter de Hooch, *A Woman Placing a Child into a Cradle* (oil on canvas, 45 × 37 cm). Birmingham, private collection on loan to Birmingham Museums and Art Gallery. Photo: museum and art gallery.

> When [children] are sick and previously you have not discovered any humility in them, approach them with great seriousness, tenderness and kindness; if there is something good in them, it will become apparent now; show them that this is the punishment of God. . . . show them how and where they have to search themselves, in particular what concerns their conversion, and faith, and salvation; and what lessons they must learn during their illness.[46]

The presence of religious symbolism in Metsu's painting is more comprehensible if tied to the contemporary belief that children's sicknesses afforded their parents suitable occasions to proselytize them. The little picture of the Crucifixion as well as the *Pietà*-like pose of the figures are probably intended to underscore the mother's opportunity to instruct her child in spiritual precepts.[47]

Although it is not certain how Metsu's contemporaries would have perceived this unusual painting, it clearly ranks among the most pathetic renditions of human frailty in any period in the history of art. The artist has poignantly conveyed the illness of the child through its feeble, lethargic pose and countenance as well as the mother's care and concern through her contemplative gaze and firm yet tender grasp of his enervated body. This painting may be small and unassuming, but it speaks volumes about parental affection for their offspring in earlier centuries.

Some social historians have been quick – perhaps too quick – to conclude that parents in early modern Europe were generally aloof and callous toward their children's suffering and even their mortality.[48] Admittedly, evidence in art of affective relationships between parents and children is slight, but this probably has more to do with pictorial traditions and, more importantly, with our ancestors' attitudes toward the display of emotions in public versus private life, than with a genuine lack of feelings.[49] Indeed, there are many heart-rending displays of parental grief over the illnesses and deaths of children in private documents of the period, among them, diaries and letters.[50] However emotionally charged these documents are, the feelings they express are filtered through the prevailing norms and customs of that specific time.[51] We cannot assume that emotional standards have remained constant since then. In fact, the scant surviving evidence indicates just the opposite: emotional life in earlier times was quite complex and even paradoxical in that expressions of parental love combined with flashes of rage in a manner that would be quite disconcerting to present-day parents and psychologists.[52] Consequently, the presumed lack of modern sentiment in seventeenth-century culture is just that, a lack of modern sentiment.[53] It cannot be used as an argument *ex silentio* to conclude that, in past ages, parents were apathetic toward their children.

In those instances where Dutch paintings do provide insight into parent–child relationships, the expression of affection that seemingly approximates its modern counterpart can be tantalizing: witness Metsu's painting. A family portrait attributed to the Gorinchem artist Gerard van Kuijl offers another telling example (Fig. 102).[54] Van Kuijl depicts a large family posed on a terrace with an elegantly tiled floor. The mother holds in her lap an infant who fingers her necklace with great curiosity; one of the baby's siblings leans against her mother's leg as she tries to attract its attention with a flower. Older children flank the father, who holds hands with his daughter while resting his other hand on her head. Such tender physical contact is atypical for portraits of this period. In light of the modern scholarly construct of inhibited parents in past eras who were indifferent to the untimely death of their offspring, it is striking to witness the commemoration in this portrait of a recently deceased, young member of their family; one of the children points to a resplendent heavenly vision unfurling above the terrace in which Jesus welcomes a small nude child escorted by an angel. The earthbound mother of this dead child gazes knowingly and confidently upward at this spectral scene.[55]

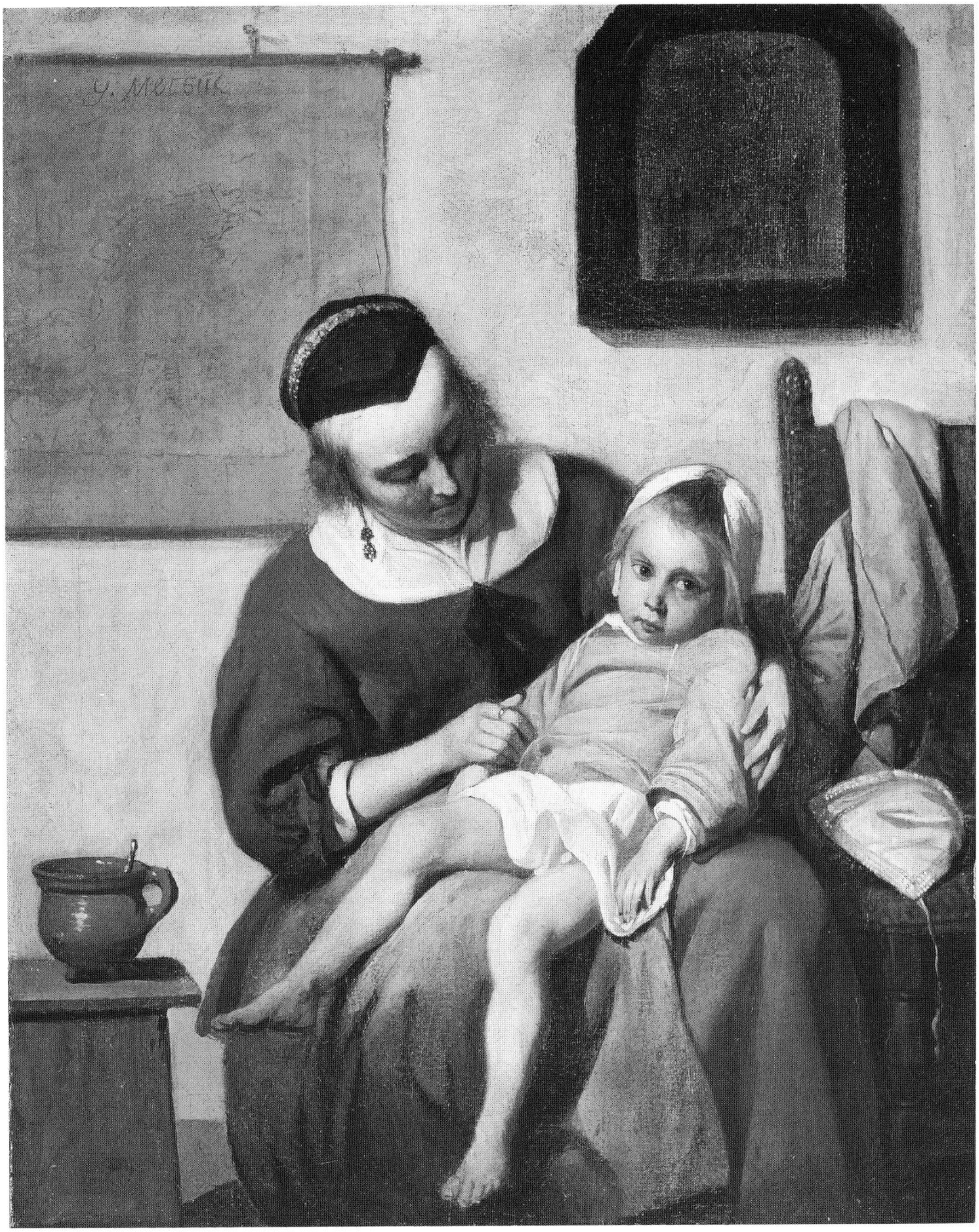

Figure 101. Gabriel Metsu, *The Sick Child* (oil on canvas, 32.2 × 27.2 cm). Amsterdam, Rijksmuseum. Photo: Rijksmuseum-Stichting.

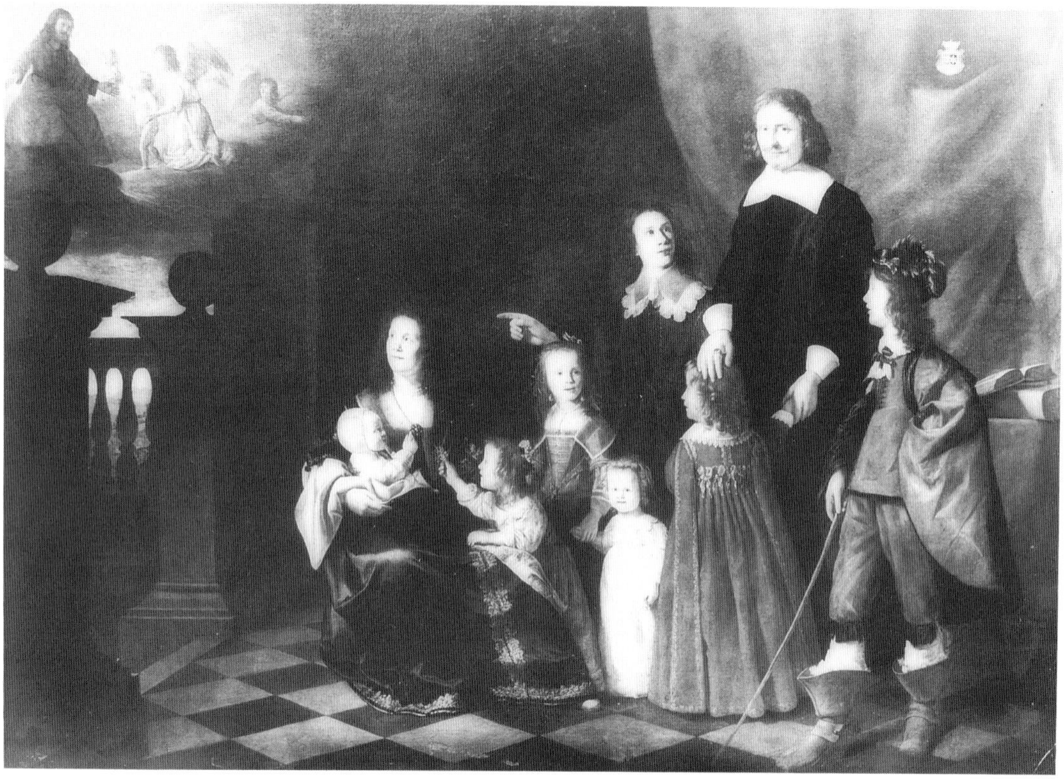

Figure 102. Gerard van Kuijl, *Family Portrait*. Present location unknown.

Metsu's *The Sick Child* is unique in Dutch seventeenth-century art. However, themes representing other maternal duties appear with far greater frequency, among them, that of women combing their children's hair. At the time, this task was performed not only for cosmetic purposes but for hygienic ones as well, since the comb was used to delouse people of all ages afflicted with head lice. A luxuriously dressed young woman combs a boy's hair in a painting by Caspar Netscher (Fig. 103). To their left, at the table, a little girl points to a mirror, sticking her tongue out at her reflection. Another woman (perhaps a maid) watches her, posed with a basin and ewer at the doorway. Various toys lie scattered on the floor before the figures. As the authors of the 1976 exhibition catalogue *Tot lering en vermaak* (For Learning and Entertainment) have demonstrated, the pedagogical symbolism of this engaging painting is somewhat complex. Because of its near programmatic complexity and stunning pictorial features, Netscher's picture was clearly intended for an elite audience skilled in habitually reading works of art in a particular manner.[56]

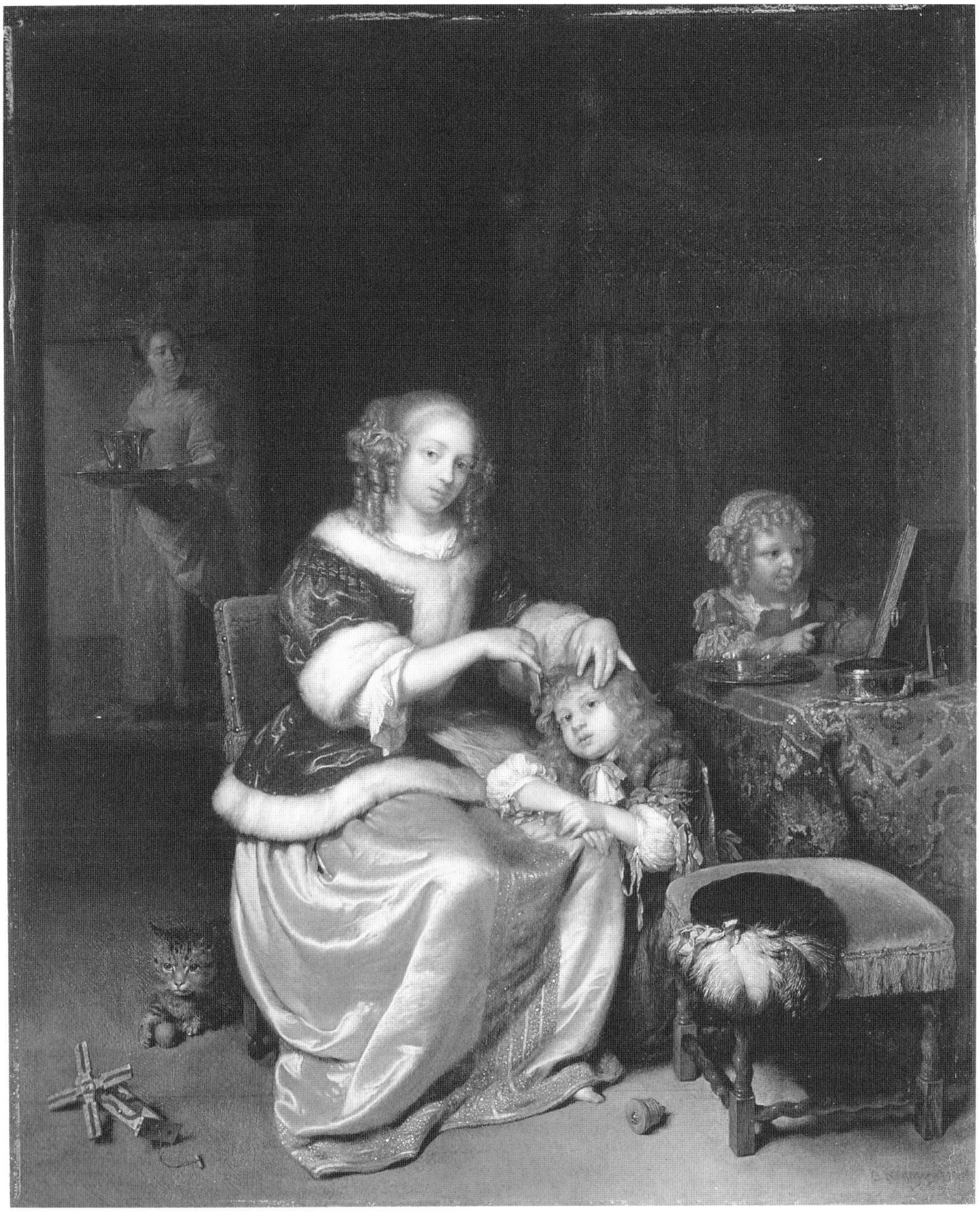

Figure 103. Caspar Netscher, *Woman Combing a Child's Hair* (oil on panel, 44.5 × 38 cm). Amsterdam, Rijksmuseum. Photo: Rijksmuseum-Stichting.

The authors of the exhibition catalogue associated the motif of the woman combing the boy's hair in the painting with an emblem by Jacob Cats. Its *pictura* shows a woman trying to comb her tangled, knotted hair (Fig. 104). The *subscriptio* explicates this scene as a symbol of the need to purify oneself spiritually on a daily basis:

> Comb, comb yourself many times, and not only your hair,
> But also what is hidden inside, to the deepest bone:
> Comb your twisted heart, and your depraved senses,
> And try to get a pure foundation.
> For he, whose head and heart are once saved,
> Although he combs many times, he combs without pain:
> But he who lets his sinful hair grow wild,
> Will not be able to pull a comb through it later,
> For everything he touches is a filthy mess,
> You, comb everyday, that is best for your body.[57]

The motif of the boy having his hair combed in the painting may have links to Cats's emblem, but this should not be overstressed; after all, the emblem is not some sort of magical key that will enable us to unlock the "symbolic secrets" of this enigmatic picture.[58] In fact, it was not even necessary for Netscher's audience to be familiar with Cats's emblem in order to grasp the pedagogical significance of this motif because it can easily be related to the widespread beliefs equating a well-groomed outer appearance with inner virtue.[59] Perhaps the maid in the background underscores this notion because she holds a basin and ewer, objects frequently symbolic of spiritual cleansing and purity.[60]

The toys scattered on the floor could well be symbols of foolishness and frivolity as playthings were often associated in contemporary texts with these vices.[61] For example, the top lying on the floor might allude to indolence. The observation that a top will not spin unless struck by a cord underlies the metaphoric significance attached to this toy in seventeenth-century literature. For Roemer Visscher, the top, an object that only spins when it is whipped, symbolizes the relationship between God and mankind because of the latter's inclination to be devout only in trying and perilous times (Fig. 105).[62] Visscher's emblem has been cited in various studies of the painting as part of an effort to interpret the top in positive terms, as a metaphor of discipline.[63] However, such interpretations overlook the fact that the top in the painting is not being driven but lies still on the floor.[64] In Cats's poem "Kinder-spel" (Children's Game), the top that falls over when it is no longer whipped is symbolic of idleness, which overtakes men when their hardships cease.[65] In light of this and other references, the top lying on the floor in Netscher's painting might possibly refer to sloth.

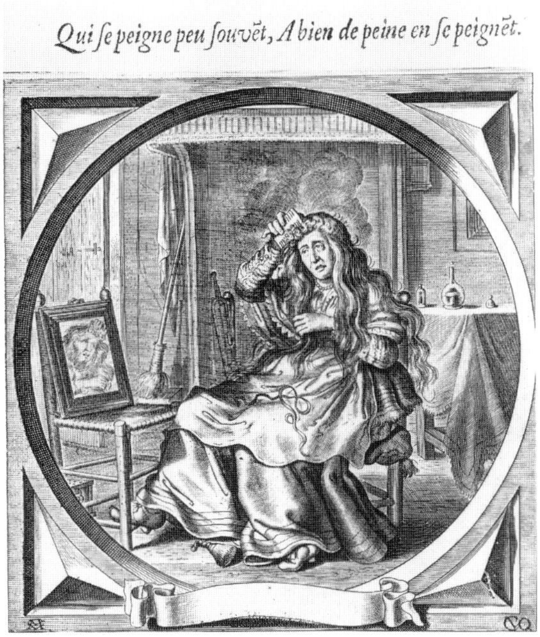

Figure 104. Emblem from Jacob Cats, *Spiegel vanden ouden en nieuwen tijdt*, The Hague 1632. Amsterdam, Universiteits-Bibliotheek Amsterdam. Photo: courtesy Universiteits-Bibliotheek.

The girl sticking her tongue out at the mirror seems naughty by comparison to her well-behaved brother. The stern, disapproving gaze of the maid in the hallway certainly suggests this. The mirror appears more frequently than any other motif in seventeenth-century literature and art as a metaphor for the necessity of self-examination.[66] At that time, the term "self-examination" did not mean "to be in touch with one's feelings" as it does today; rather it meant recognizing one's true nature as a sinful creature.[67] This is precisely the reason why so many edifying books of the period include the word "mirror" in their titles: the reader will presumably use the admonitions of the text in question as a "mirror" to examine his or her behavior. The popular emblem book by Jacob Cats, *Spiegel vanden ouden en nieuwen tijdt* (Mirror of Ancient and Modern Times), which contains the emblem of the woman combing her hair, no doubt had this intention. In the frontispiece of the first edition (1632), a personification of Truth gazes into a mirror held by Time (Fig. 106). In the preface, Cats states that his emblems serve as a "Spiegel der Waerheyt" (Mirror of Truth) for the entertainment and edification of his readers. In the explanation of the frontispiece Cats adds that the mirror is his book; he then advises the reader to "spiegelt u daer in," which is perhaps best translated loosely into English as "look into it as you would a mirror."[68]

The presence of the mirror in the painting by Netscher, then, can probably be explained as a reference to self-examination. Only through daily self-

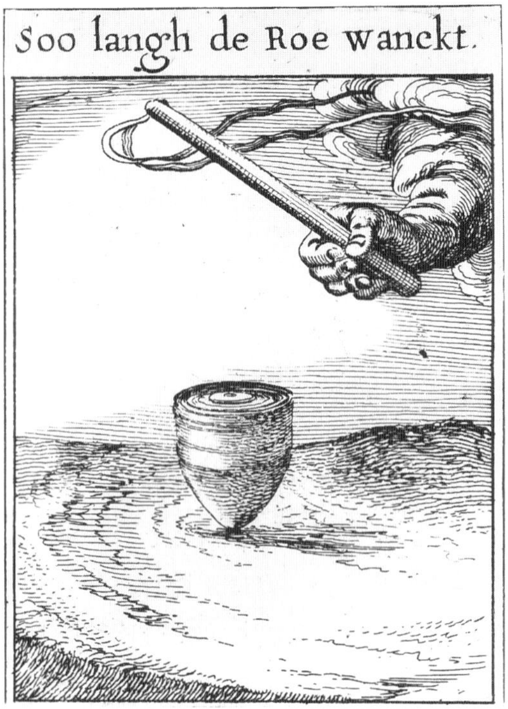

Figure 105. Emblem from Roemer Visscher, *Sinne-poppen*, Amsterdam 1614. The Hague, Koninklijke Bibliotheek. Photo: Koninklijke Bibliotheek.

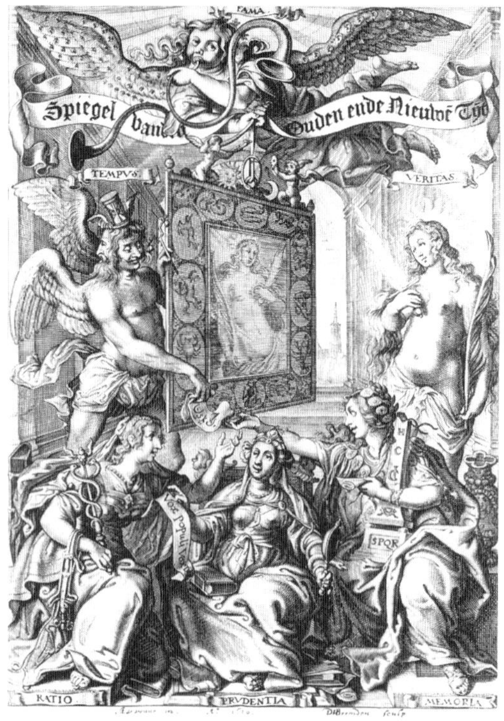

Figure 106. Frontispiece from Jacob Cats, *Spiegel vanden ouden en nieuwen tijdt*, The Hague 1632. The Hague, Koninklijke Bibliotheek. Photo: Koninklijke Bibliotheek.

examination can one be virtuous and, as the motifs of hair combing and the basin and ewer likely imply, spiritually pure. The nuances of the naughty girl's expression as she sticks her tongue out at the mirror are unclear. Is this meant as a mock expression, an indication that she will not examine herself seriously? Is the implication that she is poorly trained in contrast to her brother? In fact, the juxtaposition of poorly and well-reared children is not uncommon in Dutch art and appears in other paintings by Netscher.[69]

Other representations of women combing their children's hair lack the symbolic complexity of Netscher's painting, but they nevertheless evoke pedagogical associations. A painting by Gerard ter Borch is unusual because it depicts his stepmother, Wiesken Matthys, carefully combing the hair of a child who holds a piece of fruit (Fig. 57).[70] This picture, and its pendant of the same woman spinning (Fig. 56), seem to fall under the category of what Lyckle de Vries has termed "genrefied portraits" – works in which a sitter participates in a narrative not drawn from literary or historical sources nor from pictorial traditions normally associated with portraiture.[71]

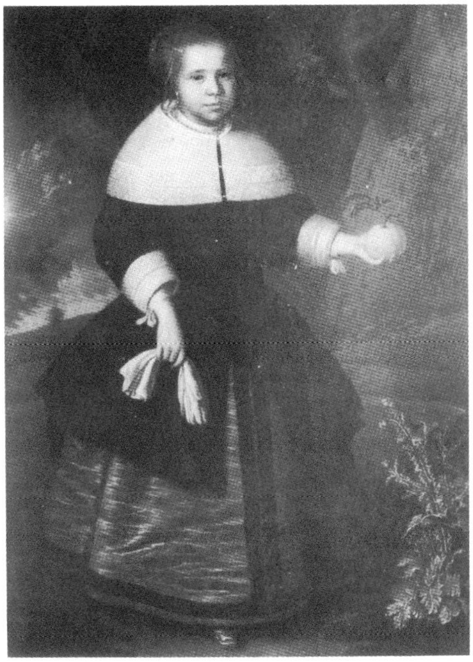

Figure 107. Jan Albertz. Rotius, *Portrait of a Girl.* Present location unknown.

Wiesken holds the comb carefully between her fingers, positioned to enable her to delouse the child patiently leaning against her. Once again, the act of combing conjures up popular notions linking grooming with spiritual and moral purity. In this context, the motif of the child holding a piece of fruit is significant. Plants, particularly fruit-bearing ones, often function as pedagogical metaphors in seventeenth-century literature because their growth and cultivation could easily be compared to the raising of children. For instance, Cats and other writers often compared child rearing to preparing ground for planting and seeding so that it would ultimately yield fruit:

> You must cultivate the infertile land so that it can bear fruit,
> Dig, uproot, make trenches,
> Pull out the weeds, from the very first day,
> So that your esteemd husband can sow there afterwards.[72]

They liken properly trained children to well-cultivated, fruitful growth, their intractable counterparts to unpruned plants or even weeds and thistles.[73] There are several seventeenth-century Dutch portraits of children who hold fruit or point to cultivated plants, an unmistakable reference to their virtuous upbringing (Fig. 107).[74]

Although it alludes to popular educational principles, we should not lose sight of Ter Borch's intention in this painting and its pendant to display Wiesken's skills and virtues as a housewife and mother. The well-reared child in the painting testifies to Wiesken's conscientious performance of her maternal duties. A contemporary proverb by Johan de Brune, which comments on the need to discipline children, best explains the link between Wiesken's actions and maternal obligations in general as it puns, in both the original Dutch and in translation, on the word "louse": "Lazy mother, lousy kids."[75]

Educational principles are likewise present in other paintings of parents and their children, especially those depicting the practical aspects of a child's training. While pedagogues and moralists charged parents with the care of the physical needs of their offspring, their obligations did not end there. Among many other duties, parents were expected to find proper callings for their children, to discipline them, and to instruct them in moral and spiritual matters.[76]

In Chapter 2, I defined a calling to be a divinely ordained duty appointed to all, "our appointed charge, and manner of life, in some honest worke, wherin we are daily to labor as we may best profit therein."[77] Parents were obliged to identify a calling for each child, that is, a future occupation for which he or she was to begin training at a relatively early age. Moralists warned them against acting despotically when choosing their children's future occupations; it was infinitely more preferable to select one suitable to the character and, most importantly, to the sex of each child.[78] Not surprisingly, parental efforts centered on finding professional callings for their sons, since daughters were predestined to be trained for the only offices available to females at this time: housewifery and motherhood. De Swaef's advice to parents to consider gender when choosing their children's callings is explicit on this point:

> Here this has to be heeded / for it is the duty of the male sex to serve in all important positions, in the Republic as well as in the Community / as well as such duties that benefit the family. On the other hand, the female sex is charged with a more general calling, namely the supervision of their children and their household / to see that the children are well taken care of / and that everything in the house goes properly.[79]

The belief that gender determined the choice of a calling was widely accepted in the seventeenth century. This precept is depicted in an illustration from Johan van Nyenborgh's *Toonneel [sic] der ambachten* (Theatre of the Trades) of children practicing skills essential for their future lives under the ever-watchful eyes of their parents (Fig. 16). The girls perform needlework while the boys study in preparation for their eventual occupations as artists

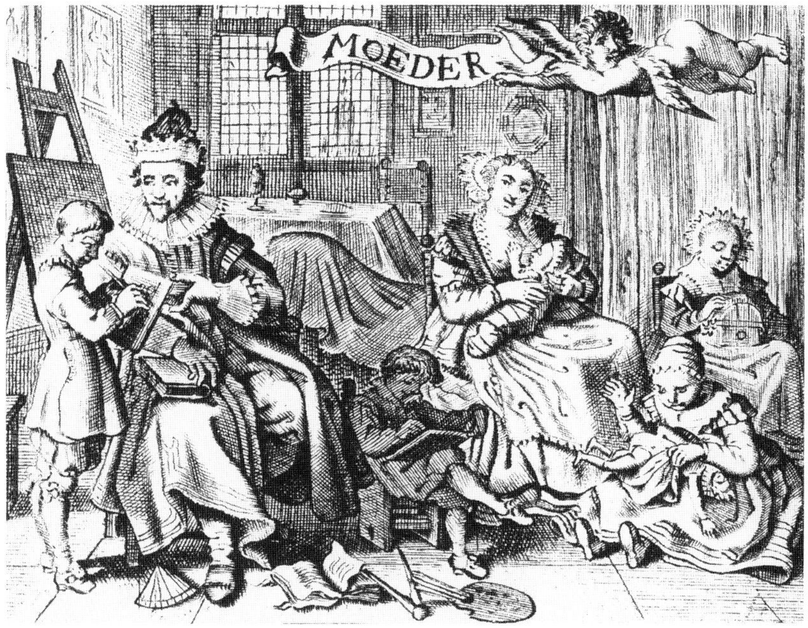

Figure 108. Illustration from Jacob Cats, *Houwelyck. Dat is de gansche gelegentheyt des echten staets*, 4th ed., The Hague 1632. Amsterdam, Universiteits-Bibliotheek Amsterdam. Photo: courtesy Universiteits-Bibliotheek Amsterdam.

and scholars, occupations that Van Nyenborgh's readers would have immediately perceived as appropriate for males. The illustration is simply but aptly inscribed "Van de goede opvoedinge der Kinderen" (On the Good Training of Children).[80]

The frontispiece to the chapter "Moeder" from the fourth edition of Jacob Cats's *Houwelyck* (1632) recalls the illustration from Van Nyenborgh's book (Fig. 108).[81] It also shows a father teaching his sons to write; here, too, an easel is present along with other artistic implements. The mother suckles an infant beside her two daughters, one of whom makes lace, a clear reference to her diligence, docility, and preparation for housewifery. The other girl plays with a doll, an activity that reflects the widely held view that, even in childhood, each sex was naturally inclined toward particular patterns of play and behavior that prepared them for their lives as adults.

In *Houwelyck,* Cats implores parents to steer children toward a calling that suits their innate inclinations and aptitudes. A charming emblematic illustration of a hen watching ducklings swim in a pond explains this idea (Fig. 109). According to Cats, the ducklings will not stay by the hen – their adopted mother – when they see water because they are inclined by nature to swim.[82] Two well-dressed women are engaged in animated dis-

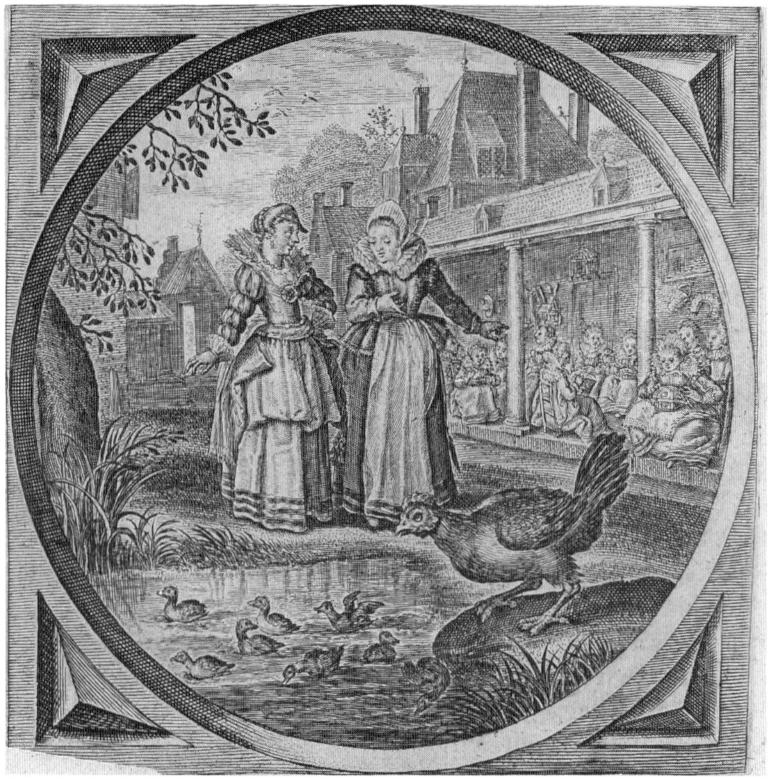

Figure 109. Illustration from Jacob Cats, *Houwelyck. Dat is de gansche gelegentheyt des echten staets*, Middelburg 1625. Collection of the author. Photo: D. Broda, Syracuse.

cussion over the significance of this event. One points to the birds and simultaneously to a group of girls sewing and making lace on a columned porch to her left. Her gestures link the two scenes, thereby demonstrating that, as ducklings are predisposed to swim, so too are females naturally inclined to perform domestic tasks.

Cats had already argued this in the introduction to *Houwelyck*, namely, in his famous poem "Kinder-spel" (Children's Game).[83] The accompanying illustration (after a design by Adriaen van de Venne) shows a crowd of children playing an assortment of games before the Voorhout in The Hague (Fig. 110).[84] In the lower left corner of the print, some girls play with dolls and small toy replicas of household utensils (Fig. 110a). A group of boys dressed as soldiers march past them to the beat of a drum. Cats interprets their actions as evidence of how gender-based aptitudes and inclinations are first revealed in childhood:

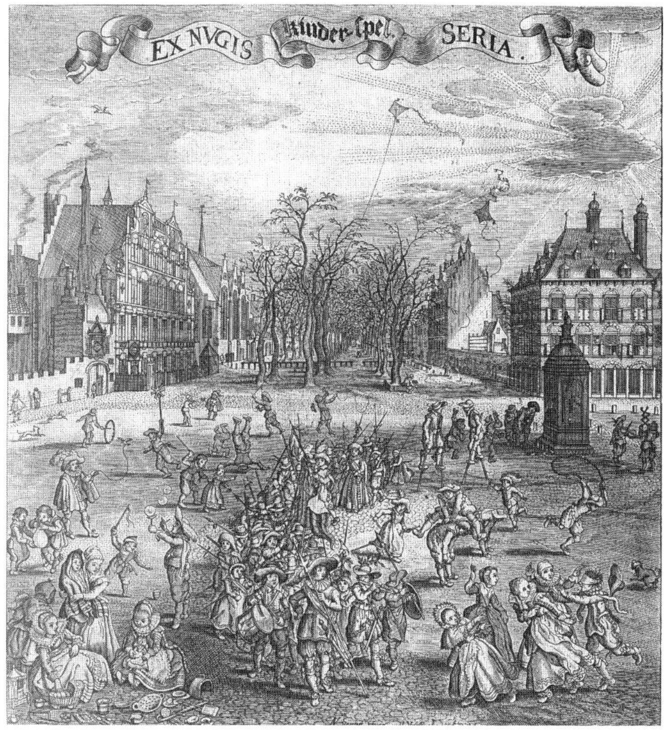

Figure 110 (right). Illustration, *Kinderspel*, from Jacob Cats, *Houwelyck. Dat is de gansche gelegentheyt des echten staets*, Middelburg 1625. Collection of the author. Photo: D. Broda, Syracuse.

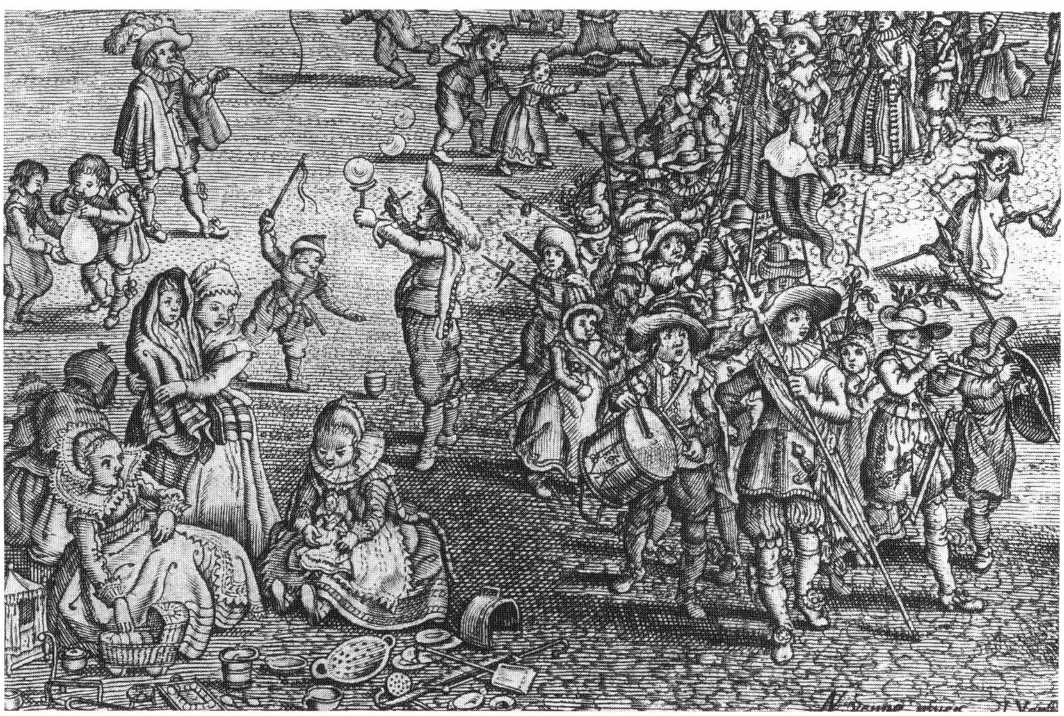

Figure 110a. Detail of Figure 110.

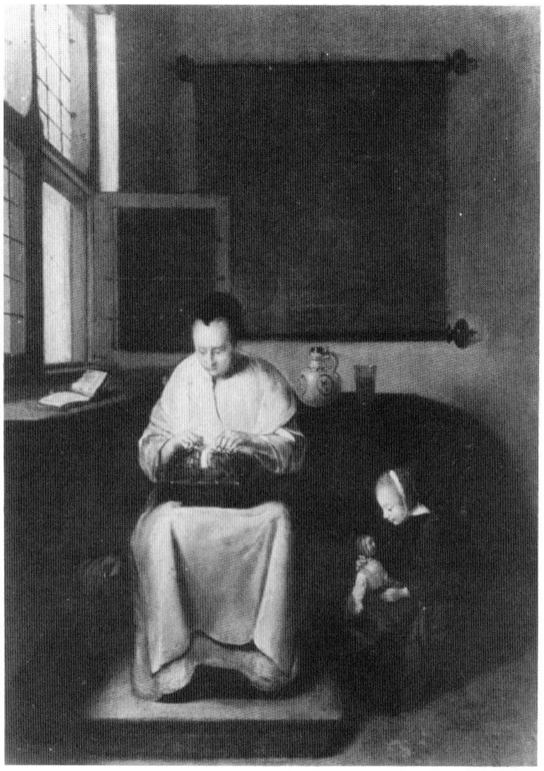

Figure 111. Quiringh van Brekelenkam, *Woman Making Lace beside Her Daughter.* Private collection.

> See how human nature
> Is revealed in early youth!
> The little girl plays with dolls,
> The little boy shows more courage;
> The little girl rocks the cradle,
> The little boy beats the drum;
> The little girl plays with small objects
> That are useful in the kitchen;
> The little boy plays with a harmless lance
> Like rough men do.[85]

In some seventeenth-century Dutch genre paintings, for example, a work by Quiringh van Brekelenkam, girls play with dolls in the presence of their mothers (Fig. 111). Moralists occasionally condemned doll playing because it was thought to teach children to love luxury and to encourage vanity.[86] However, in view of the prints and literary passages just cited, the motif in question likely refers to the presumed female predisposition to motherhood and housewifery, particularly in Van Brekelenkam's picture, where the mother makes lace. The motif also appears occasionally in con-

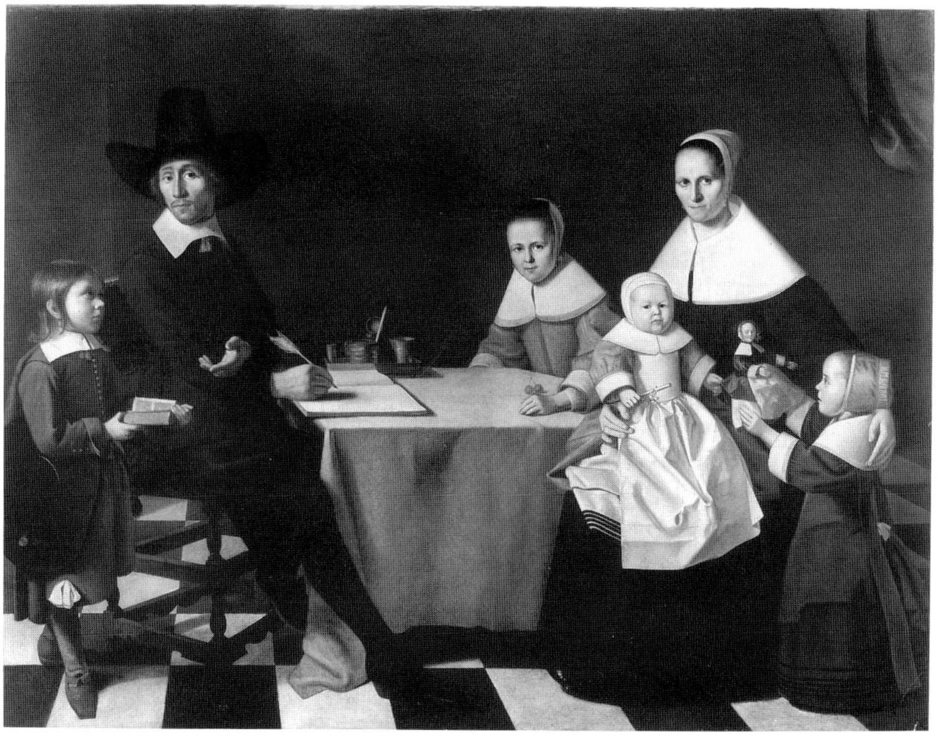

Figure 112. Michael Nouts (attributed to), *Family Group* (oil on canvas, 1.78 × 2.35 m). London, The National Gallery. Reproduced by courtesy of the Trustees, The National Gallery, London.

temporary portraiture, as in the group portrait of a soberly dressed family attributed to Michael Nouts (Fig. 112).[87] One of the young girls in this portrait holds up her doll – or perhaps, a puppet – much to the delight of the toddler seated in its mother's lap, who pulls on this toy's equally sober garment. At the other end of the table, the proud father points to his son, who holds a thick book (possibly a religious work) in affirmation of his good training in a suitably male pursuit.

The deliberate gender grouping that we find in Nouts's portrait and, for that matter, in the book illustrations just discussed, are quite common in Dutch portraiture. Children are invariably represented alongside the parent who shares their sex as if to demonstrate, literally, that instruction in gender-related offices is best learned by example. In the anonymous portrait of a family (ca. 1640) discussed in Chapter 1, the sexes are distinctly divided, leaving an odd, off-center gap in the composition (Fig. 17).[88] Once again, the children practice skills in preparation for future callings appropriate to their sex: the boys concentrate on intellectual pursuits while their sisters practice domestic tasks.

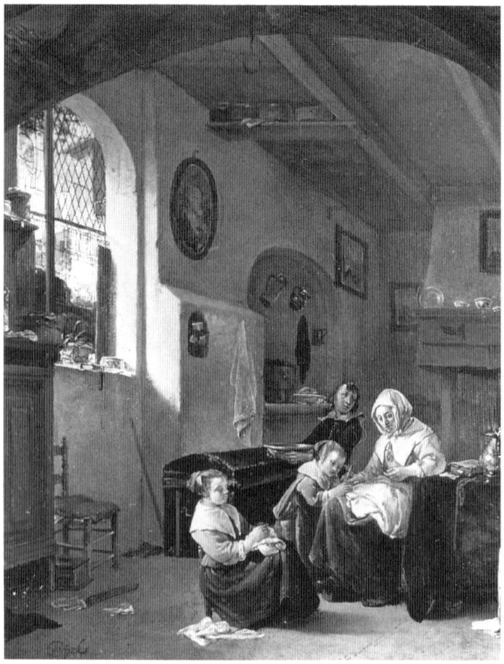

Figure 113. Thomas Wyck, *Mother with Two Daughters* (oil on panel). Present location unknown.

Genre paintings of the period frequently feature girls practicing domestic skills. On one level, these pictures can be considered constructs with unequivocal references to the proper upbringing of females for their future roles as housewives (see, e.g., Fig. 113).[89] Among the most unusual pictures of this type is Quiringh van Brekelenkam's representation of two seated girls diligently making lace in the presence of a woman (Fig. 114). A third has risen from her chair and stands behind this woman, presumably to receive detailed instruction in lace-making techniques. A purse hangs from this girl's chair, and her cloak is draped over the table behind it; she is not the woman's daughter but a visitor who has come for instruction. Cushions for making lace lie neatly on a shelf on the wall behind them. The presence of these motifs suggests that Van Brekelenkam has not represented a simple domestic scene of a mother and her children but a "school" where girls learned the art of needlework from a skilled teacher. Such schools actually existed; Schipper-Van Lottum, in her study on the history of Dutch samplers, quotes from several contemporary advertisements of schools for girls from the *Amsterdamsche Courant*. In one dated 22 May 1674, a Madame Lambert, or Anna Thibault, advertises a school where girls will learn needlework and knitting.[90] Madame Lambert's school was actually a "French School," an institution for elite females to teach them the rudiments of reading and writ-

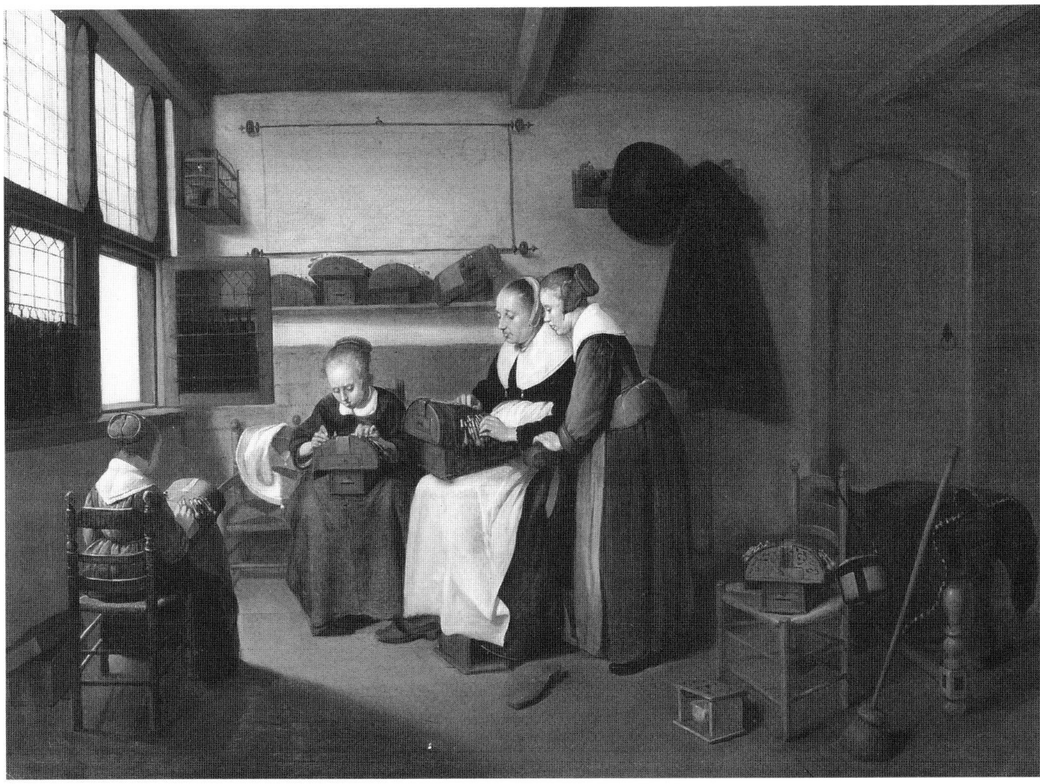

Figure 114. Quiringh van Brekelenkam, *Woman Teaching Girls to Make Lace*, 1654 (oil on panel, 73.6 × 86.3 cm). London, Richard Green Galleries. Photo: gallery.

ing, French, the needle arts, and perhaps most importantly, proper etiquette.[91]

Those less privileged would often learn the needle arts from the wife of the master of the "public" or *lagere school* (primary school).[92] Obviously, it is difficult to determine the type of school represented in Van Brekelenkam's painting. In fact, it may not even be a school since one could argue with equal plausibility that it is merely an informal gathering of girls learning how to make lace.[93] Regardless of its exact subject, the painting unquestionably depicts girls who are learning a skill apposite to their future callings as housewives. A detail from a catchpenny print (Fig. 31; discussed in Chapter 1) sheds light on the painting because it shows a strikingly similar scene (Fig. 31b). Once again, we see a group of girls learning how to make lace as well as one standing beside her teacher receiving more detailed instruction. The scene's simple inscription, "dochterkens leeren een ambacht" (Daughters Learn a Trade), enables us to understand how contemporaries perceived

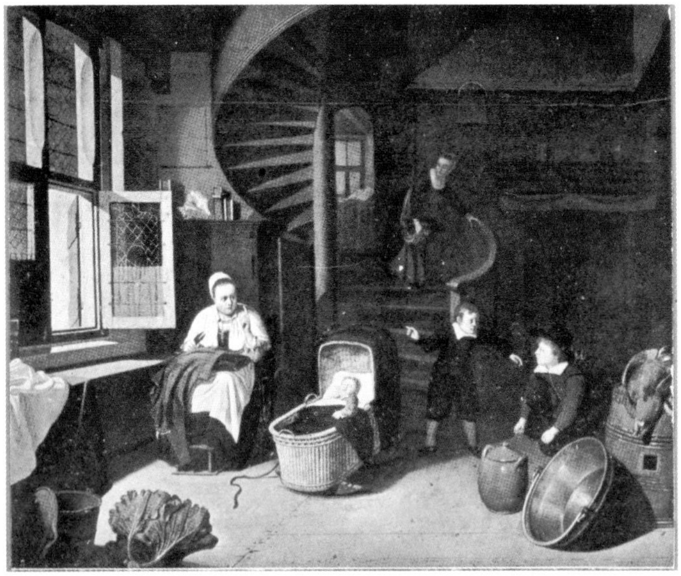

Figure 115. Pieter van Slingelandt, *Mother Disciplining Her Children* (oil on panel, 53.7 × 66.8 cm). Present location unknown.

paintings like Van Brekelenkam's. More importantly, it epitomizes prevailing convictions concerning the types of skills that females should be taught.

In addition to advising parents to find suitable callings for their children, humanists, moralists, and theologians of all religious persuasions also charged them with disciplining their offspring. Discipline played an important role in molding children's behavior because when they "strayed from the right path" they needed to be corrected. It was therefore viewed as "a physicke to purge out much corruption which lurketh in children, and as a salve to heale many wounds and sores made by their folly."[94] Some historians of childhood have interpreted the administering of discipline as evidence of the harsh and inhumane treatment of children in earlier times.[95] However, most authors urged parents to mete out physical punishment moderately, only as a last resort if stern words of correction failed to achieve the desired ends. Moreover, they urged parents to remember that children should be chastised out of love and concern for their behavior.[96]

The relatively few representations in seventeenth-century Dutch art of parental discipline usually show mothers admonishing their children for some breach of conduct, as in a picture by Pieter van Slingelandt in which a woman sternly gestures at two boys who play marbles while an infant sleeps (Fig. 115). Similarly, in a painting by Nicolaes Maes, entitled *The Naughty Drummer,* a mother threatens her sobbing son with a birch branch in order

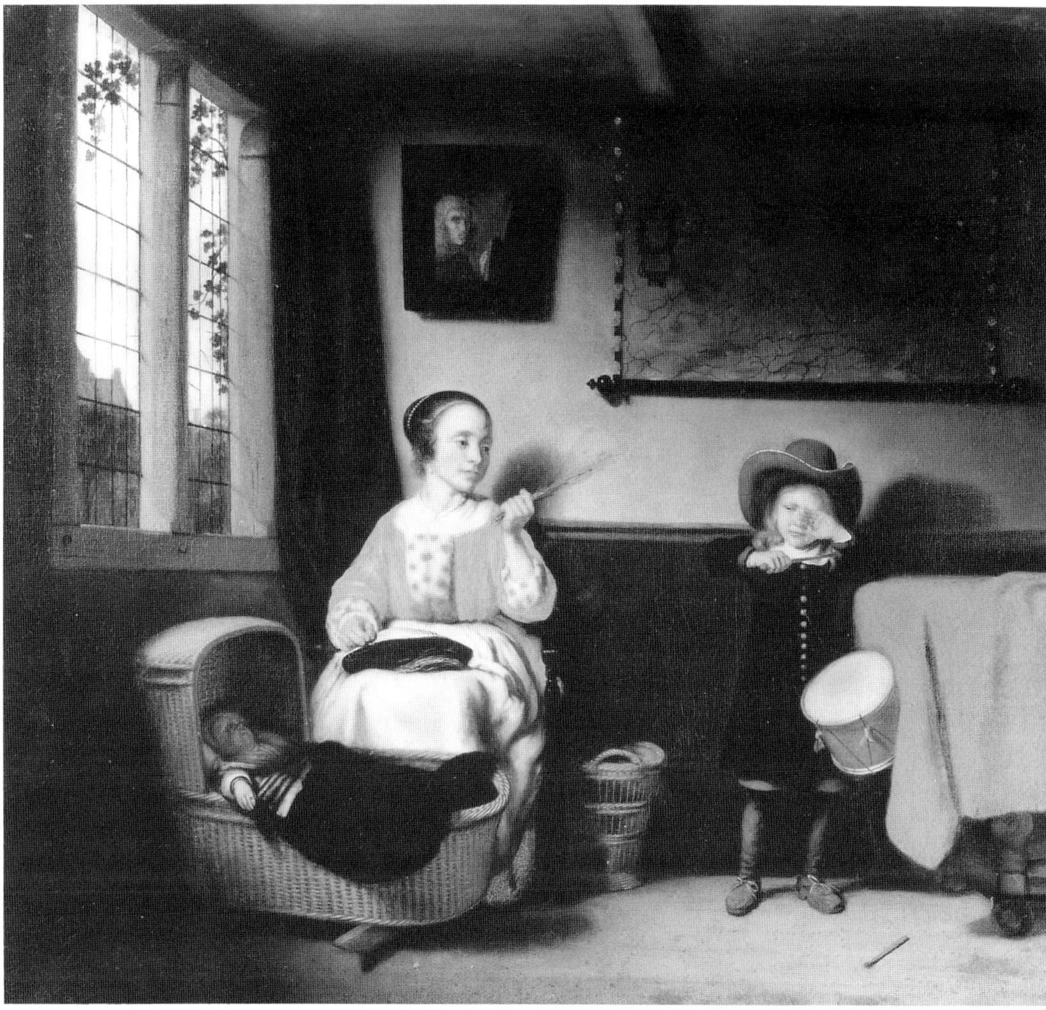

Figure 116. Nicolaes Maes, *The Naughty Drummer* (oil on canvas, 62 × 66 cm). Lugano, Thyssen-Bornemisza Collection. Photo: Thyssen-Bornemisza Collection.

to compel him to stop playing his toy drum while his sibling sleeps (Fig. 116).

Although both depict the same theme, the painting by Maes only superficially resembles the one by Van Slingelandt, because Maes has included himself posed at an easel in a mirror on the wall behind the figures. The artist's presence here led Valentiner to identify them as portraits of his wife and two small children.[97] The reasons why Maes painted himself at an easel in a mirror in this picture are uncertain. Was it simply a clever way of showing himself at work capturing an episode in his domestic life as it unfolds before the viewer?[98] Perhaps. Yet the unexpected juxtaposition of Maes at his easel and his wife chastening their son before his sleeping sibling might well be more than a shrewd display of artistic wit.

The mother's threatening posture, an indicant of her virtue as a parent, has pedagogical significance as it is adopted to discipline the boy as an integral part of his overall training. Maes's self-portrait at an easel directly above this scene of his wife and two children may not be pure coincidence because, at this time, child rearing was sometimes metaphorically likened to the activity of painting:

> Like a painter's canvas on which nothing is sketched, the painter can picture anything he likes: but does he want to? He can stain it with dirty smudges; but does he want to? He can decorate it with beautiful flowers, with landscapes or with pastoral scenes.[99]

This passage reflects the ancient pedagogical theory, widely regarded in the seventeenth century, that a child's soul is like a tabula rasa on which either good or evil can be imprinted.[100] In some religious circles, especially those of Puritans and Pietists who adhered to the strict belief that children were innately sinful, such ideas would have never been accepted.[101] Admittedly, there was no agreement over whether children were morally innocent or naturally inclined to evil; however, the necessity of a proper upbringing was universally recognized.

An emblem from the influential book (originally published in Spanish in 1640) by the courtier Diego Saavedra illustrates the necessity of good training. Interestingly, the emblem links it with the theory of the child as a tabula rasa. Its *pictura,* inscribed "Ad omnia" (To All Things), shows a blank canvas on an easel (Fig. 117). In the *subscriptio,* Saavedra explains:

> We see man is born without any manner of knowledge or propriety of speech, instruction and learning being left to draw the lineaments of Arts and Sciences on his mind as on a blank Canvass, and Education to Imprint morality thereon, not without great advantage to humane Society. . . . But 'tis necessary these measures be taken in tender years, while the mind, is fitter to Receive all manner of forms. . . . But if this be neglected in the first Age, the affections by degrees get ground, and their inclinations make so deep an impression upon the will as no Education can efface.[102]

Saavedra's book was originally intended as an aid for training princes but reached a much larger audience owing to translations in several languages, including Dutch.[103]

The painting by Maes might possibly reflect these pedagogical ideas because the artist has chosen to represent himself at an easel watching his wife dis-

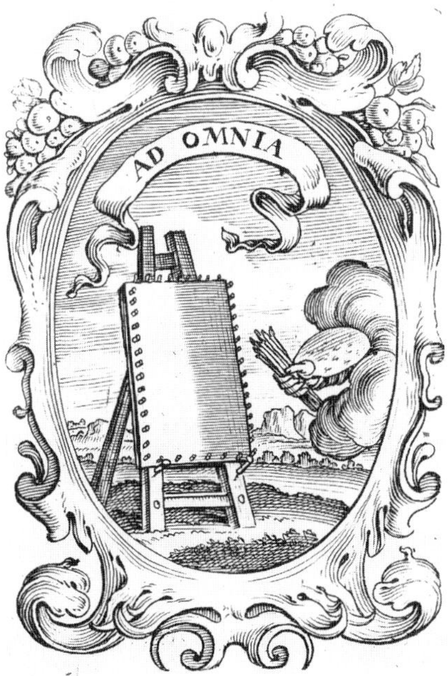

Figure 117. Emblem from D. Saavedra, *Christelyke staets-vorst . . .*, Amsterdam 1663. Amsterdam, Universiteits-Bibliotheek Amsterdam. Photo: courtesy Universiteits-Bibliotheek Amsterdam.

cipline their son.[104] We should also not overlook Maes's position as the children's father, in which he would have at least theoretically taken an active role in their training.

The last parental duty discussed in this chapter – perhaps the most important one – was to train offspring in moral and spiritual precepts or, as William Perkins puts it, "to endeavour to sowe the seedes of godlinesse and religion in the heart of the child."[105] Humanists, pedagogues, and moralists all believed that children were exceptionally malleable, permanently retaining whatever they were first taught. Thus, training or education, commencing at the earliest age possible, was essential for fashioning proper behavior: "Nature is of great effect, but instruction being more effectual, doth far exceede the same: for diligent and godly education is the fountaine of al vertue."[106]

Nearly all authors writing about the family advocated teaching children moral and spiritual precepts, but curiously, they remained silent about the practical aspects of this instruction. They advise parents to take children to church, an undisputed place of spiritual training, and to accustom them to daily catechism and Scripture readings; indeed, the imperative to inculcate godliness in the hearts of children fell squarely on the institutions of the church and school as well.[107] The only routine, secular activity mentioned as an excellent forum for instruction is the family meal. It should come as no surprise that so much attention would be devoted to child rearing during mealtimes; it provided a structured setting in which children could be trained on a regular basis.[108]

Sixteenth-century German prints, which are among the earliest depictions of the family around a table, already attest to the emphasis placed on child rearing during mealtimes.[109] Often accompanied by long inscriptions, these prints focus on the importance of good manners in children at the dinner table, hence their popular name, *Tischzucht* (Table Discipline). The *Tischzucht* by Georg Pencz, with an accompanying poem by Hans Sachs, is one of the best-known examples of this genre (Fig. 118). The poem – which seems humorous to the modern reader – exhorts children to be paradigms of good behavior at the table. Moreover, they are not to "commence eating until a blessing is said."[110] In the print, the boy at the far right with his hands folded in prayer observes this precept. This boy can be counted among the iconographic ancestors of the children who inhabit Dutch seventeenth-century paintings and prints depicting grace before the meal. Sachs's prescriptions for good behavior are strikingly similar to those expounded by Otto Brunfels and Erasmus – whose writings were so significant for Puritan and Pietist views of family life – in their contemporary books on etiquette, written for children.[111] Since Pencz's print could just as easily illustrate their ideas on the subject, it seems plausible to assume that sixteenth-century depictions of the family in art were to some extent fostered by the ideals of domestic life described in contemporary literature.[112] Yet owing to the large numbers of prints in circulation, it is equally plausible that, in turn, these works of art helped to foster the contemporary ideal of domestic life.

Prevailing domestic ideals probably affected the development of seventeenth-century portrayals of the family in art as well, particularly those depicting the theme of the family saying grace before the meal. As I already stated, mealtimes were the only daily, secular activity discussed in literature because of their potential to provide a forum for instruction. The highly structured setting of family meals was especially suitable for training children, and it lent itself rather easily to artistic representation. However, another source of inspiration was at work in these images, to wit, King David's description of family life in his celebrated Psalm 128.

The use of metaphoric imagery in this psalm to describe domestic life explains its appeal among artists and authors during the seventeenth century.[113] In an anonymous family portrait dated 1627, a grapevine has literally grown into a room where a family seated at a table says grace before a meal (Fig. 119).[114] The depiction of the grapevine in this manner clarifies its meaning as a metaphor of the mother's fecundity, a metaphor found in Psalm 128:3: "Thy wife shall be as a fruitful vine by the sides of

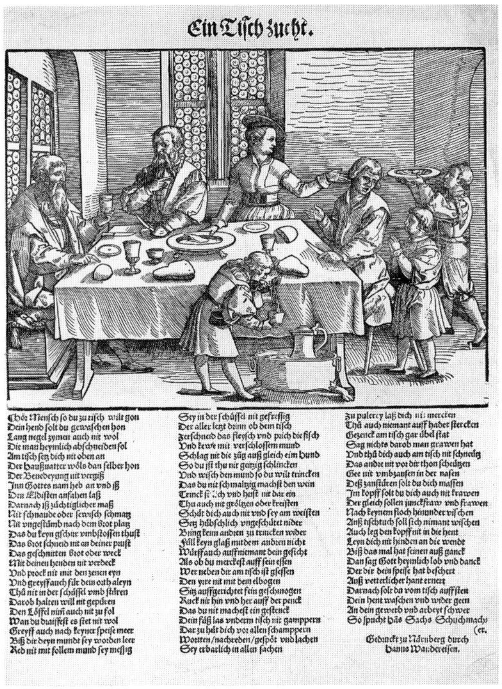

Figure 118. Georg Pencz, *Tischzucht* (woodcut). Berlin, Kupferstichkabinett, Staatliche Museen Preussischer Kulturbesitz. Photo: J. P. Anders, Berlin.

thine house." In a family portrait by Gortzius Geldorp (Fig. 120), signed and dated 1602, the artist includes a grapevine as well as olive branches placed beside the children, another motif derived from the psalm.[115]

These two portraits, with their marked air of tranquility, celebrate the commonly held conviction that having children was one of the joys of marriage. A great number of wedding poems and songs based on Psalm 128 provide literary parallels to this belief.[116] For example, in J. J. Deutel's *Huwelijckx weegh-schael* (The Scales of Marriage, 1641), the character Jacob manages to convince his cousin Maria that marriage is a desirable state by envisioning children joyfully gathered about the table.[117] Like the poems and portraits, Jacob draws his description from Psalm 128. The frontispiece of the second edition illustrates Jacob's perception of marriage as it juxtaposes a scene of grace with one of a hermit by a cave, thereby proclaiming the protagonists' antithetical viewpoints concerning the merits of marriage versus the state of being single (Fig. 121). This little scene recalls similar ones in numerous seventeenth-century prints, many of which are inscribed with verses from Psalm 128 (Fig. 122).[118]

In the two family portraits just discussed, most of the children have their hands folded (Figs. 119, 120). The pedagogical significance of their gestures would have been clear to contemporaries because learning how to

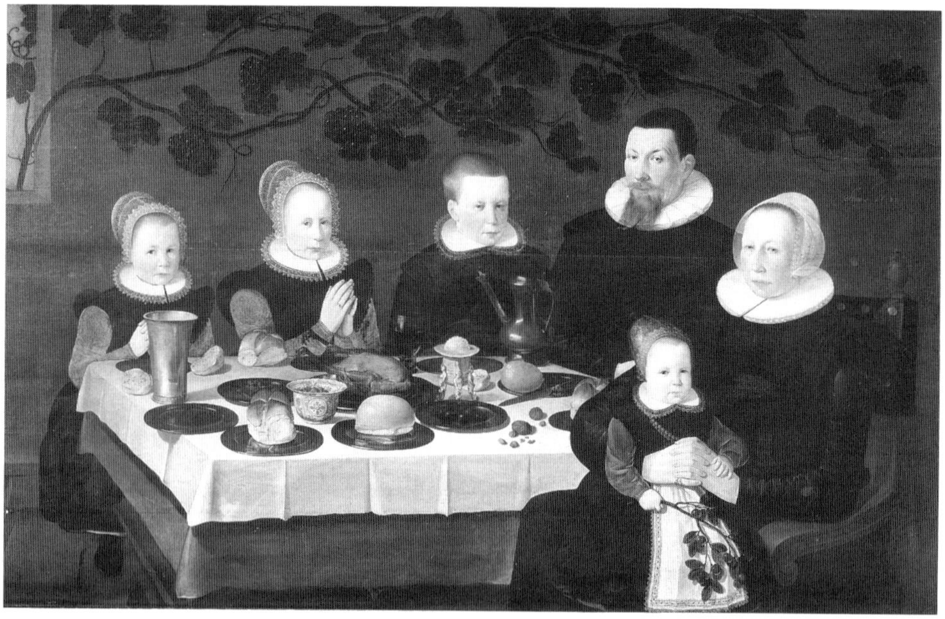

Figure 119. Anonymous, *Portrait of a Family Saying Grace*, 1627 (oil on panel, 122 × 191 cm). Utrecht, Rijksmuseum het Catharijneconvent. On loan from Amsterdam, Rijksmuseum. Photo: Rijksmuseum-Stichting.

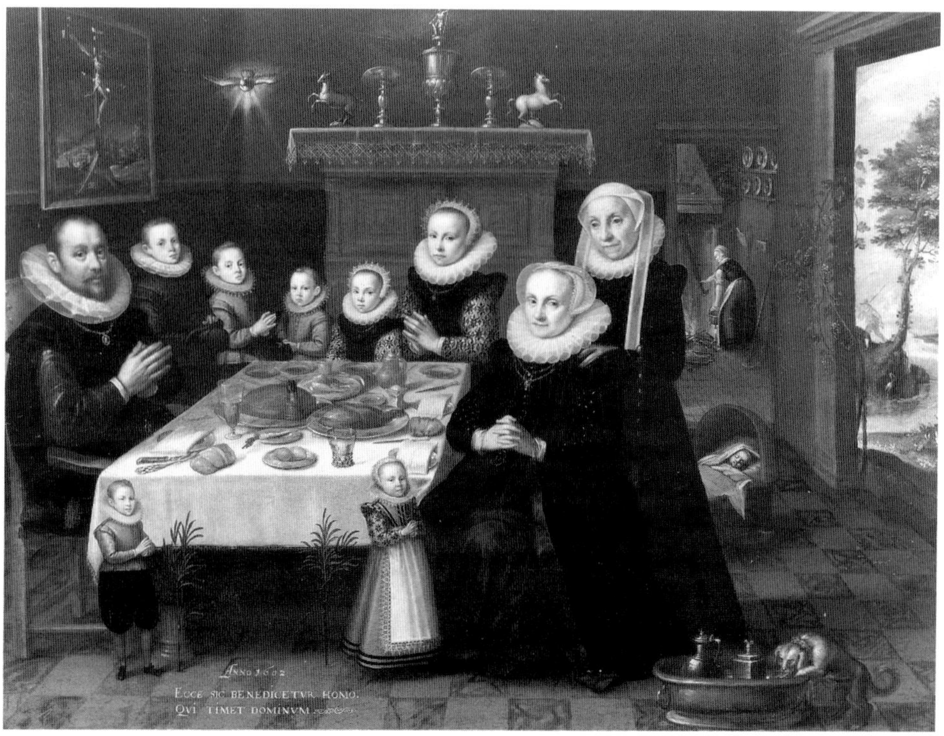

Figure 120. Gortzius Geldorp, *Portrait of a Family Saying Grace*, 1602. Private collection. Photo: courtesy Christie's, London.

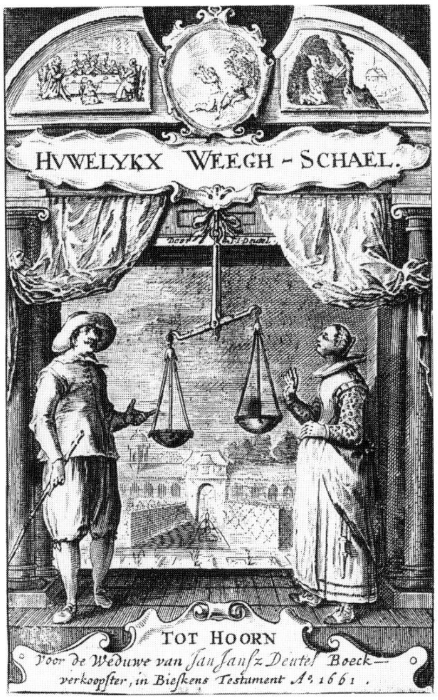

Figure 121. Frontispiece from J. J. Deutel, *Huwelijckx weegh-schael*, 2d ed., Hoorn 1662. Amsterdam, Universiteits-Bibliotheek Amsterdam. Photo: courtesy Universiteits-Bibliotheek Amsterdam.

pray was considered integral to a child's spiritual training. Parents were to teach their progeny the most appropriate language for prayer as well as the most suitable posture, that being to stand still with hands folded.[119]

The ideas underlying representations of children saying grace are also present in the family portrait by the Utrecht artist Andries van Bockhoven that I discussed at the beginning of this chapter (Fig. 90). Without question, Van Bockhoven has succeeded in displaying the virtue and concord of his family; the peaceful gathering at the table recalls an earlier print by Crispijn van de Passe I after Maerten de Vos, appropriately inscribed "Concordia" (Fig. 95).[120] As noted above, the respectful gestures of the artist's siblings and the books held by his father and two sisters clearly demonstrate the children's godliness and obedience, and by extension, their good training. Moreover, the gestures, and especially the books, refer to a specific, pedagogical and spiritual ritual conducted in many households at this time: family devotions. This ritual, which included prayer, Scripture readings, theological instruction, and edifying discussion, was led by the *paterfamilias* and played an important part in educating children.[121]

The size of the book held by the artist's father indicates that it is a Bible.[122] The Scriptures were sometimes read before meals with the exclusive purpose of sanctifying the food but, as noted, the practice always held a central place in family devotions.[123] Devotions were often conducted just before the

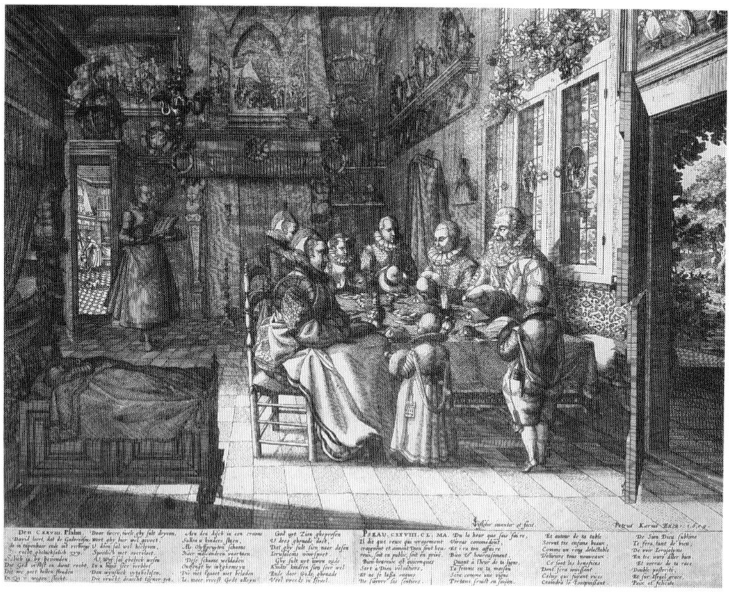

Figure 122. Claes Jansz. Visscher, *Prayer before the Meal* (engraving), 1609. Amsterdam, Rijksprentenkabinet. Photo: Rijksmuseum-Stichting.

midday meal because the entire family would be present.[124] Thus, the Bible in the portrait probably refers to this ritual as do the books held by the artist's two sisters. Because of their small format, they might be songbooks, catechism books, or perhaps one of the well-known guides to personal piety.[125] The frontispiece to one such work, Franciscus Ridderus's *Dagelijckse huys-catechisatie* (Daily Home Catechism), a popular contemporary catechism, actually illustrates devotions before the midday meal, along with the other convenient times for their practice, mornings and evenings (Fig. 123).[126]

Books like Ridderus's were highly important for training children – and older Christians as well – because they contained clear and simple explanations of all issues pertaining to the faith. If these are the types of books depicted in the painting, then they too point to the pedagogical significance of the ritual that Van Bockhoven refers to: family devotions before the meal. I deliberately use the words "refers to" because the artist has represented the salient parts of the ritual as if they were occurring simultaneously. Though no doubt based on actual events, the depiction of devotions here has been abstracted in order to stress the piety of the family and the children's proper training.

The ritual referred to in the painting likely reflects its daily occurrence in Van Bockhoven's family – the artist's father held the post of deacon in the

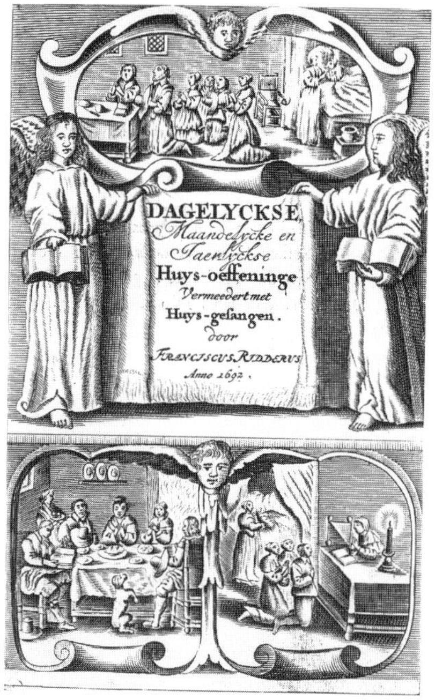

Figure 123. Frontispiece from Franciscus Ridderus, *Dagelijckse huys-catechisatie*, 10th ed., Amsterdam 1692. Amsterdam, Universiteits-Bibliotheek Amsterdam. Photo: courtesy Universiteits-Bibliotheek Amsterdam.

Reformed Church in Utrecht for several years – along with many other ones as well.[127] Fortunately, the Dutch Pietist Willem Teellinck has left an account of the ritual of devotions, based on his experiences while living with an English family in Banbury in 1604.[128] In the preface to his translation of a theological work by the English Puritan William Whately, Teellinck describes his host's daily custom during midday meals as follows:

> The whole family gathered, and then they read a chapter together; thus prepared by reading the Word, they unanimously invoked the name of the Lord. Afterwards at the table, they spoke about the things that each of them had contemplated in the chapter. After the meal they sang a Psalm together, and then everyone returned to his work.[129]

The fact that devotions were usually conducted at the dinner table provides further proof of the belief that mealtimes afforded parents the opportunity to promote godliness and courteous behavior in their children.[130] Many contemporary prints depicting grace said before the meal illustrate these underlying pedagogical aims. Some, as their titles and inscriptions imply, are iconographic descendants of the *Tischzucht* tradition (Fig. 124).[131] The inscription to Abraham Bosse's print of this subject, "spoken" by the parents and their children, emphasizes the suitability of the mealtime for paternal instruction (Fig. 125). The parents exhort their children, whose gestures are similar to those of the ones in the portraits discussed earlier, to practice obedience, virtue, and piety.[132]

Thus far we have only examined the theme of saying grace in portraits and prints. It was also represented in genre paintings.[133] In Jan Steen's *Grace before Meat*, parents prepare to serve food to their children (Fig. 126). The little girl, her hands folded in prayer, stares straight ahead, a gaze recommended for praying children by at least one contemporary writer.[134] Her brother has respectfully removed his hat and has probably folded his hands beneath it. The children's pious gestures reveal their proper training.

A dog placed rather prominently in the foreground of the composition licks a dinner pot. The presence of this slovenly creature here seems to violate the sanctity of the moment. In several contemporary emblems, the motif of a slovenly dog licking a pot is juxtaposed with one chasing a rabbit, alluding to the positive or negative effect of training on behavior (Fig. 127).[135] These emblems illustrate a parable by Plutarch from his treatise on education, a work well known throughout Europe in the sixteenth and seventeenth centuries.[136] Plutarch recounts the story of Lycurgus, the lawgiver of the Spartans, who raised two whelps from the same litter in different ways. One was trained to be a diligent hunter while his sibling was allowed to be indolent and ravenous. At a time when the Spartans were all assembled, Lycurgus told them that proper rearing, discipline, and habit were very important for the cultivation of virtue in men. To prove this statement, he brought together the two dogs and placed a pot of meat and a rabbit between them. The well-trained dog chased after the rabbit while the other began to eat the food in the pot. When the crowd could not grasp the significance of this, Lycurgus explained that habits inculcated by the dogs' upbringing had influenced their conduct, even though they were both from the same litter.[137] Plutarch's parable thus demonstrated the power of training to mold behavior, regardless of inborn character traits.[138]

The consistency and enthusiasm with which the authors of sixteenth- and seventeenth-century family literature embraced Plutarch's theories are remarkable. This attests not only to the popularity of his treatise, but more importantly, to the widespread conviction that children needed comprehensive moral and spiritual training. Contemporary moralists invariably quoted the parable of Lycurgus in order to support their contention that education ameliorates behavior. Batty, for example, recounted the parable, offering the following advice to parents:

> I wish that parents would well weigh, and deeply consider this example of Lycurgus, touching education in contrarie maner: wherof also Plato

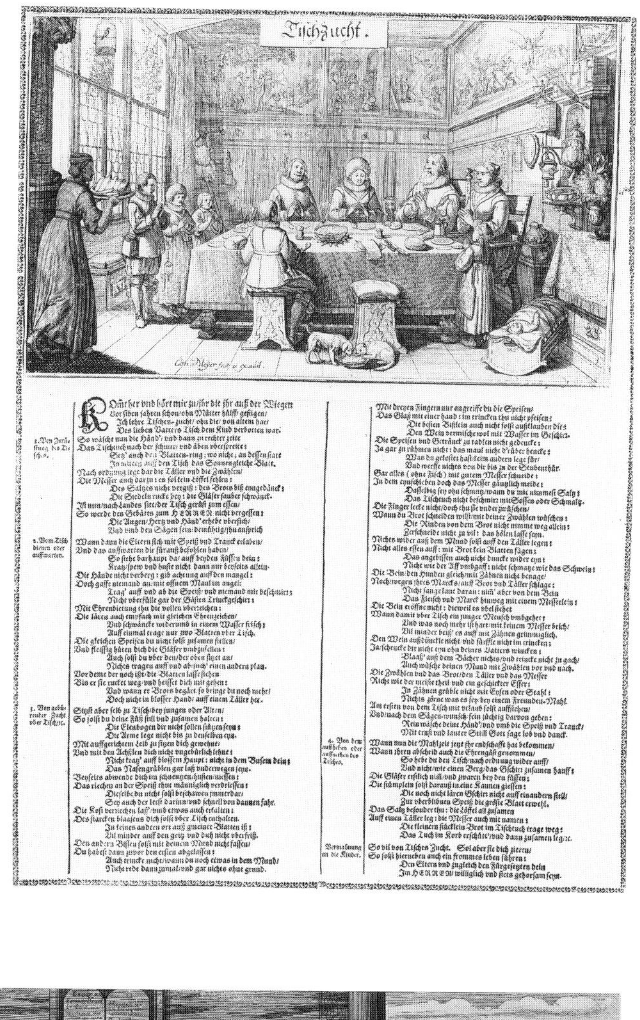

Figure 124 (right). Conrad Meyer, *Tischzucht*, 1645 (engraving). Hamburg, Kunsthalle. Photo: R. Kleinhempel, Hamburg.

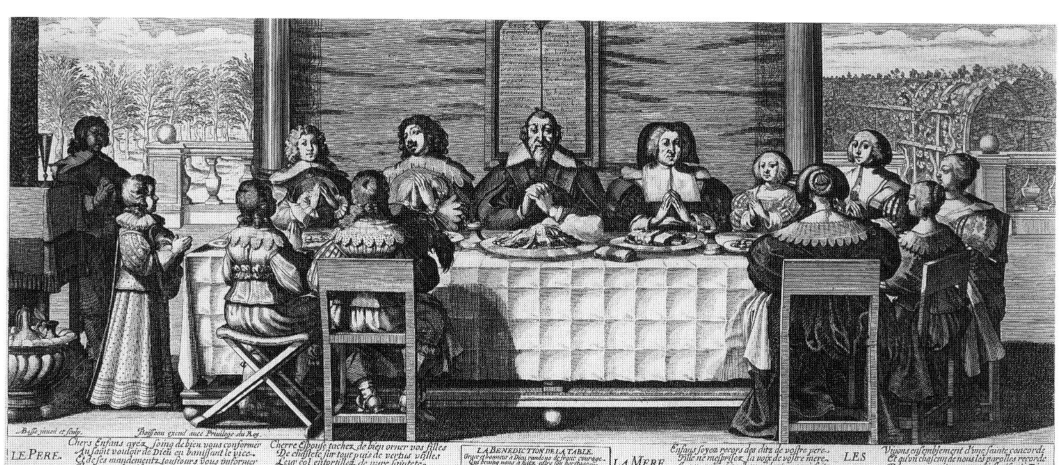

Figure 125. Abraham Bosse, *Saying Grace* (engraving). Amsterdam, Rijksprentenkabinet. Photo: Rijksmuseum-Stichting.

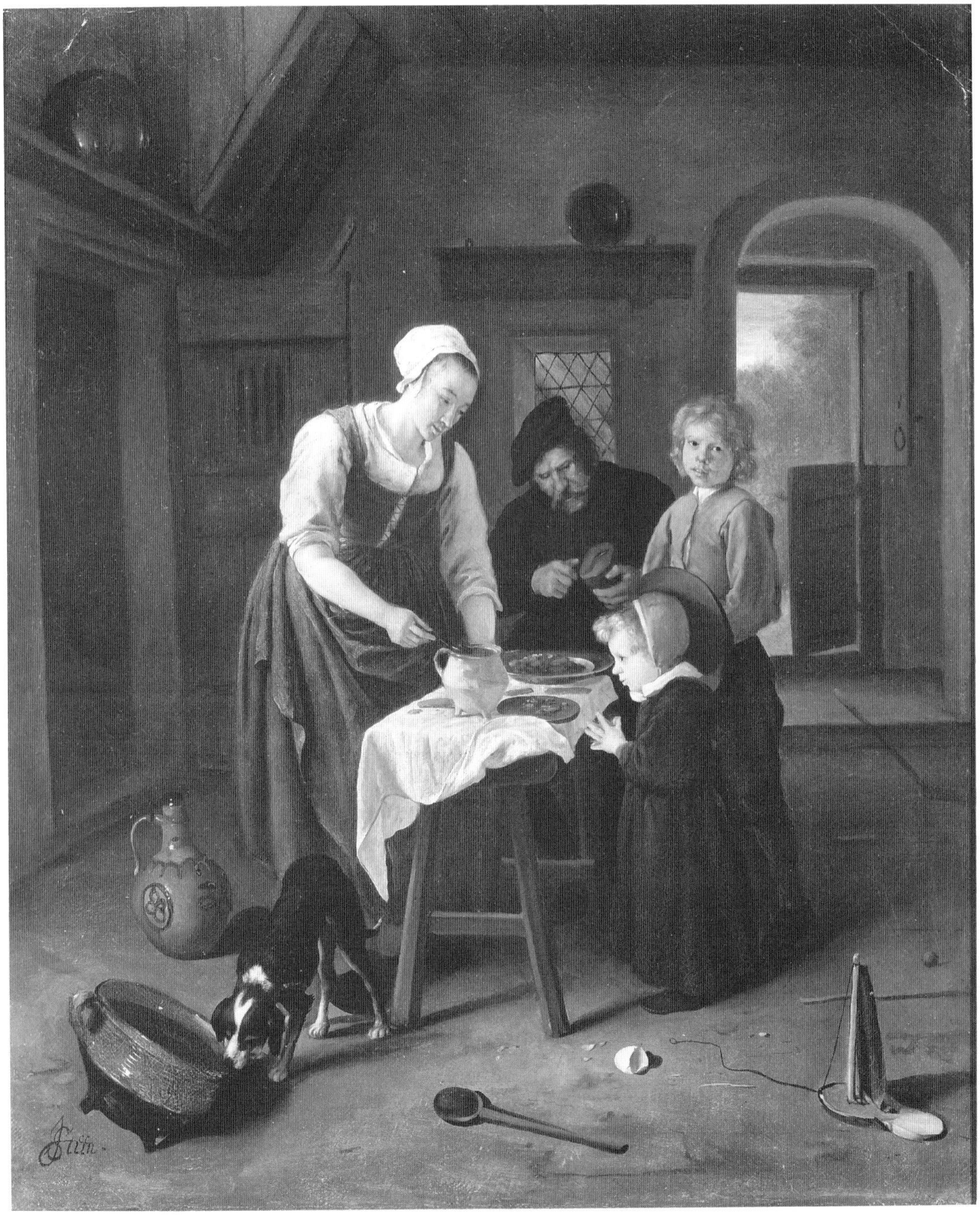

Figure 126. Jan Steen, *Grace before Meat* (oil on canvas, 44.8 × 37.5 cm). London, The National Gallery. Reproduced by courtesy of the Trustees, The National Gallery, London.

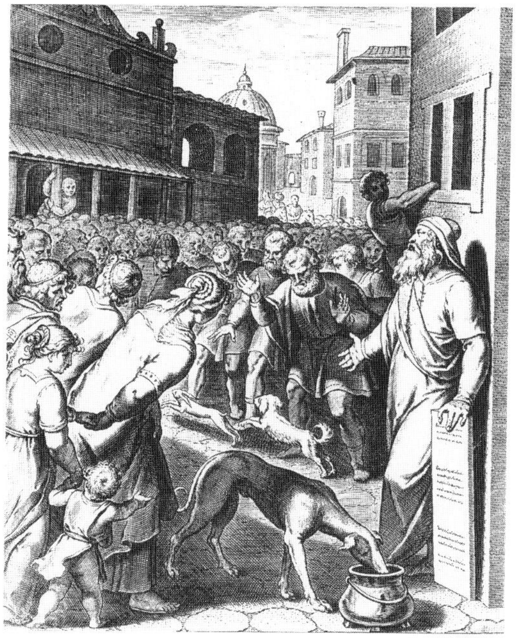

Figure 127. Emblem from Otto van Veen, *Quinti Horatii Flacci emblemata*, 2d ed., Antwerp 1612. Amsterdam, Universiteits-Bibliotheek Amsterdam. Photo: courtesy Universiteits-Bibliotheek Amsterdam.

> writeth: That a childe well and virtuously nurtured, is like to prove a divine creature: but contrarily, if it be unhappily taught, and suffered to run at libertie, then is hee like to prove a moste wicked and cruell beast.[139]

All of these books, as well as the emblems, use the motif of two dogs as antithetical pedagogical symbols. However, the motif of the dog licking the pot did not always require that of his rabbit-chasing counterpart to make the point. The slovenly dog functioned quite well alone as a metaphor for bad training as Jacob Cats's proverb demonstrates: "Accustom a greyhound to the pot, / A hunting dog becomes a kitchen fool."[140]

The story of Lycurgus, so popular with moralists and pedagogues, probably underlies Cats's proverb as well as the motif of the dog licking the pot in Steen's painting.[141] This dog is a German beagle, a breed used for hunting, like those illustrated in the emblems and the proverb. In light of the texts just cited, the presence in the painting of a German beagle licking a pot is likely meant as a metaphor of poor training to be contrasted with the pious, well-bred children who say grace.[142]

A similar symbolic contrast between poorly trained dogs and well-trained children appears in other contemporary depictions of families giving thanks at mealtime, among them, a print by Conrad Meyer (Fig. 128).[143] Meyer shows a mother teaching her children to pray before they eat, while the other

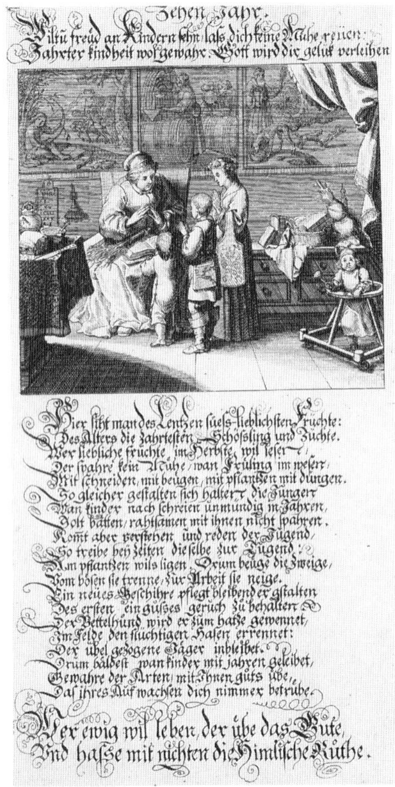

Figure 128. Conrad Meyer, *Age Ten* (engraving from the series *The Ten Ages of Man*), 1675. Amsterdam, Rijksprentenkabinet. Photo: Rijksmuseum-Stichting.

motifs in the composition refer to the importance of child rearing in general. The inscription clarifies this as do the little pictures on the wall behind the figures.[144] The picture on the right represents Lycurgus with the two dogs; the intractable pot licker is in the foreground. According to the print's inscription, this dog symbolizes poor training, thus having the same meaning as the one depicted in the painting by Steen. The only difference is that Steen has portrayed a different breed and transformed it into a "living creature," without any connection to the Lycurgus story. The painter has also depicted several toys strewn about the floor. The children have discarded them in favor of more serious matters, that is, moral and spiritual training.[145]

In another work by Steen, *Prayer before the Meal*, the motif of the dog licking the pot is once again placed prominently within the foreground of the composition (Fig. 129).[146] In this painting, the artist depicts a family of very humble means whose pious behavior confirms their faith in God, thus sustaining their meager existence. The simplicity and humility of this family is reminiscent of those in other seventeenth-century paintings and prints depicting the theme (see, e.g., Fig. 130).[147] The family in this picture may be poor, but their children are being raised properly. The mother folds

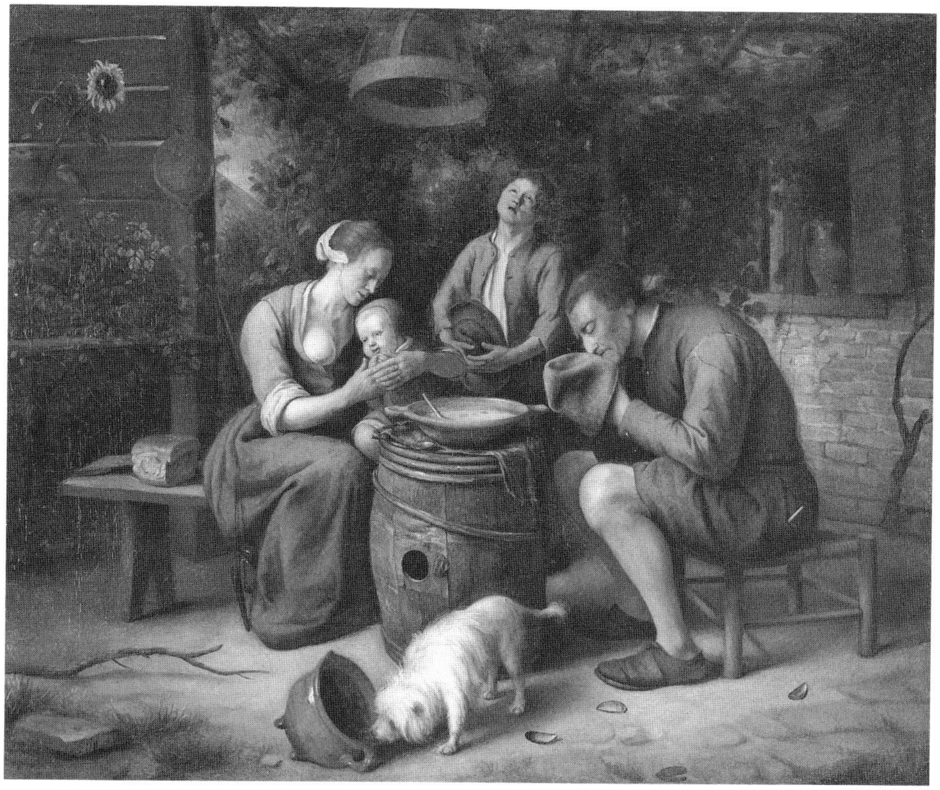

Figure 129. Jan Steen, *Prayer before the Meal* (oil on canvas, 64.2 × 79 cm). Philadelphia, John G. Johnson Collection, Philadelphia Museum of Art. Photo: museum.

her young child's hands, reflecting the contemporary notion that children must be taught not only the language of prayer but also the most appropriate gestures.[148] The older boy, who gazes piously heavenward with his hat respectfully removed, echoes his father's devout expression. The *belkroon* above the figures further underscores their piety because it is inscribed with the first two words of the Lord's Prayer, "Pa[ter]" "Nos[ter]."[149] Both the *belkroon* and the expressions of the family members heighten the solemnity of the scene.

The dog licking the pot in the foreground is a griffon, a now extinct relative of the modern-day lion dog.[150] This rare and expensive breed, of French origin, was a lap dog preferred by upper-class women and not the type of animal that lower-class, poor people would own. Thus the motif is incongruous not only with the sanctity of the occasion, but also with the social class of the family.[151] Perhaps the griffon, like the beagle in the other painting, is symbolic of poor training, to be contrasted with the pious, well-

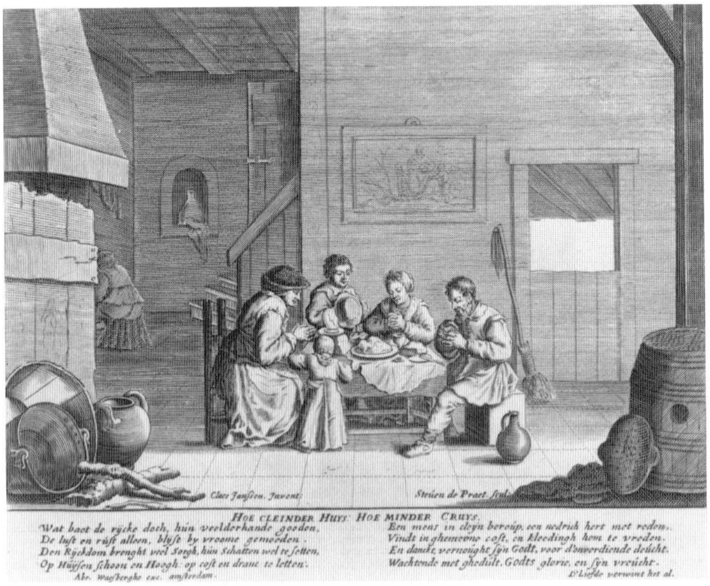

Figure 130. Steven de Praet, *The Saying of Grace* (engraving). Amsterdam, Rijksprentenkabinet. Photo: Rijksmuseum-Stichting.

reared children who say grace. However, griffons are not hunting dogs, and therefore no real parallels can be drawn with the numerous literary sources already cited.[152] Yet I believe that, in this context, the griffon functions as a pedagogical metaphor, given the very incongruity of the motif and the unlikelihood that a lady's lap dog could be a paradigm of good behavior.

In contemporary art, well-trained, obedient dogs sometimes appear beside praying children, as in a late sixteenth-century print entitled *Morning*, from the series *The Four Times of the Day* by Jan Saenredam after Hendrick Goltzius (Fig. 131). In this print, the little girl prays for her food while her brother doffs his hat after having received his. Just like the boy in the print by Meyer, the children both carry hornbooks and seem ready to leave for school.[153] On the floor beside them, a little dog squats patiently on its hind legs, hoping for a morsel of food. Like his undisciplined, pot-licking counterpart in the works of art previously discussed, this dog ultimately owes its pictorial existence to Plutarch's story of Lycurgus.[154] Therefore, this well-behaved little creature alludes to the docility of the children.

The earliest text illustration of an unmistakably obedient dog actually postdates Saenredam's print by some thirty-five years. In the illustration

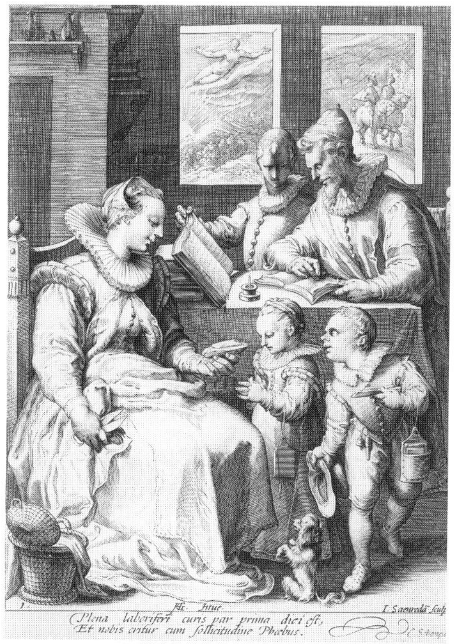

Figure 131. Jan Saenredam after Hendrick Goltzius, *Morning* (engraving from the series *The Four Times of the Day*). Amsterdam, Rijksprentenkabinet. Photo: Rijksmuseum-Stichting.

entitled *Maeghde-Wapen* (Maiden's Coat of Arms) from Cats's *Houwelyck* of 1625 (Fig. 7), a dog squats on its hind legs (in much the same manner as the one in the earlier print).[155] Underneath this creature is a banderole inscribed "Leer-sucht" (Willingness to Learn). The dog therefore alludes to the tractability of the young female personification depicted above him, as do the needlework implements that she holds.[156]

These very same pedagogical associations are evident in a Jesuit emblem whose *pictura* shows a cupid holding a piece of bread before a dog squatting on its hind legs (Fig. 132). Its *subscriptio* elucidates the significance of this scene as it appeals to parents to teach their children to pray before eating, an idea visualized by the dog who has been taught to beg for its food.[157]

The associations of the Jesuit emblem and Cats's *Maeghde-Wapen* furnish insights into the meaning of trained dogs in the presence of children in many Dutch seventeenth-century portraits (see, e.g., Fig. 133).[158] In these works, the motif of the obedient dog who squats on its hind legs or performs other tricks alludes to the docility of the children that are portrayed.

Plutarch, whose story of Lycurgus began this discussion of the dog as a pedagogical metaphor, adduced other examples from nature in order to demonstrate education's efficacy in modifying children's instincts.[159] The horse

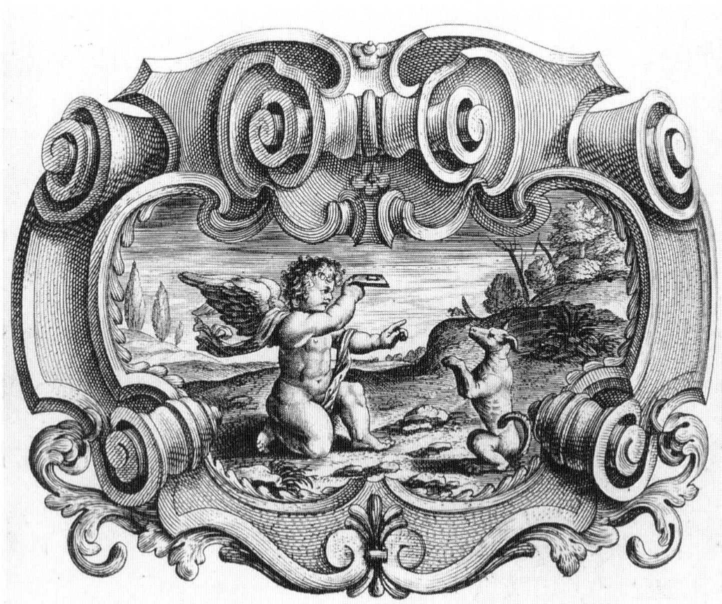

Figure 132. Emblem from *Afbeeldinghe van d'eerste eeuwe der Societeyt Iesu*, Antwerp 1640. The Hague, Koninklijke Bibliotheek. Photo: Koninklijke Bibliotheek.

figures prominently in his argument, as evidenced by the following quotation of the relevant passage from a sixteenth-century English translation of Plutarch's treatise: "What horse welle broken in youth is not after to the rider gentyll and easye?"[160] Doubtlessly inspired by this passage, contemporary pedagogues frequently employed the pedagogical metaphor of the horse. For an example, I turn once again to the treatise by Batty:

> For as the unbroken horse by reason of ignorance of what hee should doe, and of skittishnesse, is nothing apt either for pleasure or profite: so the unlearned youth which is violently led away by his own corrupt affections (which good education and learning mastereth and subdueth) is very unmeet for all companies and fellowship of life.[161]

Similar associations are even found in emblem books of the period.[162] The *pictura* to an emblem from Adrianus Hofferus's *Nederduytsche poemata* (Dutch Poems, 1635) shows an elegantly dressed youth, mounted on a

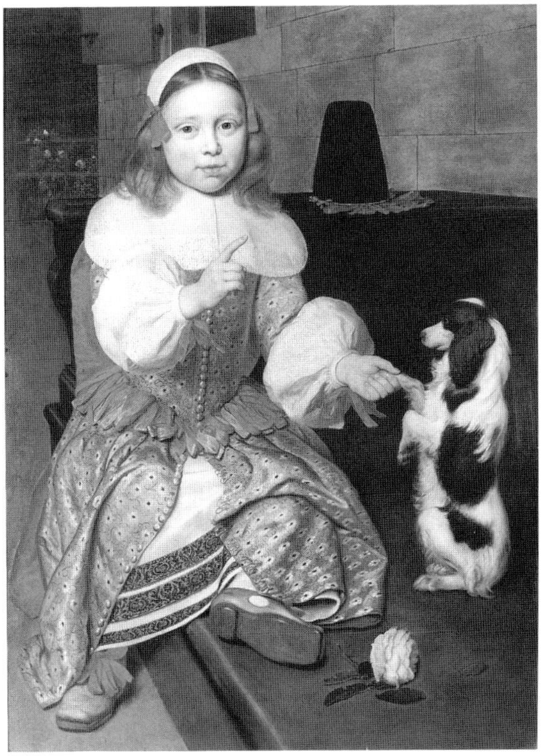

Figure 133. Ludolf de Jongh, *Portrait of a Boy*, 1661 (oil on canvas, 97.8 × 71.4 cm). Richmond, Virginia Museum of Fine Arts, The Arthur and Margaret Glasgow Fund. Photo: museum, The Arthur and Margaret Glasgow Fund.

rearing horse in a landscape (Fig. 134).[163] Pedagogical lessons are paramount as the emblem's two inscriptions confirm: "Regenda est servida adolescentia" (Impetuous Youth Needs to Be Ruled) and "Betemt de jeughd / Soo doet sy deughd" (Subdue Youth, So They Will Be Virtuous). The *subscriptio* elucidates the inscriptions and *pictura* as it describes the impulsive, tempestuous nature of youth and their resultant need to be disciplined. Hofferus likens this educational desideratum to a horse that must be spurred and bridled so that it will obey its master.[164]

Although emblems are in essence literary conceits, Hofferus's emblem, with its splendid *pictura* of a dashing youth on horseback, does facilitate our understanding of several unusual seventeenth-century family portraits that feature the motif of children on horseback or holding a horse by the reins. It would be foolhardy to argue that the emblem serves as a *clavis interpretandi* for these works of art.[165] If anything, the literary sources just discussed, namely works by Plutarch and many contemporary authors, only confirm that the associations conveyed by the emblem were not at all unique but were well known in seventeenth-century Dutch culture. It is therefore more

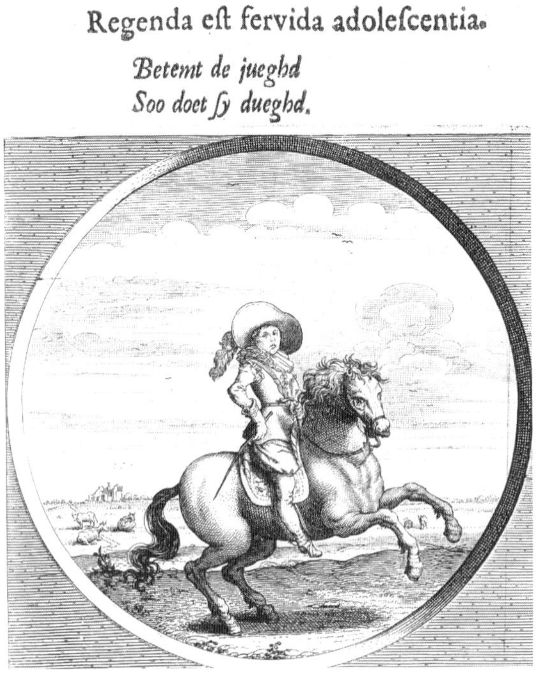

Figure 134. Emblem from Adrianus Hofferus, *Nederduytsche poemata*, Amsterdam 1635. Amsterdam, Universiteits-Bibliotheek Amsterdam. Photo: courtesy Universiteits-Bibliotheek Amsterdam.

accurate to regard the emblem and the motif in the portraits as visual analogues sharing common sources and pedagogical aims.

The first portrait to be considered, dated 1637 and attributed to Jacob Gerritsz. Cuyp, represents a family before a landscape (Fig. 135).[166] One of the children stands between his mother and father, doffing his hat. This was a common courtesy in the seventeenth century, intended to demonstrate respect for and obedience to authority. Since such behavior was – and still is – demanded of children, the occasional presence of youths doffing their hats in family portraits must be understood as a reference to their proper breeding.[167] Both the boy and his mother point toward other family members who occupy a central position in the composition: a youth who holds the reins of a pony on which his younger brother is mounted. The gesture made by this young rider directs our attention to the beast. Perhaps it belonged to the family and was included in their portrait for this very reason.[168] However, in light of the widespread pedagogical associations evoked by horses in contemporary literature, the placid pony held by the reins probably alludes to the youngster's good training.[169]

Another, equally telling example, a portrait by the Enkhuisen artist Jan Claesz, shows a well-dressed five-year-old in an arcade, posed with a little

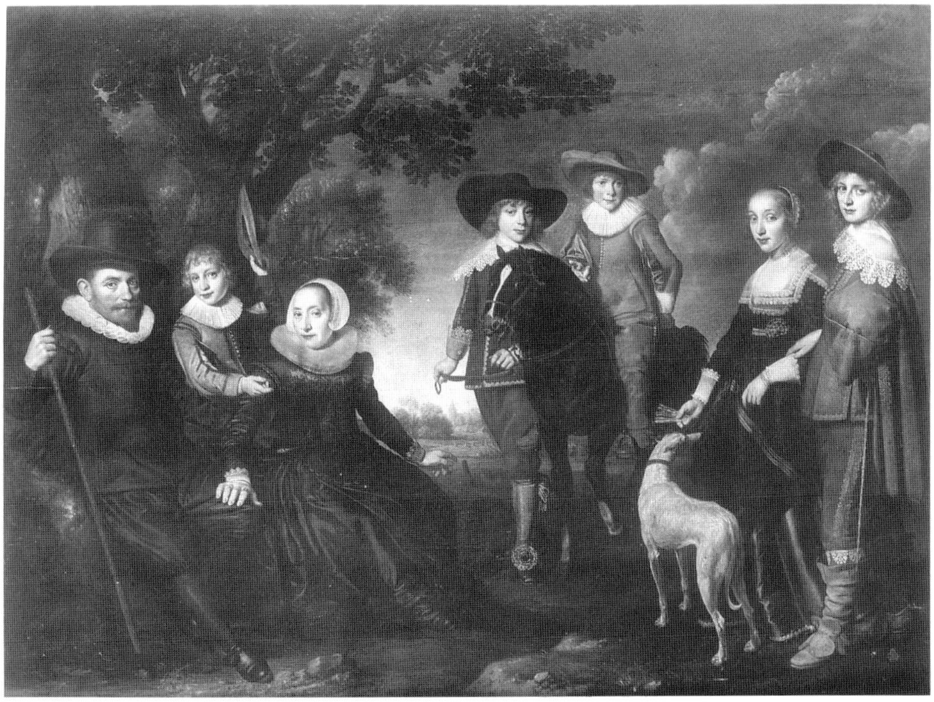

Figure 135. Jacob Gerritsz. Cuyp (attributed to), *Portrait of a Family in a Landscape*, 1637 (oil on panel, 128 × 175.5 cm). Brussels, Musées Royaux des Beaux-Arts de Belgique. Photo: copyright A.C.L.-Brussels.

horse wearing an ornate breast collar (Fig. 136).[170] Owing to the charming, provincial style of the artist, we see only the head, chest, and front legs of this woodenlike creature wedged claustrophobically between its master and one of the pilasters. Yet the pedagogical significance of the portrait is clear as the boy holds a riding whip while he tightly grips the animal's reins. This exclusive focus on child and horse, without the presence of other family members, is found in other portraits of the period.[171]

Philippe Ariès has argued that the frequent appearances of children in adult clothing in seventeenth-century portraits can be construed as evidence of the lack of an awareness of childhood at that time.[172] In the portraits just cited, the children may be wearing clothing that mimics adult fashions, but the motif of well-trained animals alludes to parental awareness of the need to correct the foibles of childhood through training.

Regardless of the extent to which the seventeenth-century concept of childhood differed from the modern-day one, the very presence of children in art

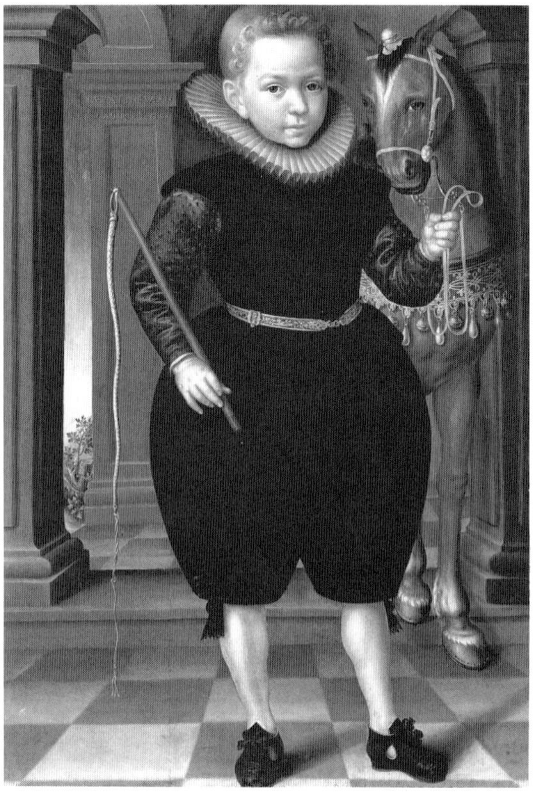

Figure 136. Jan Claesz, *Portrait of a Five-Year-Old Boy*, 1609 (oil on panel, 100.5 × 75 cm). Private collection.

and literature suggests that parents did not neglect them but were aware of the problems and needs in this distinct stage of life, separate from adulthood.[173] Although grounded in an ideal world, the art and literature of the seventeenth-century Dutch Republic bear eloquent testimony to the importance of children at that time and the belief in the home as the principal environment for training them.

Chapter 4

"WEDUWE"

Dutch seventeenth-century paintings of the elderly are surprisingly numerous, particularly when compared to the number of representations of this theme produced in other European countries during this period. From the mysterious yet renowned *tronies* (which I loosely define as paintings with unarticulated backgrounds that depict a head, bust, or sometimes a nearly half-length figure)[1] popularized by Rembrandt van Rijn, to the genre paintings by his erstwhile pupils, one is struck by the wide variety of themes involving aged protagonists. Clearly there must have been a fairly large market for such paintings. Dutch painters frequently portrayed senescent types as representatives of vices, particularly that of avarice, but just as frequently – and, for our purposes, more significantly – as representatives of a gamut of virtues.[2] The ambivalent attitudes toward the elderly expressed in these pictures are not at all unusual and, in fact, typify broader European attitudes over the centuries.[3]

Contemporary Dutch authors explored the subject of aging just as frequently as did artists. For example, in the last chapter of *Houwelyck,* entitled "Weduwe" (Widow), Jacob Cats discusses the final stages of a woman's life: senescence and widowhood. The chapter is divided into two sections. The first examines the transience of human existence (best illustrated by the decrepitude of the elderly) and the need to repent, to reject earthly matters in favor of spiritual ones. The second section contains practical instructions for widows, focusing on such matters as how they should comport themselves and whether they should remarry.[4] As we have seen repeatedly, Cats's observations and advice about womanhood reflect commonly held beliefs and ideals culled from an impressive variety of classical, humanist, and theological sources. His thoughts on widowhood and old age in general are no exception, though his descriptions of this, the final stage in life, are among the most moving ever written.[5]

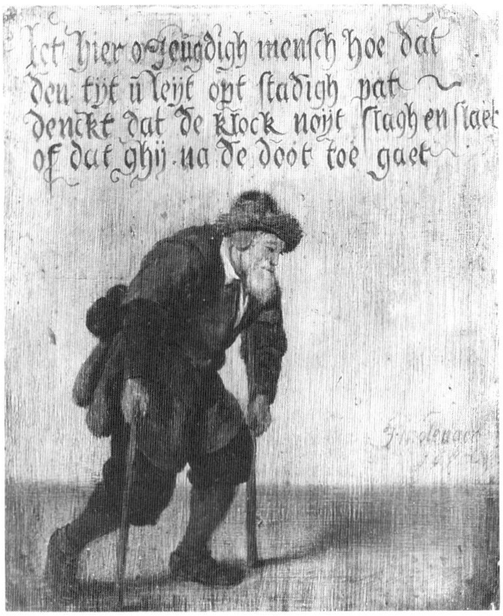

Figure 137. Jan Miense Molenaer, *Old Man on Crutches*, 1652. (oil on panel, 21.7 × 18.8 cm). Present location unknown.

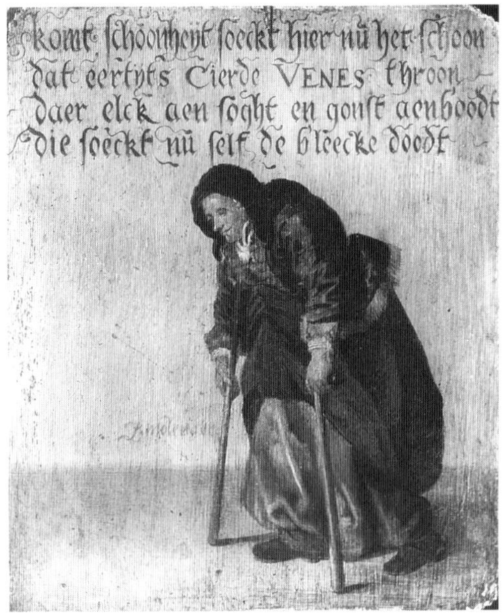

Figure 138. Jan Miense Molenaer, *Old Woman on Crutches* (oil on panel, 21.7 × 18.8 cm). Present location unknown.

Following long-standing traditions, seventeenth-century writers viewed old age itself as a "sickness," its characteristic deterioration of health ineluctably leading to death.[6] Cats's plaintive verses on the sickness of old age are particularly touching:

> Surely old age brings us to Reason,
> Or sends her messengers all through our body;
> She strikes us on our arm, chest, or weak foot
> And teaches us that soon we have to depart from here.[7]

This passage is found in Cats's *Ouderdom* (Old Age), a book written when the author himself was well into his seventies. Here as elsewhere, Cats relies on literary topoi to describe old age and the conduct most befitting it, but given the author's own elderly state, it is difficult to dismiss the possibility that the book reflects personal experience. Other writers lack his sensitivity and tact; Adriaen van de Venne simply remarks that the elderly already have one foot in the grave.[8] The vanity of old age is pathetically expressed in pendants by Jan Miense Molenaer (Figs. 137, 138). The artist depicts an elderly couple, whose withered flesh, kyphotic postures, and crutches tell us just as much – if not more – about the evanescence of human life as the admonitory inscriptions above them.

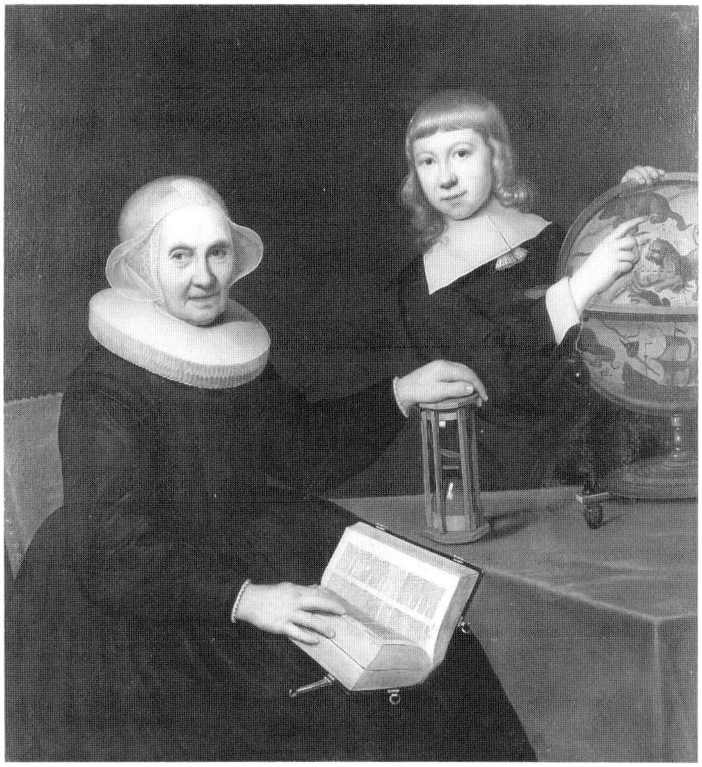

Figure 139. Pieter Danckerts de Ry, *Portrait of an Old Woman with Her Grandson.* Present location unknown. Photo: courtesy Christie's, London.

Many authors believed that the deterioration of health in old age actually had some "positive" aspects. For example, it forced elderly people to contemplate death and the hereafter. They were thus thought to possess greater wisdom than their juniors, especially with regard to spiritual matters:

> The elderly find thousands of lessons in themselves, in their infirmities, in the graveyard flowers (I am alluding to the gray hair) growing on their head and in their beard, each of which can serve as a sermon to prepare their house for their heirs, their bodies for the belly of the earth and their souls for the judgment of God.[9]

Portraits of old women, which are quite rare, focus precisely on their spiritual acumen. In Pieter Danckerts de Ry's portrait of a grandmother and (presumably) her grandson, the former, with an open Bible in her lap, gazes knowingly at the viewer while resting her hand on an hourglass, a long-standing symbol of transitoriness (Fig. 139).[10] Her young grandson, whose ruddy complexion offers a sober contrast to the wizened features of

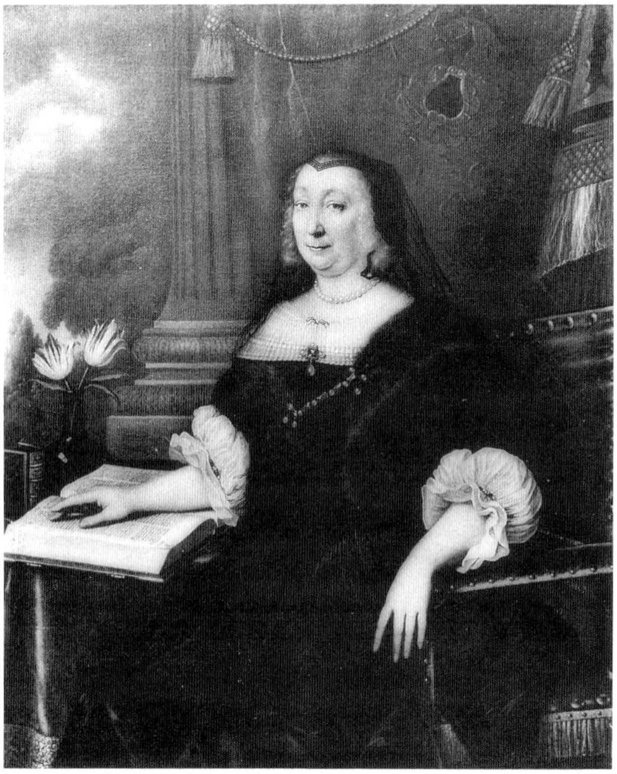

Figure 140. Abraham van den Tempel, *Portrait of a Woman* (oil on canvas, 132 × 108 cm). Present location unknown.

his grandmother, points to a celestial globe thereby completing the *vanitas* associations in this painting. A portrait by Abraham van den Tempel conveys similar ideas. Here a widow, identified as such by her mourning veil, sits in an elegant portico, her hand resting on an open Bible (Fig. 140). The tulips in the vase further underscore the ephemeral nature of existence.

As they prepared for their imminent departure for the hereafter, the aged were expected to bridle their passions.[11] What was at least theoretically difficult for younger people to accomplish was easier for the elderly as they were thought to possess, through experience and enlightened reason, virtues like temperance and simplicity.[12] For these reasons, it was argued that God looked upon old people with favor and compassion, revealing Himself to them most often because "they usually pray and pay the most / they work the hardest / and have the deepest longing for the most distinctive revelations of Himself and His mercy."[13] The elderly could thus approach death without fear because their godliness enabled them to perceive the deceitfulness and evanescence of the world and its riches.[14]

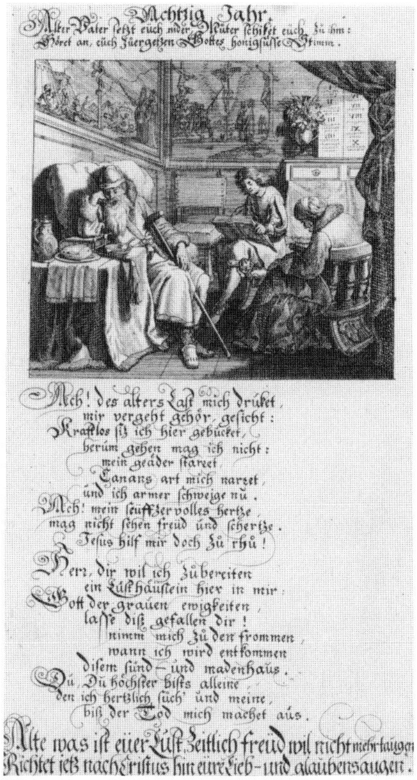

Figure 141. Conrad Meyer, *Age Eighty* (engraving from the series *The Ten Ages of Man*), 1675. Amsterdam, Rijksprentenkabinet. Photo: Rijksmuseum-Stichting.

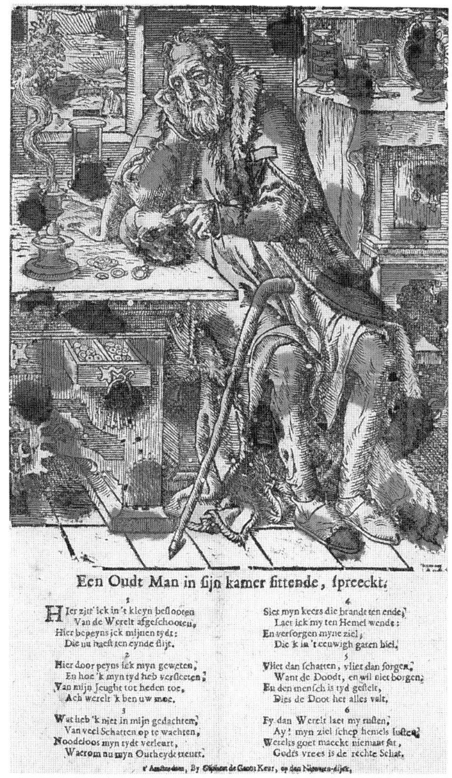

Figure 142. Catchpenny print, published by the heirs of the widow of Gijsbert de Groot. Amsterdam, Rijksprentenkabinet. Photo: Rijksmuseum-Stichting.

In many contemporary prints, the aged display the piety and spiritual foresight ascribed to them by numerous authors. In an engraving by Conrad Meyer, a child reads the Bible to a frail, aged woman and her sickly husband, whose arthritic hand rests on his crutch (Fig. 141).[15] In the inscription, this feeble man expresses the desire to leave his decrepit body in order to be with Christ. An eighteenth-century catchpenny print – cited here because it was printed from a sixteenth-century woodblock – expresses similar convictions; it shows an old man wearing a fur-lined cape, pointing to such long-standing symbols of transience as a skull beside an hourglass, coins, jewelry, and an extinguished candle (Fig. 142).[16] The advanced age of the man, expressed by his hoary features, likewise connotes mortality. According to the inscription, he realizes that his life will soon end and that all is vanity. Consequently, he forewarns the viewer that the greatest treasure one can possess is fear and knowledge of the Lord.

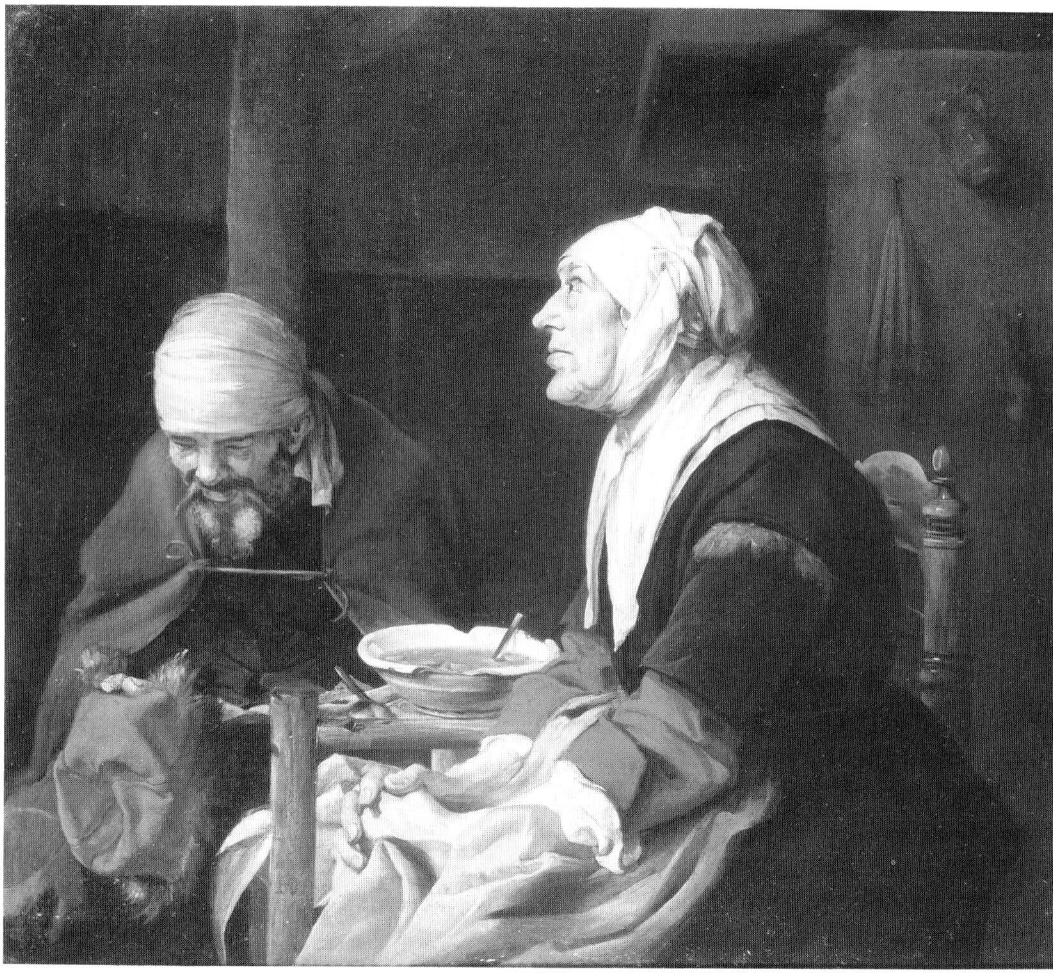

Figure 143. Abraham van Dyck (attributed to), *Elderly Couple Saying Grace* (oil on canvas, 67.3 × 75 cm). New York, Private collection. Photo: The Frick Art Reference Library.

Numerous genre paintings focus on the piety of the aged, particularly those representing the theme of old people saying grace. (That our analyses can even be classified according to such themes once again testifies to the limited thematic framework within which Dutch artists worked.) These works of art therefore image the elderly in a manner remarkably close to that of contemporary literature. In a picture attributed to Abraham van Dyck, the artist depicts an elderly couple praying before their simple meal in an unadorned interior (Fig. 143). Due to her prominence within the composition, the old woman is clearly the central focus of this painting; the serene gaze on her wrinkled face bespeaks the intensity of her supplications

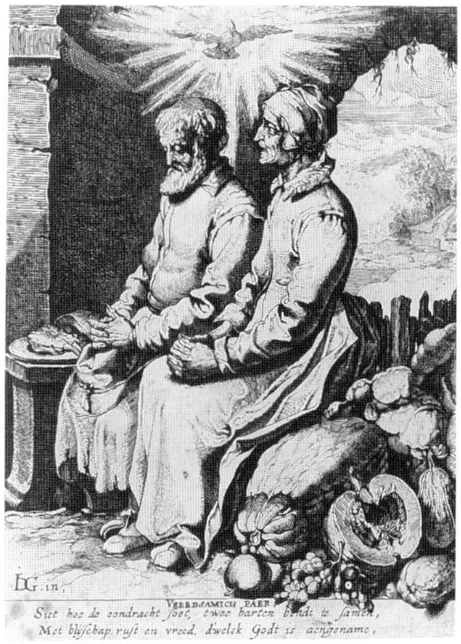

Figure 144. Jacques de Gheyn III, *Old Couple Saying Grace* (engraving). Amsterdam, Rijksprentenkabinet. Photo: Rijksmuseum-Stichting.

as do her gnarled hands, clutched tightly in prayer. Her husband sits beside her with his head lowered, his fur-lined cap covering hands presumably folded in prayer. Their serenity and even their decrepitude recall that of an aged couple who pray together before a meal in an earlier print by Jacques de Gheyn II (Fig. 144).[17] According to the inscription below, "Vreedsamich paer" (Peaceful Couple), their hearts are bound in sweet unity that pleases God. The abundant display of comestibles on the ground beside them might be construed as a sign of God's blessing, a bountiful reward for their pious and humble life-style. In contrast, the couple in Van Dyck's painting prays beside a very modest meal, a soup or stew in a chipped bowl that both of them will share.

This painting illustrates piety and simplicity, and coupled with these virtues are unequivocal references to vanity. The chipped soup bowl on the table certainly conveys this idea as broken pots were traditional symbols of transitoriness.[18] More importantly, the couple themselves represent this concept as well; as we have seen, old age was frequently equated with it in literature and in prints. Van Dyck depicts the spiritual enlightenment of these *vanitas* types, if only through their pious and humble mien. Their devoutness along with their old age – a harbinger of death – caution the viewer to practice godliness in view of life's brevity. The intrinsically admonitory content of such paintings is undoubtedly an outgrowth of their *vanitas* associations.

The poignancy of Van Dyck's painting belies the fact that it shares features with many images of the elderly. Paintings of this subject partake of time-honored pictorial traditions and, as a result, are highly conventional, more so perhaps than most other themes of domestic virtue. For example, the clothing of the old man, with his heavy garments and fur-lined hat, corresponds to that worn by old men who personify winter in print series of the late sixteenth and early seventeenth centuries that link the ages of man to the four seasons.[19] The traditional link between old age and winter is replete with references to mortality, for during the winter many living things lie dormant or have already died. A print by Johannes Sadeler dated 1580 (Fig. 145) expresses these associations along with other ones with ramifications for seventeenth-century paintings like Van Dyck's. Activities traditionally associated with winter take place within an extensive landscape, including ice-skating and hog slaughtering. In the foreground, an old man wearing thick, fur-lined clothing sits by a fire on a little hill surrounded by provisions presumably meant to tide him over during the winter months – note his gesture of prayer and the beam of light extending from heaven to the simple meal on the table beside him. According to the accompanying inscription, this man, a personification of winter, is thankful for his food and drink since they are his just recompense for having worked hard his entire life in preparation for his last years. The man's heavy fur garments, like those pictured in seventeenth-century Dutch genre paintings, therefore function as an attribute of his age, a reference to his advanced years and frail health.

A painting of December by Joachim von Sandrart from a series of the months of the year – painted during this German artist's eight-year residence in Amsterdam – sheds further light on this idea (Fig. 146).[20] Sandrart depicts an elderly woman wearing fur-lined clothing who shields a brightly burning candle in a darkened interior. This latter motif, no doubt influenced by the work of his teacher Gerard van Honthorst, subtly illuminates her wizened features, the hourglass, and especially the skull on the table as the candlelight eerily dances on the smooth areas of bone.[21] In honor of this painting (and the others in the series), Joost van den Vondel wrote a poem, which also elucidates the links between winter, old age (in this case, widowhood), vanity, and death:

> How the Winter-month grieves, like a widow in mourning.
> Her candle goes out and her hourglass is nearly empty.
> The skull predicts Death, who closes the swing-gate of life.
> The bare winter resembles a widow close to death.
> Still roasting chestnuts: her time is running out.
> What is a widow? A shadow with one foot in the grave.[22]

A theme conveying associations analogous to that of elderly people saying grace depicts women who pray for their meal alone. Many of the females in

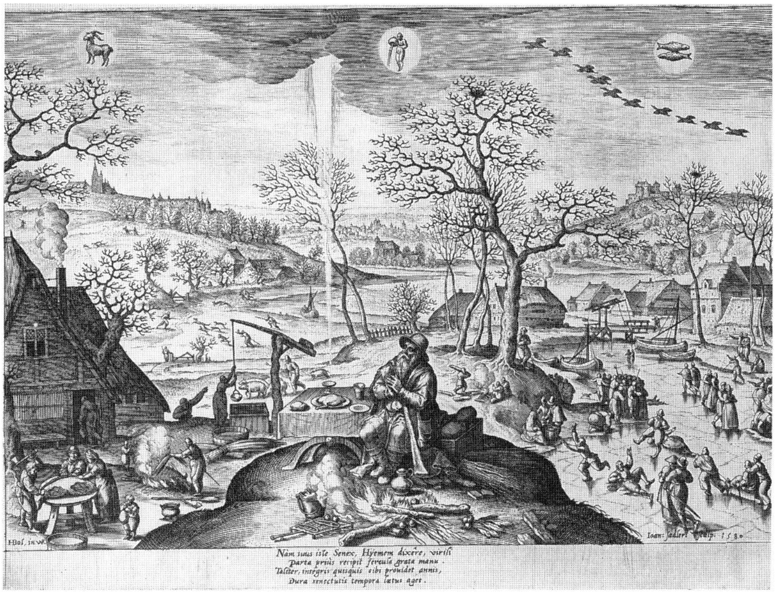

Figure 145. Johannes Sadeler after Hans Bol, *Winter*, 1580 (engraving). Amsterdam, Rijksprentenkabinet. Photo: Rijksmuseum-Stichting.

paintings of this theme would have likely been recognized as widows. However, owing to the propensity among Dutch artists to image these women as types, we cannot always be certain. Yet it is worth noting that a large percentage of women did marry at this time, and more importantly, the behavior expected of a spinster would not have been any different than that expected of an elderly widow. Therefore, whether widows or not, the females in these paintings are unmistakable paradigms of virtue.

A painting by Gerard Dou shows an old woman – wearing a garment lined with fur – in a ramshackle interior, praying humbly before her simple meal (Fig. 147).[23] Her pious demeanor would have met with the approval of Cats and a legion of other authors, some of whom wrote books addressed specifically to widows.[24] In a patriarchal society, it is only logical that rules governing women's behavior would extend to even the very last stages of their lives. According to the ideal ethical standards of the day, older women whose husbands had died were to live soberly and circumspectly; remarriage was not an option.[25] They were to remain at home, leading a pious, secluded life in honor of God and out of respect for their deceased husbands:[26]

> See what a poor human being does in misery and illness,
> He leaves everything in his room to youth;
> To be quiet, lonely, sad, and, with sweet desire

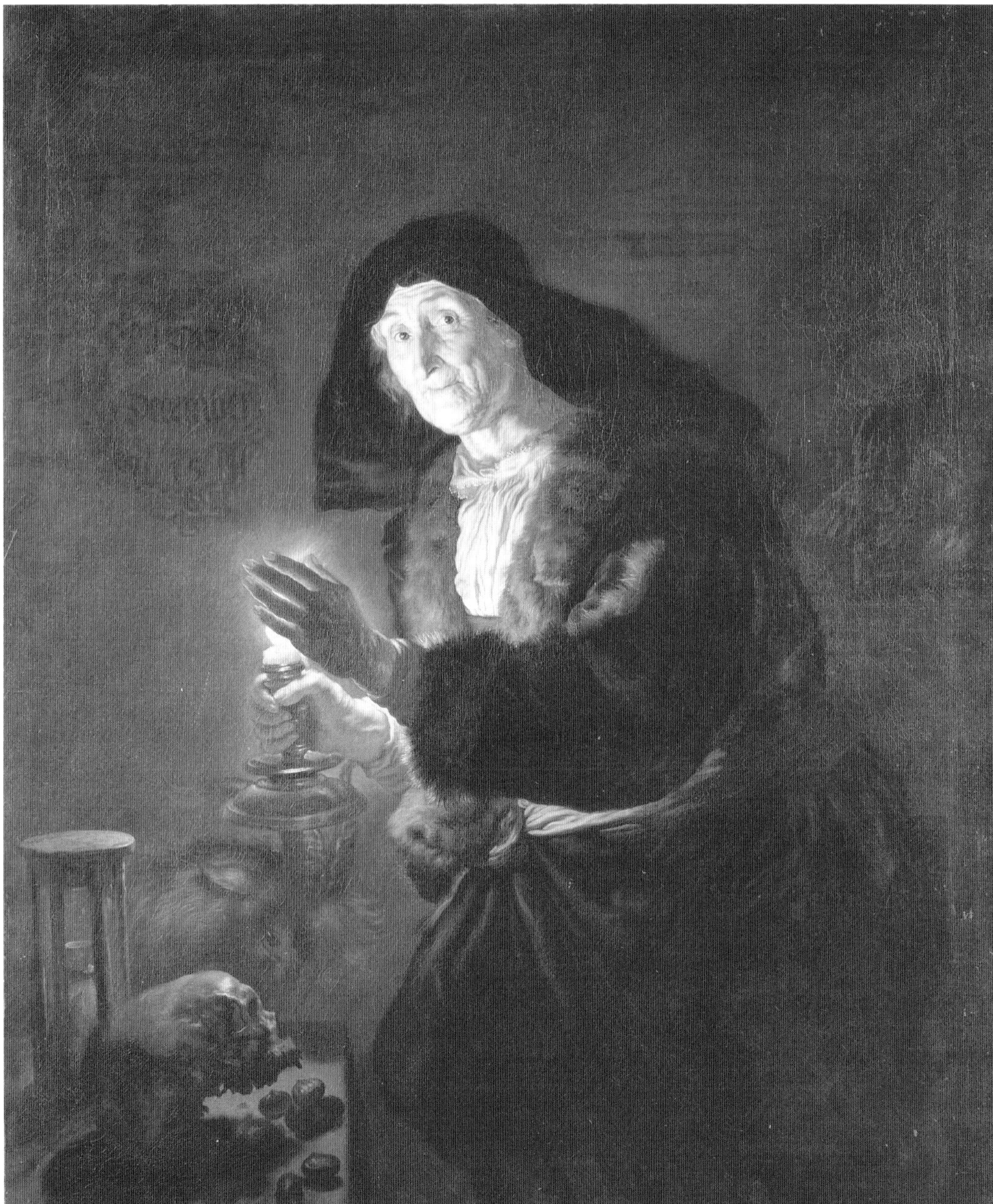

Figure 146. Joachim von Sandrart, *December* (from the series *The Twelve Months of the Year*), 1643 (oil on canvas, 146 × 122 cm). Schleissheim, Bayeriche Staatsgemäldesammlungen, Schloss Schleissheim. Photo: Bayerische Staatsgemäldesammlungen.

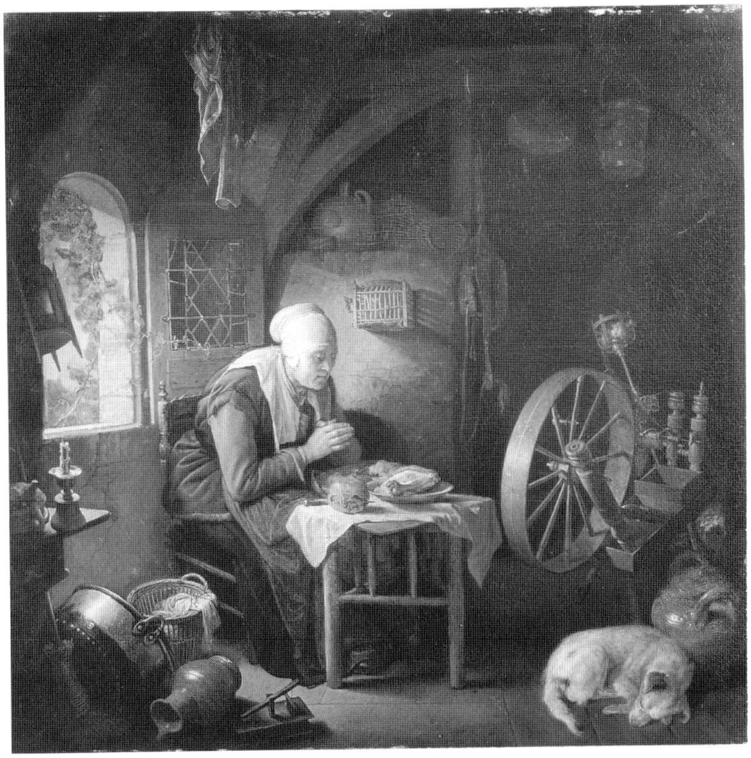

Figure 147. Gerard Dou, *Old Woman Saying Grace* (oil on panel, 27.7 × 28.3 cm). Munich, Alte Pinakothek. Photo: Bayerische Staatsgemäldesammlungen.

> Shedding many tears for the Lord that continuously roll down the cheeks, that
> is a pure face,
> That suits you best and is proper for your state:
> Much consolation in distress, much praying and sharing with generosity,
> Those are the best bridal jewels for your neck;
> Not what beautifies the body, but what strengthens the soul,
> Is appropriate for the unmarried.[27]

Dou renders the old woman in his painting with scarcely any individuality; she is objectified as a topos, her individuality effaced in the interests of depicting an idea or, more accurately, conduct appropriate for old women and widows. The frequent appearance of figures with wizened physiognomies, heavy garments, and pious demeanors in other paintings of the elderly confirms this. Furthermore, Dou has surrounded the woman with motifs, placed deliberately at conspicuous points in the composition to enable the viewer to savor their detailed naturalism and to contemplate their significance as motifs that connote virtue as well as the concept so frequently associated with the elderly: *vanitas*. For instance, the spinning wheel at the right and the sewing basket on the floor to the woman's left clearly refer to domestic virtue. The extinguished candle on the table near the window is a traditional symbol of transitoriness. The cleanly scoured metal pot in the lower left foreground likely connotes the very same concept.[28] Glittering metal objects, with their evanescent sheen, were long associated with vanity.[29] In a group portrait by Herman and Cornelis Saftleven of the second wife and family of Godard van Reede van Nederhorst, Godard's first wife, who died in 1632, lies on a bier to the right (Fig. 148).[30] An extinguished candle and several metal implements, including a gleaming pot, lie on the ground in front of the bier. In this context, they function as very poignant signifiers of *vanitas*.

The gleaming metal pot retains its association with transience in several paintings representing old women scouring pots. Godfried Schalcken's picture of an elderly woman performing this task in a nichelike enclosure is perhaps the best known portrayal of this theme (Fig. 149). As we have seen, the enclosure's artificial structure calls attention to the artist's cunning illusion of reality as it compels us to contemplate and scrutinize the objects meticulously rendered in and around it.[31] Several glistening metal implements – presumably they have already been cleaned – lie on the ledge. In addition, there is a broken earthenware vessel, a forceful symbol of evanescence, skillfully rendered in such ruinous condition that it is impossible to determine its original shape or function.[32]

Our attention to individual motifs in this painting should not blind us to the fact its very style is laden with meaning. The leathery hide of the old woman herself furnishes just as much information about transience as the motifs surrounding the enclosure; even her spectacles – a pince-nez – convey this association. In this regard, it is instructive to examine a print of Saturn by Adriaen Collaert after Maarten de Vos, from a series depicting the ages of man under the auspices of the planetary gods (Fig. 150).[33] In this print, an aged man looks at the personification of Conscientia, who points toward Saturn, seated in the sky. Various motifs symbolizing vanity lie strewn on the ground around the old man, among them, a urine flask, a smoky fire, and an hourglass with a pince-nez lying on its top.[34] The association of spectacles with transitoriness relates to the drastic weakening of eyesight in old age, another harbinger of death. In the painting, Schalcken has imbued the old woman, her task, and the objects that surround her with *vanitas* symbolism. The absence of narrative and the absolutely painstaking display of objects in the nichelike enclosure lend credence to Maclaren's tentative suggestion that "the picture may possibly be intended as an allegory of the transience of life."[35] It may be possible to go one step further and regard the elderly woman as a veritable personification of this concept.

The motifs of the cleanly scoured pot and the extinguished candle frequently appear in representations of the theme of old women saying grace,

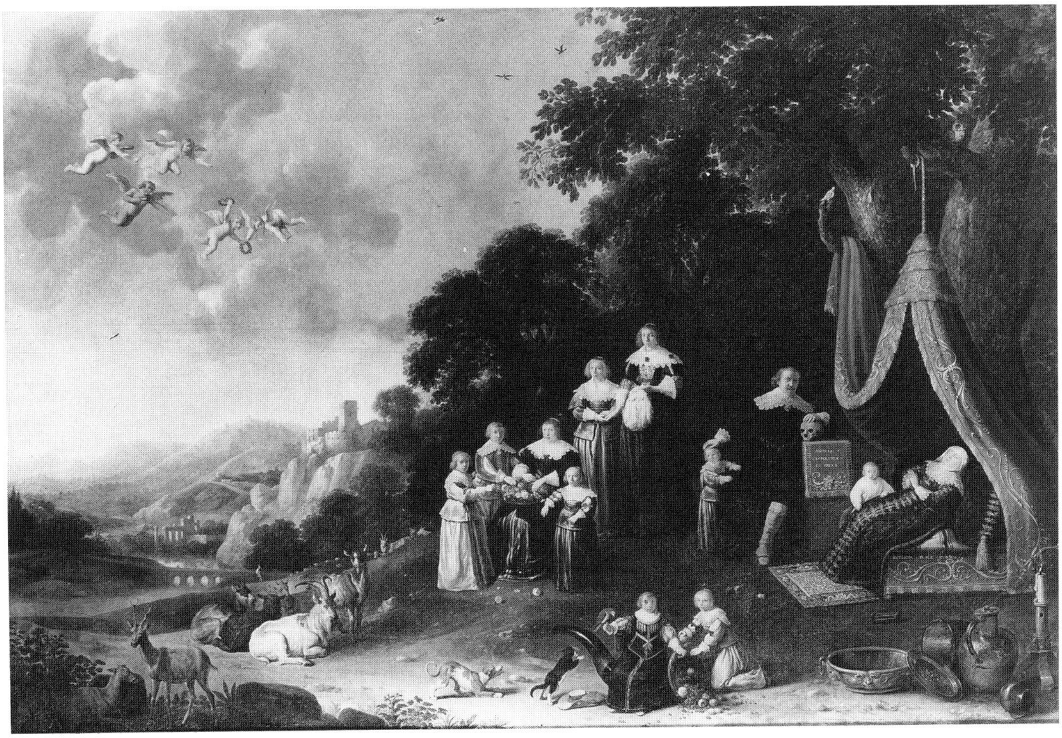

Figure 148. Herman and Cornelis Saftleven, *Portrait of the Family of Godard van Reede van Nederhorst*, 1634 (oil on canvas, 210 × 143 cm). Zuilen Stichting Slot Zuylen. Photo: copyright Stichting Iconographisch Bureau, The Hague.

among them Dou's painting previously discussed and Quiringh van Brekelenkam's *Grace before the Meal* (Fig. 151). These recurring motifs pay testimony to the highly conventional nature of this imagery as do the pious, senescent women wearing heavy clothing. As we have repeatedly seen, the very conventionality of such paintings (and other images of domestic virtue) reflects the expectations of contemporary viewers who desired to see a limited number of subjects rendered in a specific manner.[36] This bespeaks an intrinsic level of significance within the paintings themselves. The focus on the concept of vanity and on virtues like piety, humility, and simplicity is therefore tied inextricably to the mimetic qualities of these paintings. The very intensity of the facial expressions of the old women, carefully delineated in all of their shriveled detail, vividly conveys these associations. Their devout physiognomies, revealing the earnestness of their supplications, find striking parallels in the features of a praying old woman in a print by Cornelis Bloemaert (Fig. 152), sententiously inscribed "Piety Is the Weapon of the Elderly."[37]

It cannot be sufficiently emphasized that pictorial style is just as important an agent in communicating meaning in these paintings as the symbolic props

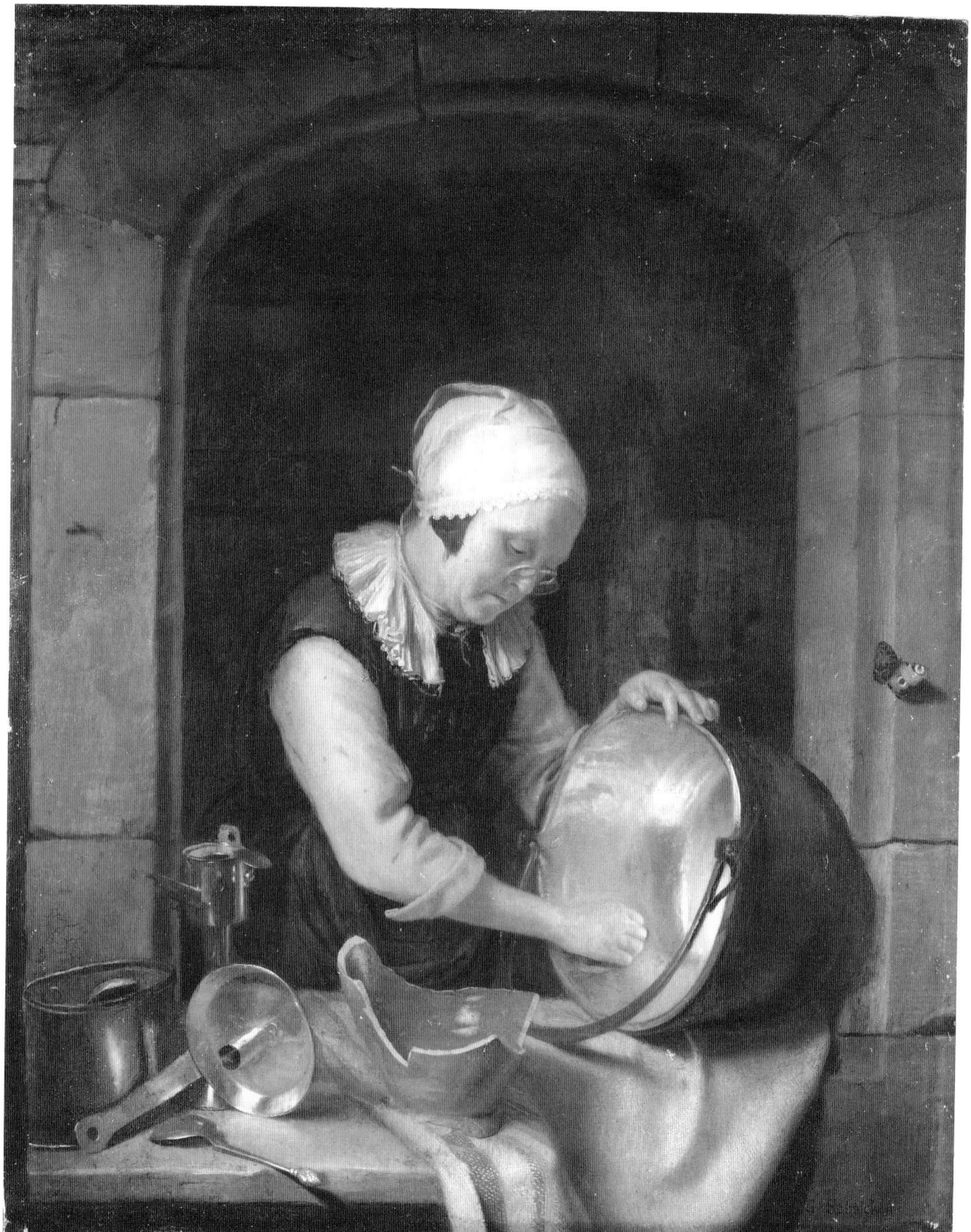

Figure 149. Godfried Schalcken, *An Old Woman at a Window, Scouring a Pot* (oil on panel, 28.5 × 22.8 cm). London, The National Gallery. Reproduced by courtesy of the Trustees, The National Gallery, London.

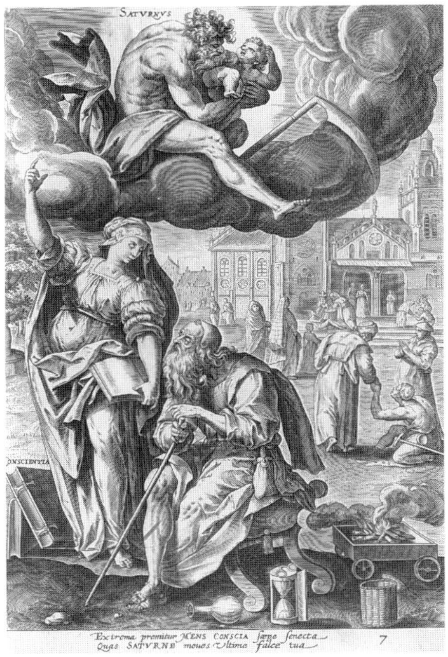

Figure 150. Adriaen Collaert after Maarten de Vos, *Saturn–Old Age* (engraving from the series *The Seven Planets and Ages of Man*), 1581. Amsterdam, Rijksprentenkabinet. Photo: Rijksmuseum-Stichting.

that continually accompany the old women. Contemporaries must have derived considerable pleasure from the skill with which artists rendered the withered, gaunt flesh and hoary heads of these elderly types.[38] *Tronies* (popularized by Rembrandt and his "school") of old women, with their heightened concentration on a single figure, offered particularly rich opportunities for close scrutiny.[39] The artists who made these *tronies* reveled in the display of wizened skin and textures of fur and heavy clothing and also in the expression of intense spiritual ardor (see, e.g., Figs. 153, 154).[40] The use of physiognomy as a vehicle to explore emotional states not only contributed to the popularity of *tronies*, but more significantly, signaled a growing fascination among contemporaries for the rendering in art of man's inner passions.[41] These works implicated viewers and articulated – through their meticulously wrought surfaces – associations centering on piety and vanity, the wrinkled skin and devout expressions instructing us more profoundly about these concepts than complicated symbolic programs.

The fervent religiosity exhibited in these *tronies* is equalled by that displayed in genre paintings of the elderly, such as Nicolaes Maes's *Old Woman Saying Grace* (Fig. 155). The woman's earnest expression in this painting, recalls the Apostle Paul's oft-quoted remark that a proper widow trusts in God, engaging in prayer and supplication night and day.[42] The woman's Lenten-like repast of fish, soup, bread, and cheese would have revealed as much for contemporary viewers about her upright character as her prayerful

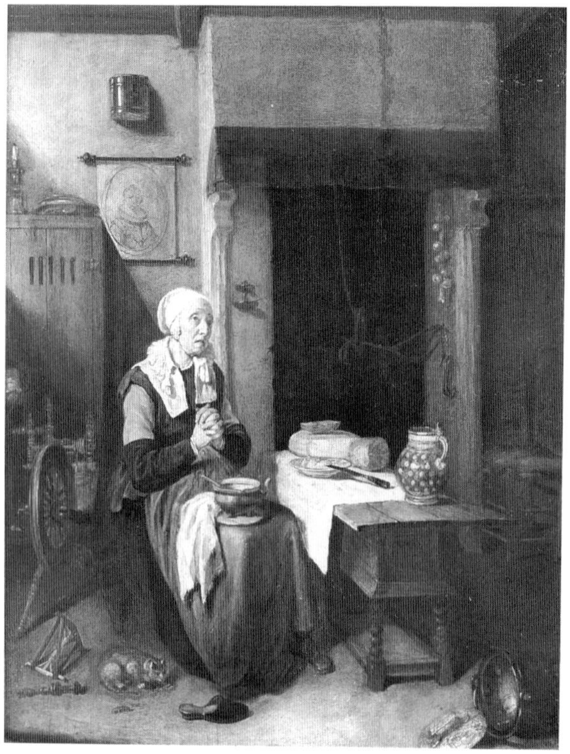

Figure 151. Quiringh van Brekelenkam, *Grace before the Meal* (oil on panel, 54.5 × 41 cm). Paris, Musée du Louvre. Photo: Réunion des musées nationaux, Paris.

gesture does. Books and tracts addressed specifically to widows exhort them to lead wholesome, simple lives, exercising moderation in all things, including the consumption of food. For example, in Pieter Ianszoon Twisck's *Troostbrief der weduwen* (Consolation Letter of Widows, 1630), the published version of an actual letter that the Mennonite Twisck wrote to his sister-in-law on the occasion of her husband's death in 1626, he states:

> The greatest honor and praise for widows is moderation in all her doings: moderation not only in food, in the care of her body, in her clothing, demeanor, and behavior but also with regard to her family, when she is in the presence of other people, in front of authorities and her familiar friends.[43]

The significance of the woman's meager meal is clarified by comparing it with one depicted in a print by Claes Jansz. Visscher after Pieter Feddes (Fig. 156). Here an elderly couple prays before their equally modest supper.[44] The inscription "records" their prayer; they ask God to "feed"

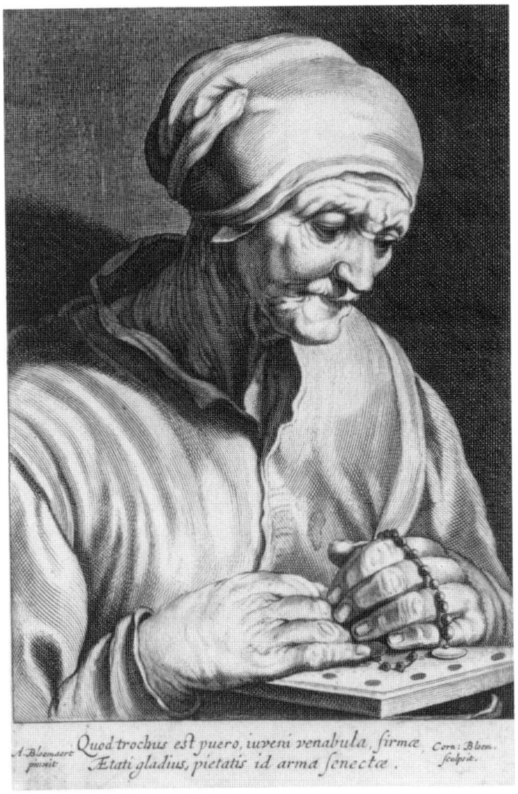

Figure 152. Cornelis Bloemaert after Abraham Bloemaert, *Old Woman Praying* (engraving). Amsterdam, Rijksprentenkabinet. Photo: Rijksmuseum-Stichting.

their souls, a request that the woman in Maes's painting could just as easily be making. This woman's ardent spirituality must be perceived in light of her advanced age and the objects on the ledge referring to *vanitas.*[45] Through motifs like the hourglass and Bible as well as the implicating naturalism of the painted surface, this picture cautions us to live humbly and piously in view of life's brevity.

The woman in Maes's painting and those depicted in some works already discussed are probably widows. Their piety and simplicity clearly mirror the image of the ideal widow set forth in contemporary literature. These paintings, like those representing younger females, present a paradigmatic image of womanhood as they display the virtues that male moralists believed most befitting women in this particular stage of their lives. In fact, Cats describes the characteristics of the exemplary widow in terms reminiscent of these paintings:

> A heart that is uplifted by reading in God's book,
> An eye that enjoys being wet with tears,
> A quiet soul that is ashamed of the world.[46]

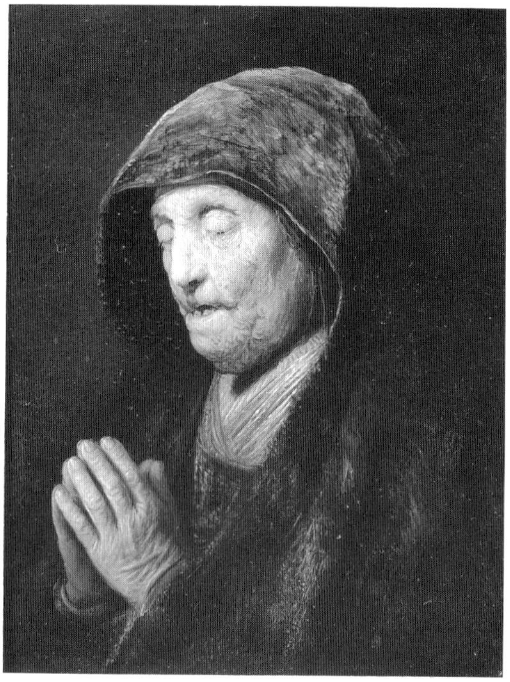

Figure 153. Rembrandt van Rijn, *Old Woman Praying* (oil on copper, 15.5 × 12.2 cm). Salzburg, Landessammlungen-Residenzgalerie. Photo: Residenzgalerie.

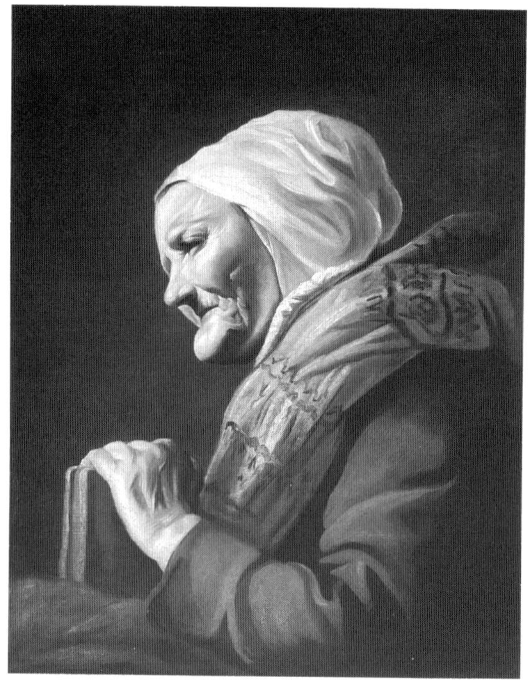

Figure 154. Jacob van Campen, *Old Woman with a Book* (oil on canvas, 70 × 56 cm). Private collection.

The virtues demanded of the elderly, among them simplicity and moderation, are also on display in paintings with a less demonstrative religious content. In a work by Dou, an old woman wearing a fur-lined cape eats from a chipped bowl in spartan surroundings that include a large spinning wheel (Fig. 157).[47] The modest interior and the utter simplicity of the woman's meal emphasize the old woman's godly lifestyle in the winter of her life. I deliberately use the metaphor "winter of her life" because of the woman's age and fur-lined cape, both compelling symbols of life's brevity. On the table beside her, a gleaming metal pot lies directly on top of a large tome, undoubtedly a Bible. As we have seen, pots are symbols of transience; therefore, its appearance here on top of a Bible – the source of much of the *vanitas* imagery known to seventeenth-century Dutch culture – is telling.[48]

Many paintings also depict virtuous widows engaged in domestic tasks. An emblematic print from the chapter "Weduwe" in Cats's *Houwelyck* is instructive in this respect since it affords insights into the type of associations that contemporaries might have attached to such paintings. The print in

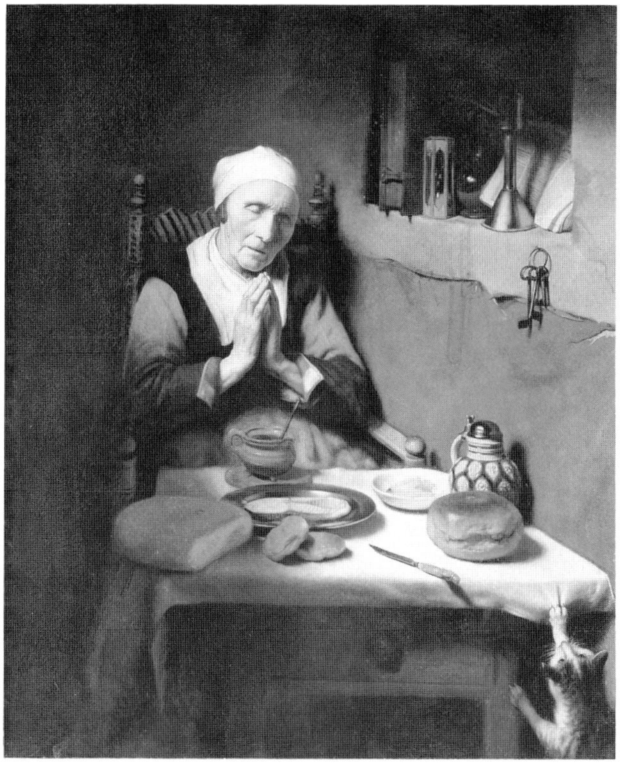

Figure 155. Nicolaes Maes, *Old Woman Saying Grace ("The Prayer Without End")* (oil on canvas, 134 × 113 cm). Amsterdam, Rijksmuseum. Photo: Rijksmuseum-Stichting.

question depicts an old woman wearing a cap with flaps and a prominent point – an accoutrement signifying her widowed state – who sews in a large interior, her basket and scissors beside her (Fig. 158).[49] In the foreground, a skeletal hand places a freshly cut tulip into a glass vase filled with water. According to Cats this tulip is the widow "severed" from her husband:

> Imagine a little flower, which cut from the stem
> With a sharp knife, has suffered its first death,
> Which now, after being picked, is put in a narrow vase, in water;
> There stands the tender plant, confined,
> There it withers, covered with tears,
> There it mourns, there it droops,
> Its consolation, even life, is a sorrowful fluid....
> See there, oh pious people, see there a true symbol
> For those whose marriage has ended and who sleep without a guardian,

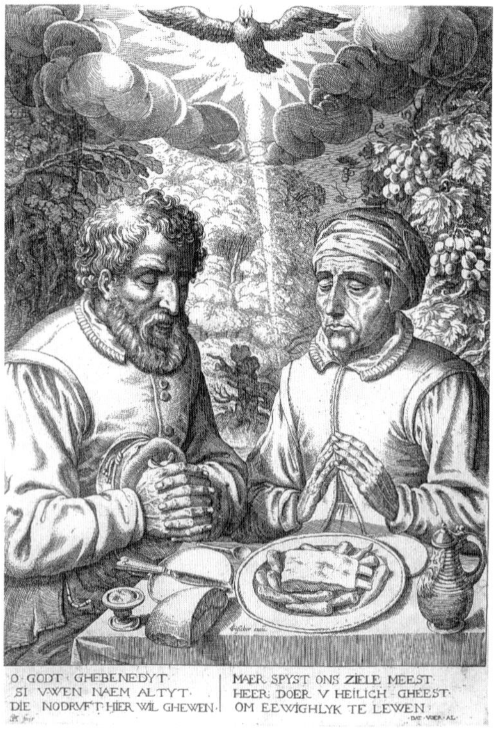

Figure 156. Claes Jansz. Visscher after Pieter Feddes, *Grace before the Meal* (engraving). Amsterdam, Rijksprentenkabinet. Photo: Rijksmuseum-Stichting.

For those who have been suddenly separated from their husband,
Just like one picks a pretty flower from a stem.[50]

There follows a long-winded discussion of appropriate behavior for women who find themselves in "dit beroup" (this calling). Ideally, they should lead secluded lives, shunning contemptible persons and all forms of profligate behavior. They should exercise caution when attending gatherings where men will be present and even when going to the market. In light of Cats's recommendations, it is easy to comprehend the meaning of the motif of the old woman sewing in the emblematic print. She sits quietly, performing a domestic chore theoretically demanded of all women. Yet her task was considered particularly suitable and praiseworthy for a woman who had been widowed: "An honorably protected widow must ease her burden by keeping herself busy."[51] In his book written for widows (a work reprinted in the seventeenth century), Erasmus also expresses this conviction. In his laudatory description of Judith, the famous widow from the Apocrypha, Erasmus informs us that she did not attend questionable social gatherings but stayed in a "secret room" with her servants. Here Judith prayed, read the Bible, or occupied herself "with some honorable handicraft."[52]

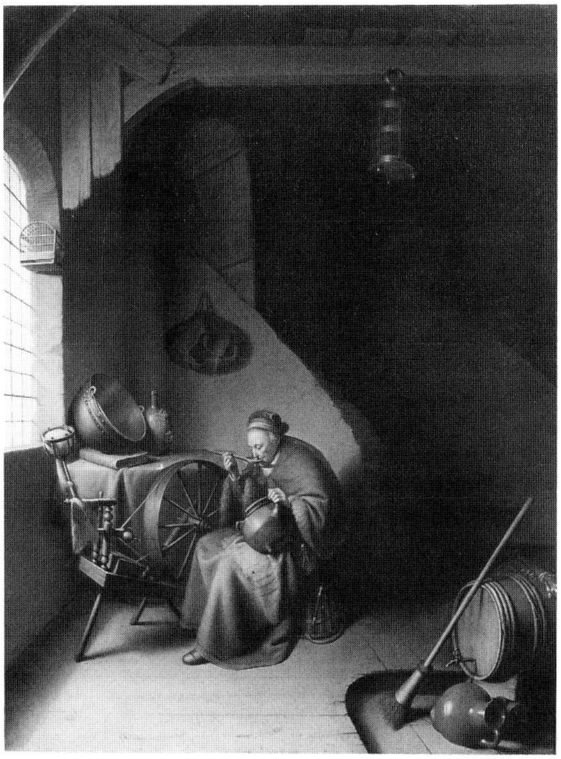

Figure 157. Gerard Dou, *Old Woman Eating* (oil on panel, 51.5 × 41 cm). Private collection. Photo: courtesy Christie's, London.

Paintings of old women performing domestic tasks are, in some respects, reminiscent of the illustration of the diligent widow in *Houwelyck.* An elderly woman with a pince-nez makes lace in a painting by Maes (Fig. 159). In another work by the artist, a senescent type is busy spinning in a darkened interior (Fig 160). In both paintings, Maes employs warm chiaroscuro and gentle spotlighting to illuminate the figures. Judging from its use here and in several other paintings examined in this book, this seems to have been a favorite pictorial device among artists who painted domestic scenes (see, e.g., Figs. 20, 79). In a peculiarly evocative manner, the light seems to adopt a preternatural dimension, as it gently illuminates the wrinkled facial features of these old women absorbed in their tasks, establishing a mood of solemnity and tranquility while transforming them into icons of industry and wholesome living.

The same can be said of another work by Maes of an aged woman peeling apples, a painting belonging to the theme of old women preparing food (Fig. 161). This woman is softly lit by warm sunlight streaming in through a

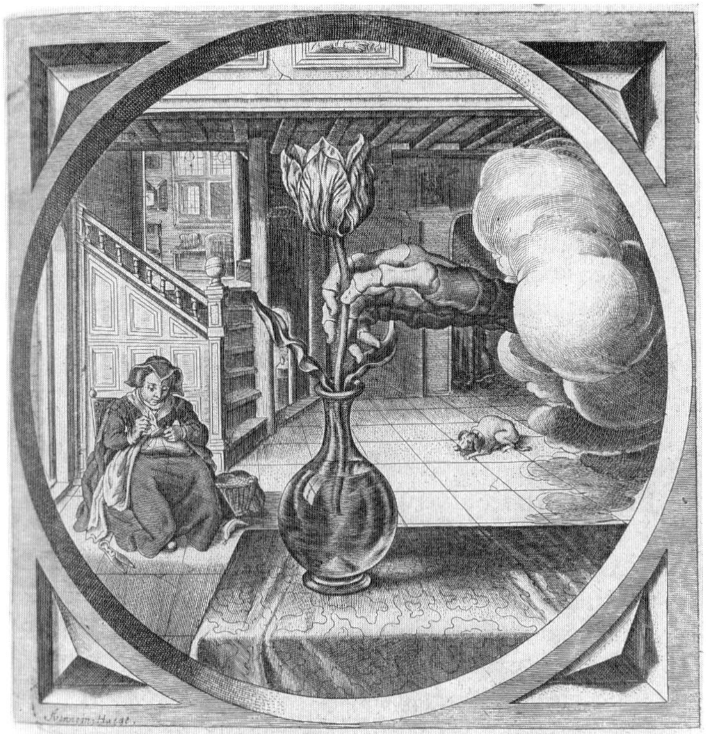

Figure 158. Illustration from Jacob Cats, *Houwelyck. Dat is de gansche gelegentheyt des echten staets*, Middelburg 1625. Collection of the author. Photo: D. Broda, Syracuse.

window, striking her open Bible and her veil, the latter reverberating with light in a manner recalling halos on female saints. The objects that surround her in the subtle penumbra enveloping the room include the conventional motif of the spinning wheel and others that, in this context, can only refer to domestic virtue in general and to her virtue as a widow in particular.[53]

An old woman is also depicted peeling apples in a modest interior in an early painting by Dou (Fig. 162). Once again, we see an elderly female wearing a fur-lined garment, which in this case has been turned up in her lap to hold the apples.[54] The artist has stocked the room with objects that appear and reappear like formulae in images of the elderly: a chipped bowl, a gleaming metal cauldron, and a lace-making cushion. The only unusual feature of this otherwise conventional image is the tiny painting of Christ and the Samaritan woman on the wall in the background. Their encounter is recorded in the fourth chapter of the Gospel of John where Christ reproves her for having had five husbands (verse 18). The questionable life-style of

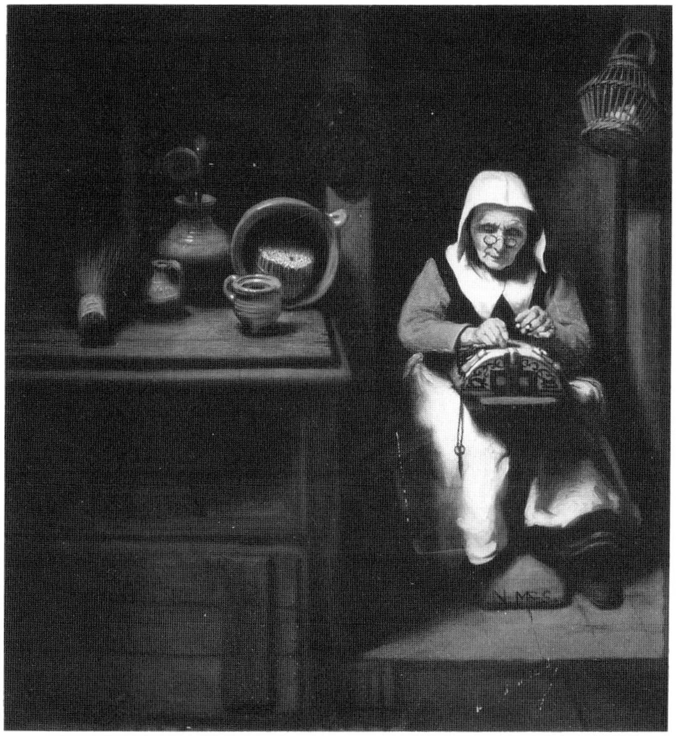

Figure 159. Nicolaes Maes, *Old Woman Making Lace.* Present location unknown. Photo: courtesy Christie's, London.

the frequently married Samaritan woman could not be in more marked contrast to the humble widow peeling fruit, living a life of pious solitude in the absence of her departed spouse.[55]

Curiously, the domestic task that elderly women most frequently perform in art is the last stage in the spinning process, when spun thread is wound from the bobbin of the spinning wheel onto a cross-reel (see, e.g., Figs. 163, 164).[56] In these pictures, elderly women often hold or actually work their bobbins and cross-reels in nichelike enclosures, pictorial devices that enable the viewer to savor the artist's mimetic skills while contemplating the meticulously rendered objects. The popularity of this conventional theme in the seventeenth century is difficult to explain.[57] Fortunately, the structure and purpose of the cross-reel itself enables us to make an educated guess about the significance for contemporary beholders of the motif of winding thread and, more importantly, why only old women perform it.

The cross-reel winds spun thread into a skein, that is, a length of thread wound in an elongated coil.[58] This is accomplished (as illustrated in some of

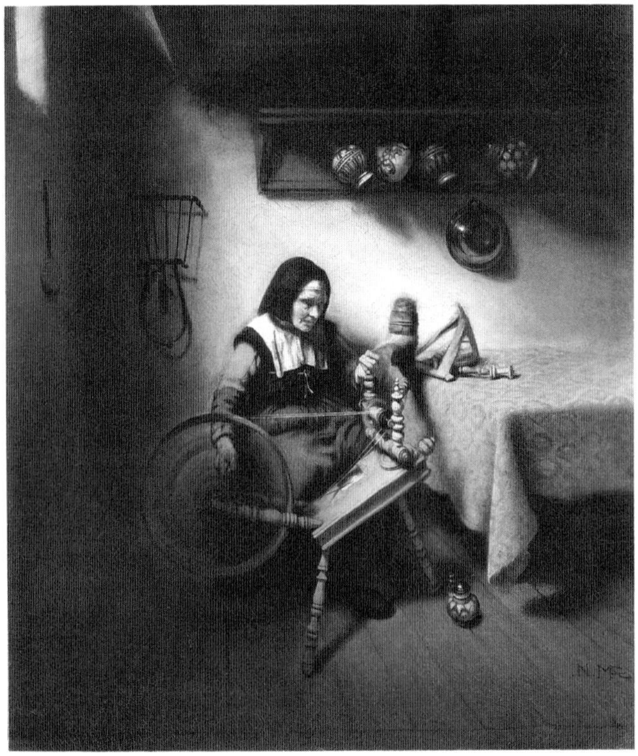

Figure 160. Nicolaes Maes, *Old Woman Spinning* (oil on canvas, 63 × 55 cm). Amsterdam, Rijksmuseum. Photo: Rijksmuseum-Stichting.

the paintings) by holding the center bar of the cross-reel with one hand while the other winds the thread from the bobbin, in succession, over the four ends of the two cross-pieces attached to it. The exact circumference of a skein would be four times the distance between the two cross-pieces. Therefore, the cross-reel did more than simply gather spun thread in an orderly fashion; it actually served as a measuring device.

In light of the cross-reel's function as a gauging implement, its presence in these paintings might allude to moderation or temperance, a virtue traditionally associated with measure.[59] If the cross-reels do convey this association in art, then it is not coincidental that only old women hold them. As we have seen, the elderly were often regarded as paradigms of virtues such as temperance because, in these final stages of life, "they acquire other blessings of the soul, such as wisdom, moderation, and other virtues befitting old people."[60] Widows themselves were admonished to exercise moderation in every aspect of their daily life, ranging from their manner of dress to eating habits.[61] The virtuous associations of the motif of elderly women winding

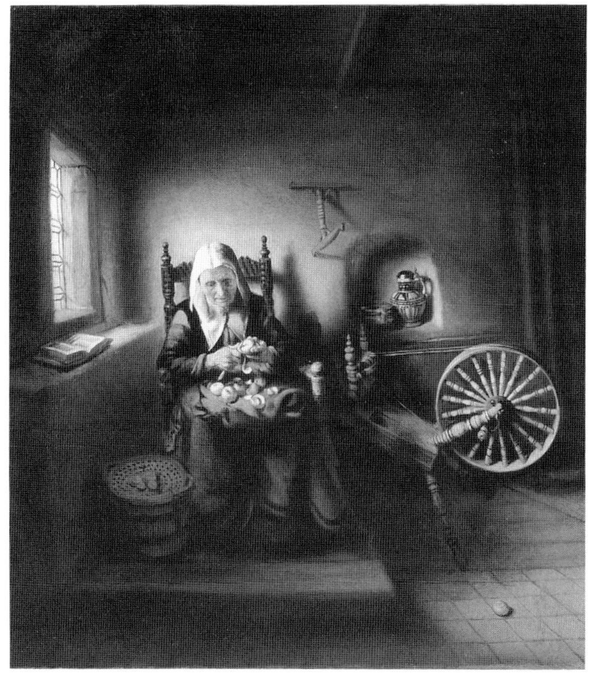

Figure 161 (right). Nicolaes Maes, *Old Woman Peeling Apples* (oil on canvas, 55 × 50 cm). Berlin, Gemäldegalerie, Staatliche Museen Preussischer Kulturbesitz. Photo: J. P. Anders, Berlin.

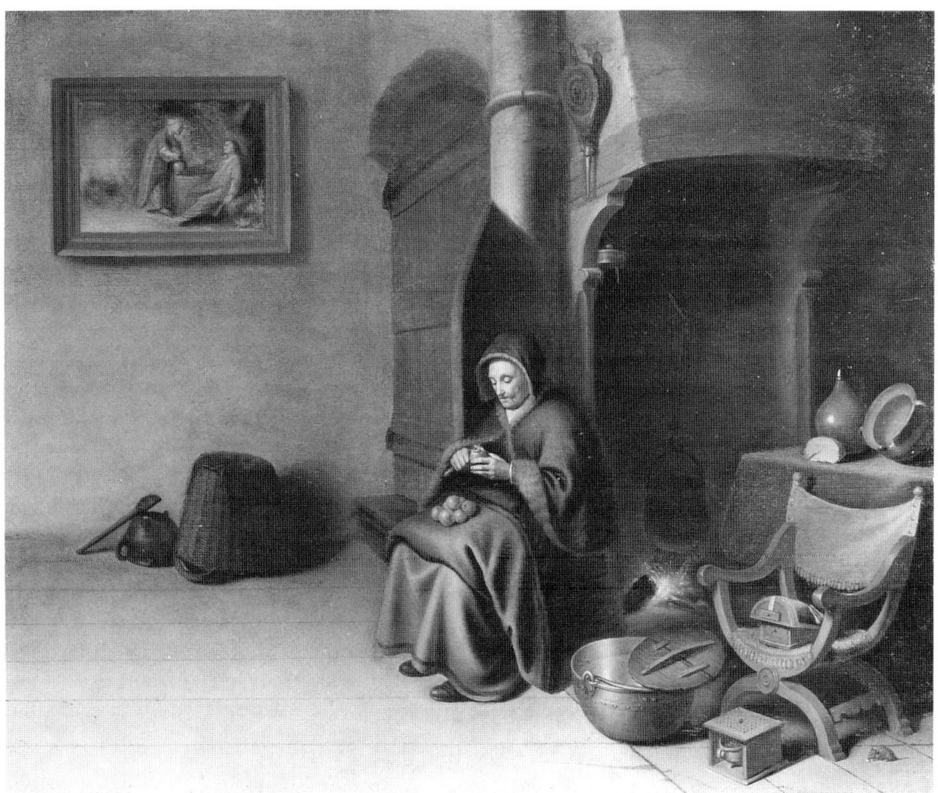

Figure 162. Gerard Dou, *Old Woman Peeling Apples* (oil on panel, 37 × 44 cm). Berlin, Gemäldegalerie, Staatliche Museen Preussischer Kulturbesitz. Photo: J. P. Anders, Berlin.

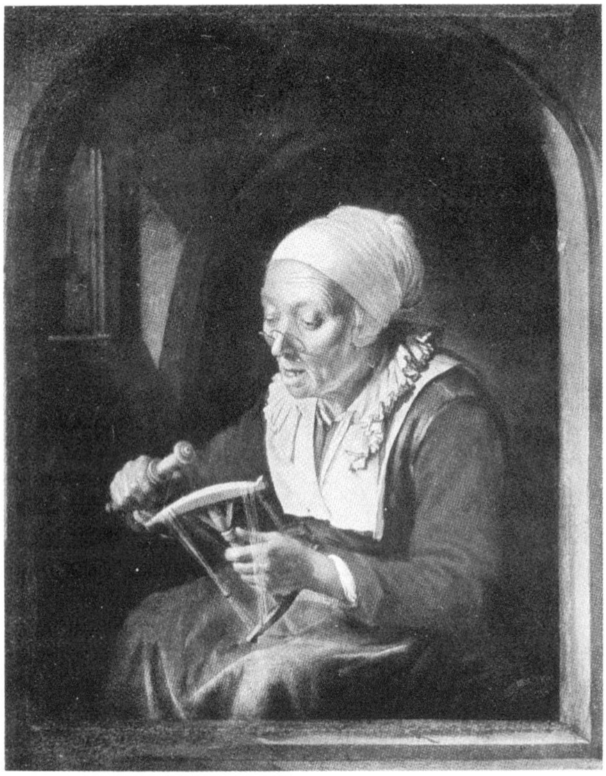

Figure 163. Gerard Dou, *Old Woman Winding Thread in a Niche* (oil on panel, 32 × 23 cm). St. Petersburg, Hermitage.

thread would explain the occasional presence of additional motifs in these paintings, like the large, clasped Bible on the table beside the woman in the picture by Quiringh van Brekelenkam (Fig. 165).

Dutch artists sometimes depicted elderly women, winding spun thread or spinning in an interior, in the company of their husbands. For example, in a painting by Abraham de Pape, a woman winds thread onto a cross-reel while her white-bearded husband warms his gnarled hands beside a small fire (Fig. 166).[62] This elderly man is the iconographic descendant of those in several late-sixteenth-century prints of winter who protect themselves from the season's chill by sitting beside a fire, the similarities even extending to the beards and the thick, fur-lined garments (see, e.g., Fig. 167).[63] These late sixteenth-century prints, as well as the motif in De Pape's painting, reveal the frail health of the aged: contemporary medical wisdom held that old age was characterized physiologically by an excessive loss of heat and moisture – hence the need to retire beside the fireplace.[64]

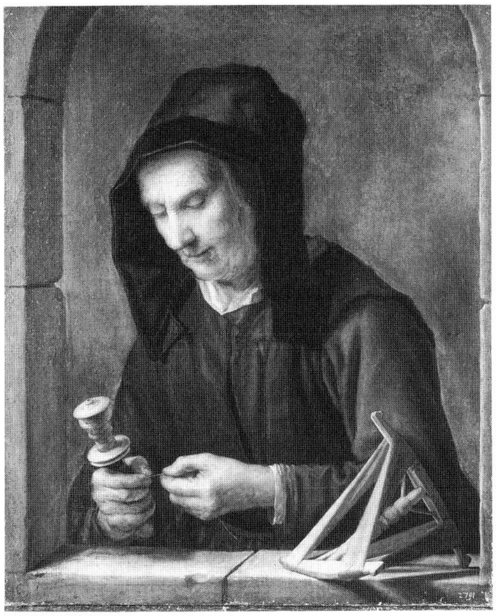

Figure 164. Pieter Verelst, *Old Woman Spooling Thread* (oil on canvas, 73 × 63 cm). Dresden, Gemäldegalerie. Photo: Sächsische Landesbibliothek Abteilung Deutsche Fotothek, Dresden.

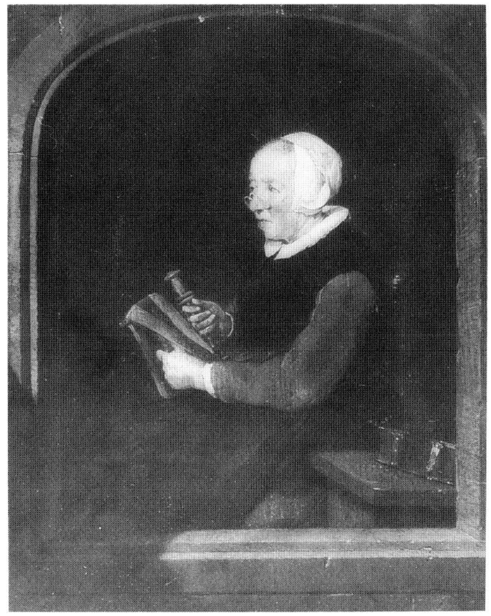

Figure 165. Quiringh van Brekelenkam, *Old Woman Winding Thread in a Niche* (oil on panel, 35 × 28 cm). Vaduz, Collection of the Reigning Prince of Liechtenstein.

It is worthwhile in this context to examine an emblem by Johan de Brune because its *pictura* recalls De Pape's painting in many respects (Fig. 168). Thus, like the painting, it too affords insights into contemporary perceptions of images of the elderly. In a rustic interior, an old woman wearing heavy clothing spins, her Bible in her lap, while her husband, likewise dressed, sits by the fire whittling.[65] The *subscriptio* explains the significance of this peaceful scene. The couple pleases God because they eke out a living by practicing crafts while waiting upon Him for their eternal reward, a description that could as easily be applied to De Pape's picture.[66] Seventeenth-century readers of De Brune would have easily recognized the suitability of the motif of the elderly couple to convey the meaning of the emblem.[67] In his *wt-legghinghe* (explanation) – a discourse appended to the *subscriptios* of this and every emblem in the book – De Brune observes that those who are pious are not deceived by the world's riches. They might have few possessions and might be held in contempt, but they perceive the transitoriness of all creation and that "their citizenship is in heaven, where they anticipate the Savior."[68] De Brune's emphasis on the virtues of simplicity and spiritual acumen explains the presence of elderly people in the *pictura:* on account of their failing health,

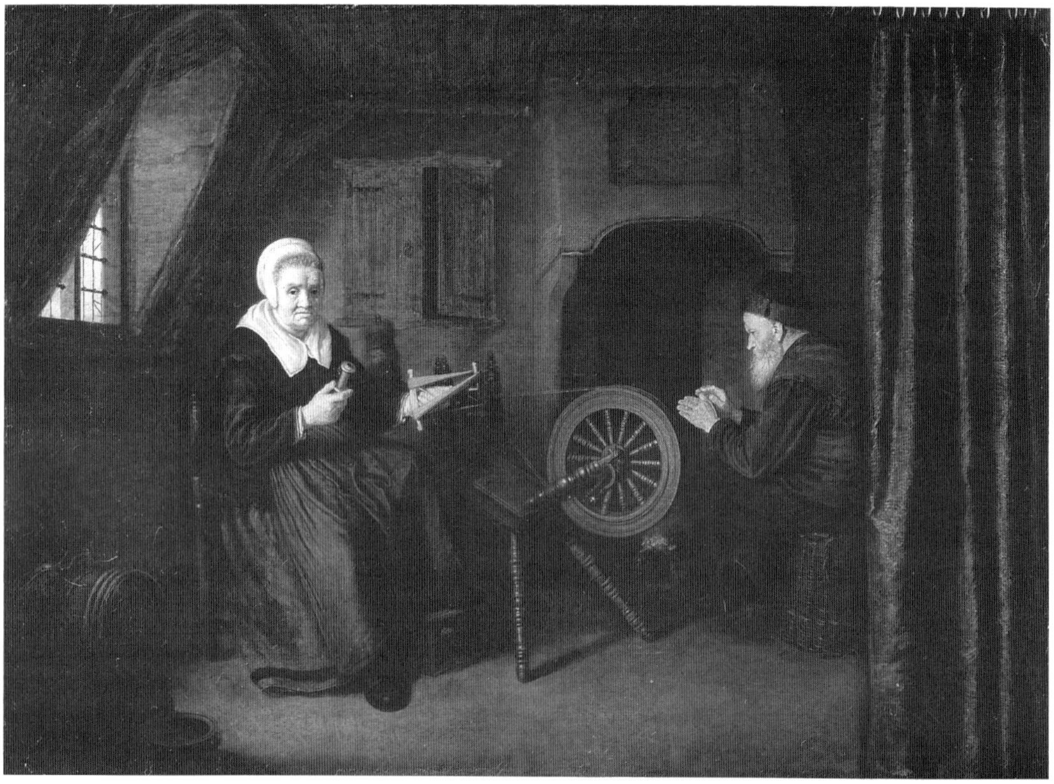

Figure 166. Abraham de Pape, *Elderly Couple in an Interior*, 1659? (oil on panel 40.7 × 56 cm). London, The National Gallery. Reproduced by courtesy of the Trustees, The National Gallery, London.

the aged were thought to possess precisely these virtues and insights.[69] Moreover, their facility in leading a simple, humble life-style was highly praised:

> That's why he [an old man] uses knowledge and reason/ and judgment/
> Wisdom and virtue, good morals and moderation/
> To appear before God/ properly and well-prepared in conduct and appearance.
> Although his limbs all grow stiff/ his heart is quick/
> He knows that no one will stay here/ which is why/
> He fixes his limits/ and pays close attention/
> To the path and Word of God/ towards the Gate of Life.[70]

Widows were called on to do far more than lead a simple, pious life. Contemporary moralists and theologians just as frequently charged them to be virtuous role models for younger women and girls. Naturally, this involved instructing them in domestic matters, since widows had extensive experience in this domain:

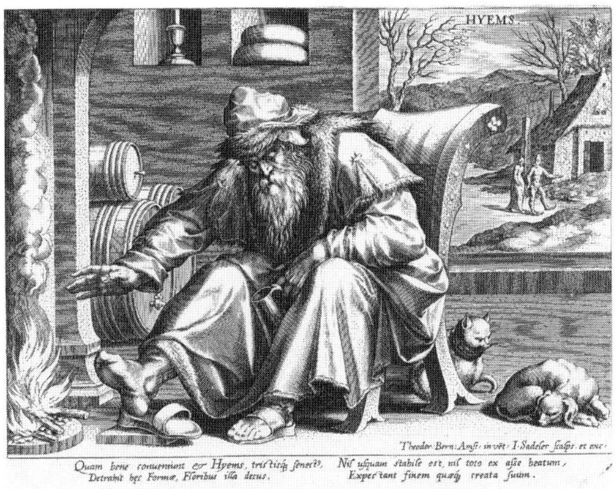

Figure 167. Johannes Sadeler after Dirck Barendsz, *Winter* (engraving). Amsterdam, Rijksprentenkabinet. Photo: Rijksmuseum-Stichting.

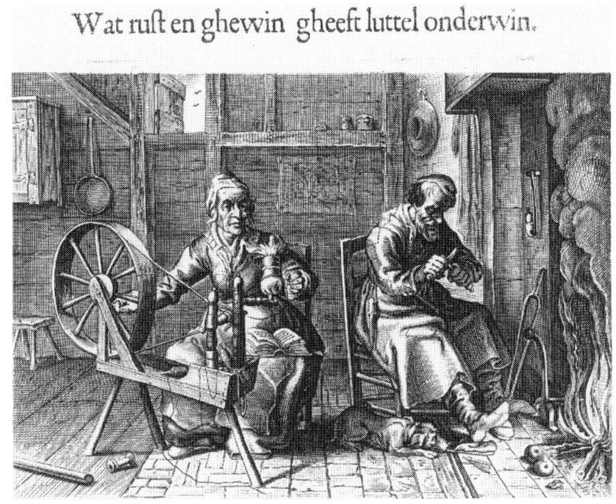

Figure 168. Emblem from Johan de Brune, *Emblemata of zinne-werck*, Amsterdam 1624. Amsterdam, Universiteits-Bibliotheek Amsterdam. Photo: courtesy Universiteits-Bibliotheek Amsterdam.

> The authority and power over maidens and young married women belongs to Widows. For it is the responsibility of Widows to teach those who are about to get married/ and those who have just been married/ how to behave with their Husbands/ their children and their Servants/ with their Friends and Relatives. It is the responsibility of the same Widows/ to discipline the Maidens; to teach them how to behave properly/ how to protect their name and reputation.[71]

Several paintings illustrate the widow's all-important duty to be a moral and domestic mentor. In what is, ostensibly, an unlikely example, a painting by Gerard ter Borch, a woman peels apples in the presence of an inquisitive girl (Fig. 169). At first glance, the apple peeler does indeed seem relatively young, but she wears a mourning veil, which signifies her widowed state.[72] Her task and the presence of a sewing basket and cushion in the lower right corner of the composition are unambiguous references to the types of activities appropriate for widows. Furthermore, in view of the presence of the attentive girl and the literary exhortations charging widows with the instruction of younger women – particularly if they were their own daughters – this painting could have a pedagogical dimension. The beautifully painted bowl of fruit on the table directly before the girl might relate to one depicted in the *pictura* of a pedagogical emblem by Roemer Visscher (Fig. 170). The emblem, inscribed "Vroech rijp, vroech rot" (Early to Ripen, Early to Rot), compares fruit that has ripened early to children who prematurely possess an adult's reasoning capacities. Such children seldom mature fully and, in

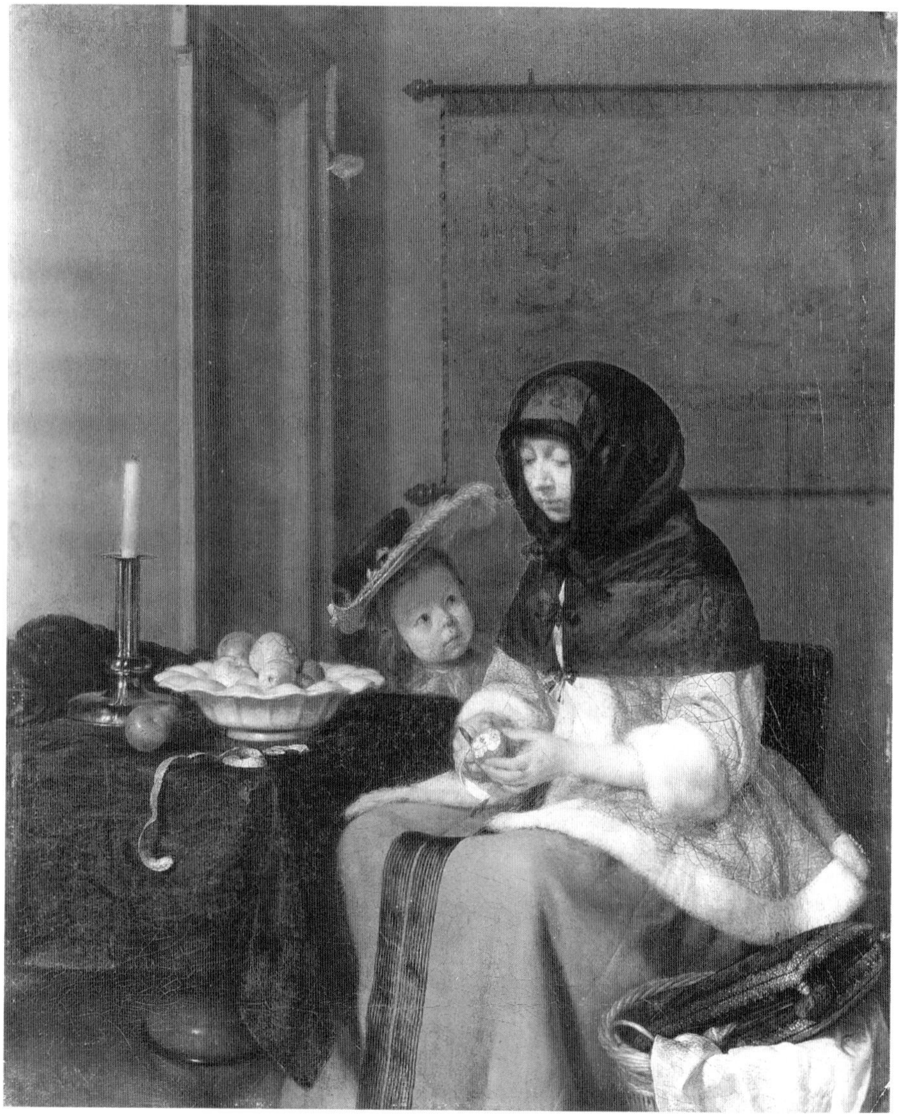

Figure 169. Gerard ter Borch, *A Widow Peeling Apples* (oil on canvas, transferred to panel, 36.3 × 30.7 cm). Vienna, Gemäldegalerie, Kunsthistorisches Museum.

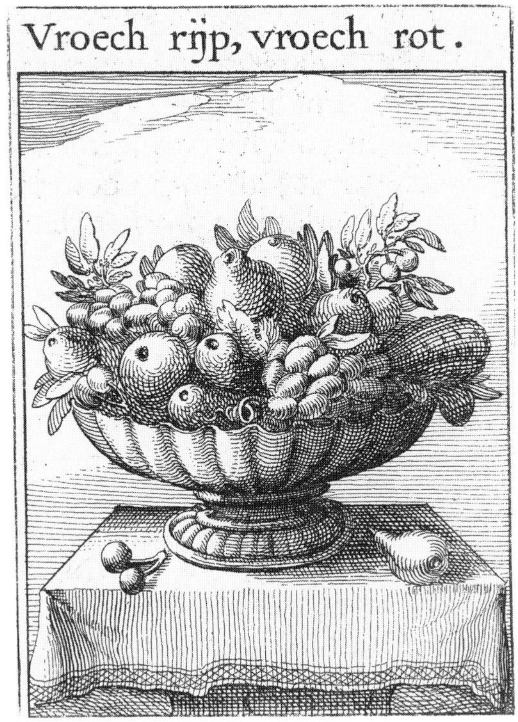

Figure 170. Emblem from Roemer Visscher, *Sinne-poppen*, Amsterdam 1614. Amsterdam, Universiteits-Bibliotheek Amsterdam. Photo: courtesy Universiteits-Bibliotheek Amsterdam.

old age, are dull and foolish.[73] These pedagogical associations might well be present in Ter Borch's painting, though only for those educated viewers who were familiar with Visscher's emblem.

Virtuous instruction is also on display in several pictures that depict elderly women combing children's hair. In a painting by Quiringh van Brekelenkam – the earliest dated work by the artist (1648) – an old woman combs a young boy's hair; her rapt attention and careful manipulation of the comb through the hair on this boy's head, which is turned so that she can inspect his scalp, suggests that she is delousing him (Fig. 171). As we have already seen, the depiction of this task in art can be linked to popular beliefs equating a well-groomed outer appearance with inner virtue.[74] Thus, the child having his hair combed in Van Brekelenkam's painting is not only well groomed, but also spiritually and morally pure, a likely consequence of his training. His hornbook and lunch, lying neatly on the floor beside him, contribute to the overall pedagogical intent of the painting since these are articles taken to school, an institution for intellectual and moral training.

The woman combing the boy's hair has been erroneously identified as his mother.[75] This cannot be correct as her leathery skin, pince-nez, and gnarled

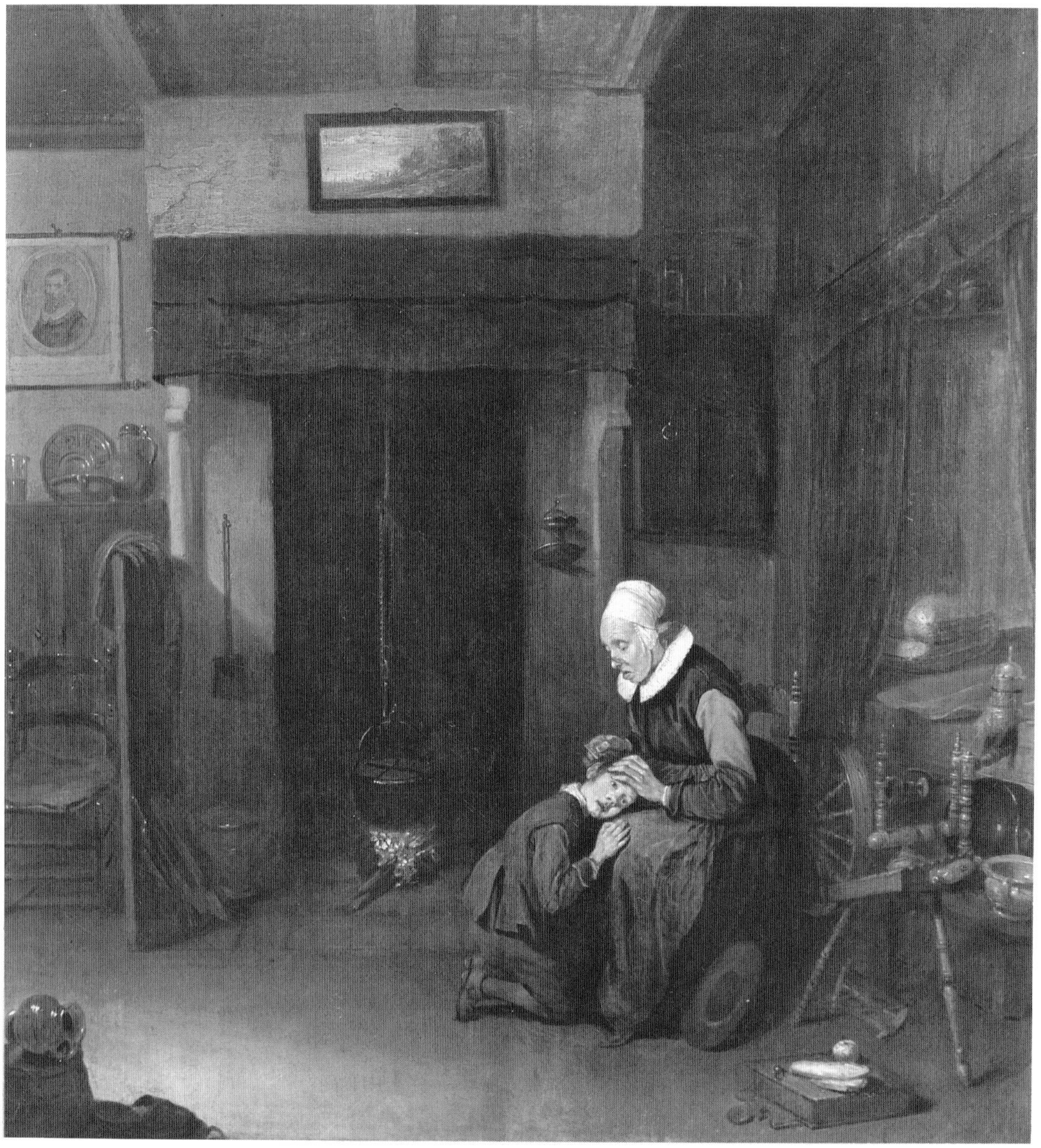

Figure 171. Quiringh van Brekelenkam, *Old Woman Combing a Child's Hair*, 1648 (oil on panel, 57 × 53.5 cm). Leiden, Stedelijk Museum "De Lakenhal."

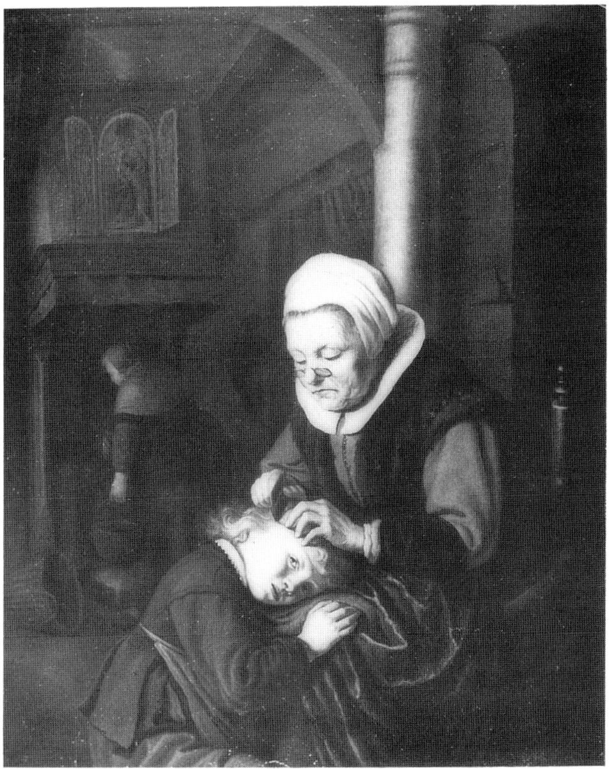

Figure 172. Abraham de Pape, *Old Woman Combing a Child's Hair* (oil on panel, 35 × 28 cm). Present location unknown.

hands reveal that she is clearly too old to be his parent. In light of contemporary beliefs concerning the piety of the aged and their charge to instruct younger women and children, Brekelenkam's decision to depict an elderly woman in this context is fitting. Perhaps Abraham de Pape's painting of an old woman – again wearing a pince-nez – combing a child's hair best clarifies the pedagogical and moral dimension of this theme since the artist has included a triptych on the back wall, one possibly representing the Descent from the Cross (Fig. 172).[76] The decision to portray elderly women in these works furnishes the artist with an opportunity not only to contrast wizened skin with the smooth, youthful flesh of children, but also to employ readily identifiable exemplars of piety and symbols of vanity – concepts pivotal to spiritual and moral training.[77]

The old women in these and other paintings share motifs, ranging from their withered faces and hands, and heavy garments, to their spectacles and pious demeanors. The references in these pictures to piety and vanity parallel the ideas expounded in seventeenth-century literature in which the elderly are purposefully cited as models of religious ardor and as evidence for the ephemeral nature of existence.[78] These women emerge as topoi, exemplary types who illustrate what males considered proper feminine virtues and roles in the final stage of life. As such, these works, like many seventeenth-century representations of women, are constructs that illuminate the role art played in espousing patriarchal values in early modern Europe.

CONCLUSION

We have now come full circle, having explored the expression in art of the virtues and obligations expected of women, from adolescence to widowhood in Dutch seventeenth-century society.

Chapter 1 examined paintings of young, unmarried women. Parallels with contemporary literature demonstrated that genre paintings and portraits of young women absorbed in household tasks reflect the importance attached to moral and domestic training. The popular theme of courtship celebrated love while illustrating the requisite behavior of maidens participating in this important premarital ritual. The young women in these representations, like those in the literature they mirror, served as topoi displaying those virtues thought to be most appropriate for females at this stage in life.

The image of the Dutch housewife at work was discussed in Chapter 2. We explored the portrayal of a gamut of housewifely duties, tasks, and activities, among them sewing, spinning, preparing food, market shopping, and supervising servants. These representations of domesticity can be linked with the image of the paradigmatic housewife expounded in contemporary literature. Both books and paintings present an ideal, yet theoretically imitable female type, thereby providing an exemplar by which the conduct of the reader or viewer could be measured. The assiduous performance of divinely ordained work was a clear component of all of these pictures as they celebrate domesticity.

The representation in Dutch art of the all-important office of motherhood was studied in Chapter 3. We examined depictions of various maternal duties (and, in some cases, paternal ones as well), including nursing, grooming, spiritual and secular training, and discipline. Although grounded in an ideal world, Dutch paintings of mothers and children, and the literary sources they reflect, bear eloquent testimony to the contemporary concern for children as well as to the belief that the home – the true microcosm of society – was the principal environment for training them.

Chapter 4 focused on works of art depicting the final stages of a woman's life: old age and widowhood. These paintings display the piety, humility, and spiritual enlightenment of widows and the aged, virtues specifically ascribed to them in contemporary literature. The elderly were thought to possess spiritual acumen because their impending deaths enabled them to perceive the deceitfulness and evanescence of the world and its material goods. Such motifs as the old women themselves, their heavy garments, and chipped earthenware allude to *vanitas.* The elderly women and widows function as topoi, exhibiting those estimable character traits and virtues demanded of females in the final stages of life.

Taken as a whole, images of domestic virtue broaden our understanding of seventeenth-century Dutch art as well as the position of women in Dutch society. As for the former, these pictures represent plausible realities, fictitious constructs that synthesize observed fact and invention. In portraits and especially in genre paintings, artists repeatedly surround women with the same, surprisingly limited number of meticulously painted objects that could only have been meant to connote virtue. Domestic imagery is therefore governed by rather strict conventions, both in themes and in the types of motifs employed to illustrate them. Their conventionality suggests that the associations evoked by these paintings were not necessarily concealed from the viewer but were an essential constituent, intimately bound up with their mimetic qualities. In other words, the presentation in these works of art of universally held ideals about women and domesticity guaranteed that access to their meanings was not normally dependent on the viewer's capacity to uncover veiled symbols. As modern viewers, we may have trouble detecting objects or motifs replete with particular associations, but this would not have been the case for seventeenth-century viewers. They would have immediately perceived them on the surface of paintings since these objects or motifs were intrinsic to the artist's engaging presentation of a plausible reality. The propensity in much current scholarship to divorce form, that is, pictorial style, from content is therefore anachronistic for both are inextricably bound together.

Seventeenth-century Dutch paintings of domestic scenes also furnish much information about the position of women in contemporary Dutch society. These pictures do represent plausible realities, but these realities were fundamentally structured by a culture that privileged males. They therefore resonate with an entire system of values, ideals, and even prejudices, all of which reflect common attitudes toward women at that time. This even extends to questions of style. In portraiture, a different aesthetic governs the representation of women as opposed to men. Not only are they subject to the heraldic convention of being placed to the left of their husbands, but the differences even extend to their depiction in passive poses with their features rendered in a flat, superficial manner. In genre paintings, which represent a limited number of themes, the individuality of women is very often downplayed in the interests of having them signify, like the highly conventional motifs that surround them, an appropriate feminine virtue. In this sense, the pictures are visually analogous to the prescriptions of contemporary literature as they literally illustrate the housewifely and motherly roles and tasks assigned to females in early modern Europe, ones for which they trained from childhood. As such, they illuminate the subordinate position of women in Dutch society, a position oriented to the home in obedience to husbands who had more "significant" public careers. (I must add that, for the most part, it seems unlikely that men were always consciously aware of their privileged positions in society, nor were women always consciously aware of what we today would perceive as their unjust subordination to men.) With their quite literal demonstration of the female place in society, it would be reductive to assume that these pictures simply reflected prevailing gender norms; such norms were not passively reflected but were actively and gracefully articulated in images that celebrate the virtues of home life with unparalleled beauty and subtlety.

NOTES

INTRODUCTION

1. My discussion in Chapter 1 of images of courtship falls outside the parameters of this definition. Nevertheless, this subject is important if we wish to understand more fully what contemporaries considered proper behavior among young, unmarried women.
2. Representations of virtuous subjects have not been completely ignored; see, e.g., De Jongh 1974; 1975–6; D. Smith 1982; Bedaux 1983; Exhib. cat. Haarlem 1986; Franits 1986; Van Thiel 1987; Bedaux 1987; 1990, pp. 71–160.
3. Schama 1987. The author's chapter on women was anticipated by his 1980 article.
4. Reviewers such as Elliott 1987, p. 30; and Dekker 1988, p. 31, have pointed out that similar tensions between morality and prosperity existed in other European countries.
5. Schama 1987, p. 389.
6. I plan to explore representations of "wanton woman" – to borrow Schama's term – in a book that will serve as a "sequel" to this one. The reason that such images are not included here is quite simple: if they were, this would no longer be a study purely of domestic virtue.
7. Schama 1987, pp. 467, 480.
8. Art historians have analyzed individual genre paintings that represent a few isolated themes; see, e.g., De Jongh 1967, p. 65; Exhib. cat. Amsterdam 1976, cat. nos. 3, 5, 6, 19, 41, 49, 77; Slatkes 1981, pp. 33–4, 94, 113, 114, 124, 126, 146, 158; Exhib. cat. Philadelphia 1984, cat. nos. 14, 16, 17, 32, 34, 50, 54, 55, 65, 102, 124. See also the comments of Sutton 1980, pp. 45–9.
9. See Stone-Ferrier 1983, pp. 10–11; McGrath 1984; Renger 1984.
10. For the value of portraiture in revealing contemporary ideals, see D. Smith 1982; Exhib. cat. Haarlem 1986; Bedaux 1990.
11. Cats 1625. For the influence of *Houwelyck* on Dutch seventeenth-century painting, see De Jongh 1974, pp. 166–80; Sutton 1980, pp. 46–8; D. Smith 1982, pp. 26–7, 31–2, 67–8, 130–1. For *Houwelyck* itself, see Meertens 1943, pp. 267–83; Ten Berge 1979, pp. 77–95; Dresen-Coenders 1989b, pp. 20–39.
12. De Jongh 1974, p. 174.
13. See, e.g., Dod and Cleaver 1612; Gouge 1622; Wittewrongel 1661. There are even precedents for its division into chapters corresponding to specific life stages of women. See, e.g., Vives 1547; Houwaert 1622–3.
14. De Jongh 1974, p. 173, states that "the Amsterdam publisher Ian Iacobszoon Schipper, who brought Cats's collected works out no fewer than four times between 1655 and 1665, estimated in mid-century that the number of copies of *Houwelyck* in circulation could not be less than 50,000." By seventeenth-century standards, this is truly an astonishing number; see further ibid., p. 173 n. 14.
15. I have translated "Vrijster" as "Sweetheart" for lack of a better term; De Jongh 1974, p. 168, and other scholars have translated it "Spinster," but in American English, spinster connotes an older woman who has remained single beyond the typical marrying age. The division of *Houwelyck* according to

life stages testifies to the enduring interest in the centuries-old concept of cyclically dividing human life into specific phases. Other books of the period along with print series reflect this interest, thus demonstrating that this traditional concept, far too often associated exclusively with the Middle Ages, survived into the seventeenth century and beyond. See, e.g., Cuffe 1607; Messiae 1607, pp. 163–8; C. Udemans 1659, pp. 99–102; Croon 1665; Van Royen n.d. (before 1730). For the concept of the ages of life in general, see Chew 1962, pp. 153–73. For the survival of medieval symbolism in Dutch art of the seventeenth century, see Bruyn 1961; 1981, pp. 10–16; 1987. See also J. Bruyn et al. 1978.

16. In the preface to the book, its publisher and illustrator, Adriaen van de Venne, explains the significance of the frontispiece: "Dat de Titel hier voren ghestelt is afgebeelt in ghedaente van een Heuvel, rijsende aende eene ende dalende aende andere sijde, met byvoughsel van ses paer menschen, die den berch, elck te sijner plaetsen, over weder-sijden bewandelen; alles op dat yeder daer uyt mochte bemercken den ganschen ommegang des menschelicken levens hier vertoont te worden in ses deelen, maeckende als ses dagen, ende mitsdien uyt-brengende den vollen loop van een gheheele weke, daer selfs de Rust-dach, ofte den dach des Heeren niet aen en ontbreeckt, afgebeelt inden voorschreven tijtel door het laetste woonhuys alles vleesch, twelck is het graf" (Cats 1625, sigs. I (*)^{v}–I (*) ij).

17. For prints representing the steps of life, see Englert 1905; 1907; De Meyer 1962, pp. 393–6; and, more recently, Exhib. cat. Kleves 1983–4, cat. nos. 12–21. See also ibid., cat. no. 11, for a painting of the same subject (ca. 1650) by an anonymous Haarlem artist. See also Hazelzet 1989. For print series of the ages of life, see, e.g., Figs. 14, 96, 124, 128, 141. See also Veldman 1980, pp. 149–69; 1983, pp. 37–46; Exhib. cat. Kleves 1983–4, cat. nos. 9, 10. There are also some paintings in which the concept of the ages of life is a factor; see Exhib. cat. Haarlem 1986, cat. no. 47, and several pictures by Brekelenkam including one formerly at Trafalgar Galleries, London (1977 annual catalogue, cat. no. 7).

18. It is well known that the naturalistic appearance of Dutch seventeenth-century paintings led nineteenth-century viewers to regard these works as objective representations of the everyday world; see, e.g., Demetz 1963; De Vries 1977, pp. 102–3; Sutton 1984, pp. xx.

19. See, e.g., De Jongh 1967; 1971; 1975–6; Exhib. cat. Amsterdam 1976. Among the earliest studies that explored the symbolism of Dutch painting were Van Gelder 1938; Rudolph 1938; Kauffman 1943; Bergström 1955; De Jongh and Vinken 1961. For a brief essay on the history of the scholarly investigation of meaning in Dutch art, see Renger 1978, pp. 34–8.

20. See De Jongh 1967, pp. 21–2, and especially De Jongh 1971, pp. 143–6. Panofsky first used the term "disguised symbolism" in his seminal article on Jan van Eyck's *Arnolfini Portrait,* published in 1934; it was subsequently explored in a number of his books.

21. See, e.g., Visscher 1614, pp. iv–v; Johan De Brune 1624, sig. * 1^{v}; Cats 1632b, sigs. * iij^{v}–* iiij. These passages have been cited in several studies by De Jongh; see, e.g., De Jongh 1967, pp. 8–9; 1976, p. 20; 1982, pp. 27, 36 n. 4. For Horace's doctrine of *ut pictura poesis* and its ramifications for art and literary theory of the sixteenth and seventeenth centuries, see the excellent study by Lee 1967. See also Hagstrum 1958; Silver 1983.

22. Van Mander 1604, bk. 6, *Wtbeeldinge der figuren,* dedication, "Aen Const-rijcken, cloecksinnighen Mr. Cornelis Ketel, Schilder en Dichter," sig. 123^{v}; Van Hoogstraten 1678, p. 90. For these passages, see De Jongh 1976, p. 20.

23. This point is made by Sutton 1984, p. xxi; Bedaux 1990, p. 13. For a critique of Bedaux's book, in which the author defends De Jongh's concept of *schijnrealisme,* see Miedema 1991. See also De Jongh 1990.

24. Sutton 1984, p. xxi, came to this conclusion as well, stating that "the implication that the work's outward realism was only at the service of symbolic elements there encoded is inconsistent with the Dutchman's celebration of naturalism – his delight in mimicry and the accurate recording of the particular." See also Sluijter 1988a, pp. 15–16; 1990, pp. 22–6.

25. See Sluijter 1988a, p. 11; Goedde 1989b, p. 15. See also Sluijter 1990, pp. 27, 30.

26. For the thematic hierarchy of art in seventeenth-century art theory, see Albert Blankert's remarks in his introductory essay to Exhib. cat. Washington, D.C., 1980–1, pp. 15–19. See also Miedema 1975, pp. 3–5; Sutton 1984, pp. xiv–xv.
27. Van Hoogstraten 1678, pp. 75–87. See also Sluijter 1988a, p. 11. Genre paintings or scenes of everyday life, as we identify them today, were not defined as such in the seventeenth century. In fact, as De Jongh 1976, p. 20 n. 21 has observed, our modern definition of genre painting would suit some of the subjects that Hoogstraten assigns to the middle stratum of his artistic hierarchy and some that belong to his lowest stratum. In the seventeenth century, genre paintings were designated by descriptive terms such as "bordeeltje" (brothel scenes), "cortegarde" (guard room scenes), "geselschap" (merry companies), etc. See further De Pauw-De Veen 1969, pp. 167–79; Miedema 1975, pp. 3–5; Sutton 1984, pp. xiv–xv. For the history of our modern designation "genre painting," see Stechow and Comer 1975–6. See also Albert Blankert's interesting attempt to define genre painting in Blankert 1987.
28. Hoogstraten 1678, p. 90.
29. For criticisms of De Jongh's method, see De Vries 1977, pp. 108–9; Raupp 1983, p. 403 n. 10; Müller-Hofstede 1984, p. xv; Moxey 1989a, p. 35; Bedaux 1990, pp. 12–16. For criticisms of Panofsky's concept of "disguised symbolism," see Pächt 1956, pp. 275–9; Benjamin 1976, pp. 15–16; Bedaux 1986, pp. 5–7; Marrow 1986, pp. 150–1; Moxey 1989a, pp. 34–5; Bedaux 1990, pp. 10–12.
30. See the reviews by Gombrich 1983; Gaskell 1984; Glynne 1984; De Jongh 1984; Schama 1984; Stumpel 1984; Veltman 1984; Bialostocki 1985; Bruyn 1985; Grafton and Kaufmann 1985. See also Stone-Ferrier 1983, pp. 15–24; Sutton 1984, p. lxiii n. 49; Cropper and Dempsey 1987, pp. 506–7; Haverkamp-Begemann 1987, pp. 510–11; Honig 1990, pp. 33–9.
31. Sluijter 1988a. Sluijter's primary witness is Angel 1642. Miedema 1989 has analyzed this work in detail. His article contains some important observations concerning the negligible impact of art theory on painting in the seventeenth century. See also Sluijter 1986, pp. 281–92; 1990, pp. 22–7.
32. Ample documentation for this – at least for the Leiden *fijnschilders* – is provided by Sluijter 1988b, pp. 15–23. Sluijter's ideas are followed by Bedaux 1990, p. 13, who likewise argues that "the demand and supply for pictures could be determined solely by the visual pleasure they provided, and that people could enjoy a picture without it having an intentional didactic content." See also Pace 1987.
33. See Hagstrum 1958; Mace 1971; Porteman 1979; 1983, pp. 109–10; 1984a, pp. 96–8, Gent 1981.
34. See Porteman 1984a, pp. 96–7.
35. Porteman 1983, p. 109: "Het pictorialisme is bij hem een artistiek beginsel geworden en blijkens de voorreden op vele treurspelen zelfs een programma. Vondels picturale schrijfkunst, zijn emfatisch-visuele stijl, zijn zin voor schilderkunstige ordening en beweging, sluiten in eerste instantie bewust aan bij de in hogere kringen erg bewonderde internationale historieschilderkunst, maar globaal zijn in zijn werk onmiskenbaar ook veel sporen van de zo intense inlandse schilderscultuur aanwezig." See also ibid., pp. 109–10; 1979; 1984a, pp. 96–7. See also Brom 1957, pp. 256–9.
36. Bredero 1622/1971, p. 8: "Wat my belangt, ick heb anders geen boek geleerd als het boek des gebruiks; zo ik dan door onwetenheid der uytlandser spraken, wetenschappen, en konsten hebbe gedoold, verschoont mij ongeleerde lekebroeder, en geeft den Duitse wat toe, want ick heb als een schilder, de schilderachtige spreuke gevolgd, die daer zeit: Het zijn de beste schilders die 't leven naast komen . . . Ik hebbe zo veel als ik vermocht de boerterijen met de zoetste boere-woorden uitgedrukt." Part of this passage is cited by Porteman 1984a, p. 100. See also Porteman 1983, pp. 111–14; 1984a, p. 100, where he remarks that "men kan zich bijvoorbeeld met evenveel recht afvragen of Bredero's beroep op de schilderkunst geen modieuze inkleuring is van *literaire* opvattingen." See also Miedema 1977, pp. 214–15, n. 45; 1981a, p. 198. However, we do know that Bredero worked with the Flemish artist Francois Badens, and there are records of now-lost paintings by him; see Alpers 1975–6, p. 117 n. 7.
37. See Porteman 1983, p. 113; 1984a, p. 100, who notes that this passage also constitutes

an "uitval tegen het geleerde concept van literatuur en de maniëristische schilderkunst."

38. See Emmens 1955/1981; Goedde 1989a; 1989b. See also Porteman and Brems 1979; Porteman 1984a, pp. 103–9; Land 1990.

39. See Emmens 1955/1981; Goedde 1989a, pp. 38–43; 1989b, pp. 18–20, 119–28.

40. See Goedde 1989a, pp. 37–40; 1989b, pp. 123–30.

41. Among the few ekphratic poems about genre painting is Vos 1726, vol. 1, p. 388: "Op de Schildery van een Kraamvrouw . . . door G. Moetsu [Metsu] geschildert." Obviously, the narrative capacity of some genre paintings is more pronounced than that of others. In domestic subjects there is generally less emphasis on narrative.

42. See Goedde 1986; Sluijter 1988a, pp. 14–15; Goedde 1989b, pp. 16, 20, 163–4; Sluijter 1990, pp. 21–2; 1991, p. 51.

43. Schneede 1968, pp. 54–61, came to these conclusions about the genre paintings of Gabriel Metsu. See also Miedema 1975, pp. 8–10; 1984, pp. 10–12. De Vries 1977, pp. 103–6, adduces seven qualities inherent to "realism" in Dutch art.

44. Goedde 1989b, p. 16, states that "even when followed thoughtlessly, a convention or formula communicates meaning and can be analyzed for evidence of what contemporaries expected to see – or not to see – and what they found significant and worthy of representation out of all the multiple possibilities of existence." See also Goedde 1986, p. 146.

45. The following discussion is indebted in part to Wolff 1981; Moxey 1989b, pp. 7–9.

46. My reasoning here is inspired by the work of several scholars, among them Bauch 1967, pp. 123–51, who has written an illuminating essay about Rembrandt's manner of depicting stories from the Bible. Bauch employs the term "iconographic style" to denote the peculiar features of the artist's Bible paintings, images that so often deviate from firmly established pictorial traditions. In this sense, Bauch argues, one can speak of an iconographic style in the same restricted sense that one speaks of a drawing style, a compositional style, etc. For the symbolic or signifying aspects of style, see also Schapiro 1961, pp. 81–2, 105–6; Ackerman 1961–2, pp. 229, 233; Kubler 1981, pp. 23–4. I am also indebted (obviously) to semiotic approaches; see, e.g., Geertz 1976; Mukarovsky 1988, p. 4; and some of the more recent formulations by, among others, Bryson 1988, pp. xvii–xxviii; Moxey 1989a, pp. 36–7; 1989b, pp. 6–9; Bryson 1991. However, I do not entirely agree with a semiotic view of representation that dismisses the notion of the pursuit of mimetic naturalism in Western art as ahistorical in favor of realism as a purely cultural construct. For example, Moxey 1989a, p. 37, argues: "Far from having unmediated access to nature, a nature which is then reproduced through a process of mimesis, the artist is forever alienated from nature and has only the artistic conventions of his time with which to suggest its appearance. A naturalistic style, in other words, is a 'reality effect.' " Although much seventeenth-century Dutch art is ideologically freighted – and nowhere is this more unequivocal than in the depiction of women – I also believe that, paradoxically, a seemingly value-free pursuit of mimetic naturalism can be historically defined; one only has to take into account such diverse phenomena as the vast numbers of alfresco landscape drawings or the contemporary art theorists' and collectors' purely aesthetic appreciation of the naturalistic qualities of paintings. See further the criticisms of Moxey's position by Koerner 1991, p. 149.

47. This view differs somewhat from that of Schama 1987, p. 413, who argues that "what is certainly apparent in Dutch pictures of women at their domestic chores, reading letters, or being courted, is that artists went to unusual pains to trace expression of feature, bodily attitude and gesture in the female with a relaxed clarity that is missing from the conventions of classical and baroque depiction elsewhere."

48. See especially D. Smith 1982, pp. 44–9; see also, Exhib. cat. Haarlem 1986, pp. 36–40; Möbius 1987, pp. 69–83.

49. Bedaux 1990, p. 152, refers to the symbolic motifs that appear in portraits as "accessories." He rightly observes: "The emphasis which iconology tends to place on them suggests that they constitute the main aspect of the painting. To an increasing extent accessories have been used as a point of departure from which to examine a cultural and his-

torical setting. This has resulted in an exaggerated view of the painter's invention with respect to the content of his work" (ibid.).

50. Exhib. cat. Amsterdam 1989–90, p. 55. Hecht's deliberate attention to aesthetic issues at the expense of questions of meaning and interpretation in his exhibition catalogue has been sharply criticized; see, e.g., Bruyn 1991; Sluijter 1991. See also Hecht's response – along with Eddy de Jongh's criticisms – in Raben and Vermeij 1990, an article that made use of interviews with the two scholars.
51. See Wolff 1981, p. 70. See also Sluijter 1991, p. 51.
52. The principal contemporary viewers of Dou's paintings – at least the ones that are recorded – were a special group indeed, one that included King Charles II of England; see further p. 84, this volume. According to Blankert 1987, pp. 30–1, 32 n. 20, it is possible that artists attempted to make their paintings as realistic as possible in order to enhance their meanings – or as he terms it, their "moralizing impact" or "ulterior significance."
53. Nochlin 1989, p. 34. Nochlin's comments refer to Orientalism in nineteenth-century art, where the realism of paintings is grounded in European colonialist ideologies. See also Nochlin 1991.
54. It is extremely unlikely that men were consciously aware of their privileged place in society or that women consciously considered themselves unfairly subordinated. See further Ozment 1983, p. 202 n. 12: "In the sixteenth century being 'fraw im Hawse' was looked on by neither women nor men as demeaning in any way to womankind; it was a respected identity and vocation that lifted women above the rank of 'just wives.' "

CHAPTER 1. "MAEGHT" AND "VRYSTER"

1. Cats 1625, chaps. 1–2. The distinctions made by Cats between these two phases in a young, unmarried woman's life may seem vague to the modern reader – which is one reason why I combine them here – but they were not for the seventeenth-century one; see the preface to the book by its publisher, Adriaen vande Venne, sig. I (*)^{v}. Cats has also included a special index for these two chapters. For the first two chapters of *Houwelyck*, see Meertens 1943, pp. 268–9; Carter 1974, pp. 105–6; Ten Berge 1979, pp. 80–2; Dresen-Coenders 1989b, pp. 27–31.
2. Cats's avowed intention here is to offer a guide to marriage from out of the maze of "calf love," the seventeenth-century Dutch equivalent of our expression "puppy love." See further Cats 1625, chap. 1, preface, sigs. I (***)–I (***)ij^{v}, which includes an illustration of a maiden entering the maze of "kalver-liefde" (calf love) with Cupid as her guide.
3. Cats 1618. The rhymed dialogue of Phyllis and Anna in the first chapter of *Houwelyck* originally appeared in a more concise form in this book; see Smilde 1938, p. 128; Ten Berge 1979, p. 80. See also De Jongh 1974, pp. 166, 168. Cats 1632b also contains an extensive section on courting.
4. E.g., Anon. 1591; Godewycx 1641; Den Heussen 1657. See also the many works cited in Daalder 1950.
5. Seventeenth-century ideas regarding the dangers confronted by youth are discussed by Peeters 1966, pp. 238–42; S. Smith 1974–5, pp. 495–500; Davis 1975, pp. 108, 112; Fox 1977, pp. 273–83; Grootes 1979–80, pp. 484–9; Vandenbroeck 1983–4, p. 43.
6. See, e.g., the diaries of Constantijn Huygens, Jr., which contain descriptions of the problems that he had with his college-age son, Tien. These are examined in Dekker 1989.
7. See Peeters 1988, p. 28; Spierenburg 1989, pp. 624–5; and the important study by Fox 1977. Fox's article and the work of the other authors cited in note 5 have effectively countered the theories of some social historians concerning the conceptual origins of adolescent behavior. These were largely formulated by Ariès 1962, pp. 25, 29–30, 261–2. Although our ancestors were conscious of the life stage of adolescence, we cannot precisely define their concept of it nor, for that matter, the extent to which it differed from our notions. Grootes 1979–80, pp. 481–2, reaches similar conclusions.
8. Messiae 1607, p. 164; Gouge 1622, p. 526; and Wittewrongel 1661, vol. 1, p. 171, distinguish between various phases in the life of children, including one called "youth"; see

Groenendijk 1984, pp. 139–40. See also Groenendijk 1989, pp. 658–9.

9. Seventeenth-century pedagogical theories are discussed in detail in Chapter 3.

10. Gataker 1637, p. 142, has the following advice for parents who are raising young girls: "... but labor to traine them up in true wisedome and discretion in the feare of God, and such graces, as may make them truely amiable, as well in Gods sight as in mans eyes, in housewifery, and industry, and skill to manage houshold affaires: that so they may be helpers to their husbands (and not hinderers;) as to that end they were made at first." Gataker's book was known in the Netherlands at this time through three Dutch editions of his complete works, published in Amsterdam in 1659, 1660, and 1662; see Van der Haar 1980, p. 58. For contemporary ideas on training maidens in general, see Kelso 1956 pp. 38–57. See also Chapter 3, pp. 130–5.

11. See Cats 1625, chaps. 1–2. Cats's and his colleagues' ideas on this subject display remarkable continuity with those expressed by several sixteenth-century humanists, most notably Juan Luis Vives 1524. This influential advice book adumbrates *Houwelyck* in its division of its subject into female life stages, in this case three: maidenhood, motherhood, and widowhood. A Dutch translation of the book was published in Antwerp in 1554. For my study, I will cite the English translation of 1547. For Vives's influential book, see, Nauwelaerts 1975; 1976; Kaufman 1977–8. Cats was quite familiar with it, as he repeatedly quotes it in *Houwelyck.* Vives's work was also an important source for Cats 1618; see Nauwelaerts 1976, p. 141; Friesendorp and Joosse 1983.

12. On the basis of the sitter's clothing, Baer 1990, cat. no. 34, dates the painting to ca. 1640–4. Baer adds that it might have had a pendant, due to the motifs contained therein, the young woman's position to the heraldic left, and because of "the ring on her third finger, possibly a wedding band, which may indicate that the woman at one time had a mate." This is possible, but as De Jongh observes in Exhib. cat. Haarlem 1986, pp. 138–40, there were no set rules in the seventeenth century governing the wearing of wedding rings. He further notes (p. 140): "Maar waar de calvinist Jacob Cats, in zijn *Houwelick*, per implicatie over de rechterhand van de bruid als plaats voor de trouwring komt te spreken, denkt hij ongetwijfeld aan geloofsgenoten. Cats klaagt trouwens over het gebruik dat in zijn tijd, vooral in de steden, bestond om de ring niet aan de ringvinger, maar aan de 'de voorste vinger' te dragen." In Dou's painting, the woman wears the ring on her left hand, not on her right as Cats advises. Moreover, the ring is not on her "voorste vinger."

13. For the stylistic conventions that portraitists adopted for each sex, see D. Smith 1982, pp. 44–9; Exhib. cat. Haarlem 1986, pp. 36–40; Möbius 1987. For similar conventions that extend beyond portraiture to include history painting, see Held 1985–6, p. 48.

14. The book standing on end on the table is likely a Bible because of its thickness and the fact that it is equipped with clasps, a device commonly used to keep Bibles tightly closed in order to protect them from dust and moisture.

15. Overbury 1614, sig. B4, argues that the realms of books and learning should be left to men, remarking: "Domesticke Charge doth best that Sex befit,/ Contiguous buisnesse, so to fixe the Minde,/ That Leasure space for Fancies not admit:/ Their Leasure tis corrupteth Woman-kinde,/ Else being plac'd from many vices free,/ They had to heav'n a shorter cut than we." See also [Du Bosc] 1643, pp. 1–33, 135–44. For the often vociferous contemporary controversy concerning the degree to which women should be educated, see Kelso 1956, pp. 58–77; Kaufman 1977–8; Wright 1980, pp. 103–18; Friesendorp and Joosse 1983; Noël 1986; Garrard 1989, pp. 150–1. See also Spies 1986; Schama 1987, pp. 408–12; Van der Stighelen 1987, p. 22. The "notable exceptions" that I refer to are the leading female intellectual luminaries of the day, Anna Maria van Schurman and the daughters of Roemer Visscher, Anna and Tesselschade. For the former, see Schama 1987, pp. 410–12; Van der Stighelen 1987. For Anna and Tesselschade Visscher, see Schama 1987, pp. 408–10, who astutely observes that "while they strayed far from the conventional realms of

Dutch housewifery, the talented Visscher women did not pose a serious threat to male sovereignty over female options. . . . In most respects, then, their unofficial careers as learned women remained ornamentally designed to please men" (p. 410).

16. See the advice on the types of reading suitable for young women offered by Salter 1579, sigs. B3–B3^v, B7^v, C3–C4; Hazart 1678, pp. 285–94. (Salter's book is a close translation, without acknowledgment, of the famous work by Bruto 1555; see Kelso 1956, p. 344, no. 161.) Among the popular books intended for women at this time was Anon. 1591. There were also several seventeenth-century books about Lucretia and Penelope, two virtuous women from classical history who were frequently invoked as role models; see Chapter 2, note 52. See also the numerous works cited by Wright 1980, pp. 108–18, as well as the important study by Hull 1982.

17. One of the most popular songbooks of sacred music was Camphuysen 1624, first published in an oblong format. An enormous number of secular songbooks were published during this period, often containing amorous songs. Since these also professed to have edifying intentions, it is impossible to state unequivocally that the songbook in Dou's portrait is a spiritual one. See further, pp. 37–8, this volume.

18. Cats 1625, chap. 1, preface, sigs. I (***) iij–I (****).

19. See Bedaux 1983, pp. 56–7; 1990, p. 119.

20. Similar conclusions about women in quattrocento portraiture have been reached by Simons 1988, p. 15.

21. For this work, see Schipper-Van Lottum 1975, pp. 145–51; Lowenthal 1986a, cat. no. A-98; Exhib. cat. Haarlem 1986, cat. no. 4, where similar conclusions are reached as those presented here. There are several studies that examine the needlework of the period in detail, often from a technical standpoint; see Groves 1973; Schipper-Van Lottum 1980; Levey 1983; De Bodt 1987.

22. Fig. 9 reproduces a painting presently located in the Maagdenhuis, Antwerp, where it is attributed to Cornelis de Vos. The painting has also been attributed to Jan Albertsz. Rotius. According to Levey 1983, n.p., it depicts an orphan.

23. For this painting, part of a group of portraits by Wtewael of members of his family, see Lowenthal 1986a, Cat. no. A-96.

24. See p. 14, this volume.

25. For this painting, see Naumann 1981a, vol. 1, pp. 64, 66–8, 124, vol. 2, cat. no. II 54. Naumann argues that this work may belong to a series of four, all showing women at knee-length engaged in domestic or frivolous activities (ibid., vol. 1, p. 66). The series would have represented four of the five senses. See further Moiso-Diekamp 1987, pp. 375–6. According to C. White 1982, p. 79, cat. no. 113, the subject of Van Mieris's painting was first treated by Dou and probably originated with that artist. See, e.g., Dou's *Girl with a Parrot,* formerly in the collection of Count Gagarin, St. Petersburg; illustrated in Martin 1913, pl. 111.

26. This probably explains this bird's presence in several seventeenth-century portraits of children where it alludes to proper rearing; see Bedaux 1983, p. 63, figs. 21, 23. See also Bedaux 1990, p. 122, fig. 57. In Ripa 1644, pp. 283–4, the parrot is an attribute of *Leersaemheyt* because of its ability to learn how to speak. See Zaunschirm, 1985, pp. 14, 17. A parrot in a cage is given a pedagogical meaning in an emblem from Cats 1627, pp. 82–3, no. 14. Its *subscriptio* likens the training of a parrot to the discipline that one must undergo when seeking honors, as well as to the discipline required in child rearing. The emblem has been cited by De Jongh 1967, p. 19; Durantini 1983, pp. 63–4; Bedaux 1990, p. 122. De Jongh 1967, p. 19, notes that in keeping with Cats's approach in this emblem book, the very same *pictura* also had amorous and spiritual meanings. These three different *subscriptios* for each *pictura* were not meant to be read independently of one another, as Cats himself states in the preface to the book: "Het eene een aenleydinge zijnde tot het andere." Therefore, each *subscriptio* begins with an amorous interpretation and continues with a social one, both designed to lure the reader into confrontation with the final one, the spiritual. See also Meertens 1943, pp. 254–5; Warners, 1972, pp. 115–16; Porteman 1984b, pp. 3–4. For a different explanation of the significance of this arrangement, see Alpers 1983, p. 231.

27. In seventeenth-century Dutch art, birds

sometimes function as erotic metaphors. Such associations are extremely unlikely here because we see demure maidens engaged in domestic tasks. For birds as erotic metaphors in Dutch art, see De Jongh 1968–9, pp. 22–52. See also p. 90, this volume.

28. De Swaef 1621/1740, p. 312: "...de Dochters moeten sy leeren wat dat tot huyshouden behoort/ hoe sy in aller ootmoedigheyd hare mannen (als God haer tot het houwelyck roept) sullen onderdanigh syn/ en lief hebben/ hoe sy met de kinderen moeten ommegaen/ hoe sy haer huysgesin moeten regeeren/ wat het sy van kopen/ van naeyen/ spinnen/ hoe sy reyn en vlytigh moeten syn/ en diesgelycke dinghen die tot vrouwen beroep behooren." For De Swaef's treatise, see Groenendijk 1989, pp. 656–7. See also V[an der] D[oes] 1622, sigs. D1^{v}–D2; Den Heussen 1657, p. 94. De Swaef mentions the need for maidens to learn to spin, an exhortation repeated by many of his contemporaries. Curiously, seventeenth-century Dutch portraits of women – of any age – spinning are rare; see pp. 72–6, this volume.

29. The series, dated 1675, is entitled *Nützliche Zeitbetrachtung;* see Hollstein, *German,* 1954–, vol. 27, pp. 117–21, no. 191.

30. Veldman 1983, p. 42, fig. 20, reproduces and discusses this print, one in a series of the ages of man by Adriaen Collaert after Maarten de Vos.

31. See, e.g., Fig. 58.

32. Contemporaries attached great importance to diligent habits; see Wright 1980, pp. 170–85. The educational principles outlined here are discussed in detail in Chapter 3, pp. 111–13.

33. Van Nyenborgh 1659, pp. 90–2. The illustration recalls one that appeared in the fourth edition of Cats's *Houwelyck* (1632), at the beginning of the section "Moeder" (p. 380). See Chapter 3, p. 131 and Fig. 108.

34. Van Nyenborgh 1659, p. 90: "Gewent men haer tot den arbeyt,/ Soo blijven sy in besigheyt,/ Maer laet men haer luy en traeg blijven,/ Soo sullen sy daer in beclijven,/ En beminnen de ledigheyt."

35. For the idea that boys and girls were to receive particular training in the roles and duties considered intrinsic to their sex, see Chapter 3, pp. 130–5.

36. Pattern books were very popular, helping to disseminate decorative patterns throughout Europe. Prior to the appearance of these books in the early sixteenth century, embroidery patterns were handed down from one generation to the next. See Groves 1973, p. 122; Schipper-Van Lottum 1980, pp. 38–47.

37. Sibmacher 1604, frontispiece. For this frontispiece, see Schipper-Van Lottum 1975, p. 159, fig. 21. A similar illustration, undoubtedly based on the one cited here, appeared as the frontispiece to an English pattern book of the same period: Taylor 1634. For this latter work, see Hull 1982, pp. 46–7, 207–8.

38. See, e.g., Sibmacher 1604, n.p.: "Gott der aller Menschen Gemüt// In Händen hat/ regiert und bhüt// Der geb das all Jungfräwlein schon// All bös Gesellschafft meiden thon// Und für das schändlich müssiggehen// Mit fleiss lernen die Kunst des Nähen// Damit zu schaffen ihrn frommen// Und hie zeitlich zu Ehrn kommen." Taylor 1634, sig. A1^{v}, calls needlework "a mortall enemy to idlensse."

39. For this portrait, and its pendant of a man with an accounting book and coins, see Bruyn 1955; Grosshans 1980, cat. nos. 3, 4.

40. This point is made by Schipper-Van Lottum 1975, p. 151, and De Jongh, in Exhib. cat. Haarlem 1986, cat. no. 4. See also D. Smith 1982, p. 70.

41. I owe this observation to H. Perry Chapman. De Jongh, in Exhib. cat. Haarlem 1986, p. 75, observes that during the course of the eighteenth century, portraits of women performing domestic tasks practically disappeared: "De vrouw uit de hogere stand, en zij was het vooral die geportretteerd werd, wenste zich daarmee niet meer te associëren."

42. See the monumental study by Posthumus 1910–22. See also Zimmermann 1956, pp. 193–254; Stone-Ferrier 1985, pp. 1–40, 83–4; Israel 1989, pp. 35–6. The *spinhuizen,* reform houses where female delinquents spun as part of their punishment, probably helped bring about the decline of domestic spinning as well, though they certainly did not have the same impact as the flourishing industries. For the *spinhuizen,* see Baines 1977, p. 179.

43. This survey, which was conducted at the Gemeentelijk Archief in Amsterdam, consisted

of a random sample of thirty inventories for each decade of the seventeenth century of the possessions of persons of varying social status and religion. The average number of spinning wheels present in each decade was about seven, a statistic that tapered off to three for the years 1690–1700. Baines 1977, p. 90, cites a study of household and farm inventories in Oxfordshire for the years 1550–90 in which spinning wheels were recorded in 25% of the households. I wish to thank John Michael Montias for his assistance at the archive. It was Montias who first suggested to me that domestic spinning was possibly on the wane during the seventeenth century.

44. Representations depicting spinners of questionable behavior belong to a different category; see the examples reproduced in Stone-Ferrier 1985, figs. 38, 49, 50, 53.

45. See the quotation from De Swaef 1621/1740 on p. 26, this volume. See also Salter 1579, sig. C8v; Den Heussen 1657, p. 97.

46. For the virtuous associations of spinning, see Chapter 2, pp. 71-6. See also the charming poem that Constantin Huygens wrote on the occasion of his presentation of a spinning wheel to his daughter: Huygens 1672, vol. 2, p. 379. He focuses on the "profijt, eer en vermaeck" that the apparatus will give her. The maiden in the Netscher painting seems to be wetting something in her mouth. Baines 1977, p. 103, notes that spun flax must be kept damp. Perhaps she is wetting her fingers or more likely, a piece of flax that she will spin.

47. This maiden, possibly a servant, works beside what is the seventeenth-century equivalent of a baby's high chair. For the symbolism of the lantern, depicted in the foreground, see Chapter 2, pp. 83–4.

48. It is noteworthy that virtuous women are often compared to bright light (including sunlight) in contemporary literature; see, e.g., D[oes] 1622, sig. C2: "Als in den dagheraet den Hemel door de Sonne/ Wordt door een deughtsaem Vrou 't cieraet van't huys begonnen." See also, Cats 1625, chap. 4, sig. 30; Hofferus 1635, pp. 86–7; Sprankhuisen 1658, pt. 1, p. 150; Schaep 1671, pp. 241–2; Wits 1706, pp. 173–4.

49. Cats 1618. The dialogue, between Phyllis and Anna, was rewritten for the first chapter of *Houwelyck*. The *picturae* of the emblems reappear in reverse in Cats 1627, in the second section entitled *Emblemata moralia et oeconomica*. Cats wrote new *subscriptios* for them. Smilde 1938, pp. 128–9, outlines these and other changes.

50. The renowned Anna Maria van Schurman, celebrated for her artistic and intellectual accomplishments by Cats and others, represented herself as a personification of chastity by depicting a veil over her head; see Van der Stighelen 1987, pp. 72–6, fig. 5. See also Schama 1987, pp. 410–12.

51. Soet 1641, sigs. A3–A7v, p. 297. Marriage was the ultimate aim of courtship and, as Jan Soet would say, a safe and restful harbor, a metaphor literally taken to heart by many other seventeenth-century authors. The motif of ships and harbors as metaphors of marriage was especially popular in epithalamia; see, e.g., May-Vogel 1680, pp. 112–13; Brandt 1727, vol. 2, pp. 25–7: "De haven, van A. Leceuter en Juffrouw H. Maas" (the couple was married in 1644). It is obvious that the bride's name, Maas, which is the same as the Dutch name for the Meuse River, easily lent itself to the use of ship and harbor metaphors. These metaphors also appear in the frontispiece to Joost van den Vondel's wedding poem published in Amsterdam in 1629 in honor of the marriage of Roemer Visscher's daughter, Tesselschade, and Alard Krombalck. This frontispiece, based on a *pictura* from Visscher 1614, shows a ship sailing into a harbor and is inscribed: "Geeft Tesselschade baet, / Sprack Adelaert aen 't land, / Myn schip is dan te laet / In Tessels schoot gestrand." The frontispiece and full text of the poem are reproduced, with commentary, in Vondel 1927–, vol. 2, pp. 460–79.

52. Cats 1618, pp. 26–7, no. 13.

53. In reality, children often exercised far greater freedom in their choice of a spouse than moralists like Cats and Soet would allow; see Marshall 1987, pp. 35–8; Schama 1987, pp. 441–2; see further pp. 60–1, this volume. For the "rules" and ideas just outlined, see Cats 1625, chaps. 1–2; Soet 1641. See also [Du Bosc] 1643, pp. 33–52; [Earle] 1647–8, vol. 2, pp. 63–6. For Earle's book, which was first published in English in 1628, see Chapter 3, note 100. See also Scheltema 1832; De Roever 1891; Haller 1946, p. 82;

Goode 1959, p. 44; Carter 1974, pp. 105–6; Schama 1987, pp. 436–8; Exhib. cat. Apeldoorn 1989. For marriage itself, see pp. 64–70.

54. Cats 1627, no. 38 and sig. C3. The English translation that I have quoted appears in the back of this edition of the book, along with translations of most of the amatory versions of the emblems. See Smilde 1938, pp. 125–8. The book also includes an emblem whose *pictura* shows a maiden embroidering with a cupid (no. 9). It conveys similar associations as the emblem in question here.

55. According to Stone-Ferrier 1985, p. 95, the *subscriptio* to this emblem (and another in Cats's text whose *pictura* illustrates a maiden and cupid embroidering) suggest an explicit analogy to lovemaking, an interpretation that is surely incorrect. The Petrarchan conceits evoked by the needle appear in other amorous poetry of the period; see, e.g., Blasius 1663, p. 10.

56. Forster 1969 remains the principal study of Petrarchism in European literature.

57. See Ypes 1934, pp. 69–193. See also Hooft 1611/1983, pp. 22–4.

58. The following discussion is greatly indebted to the work of Alison Kettering, specifically Kettering 1993, in which she examines Petrarchan notions in the courtship paintings of Gerard ter Borch.

59. See Ypes 1934, p. 46; Forster 1969, pp. 8–23; Roose 1971, p. 23; Hooft 1611/1983, pp. 22, 25.

60. Heinsius 1616, nos. 32, 39, 44, 46. Ypes 1934, p. 157, lists these direct quotations. See also Praz 1964, pp. 88–98; Porteman 1977, p. 66; Hooft 1611/1983, p. 17.

61. See, e.g., Van Veen 1608, p. 185; Hooft 1611/1983, nos. 3, 15, 21, 24; Heinsius 1616, nos. 32, 39.

62. E.g., Anon. 1607; Anon. 1610; Stam 1613; Anon. (ca. 1620).

63. See Keersmaekers 1981; 1985, pp. 9–11, 119; Grootes 1987, pp. 73–5; Spies 1987, pp. 90–6. See also Snoep 1968–9, pp. 78–81.

64. See Hooft 1611/1983, pp. 7–8, 28; Keersmaekers 1985, p. 11; Spies 1987, pp. 93–4. Grootes 1987, has perceptively analyzed the complex social, demographic, and economic factors that underlay the production of songbooks, concluding that publishers aimed their products at affluent young people. His findings are limited to the market for songbooks in Amsterdam during the first quarter of the seventeenth century; the market would flourish throughout the century with the introduction of cheaper editions, often furnished with rather crude woodcut illustrations. Scheurleer 1912, provides a comprehensive bibliography of songbooks published in the Netherlands during the sixteenth and seventeenth centuries.

65. See Hooft 1611/1983, pp. 25–9, 66.

66. See Snoep 1968–9, p. 78, fig. 2.

67. In vogue at this time were so-called *juffer-boekjes*, handwritten, frequently illustrated albums composed for and by young ladies containing verses from some of the most popular songs and poems. See Snoep 1968–9; Hooft 1611/1983, p. 25; and Kettering 1988, pp. 416–614, who reproduces the poetry book by Gesina ter Borch, the sister of the famous painter Gerard. For Gesina's album, see also Luijten 1988. *Alba amicorum* sometimes contain love songs and poems; see, e.g., Exhib. cat. The Hague 1990, cat. no. 32.

68. Among the most popular were Van Heemskerck 1622; Westerbaen 1665. For these two works, see Van Boheemen 1989.

69. See Forster 1969, p. 66; Hooft 1611/1983, pp. 23, 25, 29.

70. Vinckboons's illustration also appears on the title page of Anon. 1607. There, it carries the following inscription, with a gentle admonition: "Al zijt ghy, O Ieught, daarmen gheneucht, t'hanteren, spoort / Brenght Musijck, en Rethorijck, in deught, en eeren, voort." Goosens 1977, pp. 98–9, detects a satirical note to this inscription, which he regards as "een lakende zinspeling op die gezelschappen." See further Keersmaekers 1985, p. 115.

71. For the pictorial traditions that underlie the theme and for its general development in Dutch seventeenth-century art, see Würtenburger 1937, pp. 12–37; Banks 1977, pp. 156–202. For Vinckboons's contributions to its development, see Exhib. cat. Amsterdam 1976, cat. no. 72; Goossens 1977, pp. 89–100; Exhib. cat. Philadelphia 1984, cat. no. 121.

72. For this painting, see Exhib. cat. Philadelphia 1984, cat. no. 121.

73. See, e.g., Judson 1970, pp. 95–8; Stechow

1972, pp. 165–75; Exhib. cat. Amsterdam 1976, cat. no. 72; Goossens 1977, pp. 98–9; Exhib. cat. Philadelphia 1984, cat. nos. 112, 121; Keyes 1984, pp. 77–80; Exhib. cat. Pittsburgh 1986, pp. 46–7. The theme can also be traced to such late medieval and sixteenth-century series as the months and seasons of the year, the ages of life, the four temperaments, the five senses, the children of the planets, etc. In these series, which were often linked to one another, we frequently find the topos of young people enjoying themselves in lavish, cultivated gardens or pastoral settings. This is because youth, governed by the planet Venus (see my Fig. 15), was traditionally associated with spring; see Veldman 1980; Exhib. cat. Pittsburgh 1986.

74. In fact, both the theme of the garden party and that of the Prodigal Son can be linked, independently, to late medieval images of love gardens.

75. Goodman 1982, pp. 247–59, took a significant step in recognizing that such images – her study focuses on Rubens's *Garden of Love* – were "viewed as secular, light-hearted works, not as abstruse allegories (p. 255)." Hellerstadt wisely argues in Exhib. cat. Pittsburgh 1986, p. 47, that the interpretation of such scenes should rest on the degree to which the festivities represented are excessive.

76. For drinking in seventeenth-century Dutch culture, see Pers 1628/1978. See also Van Deursen 1978–81, vol. 2, pp. 38–42; 1991, pp. 100–102; Schama 1987, pp. 189–93, 199–203, 208–12, 218–20. Dancing is also occasionally represented in paintings of garden parties. This activity likewise aroused the ire of theologians; see Van Deursen 1978–81, vol. 2, pp. 17–19; 1991, pp. 85–7.

77. Fig. 28 is an illustration from Stam 1613, p. 25.

78. See, e.g., the preface to Hooft 1611/1983. See also Porteman's comments in ibid., pp. 20–1, 46–7. Obviously, in more blatantly scabrous literature, warnings and pronouncements of didactic intent did little more than pay lip service to the concept of edification; see De Jongh 1968–9, p. 57.

79. See Hooft 1611/1983, pp. 20–2, 46–7; Keersmaekers 1985, pp. 56, 78, 119; Grootes 1987, p. 84.

80. For example, in one passage, Ovid suggests that a suitor become acquainted with his lover's husband so that the latter will not become suspicious (Bk. 1, lines 599–600). Heemskerck 1622, sig. B7v, cleverly avoids this reference to adultery by changing the original lines to "soeckt van haer Broeder oock te zijn een goeden vriend." See further Van Boheemen 1989, p. 54.

81. For Esaias van de Velde's garden parties, see Keyes 1984, pp. 29–30, 77–86. See also Exhib. cat. Philadelphia 1984, cat. nos. 112, 113.

82. For this painting, see Goodman 1982, p. 250; Keyes 1984, p. 84 and cat. no. 65.

83. For the significance of gardens as a focal point for dalliance, see especially Goodman 1982.

84. For this painting, see Exhib. cat. Philadelphia 1984, cat. no. 43; Exhib. cat. Pittsburgh 1986, cat. no. 27.

85. See Forster 1969; Goodman 1982, p. 256–8; 1989, p. 80.

86. According to Kettering 1988, pp. 426, 435, 449, Gesina ter Borch used the motif of the fan several times in her poetry album to suggest the coldheartedness of the lady who spurns her suitor's affection. For the symbolism of the fan in Dutch art, see further D. Smith 1982, pp. 81–9.

87. See pp. 12–13, this volume. See also Kettering 1993, pp. 108–9.

88. For the motif of the fan, see note 86.

89. The woman raises her hand as they sing, a gesture that appears in other representations of music makers. This gesture is commonly assumed to signify temperance. Goodman-Soellner 1989, argues that according to the musical practices of the time, no one would be required to set the pace of an informal performance. Therefore it is much more likely that gestures underscore the expressive effects or content of the song. In October 1989, at the Historians of Netherlandish Art meeting in Cleveland, Kenneth Be gave a paper on Pieter de Hooch's *Family Making Music,* in which the very same gesture appears. In explaining this gesture, Be cited several contemporary treatises that stress the importance of keeping the beat with one's hand.

90. There is an enormous amount of literature on melancholia and art; see, e.g., Klibansky, Panofsky, and Saxl 1964; Bedaux 1975, p.

27. See also Kettering 1988, pp. 499, 587, for two illustrations of melancholic lovers from Gesina ter Borch's poetry album.

91. See, e.g., Bedaux 1975, figs. 23–4.

92. See, e.g., Hooft 1611/1983, emblem no. ix. See also fol. 75 of Gesina ter Borch's poetry album; illustrated and discussed in Kettering 1988, pp. 457–8, 565.

93. See Grootes 1987, pp. 82–3. For a valuable overview of the prosperity of the Dutch Republic during the seventeenth century, see Schama 1987, pp. 289–371.

94. See, e.g., the poem by Karel van Mander celebrating a feast held in the woods outside of Haarlem, quoted in part in Exhib. cat. Amsterdam 1976, pp. 274–5. See also Schama, pp. 290–3.

95. Alpers 1983, pp. 194, 262 n. 14, convincingly suggests that such imagery was popular because it combined "actual social rituals . . . with established fictional or artistic forms."

96. See Forster 1969, p. 63.

97. For the term *gezelschapjes* in the seventeenth century, see Pauw-De Veen 1969, pp. 171–2, 178–9.

98. For an overview of the stylistic development of merry company scenes, see Blankert 1978, p. 24; and Peter Sutton's essay in Exhib. cat. Philadelphia 1984, p. xxxii. Gerard ter Borch was one of the catalysts in the development of new subject matter in genre painting; see Gudlaugsson 1959–60, vol. 1, pp. 72–101.

99. For Van Loo's influence, which has not been sufficiently assessed, see Blankert 1978, pp. 24–5; Exhib. cat. Philadelphia 1984, cat. no. 64.

100. Eighteenth-century publishers of catchpenny prints usually possessed large inventories of woodblocks, many of them dating from the sixteenth and seventeenth centuries; see De Meyer 1962, pp. 10–11, 25–53. These prints are valuable sources for measuring the popular attitudes of past eras since they were published in enormous editions intended for mass distribution. See ibid., p. 9. See also Coupe 1966, vol. 1, pp. 225–6, who notes that "the importance of the broadsheet was that it was in truth the literature which the people studied and the student of the seventeenth century who ignores that literature and draws solely on the evidence of esoteric "literary" literature for his conclusions, does so at the cost of complete accuracy."

101. See Slatkes 1981, p. 132.

102. See Van der Pluym 1954, pp. 40–50. This text is cited in Exhib. cat. Haarlem 1986, pp. 179, 180 n. 5, where it is noted that separate bedrooms came into vogue only later in the seventeenth century. There are many other paintings where beds are depicted in what clearly is not a bedroom; see e.g., ibid., cat. no. 35. For beds in Europe in the seventeenth century, see further Thornton 1983, pp. 149–79.

103. See, e.g., the title page to Anon. (ca. 1620).

104. Krul 1644, pt. 1, p. 316: "Mijn plicht vereyscht mijn werk, maer Min gund my geen rust,/ In alles wat ik doe vind ik my zonder lust;/ 't Gedacht voed op de Min, de Min voed mijn gedachten,/ Zoo ik 'er tegen strij vind ik my zonder krachten;/ Al wat ik doe oft maek 't is tegen wil, en zin,/ Vermits dat gy my steurt, ô rustelooze Min!" The same *pictura* appears in *Krul* 1634, pt. 2, p. 6, with a different meaning, focusing on winning the maiden's affections with a letter.

105. For amorous symbolism in this painting, see De Jongh 1967, pp. 50–2. See also Exhib. cat. Amsterdam 1976, cat. no. 71; Slatkes 1981, pp. 73–4; Goodman 1989, pp. 78–9. In general, scholars have approached the question of symbolism in Vermeer's art with only limited success; the evocative yet enigmatic nature of his art often masks its conventionality.

106. Slatkes 1981, p. 132, cites this emblem; yet its *subscriptio* actually undermines his argument that the picture depicts an elegant brothel.

107. Visscher 1614, p. 178: "Die dan by henlieden de tweede plaetse van gheacht te wesen wil bejaghen, die moet hem stellen om haer te dienen met een soete boertighe, vermaeckelijcke praet, mydende alle dorperheyd en vilonie, sonder haer kaeckelen ende snappen te berispen, nimmermeer haer puys pronckende kleederen te bejocken; maer al prysen wat zy doen en voortstellen, dan sal hy in haer gheselschap voor een volmaect Courtisaen ghepresen worden."

108. Half-length figures of musicians, popularized by the Utrecht Caravaggisti, were also critical for the development of this imagery; see Exhib. cat. Philadelphia 1984, pp. xxxi–xxxiii.

109. See, e.g., Mirimonde 1961; De Jongh 1967, pp. 50–6; Fischer 1975; Exhib. cat. Amsterdam 1976, cat. nos. 8, 21, 45, 53, 60; Slatkes 1981, pp. 60, 66, 88, 91–2, 150; Exhib. cat. Philadelphia 1984, cat. nos. 77, 115, 117, 119; Goodman 1989.
110. See Exhib. cat. Philadelphia 1984, p. 336.
111. It is not difficult to imagine that the young, affluent, cultured members of a group like the Ordre de l'union de la joye (to which Johan de Witt once belonged) would have purchased such paintings; for this exclusive circle of sophisticates, see Haks 1982, p. 113; Schama 1987, pp. 439–40.
112. For this painting, one of several variations on this theme by the artist, see Gudlauggson 1959–60, vol. 1, p 159, vol. 2, p. 230, no. 270.; Exhib. cat. The Hague 1974, cat. no. 60; Scott 1987, cat. no. 6. I disagree with the latter's opinion that this painting represents a music lesson with an older instructor (an entirely different theme in seventeenth-century Dutch art; see ibid., p. 26, fig. 1).
113. Kettering 1993.
114. See Forster 1969, pp. 11–12; Goodman 1983, p. 181.
115. For this painting, see Kuretsky 1979, cat. no. 63; Slatkes 1981, p. 150; Exhib. cat. Philadelphia 1984, cat. no. 88.
116. Naumann and others who have written about this picture argue that it could have been the pendant to the artist's *Oyster Meal,* also in the Mauritshuis; see Naumann 1981a, vol. 1, pp. 60, 110, vol. 2, cat. no. 35; Exhib. cat. Philadelphia 1984, cat. no. 75; Exhib. cat. Leiden 1988, cat. no. 23. Moiso-Diekamp 1987, p. 382, disagrees – as do I – pointing out that they have different provenances and that the shapes of their arched tops differ as well.
117. Naumann 1981a, vol. 1, p. 110; Exhib. cat. Philadelphia 1984, cat. no. 75; Exhib. cat. Leiden 1988, cat. no. 23, all interpret the female's gesture as one by which she shuns the man's sexual advances. This interpretation is typical of our modern-day propensity to read sexual significance into Dutch seventeenth-century art with alarming frequency. Although it is true that many Dutch paintings have erotic content, too often our assumptions that they do rest largely on our own modern sensibilities.
118. Blasius 1663, p. 245; "Gelukkig Hondje, uw voorspoedig Lot benijd is:/ Gelukkig Hondje die de schoot/ Van Celestyn so vaak genoot/ En wierd van haar gestreelt, so sacht, dat het my spijt is." See also Van Overstege 1661, pp. 36–7; Vander Minnen 1684, pp. 98–100. In one of the songs from Gesina ter Borch's poetry album, the speaker declares that he will never turn into a "juffers hont," a lady's lap dog; see Kettering 1988, p. 462. Goodman 1983, p. 183, arrived at similar conclusions to those reached here about the lap dogs in the Prado and Berlin versions of Titian's so-called *Venus and Musician* paintings. She also cited Italian and English poems in which frustrated suitors must compete with their lady's lap dogs, poems whose tenor accords with those by Dutch authors.
119. For this painting, see Exhib. cat. Amsterdam 1989–90, cat. no. 47.
120. Suitors make similar gestures in several folios in Gesina ter Borch's album; see the illustrations in Kettering 1988, pp. 548–9, 559, 588. In De Hooch's painting, there is a strong possibility that the man is a servant of the actual suitor who has been called on to deliver a letter to the lady. Many of the practical guides to the art of courting urged lovers to use servants as go-betweens in their relationships, especially for the purpose of delivering letters; see, e.g., Van Heemskerck 1622, sig. 15v.
121. Kettering 1993, pp. 109–15, contains an interesting discussion of how contemporary male and female viewers would have responded to these images.
122. See, e.g., Stone-Ferrier 1985, pp. 163–227. See also Goodman 1982, pp. 255–9; Kettering 1993, pp. 96–8.
123. See, e.g., Cats 1618, pp. 26–7, no. 13 (discussed on pp. 33–4).
124. Forster 1969, p. 2; Kettering 1993, pp. 112–13. Songbooks and related works of the period may celebrate female beauty and the power that it exerts over males, but they simultaneously celebrate the virtues that men considered most befitting women.
125. See further Kettering 1993, pp. 112–13.
126. For the comparatively late age at which people married in the seventeenth century, see Haks 1982, pp. 128–9; Marshall 1987, pp. 35–6, 41–3; Noordam 1987a, pp. 89–91, 102–3; Schama 1987, p. 436. Their research suggests that Cats's advice that men ideally

marry at age twenty-eight and women at twenty-one often went unheeded.

127. See, e.g., Moryson 1617/1971, pt. 3, p. 34. See also Van der Pol 1978, p. 63; Schama 1980, p. 6; 1987, p. 438; Spierenburg 1989, pp. 619–22.

128. See Van Deursen 1978–81, vol. 2, pp. 16–17; 1991, pp. 84–5; Haks 1982, p. 109; Schama 1987, p. 438; Dresen-Coenders and Van Haaren 1989; Roodenburg 1990, pp. 242–3. There was also the practice of *kweesten,* a time-honored custom of night courting in several European countries by which young men would spend the night unsupervised in the bedrooms of their sweethearts. This practice seems to have been fairly well known in the Netherlands – it was not restricted to the more remote parts of North Holland and Friesland, as is commonly assumed; for example, Roodenburg discusses cases of *kweesten* handled by the consistories (assemblies of ministers and elders who administered church discipline) in Amsterdam (ibid. pp. 234–6). For *kweesten* in general, see the old but still-valuable study by Wikman 1937. See also Spierenburg 1989, pp. 617–18.

129. See, e.g., Van Heemskerck 1622; Westerbaen 1665; Van Boheemen 1989, p. 54. There are also somewhat questionable reports of several country towns that had "courting markets" where a matchmaker would introduce prospective couples; see Haks 1982, p. 112; Schama 1987, p. 439.

CHAPTER 2. "BRUYT" AND "VROUWE"

1. For this portrait, see Van Thiel 1969. There are precedents in sixteenth-century art for representing married couples with attributes of their roles, for example, Maarten van Heemskerck's well-known pendants, now in the Rijksmuseum, Amsterdam. In these pendants, formerly identified as Pieter Bicker and Anne Codde, a man is shown with his bookkeeping while his wife spins. Bruyn 1955, pp. 30–1, has demonstrated that the implements and activities depicted in these pendants refer to the sitters' professions in life. I would define these objects as references to their callings; see p. 68, this volume.

2. For a slightly different interpretation of this portrait, see D. Smith 1982, pp. 70–1. The portrait of Pieter de la Court and his wife Elisabeth Tollenaer by Godaert Kamper (Exhib. cat. Haarlem 1986, cat. no. 35) likely conveys similar ideas, as do the portrait pendants by Joachim Wtewael and Gerrit van Honthorst of themselves and their wives (Exhib. cat. Haarlem 1986, cat. nos. 65, 66); see Franits 1988, pp. 253–4.

3. For these print series, see Hollstein 1949–, vol. 4, p. 23, nos. 201–9; vol. 15, p. 187, nos. 478–87.

4. For these portrait pendants, see Exhib. cat. Amsterdam 1984, cat. no. 45. The Rijksmuseum has on loan from the city of Amsterdam portrait pendants by Michiel van Musscher that have frames carved in a manner similar to those by Spruyt; see Cat. Amsterdam 1976, p. 403, cat. nos. C13, C14.

5. See Zaretsky 1973; Hamilton 1978. The theories of these two scholars have been generally accepted by many feminist historians; see, e.g., Kelly-Gadol 1976, pp. 817–23; Vann 1977, pp. 204–5; Ferguson et al. 1986, pp. xviii–xix. For an excellent critique of some of the more problematic aspects of Zaretsky's work, see Kloek 1989. Curiously, Kloek does not discuss Hamilton's book.

6. It is important to note however that a sizeable number of women were active in the economic sector of the Dutch Republic; see Spies 1986, pp. 347–50. For the female activity in this sector during the centuries preceding the formation of the republic, see Howell 1986, pp. 49–94, who has written about the role of women in the textile industry in Leiden during the late Middle Ages. Women also participated, albeit on a smaller scale, in the economic sectors of other European countries; for England, see Clark 1919; for Germany, Wiesner 1986.

7. Domestic responsibilities had certainly been the domain of women in earlier centuries. As Hamilton 1978, p. 26, points out, there was a division of labor along sexual lines "but it did not correspond to 'natural' functions (what women do) and 'real work' what men do: the feudal woman would not be asked 'do you work or are you a housewife?' " See further Kloek 1989, p. 77.

8. For an excellent overview of Luther's ideas about marriage and family life, see Ozment 1983; 1984. See also Harkness 1931, pp. 135–6; Hoffmann 1959, p. 34; Biéler 1963; Col-

linson 1988, pp. 65–7. For Erasmus and Vives, see Telle 1954, pp. 153–477; Leites 1982, pp. 385–6; Todd 1987, pp. 96–117.

9. See Ozment 1983, pp. 1–25; Todd 1987, pp. 97–8; De Mol 1989, pp. 97–8. See also the literature cited in note 10.

10. E.g., Luther 1522; Vives 1524; Erasmus 1526; Menius 1529; Bullinger 1541; 1563; Coornhert 1586/1942. Bullinger's work, as these translations suggest, was popular throughout Europe. For Coornhert's treatise, see Van Thiel 1987, pp. 92–5. For Luther's writings, see Ozment 1983, pp. 50–72, 132–54; 1984, pp. 43–53. See also Hoffman 1959, pp. 34–40. For Erasmus's book, see Telle 1954, pp. 347–420. There were also several works concerning marriage and the family published before the Reformation, e.g., Von Eyb 1472.

11. E.g., Dod and Cleaver 1612; Perkins 1613; Gouge, 1622; Wittewrongel 1661; and Cats 1625, which actually belongs to this genre despite our tendency, because of its immense popularity, to regard it as the lone seventeenth-century book devoted to marriage and family life; see pp. 5–6, this volume. For the treatise by Wittewrongel, see Groenendijk 1984; De Mol 1989, pp. 107–14. For domestic conduct books, see ibid.; Hoffman 1959; Powell 1972, pp. 101–46; Wright 1980, pp. 201–27; Hull 1982, pp. 31–70, 144; Op 't Hof 1987. See also Franits 1986, pp. 38–9.

12. See Hoffmann 1959, pp. 5–33; Todd 1987, pp. 96–117.

13. See Groenendijk 1984, pp. 14, 41. This fact is noteworthy; as Roodenburg 1990, pp. 40–2, has recently argued, Dutch seventeenth-century culture was still primarily an oral culture and not a literate one despite the comparatively low levels of illiteracy in the Netherlands versus other European countries.

14. According to Wright 1980, p. 226, "It is reasonable to suppose that few households among the substantial middle class were without benefit of printed guidance in the management of their affairs." It also should be pointed out that cheaper editions of some of the books discussed here, e.g., Cats's *Houwelyck,* were available to less affluent readers.

15. See, e.g., the works cited in note 11.

16. This movement had originated in England in the late sixteenth century and quickly spread to the Netherlands and eventually to the rest of the Continent. The English Pietistic Puritans and their Dutch colleagues believed that the Reformation had only purified the true Christian faith from Catholic heresies; a further reformation (*nadere reformatie*) was still needed in order to cleanse the hearts and minds of Christians living under the corrupting influence of secular society. Christians were charged to make religion a matter of the heart, to express renewed spiritual zeal in practical terms by leading a pious or, what the Pietists termed, a godly life. The *praxis pietatis* was grounded in Pauline ethics and directly applied to all aspects of daily living, in particular to marriage and family life. See Meertens 1943, pp. 168–85; Stoeffler 1965; Graafland 1983; Groenendijk 1984, pp. 13–34; 1989, p. 647.

17. Davies argues that many of what are commonly viewed as distinctly Puritan contributions to the idea of marriage actually existed in earlier writings by Catholic authors that predate the Reformation (1977; 1981); see further Kloek 1983, pp. 122–3. Although pre-Reformation books on marriage were written for priests, and although they stressed celibacy, they did contain advice for the clergy about how to counsel the laity on marriage problems, advice that is remarkably similar to that given in later Protestant manuals specifically addressed to the laity. In fact, during the period in question here, Catholic teaching on marriage and family life, despite the higher theological status routinely ascribed to celibacy and the stronger emphasis placed on procreation, was similar in many respects to that by Protestants. Nevertheless, Protestant books on marriage and family life far outnumber those written by humanist and Catholic authors as Protestants approached the subject in a comprehensive, systematic manner. Groenendijk 1989, p. 650, observes that the ideas of Anglicans, Catholics, Lutherans, and philosophers from antiquity about family life are similar in many respects to those of the Puritans. He also outlines several significant differences. See also Van Thiel 1987, p. 92; Todd 1987, pp. 96–117; Collinson 1988, pp. 90–3; De Mol 1989, pp. 114–20.

18. For example, a Dutch edition of Perkins 1613

was published in 1614. See Groenendijk 1984, pp. 45, 57 n. 42. Furthermore, a Dutch edition of all of Perkins's works was published in three volumes in Amsterdam in 1659–63. Perkins's writings were well known in the Netherlands; see the bibliography in Perkins 1970, pp. 612–32; Op 't Hof 1987, pp. 280–320. See also note 32 this chapter. For a bibliography of English works translated into Dutch at this time, see Van der Haar 1980; Op 't Hof 1987. See also the important study by Schoneveld 1983. For the influence of English Pietists on their Dutch colleagues in general, see Stoeffler 1965, pp. 109–61; Graafland 1983; Groenendijk 1984, pp. 18–19; 1989, pp. 647–8, who observes that "Gedurende de 17e eeuw speelde het – vertaalde – puriteinse boek een grote rol in de instructie van het gereformeerde gemoed en gezin" (p. 648).

19. To cite just one of many examples, in the second edition of *Houwelyck* (1628), Cats quotes William Gouge's *Of Domesticall Duties . . .*, published in London in 1622. See Carter 1974, pp. 97 n. 9, 105 n. 33. Wittewrongel was also influenced by Gouge's book; see Groenendijk 1984, pp. 50–1, app. C and pp. 49–52, where he discusses the importance of other English works for Wittewrongel's conception of family life. See also Schoneveld 1983, pp. 122–3; Op 't Hof 1987, pp. 587, 628, 630. Cats was also close friends with one of the leaders of the movement in Middelburg, William Teellinck. Cats wrote a number of *lofdichten* for works by Teellinck and other Pietists. According to Meertens 1943, p. 288, "De toon en inhoud van deze lofdichten verraden zijn grote sympathie voor deze voorvechters van het Piëtisme, en evenals zij heeft ook hij de praxis pietatis in zijn leven en zijn werken tot uiting gebracht." These contacts helped him to formulate his ethical and spiritual views, thus influencing his concept of marriage and the family as expounded in *Houwelyck*.

20. See Ozment 1983, p. 55; De Mol 1989, pp. 119–20; and Hekma and Roodenburg 1988, pp. 12–13, who observe that it is possible that the same admonitions and exhortations needed to be continually repeated in these books because the public found them so unappetizing.

21. See, e.g., the findings of Van Deursen 1978–81, vol. 2, pp. 23–31; 1991, pp. 90–5; Haks 1982, pp. 175–218; Noordam 1987b, pp. 134–8, 140–1; Schama 1987, pp. 405–7; Van de Pol 1988a, pp. 178–80; Roodenburg 1990, pp. 230–301, 362–9. See also Leuker and Roodenburg 1988; Van de Pol 1988b; De Mol 1989, p. 120; Spierenburg 1989, p. 623.

22. See Leuker and Roodenburg 1988; Roodenburg 1990, pp. 39, 43, 244–54, 386. See also Koorn 1987, pp. 96–7, who came to similar conclusions concerning court cases involving unwed mothers in Twente during the eighteenth century.

23. Many of the ideas set forth by Cats and others were echoed in the writings of humanists and Catholic theologians, among them Vives 1553; David 1607; Hazart 1678.

24. For example, Perkins 1613, p. 668, considers the "marriage" of Adam and Eve "as the roote wherein mans whole posterite was virtually contained and whence in ages succceeding [*sic*], both Church and Commonwealth should spring and grow to perfection." See also Van Renesse 1639, p. 4; Wittewrongel 1661, vol. 1, p. 2. In Cats 1637, pp. 5–35, a book written for bachelors considering marriage, Adam and Eve's marriage is called the "gront-houwelyck" since it provides the foundation for those of all posterity. See also Johnson 1970, pp. 103–4; Groenendijk 1984, p. 74; De Mol 1989, pp. 85–7.

25. The term "oldest political society" is taken from Thomas 1958, p. 42. This term reflects the belief that the family, in its structure and system of authority, is a microcosm of the state; see further, Chapter 3, p. 112.

26. See Johnson 1970, p. 6; Groenendijk 1984, pp. 74–6. The conviction that procreation was a consequence of marriage and not its main purpose had been previously argued by Calvin; see Harkness 1931, pp. 135–6, 144–5; Biéler 1963, p. 89; Haks 1982, pp. 11–12. Davies 1981, p. 63, observes that this point of view was not shared by all Puritan writers and that some contemporary Catholic theologians were also arguing that sexual intercourse in marriage had other benefits besides that of procreation. See also Leites 1982, pp. 383–5. Todd 1987, pp. 99–100, notes that companionship is stressed over procreation in Elizabethan marriage homilies and the writings of Christian humanists.

27. See Leites 1982, pp. 387–8. Leites considers the concepts of companionship and friendship in marriage salutary Puritan contributions to this institution. See also Groenendijk 1984, pp. 75–6, who also discusses the Protestant argument that marriage provided the natural and proper setting for channeling one's sex drives versus the Catholic view of celibacy as a life-style preferred over that of wedlock. Protestants believed that if sexual relations were conducted chastely and moderately in the confines of marriage, it afforded spouses a necessary remedy against the powerful temptation of fleshly desires. However, a few Catholics held this view as well; see the literature cited in note 17.

28. See Groenendijk 1984, p. 75.

29. See, e.g., Perkins 1613, pp. 688–9, 692; Wittewrongel, 1661, vol. 1, pp. 108–19, 126. See also Groenendijk 1984, pp. 81–9.

30. See, e.g., Perkins 1613, p. 692; Gouge 1622, p. 267; Wittewrongel 1661, vol. 1, pp. 108–19. See also Groenendijk 1984, pp. 89–93. These authors usually cited the Old Testament and especially the Pauline Epistles in support of their views concerning wifely submission and obedience. The writings of Christian humanists on this subject were equally important; see Todd 1987, pp. 115–16.

31. See, e.g., Cats 1625, chap. 4, preface, sigs. 2 ** iij^{v}–2 ** iiij^{v} ("Cort begrijp vande plichten des houwelijcks"); Van Renesse 1639, p. 119; Taffin 1640, sigs. 186^{v}–194. For English Puritan views on marriage as a covenental relationship, see Johnson 1970, p. 19, 89; Schama 1987, pp. 420–3. See also Todd 1987, pp. 98–100.

32. Dod and Cleaver 1612, sig. D7. The concept of callings was already discussed in detail in the sixteenth century, namely by Calvin in his *Institutes of the Christian Religion;* see Calvin 1960, vol. 1, pp. 724–5. The *Institutes* were frequently reprinted in the Netherlands throughout the sixteenth and seventeenth centuries. For Calvin's concept of callings, see Harkness 1931, pp. 210–12; Wallace 1982, pp. 154–6. The most important work on the concept of callings is Perkins 1609a (first published in 1603). Dutch editions of this influential treatise appeared in 1605 and 1610. Furthermore, a Dutch edition of all of Perkins's works was published in three volumes in Amsterdam in 1659–63. For these books and translations of other writings by Perkins, see Perkins 1970, pp. 613–32; Op 't Hof 1987, pp. 280–320. See also Wright 1939–40, pp. 171–96; Carter 1974, pp. 98 n. 11, 103, where it is noted that Cats attended some of Perkins's lectures at Cambridge University. For *A Treatise of the Vocations* (Perkins 1609a), see Wright 1939–40, pp. 181–3; 1980, pp. 170–85. For the concept of callings, see ibid.; Weber, 1958, pp. 79, 155 (Weber's study was originally published in German in 1904–5); Tawney 1962, pp. 240–6; H. White 1973, pp. 241–6, 253–4; Larsen 1979, pp. 9–11.

33. Gouge 1622, p. 19. The passage by Joannes de Swaef that I quoted in Chapter 1 admonishes maidens to learn those skills that belong to a woman's calling; see pp. 25–6. Marriage itself was defined as a calling; see Van Renesse 1639, p. 109. Griffith 1633, p. 415, accused women of forsaking their callings if they did not tend to their household affairs. See also Cats 1625, chap. 4, sigs. 88^{v}–89, 110^{v}–111. Motherhood and its attendant duties were regarded as a calling as well; for example, Gouge 1622, p. 510, even states that breast feeding is a calling; see further Chapter 3, pp. 113–19.

34. See Gouge 1622, p. 367. The wife's diligent fulfillment of her responsibilities in the home would benefit the family, guarantee her chastity, and thwart idleness "because it is a direct rode to become idle persons, that forsake their callings, which ought to be their stations; they must see good order observed at home" (Griffith 1633, p. 415). Dod and Cleaver 1612, sig. o6, state that a woman is called a housewife "to shew that a good wife keepes her house: and therefore Paul biddeth Titus [Titus 2:5] to exhort women that they be chast, and keeping at home: presently after chast, he saith, keeping at home, as though home were chastities keeper." See also Niccoles 1615, p. 33. There were no Dutch translations of the three works cited in this note. Nevertheless, they are important sources because their outlook, their style, and even their organization closely correspond to contemporary Dutch works.

35. Whately 1617, p. 24, states that, "in such

things [i.e., housework] he should let his wife rule under him, & give her leave to know more than himselfe which hath greater maters and more neerely concerning the family to exercise his knowledge." A Dutch edition of Whately's book, translated by the influential Pietist theologian Willem Teellinck, was published in Middelburg in 1633. See also Gouge 1622, p. 367; Cats 1625, chap. 4, sig. 2.

36. C[olerus] 1663b, p. 6: "Een huys-moeder sal het gene/ welck haren man t'huys brengt/ wel bewaren en op-leggen op sijn behoorlijcke plaets/ en gewilligh daer of halen wat men verteeren: maer wat men behouden wil/ wech sluyten . . . sy moet het oock niet qualick nemen/ so haer meerder sorge als andere huysmoeders op-geleyt wordt: want sy heeft mede het ghenot van het geheele huys/ gelijck een heerscherse en besitster." Colerus's book, originally published in German in six parts between 1591 and 1605, was one of the most popular family books during the seventeenth century; see Ozment 1983, p. 112. For other contemporary references to wives remaining at home in order to administer the goods provided by their husbands, see, e.g., Dod and Cleaver 1612, sig. L4; Van Marconvelle 1647, pp. 5–6; Wittewrongel 1661, vol. 1, p. 105.

37. See Siegel 1950, pp. 45, 48, 51; Kelso 1956, pp. 17, 31, 110–11; Hoffmann 1959, pp. 5–33; Johnson 1970, pp. 97–9; Maclean 1980, pp. 57–60; Haks 1982, pp. 150–1.

38. See Maclean 1980, pp. 57–60; Elshtain 1981, pp. 41–54.

39. Xenophon 1557, sigs. xxiii^{v}–xxiiii.

40. Smilde 1938, p. 104; Schama 1987, pp. 418–20.

41. Van Beverwijck 1639, pp. 298–99: ". . . dat den lof van een Vrouw meest bestaet in de sorgh van haer huys-houdinge. Want de schilt-padt is altijt t'huys, ende draeght het selve allesins mede." For the original parable, see Plutarch 1575, no. 27.

42. Van Beverwijck 1639, p. 299: "Man, alle buyten-werck / Is uwer daden perck. / En al wat binnen past / Dat is uw wifjes last." Schama 1980, p. 8, suggests that the figures working in the background of the print in Beverwijck's book might represent Adam and Eve. This is possible because there is an iconographic tradition for representing them at work; see, e.g., the late-fifteenth-century German book illustration reproduced in Strauss 1978–, vol. 81, p. 88.

43. See, e.g., Taffin 1640, sig. 197^{v}; Wittewrongel 1661, vol. 2, p. 722. The snail was used interchangeably with the tortoise as a metaphor of domesticity; see Pers 1624, p. 6; Cats 1625, chap. 4, sig. 93^{v}; Griffith 1633, pp. 413–14. See also Exhib. cat. Haarlem 1986, cat. no. 25, in which the motif of the snail as a symbol of domesticity is discussed in relation to a portrait of a woman drawn by Guilliam de Heer. See also Groenendijk 1984, pp. 114, 126 n. 24. Other creatures besides tortoises and snails were regarded as metaphors of domesticity. In Heyns 1625b, pt. 2, sigs. 18^{v}–19^{v}, the behavior of the spider, a creature that hunts and repairs its web, is interpreted as a metaphor of the proper manner in which to manage a household because "het huyshouden in verscheyden ampten bestaet, wijst ons het manneken, synde op jacht gestelt om den kost te saemelen, dat een goedt Huyshouder den kost voor het huysgesin winnen en besorgen moet, ende het wijfken gedurich het gebroocken net stoppende, dat een goede huysvrouwe haer huys moet gade slaen, vlijtich naeyende ende spinnende gelijck" (sig. 19^{v}). Heyns invokes the authority of Aristotle and Xenophon to support his views. The same observations about the behavior of the spider as a metaphor of household management are present in Cats 1625, chap. 4, sig. 49^{v}.

44. Whitney 1586, pt. 1, p. 93. Exhib. cat. Haarlem 1986, p. 162, fig. 30B, reproduces the *pictura* of an emblem from H. Junius 1562, no. 50, which is identical to the *pictura* from Whitney's book. See also Stallybrass 1986, p. 127, who terms this construction "the production of a normative 'Woman'." See also a sixteenth-century woodcut by Wolfgang Resch of a woman depicted in the same allegorical manner; reproduced by Ozment 1983, pp. 66–7. He notes that although the woodcut is a traditional Catholic portrayal, the virtues it displays were those desired in women by moralists of every religious persuasion. Veldman 1986, pp. 113–14, fig. 1, reproduces and discusses a sixteenth-century woodcut, attributed to Cornelis Anthonisz., that depicts an ideal married couple. Two long, accompanying poems explain the figures' attributes and the qualities most befitting men and women. Veldman (p. 114) believes that Anthonisz. was likely influenced by the German woodcut just mentioned, though she attributes it to Anton Woensam.

45. See, e.g., Whately 1617, pp. 38–40; De Brune 1660, vol. 1, p. 206, no. 556; Gouge 1622, pp. 280–2. See also Cats 1632b, pt. 1, pp. 68–70, no. 22. See also Kelso 1956, p. 105.

46. Cats 1625, chap. 4, sig. 1^v; Ridderus 1664, p. 460.

47. For Fig. 57, see Exhib. cat. Haarlem 1986, cat. no. 30.

48. Perkins 1613, p. 700. For Perkins, see notes 17 and 31, this chapter.

49. Cats 1625, chap. 4, sig. 120: "Ghy, kiest, o jonge vrouw, de spille voor het spel./ Doorsouckt den ouden tijt en al het voorich leven;/ De rijckste dochter span, de moeder konde weven;/ Princesse van het lant, de grootste dieder was,/ Ging om met reyne wol, of met het witte vlas./ Besiet de weerde vrou door Salomon beschreven,/ Sy wort door enckel lust tot spinnen aengedreven;/ Sy maeckt dat haer gesin de spille drayen kan/ Ten goede van het huys, ten dienste vanden man." The line "Sy maeckt dat haer gesin de spille drayen kan" is difficult to translate. Perhaps this line, which is literally translated here, exhorts the housewife to make the family the center of her attention, to keep the family going, etc.

50. See, e.g., Vives 1547, sig. 62; Dod and Cleaver 1612, sigs. $F5^v$–$F7^v$; Hannay 1619, sig. $C4^v$; Taffin 1640, sigs. 198^v–200; Wittewrongel 1661, vol. 1, pp. 246–7.

51. I reproduce here the print of the virtuous housewife and her maids spinning that illustrates verses 13 and 19. This series is cited by Bruyn 1955, p. 31 n. 1. Veldman 1986, pp. 114–15, figs. 2–7, reproduces the series in its entirety.

52. For the tragic story of Lucretia, see Livy, *Ab Urbe Condita,* bk. 1, chaps. 57–8; Ovid, *Fasti,* bk. 2, lines 761–852. Lucretia was praised not only as a paradigm of chastity, but also as the virtuous housewife par excellence. In early seventeenth-century plays by Pers 1624 and Heywood 1608, she emerges as a type because the authors use the story as a pretext to sermonize about the qualities of the good housewife who remains at home, diligently caring for her husband's goods and supervising her maids. The ancient heroine Penelope was also regarded as a model for her seventeenth-century sisters to emulate. Homer recounts in *The Odyssey* how Penelope waited over twenty years for her husband Ulysses to return from the Trojan War. During his absence, she was continually besieged by suitors. Penelope resisted their advances saying that she would not be wooed until she finished weaving a shroud for her father-in-law, a work which she unraveled every night. Although this ruse was eventually discovered, Penelope succeeded in frustrating many suitors until her husband's eventual return. Penelope was praised by seventeenth-century moralists for her chastity and fidelity during her husband's absence; see, e.g., Moerman 1608, sigs. $O2^v$–O3. The *picturae* of Moerman's emblem book also appear, with new *subscriptios,* in Vondel 1613; see the introduction by J. Becker to the 1978 reprint of this book, pp. vii–xi. See also Colse 1596; Brathwait 1631, pp. 103–4. See also Jan de Bray's *portrait historié* of a couple as Ulysses and Penelope, in Exhib. cat. Washington, D.C., 1980–81, cat. no. 62.

53. Support for this hypothesis was also found in the existence of flourishing commercial textile enterprises in Haarlem and Leiden at that time, as well as in contemporary death inventories in which only a relatively small percentage of households contained spinning wheels. See Chapter 1, p. 30.

54. De Vries 1990a, pp. 55–6. (Another example is Fig. 75.) Even if one does not accept the hypothesis that these pendants are portraits, it does not substantially alter my reading of them. See also Slatkes 1981, p. 113. D. Smith 1987, discusses the settings and social milieu that genre paintings and portraits share, arriving at the controversial conclusion that genre paintings ironically invert the social meanings of portraiture. The strong genre-painting-like character of Ter Borch's pendants has long been noted; see Gudlaugsson 1959–60, vol. 1, pp. 87–8, vol. 2, cat. nos. 95, 96; Exhib. cat. The Hague 1974, cat. nos. 24, 25; Exhib. cat. Amsterdam 1976, cat. no.

3. Moiso-Diekamp 1987, pp. 481–2, strongly doubts that the paintings are pendants. Elizabeth Honig, writing in Exhib. cat. Leiden 1988, p. 81, points out that there is a precedent for pendants of this type of domestic subject matter in the work of Judith Leyster. Leyster painted pendants of a *Mother Sewing with Children by Lamplight and Fire* (Dublin, National Gallery of Ireland) and a *Mother Cleaning a Child's Hair* (present location unknown); for these pendants, see Hofrichter 1989, cat. nos. 22, 23. For the pendant of Wiesken combing a child's hair, see further Chapter 3, pp. 128–9.

55. See pp. 21–31.
56. Slatkes 1981, p. 113, believes that the pendants can be linked on pedagogical grounds. According to him, both the motifs of spinning and hair combing refer to training or education. The motif of hair combing certainly conveys this idea (see Chapter 3, pp. 124–30), but whether spinning does as well is open to question.
57. Fifteenth-century book illustrations provide iconographic precedents for these prints; see Olyslager 1985, pp. 22–3, fig. 5. See also Exhib. cat. Nijmegen 1985, pp. 53–5. Bruyn 1955, p. 31, states that spindles were used as attributes for personifications of virtue in the theater during the sixteenth century.
58. The print reproduced here is part of a series depicting virtues. Van de Passe I also engraved a series of prints depicting vices that correspond to these. The print corresponding to that of diligence illustrates negligence and includes a sleeping figure who has abandoned her spinning. For these two series, see Hollstein 1949–, vol. 15, pp. 180, nos. 426–32, 184, nos. 455–61. Van de Passe's prints representing diligence and negligence were copied as *picturae* in Oraeum 1620, nos. 29, 31. In my Fig. 58, there is also a hen with her chicks beside the personification of diligence. In contemporary literature, the hen was regarded as a symbol of diligence because of her vigilant care for her brood; see, e.g., Biens 1635, p. 55.
59. Cats 1625, chap. 3, preface, sig. *** iij. See De Vries et al. 1882–, vol. 4, col. 291; De Cock 1911, p. 23, no. 49.
60. See De Swaef 1621/1740, p. 312; V[an der] D[oes] 1622, sig. D1[v]; Brathwait 1631, p. 49. Cats 1625, chap. 4, sig. 121[v], advises women to sew if the whir of the spinning wheel bothers their husbands; De Jongh quotes this passage in Exhib. cat. Haarlem 1986, p. 75.
61. For the print, see Andrews 1977, pl. 92. For its possible meaning in this context, see note 76.
62. This design also resembles several that appeared in contemporary pattern books; see, e.g., Sibmacher 1604, pl. 31. For pattern books, works responsible for the transmission of embroidery patterns throughout Europe, see Chapter 1, pp. 27–9. This very same symbol of clasped hands appears on pairs of embroidered bridal gloves that have actually survived to this day; see Du Mortier 1984.
63. For the motif of clasped hands, see Exhib. cat. Haarlem 1986, p. 54, cat no. 28.
64. See Carter 1627, p. 77; Brathwait 1631, pp. 1–25; Taffin 1640, sigs. 197[v]–198. See also Kelso 1956, p. 107.
65. For the symbolism of the broom, see further pp. 97–100.
66. See, e.g., De Jongh 1968–9, pp. 36–7; Broos 1971, p. 25; Exhib. cat. Amsterdam 1976, cat. nos. 64, 68. Perhaps the most famous footwear in Northern European art are the pair of patterns that appear in the foreground of Jan van Eyck's *Arnolfini Portrait.* Bedaux 1986, p. 12, convincingly argues that the patterns in this portrait, once widely regarded as a sacred symbol, should be linked to late medieval marriage rituals. See also Bedaux 1990, pp. 29–30.
67. *Conjugalia praecepta* originally appeared in the second book of Plutarch's *Moralia.*
68. Plutarch 1575. A reprint of Plutarch's book is appended to Van Marconvelle 1647, pp. 200–245. Curiously, the 1575 reprint contains only forty-three "laws" while Van Marconvelle and all other sources list forty-nine. For the frequent quotation of Plutarch's work by seventeenth-century authors, see the literature cited in note 71.
69. Plutarch 1575, no. 25. The version of the "law" recounted in Van Marconvelle 1647, pp. 224–5, no. 31, is quoted here: "De Egyptische Vrouwen/ nae des landts wijse/ en hadden geen gewoonte schoenen te dragen/ op dat sy haer-lieder schamende barvoets te gaen/ souden leeren t'huys te blijven."
70. E.g., Houwaert 1622–3, vol. 2, p. 651; Hazart 1678, p. 259. The duty of women to remain in the home in order to manage the

practical affairs of the household is discussed in detail on pp. 68–9.

71. De Jongh, in Exhib. cat. Haarlem 1986, cat. no. 25, reproduces and discusses a drawing of a newly married woman with a snail on the ground before her. He cites several contemporary texts – including Van Marconvelle 1647 – that cite the creature as a metaphor of domesticity because it carries its house on its back. This idea, found in Plutarch 1575, no. 27, was the "law" most often cited in seventeenth-century literature. In these later texts, a snail or a turtle are used interchangeably to illustrate it. See the works cited in Exhib. cat. Haarlem 1986, p. 144. De Jongh also cites Plutarch's book as an important source for interpreting portraits of families playing instruments as metaphors of concord (ibid., pp. 44–5); see Plutarch 1575, no. 8, and pp. 88–9, this volume.
72. Coornhert 1610, no. 23.
73. See Exhib. cat. Amsterdam 1976, cat. no. 51; Cheney 1987.
74. Van de Venne 1623, p. 97: "Vorsse-mossels, zijn gheleken/ Met de seegbaer vrouwenlien,/ Die beset, en eerbaer spreken,/ En na 't huys staegh ommesien;/ Wijven moeten al sté-vast/ Dregen, mossel-huysigh-last." The mussel also functions as a metaphor of domesticity in a poem in ibid., pp. 98–9, entitled "Vorsse-Mossels eyghenschap, gheduydet op de ghelijckenisse der menschen seden, en leven." This section of the book, beginning with the print of a mussel vendor on p. 95, was also published as a large block print in 1650; see F. Muller 1863–82, vol. 4, no. 1983.
75. Cats 1625, chap. 4, sig. 91^{v}. Cats 1632b, appendix of proverbs, "rakende de onderlinge plichten tusschen man en wijf," after pt. 2, p. 9, contains the following proverb on the housewife's duty to remain at home: "Blijft binnen u schelpen, Dat sal u helpen." The section in which this proverb appears is entitled "Eygen huys."
76. Netscher undoubtedly intended the print on the background wall to convey some specific idea because the woman faces it. Unfortunately, its meaning in this context is unclear. As noted, it resembles Goudt's *Flight into Egypt* after Elsheimer, particularly in the compositional line created by the tops of the trees, descending to the left. One major difference, however, is the absence of figures in the fictitious print. Since it represents a landscape, the print could refer to some far-off locality to which the lace-maker's husband has journeyed. The woman's domestic activity and the motifs around her would then refer to her virtuous behavior during her husband's absence. Because of Holland's extensive mercantile relations with distant lands during the seventeenth century, Dutch men spent considerable amounts of time away from the home on business. In fact, books were written specifically for traveling merchants and their wives, prescribing specific conduct during their trying times of separation; see, e.g., Westermannus 1631. Cats 1625, chap. 4, sig. 108, offers much advice for women and their husbands about how to conduct themselves during times of separation.
77. For the *nisstuk*, a device not invented but nonetheless popularized by Gerard Dou, see F. Robinson 1974, pp. 89–91; Naumann 1981a, vol. 1, pp. 38, 58; Exhib. cat. Leiden 1988, p. 101; Exhib. cat. Amsterdam 1989–90, p. 46; Baer 1990, pp. 72–4; Sluijter 1990, p. 15.
78. Among the most insightful studies on illusionism is Hobson 1982, a book that studies this phenomenon in eighteenth-century French culture; her findings are deftly summarized by D. Smith 1987, p. 425.
79. For this motif, see also pp. 81–2, this volume.
80. Cats 1627, pp. 80–1, no. 14.
81. Cats 1632b, pt. 1, p. 69: "Femme qui va de place en place, parle de tous & tous d'elle. Femme bonne est oiseau de cage."
82. Van der Minnen 1684, pp. 76–7: "'K Sagh in 't Salet daer hangen / Den groenen Papegay, / Al sat hy daer ghevanghen, / Hy klapten wonder fray. . . . En hy / Was daer soo bly / In sijn ghevangen kluys, / Als in een Bruyloft-huys. . . . Soo ick uw slaef magh zijn / Neemt my, / In slaverny, / Bindt mijn hant aen uw hant, / Den Trouw-rinck zy den bant."
83. See De Jongh and Vinken 1961, p. 118; De Jongh 1967, pp. 28–31; Exhib. cat. Haarlem 1986, cat. no. 20.
84. See De Jongh 1974, pp. 179, 189–90; Franits 1986, pp. 40–2. See also Chapter 3, pp. 142–3.

85. The metaphor of the wife as a fruitful vine influenced many works of art, most notably representations of families saying grace before the meal. In these, grapevines sometimes grow literally into the house as a reference to a woman's fertility, that is, to the offspring created through chaste marital love (see my Figs. 119, 120). See also De Jongh 1974, pp. 187–90; Exhib. cat. Haarlem 1986, pp. 47–50, 295; Franits 1986, p. 40; Van Thiel 1987, pp. 128–41. See also Bedaux 1987; 1990, pp. 69–108. See also Chapter 3, pp. 142–3.

86. Baardt 1645, p. 373: "De Propheet [David] / dan willende een deugdelijcke huys-vrouwe van eerbaer Zeden / gelijcken by een vruchtbaren Wijn-stock / heeft-se niet willen planten aen de wegen buytens Huys / maer beklemste binnen de Muyren harer Woninghe." In a wedding poem based on this famous psalm, Baers 1629, p. 18, states that verse 3 teaches women to stay at home and know that nothing ornaments a house better than their presence. Baers's pamphlet is a published version of the sermon that he delivered at a wedding on 23 January 1629.

87. For *andachtsbilder*, see Panofsky 1927; Ringbom 1965; Marrow 1986, pp. 152–3; Falkenburg 1988, pp. 22–3.

88. In this painting and several others discussed here (e.g., Figs. 20, 79), women are seated near open windows with light streaming in on them. In a painting by Nicolaes Maes in the Wallace Collection (see Valentiner 1924, pl. 21), a woman working next to a window gestures to a child who presses against the glass outside. The woman is strongly illuminated by sunlight, and her rhetorical gesture toward the young boy seems to call attention to the light streaming in through the window. Its precise significance in these contexts is unclear, but it is noteworthy that virtuous women are often compared to bright light (including sunlight) in contemporary literature; see, e.g., V[an der] D[oes] 1622, sig. C2: "Als in den dagheraet den Hemel door de Sonne / Wordt door een deughtsaem Vrou 't cieraet van't huys begonnen." See also, Cats 1625, chap. 4, sig. 30; Hofferus 1635, pp. 86–7; Sprankhuisen 1658, pt. 1, p. 150; Schaep 1671, pp. 241–2; Wits 1706, pp. 173–4.

89. During the seventeenth century, illuminated lanterns were often associated with wisdom. Logically, unlit lanterns conveyed the converse meaning: mental or spiritual ignorance. For the lantern as a symbol of reason as well as ignorance, see Emmens 1963, p. 133 and n. 18. However, it is unlikely that unlit lanterns are symbolic of ignorance in the scores of pictures celebrating the virtues of domesticity and motherhood. In Proverbs 31, the oft-cited chapter written in praise of the virtuous housewife, Solomon extols the woman whose "candle goeth not out by night" (vs. 18). Seventeenth-century authors usually quoted this verse to justify their belief that housewives were obligated to continue their work long after the sun had set. Women were exhorted to keep their candles or lanterns lit at night, that is, to continue working after daylight hours – in fact, there are several paintings in which women sew by candlelight. Dod and Cleaver 1612, sig. F5^{v}, mention Proverbs 31:18, commenting that a housewife "borroweth of the morning and the evening, for to dispatch her businesse." Lanterns and candles are usually discussed in contemporary literature in connection with the need for housewives to continue working on into the night. Wittewrongel 1661, vol. 2, p. 722, states that "dewijle de Vrouwe haer werck meest binnens-huys heeft / soo kan sy oock door het ontsteecken van een keersse, hare sonne oock in den nacht doen open-gaen". See also V[an der] D[oes] 1622, sig. C2; Gouge 1622, p. 674; Cats 1625, chap. 5, p. 5. Perhaps the presence of lanterns in so many paintings of domestic subjects refers as well to the woman's obligation to work on into the night. Unfortunately, this cannot be determined as the lanterns depicted are almost always unlit.

90. For a representation of one of these lanterns, see the print in Cats 1625, chap. 4, sig. 57. See also the large lantern on the fish woman's stall – for use when selling fish at night after a catch had been brought in – in a portrait by Emanuel de Witte of Adriana van Heusden and her daughter at a fish market, perhaps the New Fishmarket in Amsterdam (Fig. 75).

91. The painting, a tour de force in the *fijnschilder* style, demonstrates why Dou was so famous during his lifetime. Along with one other picture by the artist, it was actually purchased by the States General and sent as

a gift along with other works to Charles II of England; see Martin 1902, p. 57; Mahon 1949a, p. 304 n. 21; 1949b, p. 350; Logan 1979, pp. 75–86; Broos 1987, pp. 111–18; Exhib. cat. The Hague 1988–9, cat. no. 9; Exhib. cat. Amsterdam 1989–90, cat. no. 7; Baer 1990, pp. 93–7, cat. no. 76.

92. In this regard, see the important observations of Baer 1990, p. 75. P. Hecht, in his entry in Exhib. cat. Amsterdam 1989–90, p. 54 and n. 3, cites John Evelyn's description of the painting as a "drollerie" – an English term often used to describe Dutch paintings during this period – as probable evidence that it was more esteemed for its mimetic qualities than for its potential meaning. This may indeed be true but it clearly does not negate the possibility that due to its conventional use of imagery, the painting evoked common associations about women and domesticity for some of its viewers; see further pp. 16–17, this volume. On the basis of the coat of arms in the window to the sewing mother's left, and of the fact that the date on it has been changed to 1658, Broos 1987, p. 117, has hypothesized that the picture was originally commissioned by Dirck van Beresteyn and Magdelena van Adrichem on the occasion of their marriage in 1652. Dirck van Beresteyn died shortly after, and his widow might have canceled the commission. Broos's hypothesis is ingenious but highly speculative. Moreover, it does not explain the presence of children in the painting.

93. The presence of a cupid on the column in front of the bookcase is difficult to explain. Egbert Haverkamp-Begemann has suggested that because of its placement in the composition, the cupid might refer to marital love that connects the realms of the man and woman. The motif of a cupid on a column appears in several other paintings by Dou; see Sumowski 1983–, vol. 1, pp. 572, no. 275, 599, no. 302.

94. For the cap, see Le Francq. van Berkhey 1769–, vol. 3, pt. 1, pp. 599–600.

95. Analogous ideas are present in a painting by Esaias Boursse that depicts a woman spinning beside a chair on which some male garments and accoutrements are draped (see Fig. 55).

96. See Cats 1625, chap. 4, sig. 81[v]. Jacob Bierens's daughter, who plucks a bird in the family portrait by Sorgh discussed later in this chapter, (see Fig. 67), has evidently learned her lessons well.

97. Markham 1637, p. 62. This book contains a wide variety of cooking recipes along with instructions for brewing beverages, directions for preparing herbal remedies, and the like. These were skills that most housewives were required to know, especially those living on the great English country estates. For recipe books of this period, see Hull 1982, pp. 37–45; Rose 1989. See also Cats 1625, chap. 4, sig. 81, who recommends several recipe books and discusses many practical aspects of cooking, e.g., how to preserve fruit to be eaten during the winter. Schama 1987, pp. 150–88, provides an illuminating account of Dutch attitudes toward food and feasting.

98. The authors of domestic conduct books invariably cite this verse as proof that a woman must be capable of preparing food for her family; see, e.g., Wittewrongel 1661, vol. 2, p. 724.

99. This is not to imply that all representations of women cooking can be interpreted in this manner. Sumowski 1983–, p. 532, no. 279, has suggested that Dou's *Cook in a Niche* in Karlsruhe might be understood as an allegory of the four elements. For this painting, see also Exhib. cat. Amsterdam 1989–90, cat. no. 4. Emmens 1968, pp. 112–13, fig. 3, had earlier demonstrated that another painting by Dou of a cook, in Montepellier, actually illustrated the proverb "Wel ghecoockte rapen is goe pottage" and, as such, alluded to artistic training. Emmens fails to explain why the woman is not scraping turnips (*rapen*) but parsnips.

100. For this portrait, see Exhib. cat. Haarlem 1986, cat. no. 58.

101. See pp. 14, 21–2.

102. For this husbandly duty, see pp. 67–8. Writing in Exhib. cat. Haarlem 1986, p. 248, De Jongh states that the Bierens house was located close to the Amsterdam fish market, which might explain the motif of the elder Bierens holding the fish in the portrait. De Jongh acknowledges that the motif could very well have a "diepere betekenis, maar in dat geval ontgaat ons de kwintessens, of het moest zijn dat de vis refereert aan het begrip soberheid, zoals in Ripa's *Iconologia* een vis

tot de attributen van de verpersoonlijkte soberheid behoort." The motif of the fish could very well symbolize sobriety, but it is more probable that it illustrates the father's provision for his family. This interpretation is supported by the visual context in which the motif appears – the women are preparing other foods – and also the widespread references to husbands as providers in contemporary literature. See Franits 1988, p. 253. The fact that the Bierens family were Mennonites poses no problems in this regard; there were domestic conduct books written by Mennonite authors at this time; see, e.g., Van Wormerveer 1677. Their ideas closely correspond to those of their Pietist counterparts.

103. See Exhib. cat. Haarlem 1986, pp. 40–5, cat. nos. 69, 70, 71.

104. De Jongh in Exhib. cat. Haarlem 1986, p. 248, was the first to interpret the motif of the son playing the *viola da gamba* as a symbol of harmony. He also notes the Plutarchian source of this motif and discusses other examples of its use in art; see ibid., pp. 40–5 and cat. nos. 69, 70, 71. For a critique of De Jongh's analysis as well as for the following discussion, see Franits 1988, p. 253.

105. Dod and Cleaver 1612, sig. L4.

106. For this painting, see Exhib. cat. Basel 1987, cat. no. 22. I do not agree with the author's suggestion that several motifs in this painting (e.g., the dead duck) are symbols of love.

107. See Exhib. cat. Philadelphia 1984, cat. no. 65. See also Sutton 1990, p. 191, who observes that although the painting "would seem to deal generally with those ideals of domesticity that served to inspire so many scenes of Dutch home life around mid-century . . . it may also convey a veiled erotic message and an admonition, functioning as footnotes to the popular theme of bourgeois tranquility." See also Exhib. cat. The Hague 1990–91, pp. 328–9.

108. De Jongh 1968–9, pp. 22–52.

109. This point was made in Exhib. cat. Philadelphia 1984, cat. no. 65. See also Sutton 1990, pp. 190–1. For raucous scenes, see De Jongh 1968–9, figs. 1, 12, 13, 14.

110. Other paintings of women plucking fowl, among them one by Pieter de Hooch (Danzig, National Museum), exhibit the same aura of warm, domestic intimacy and serenity as Maes's work; for this painting, see Sutton 1980, cat. no. 73. For the duties and obligations of servants, see pp. 100–8. The meaning of the prowling cat – if it really is prowling – in this context is difficult to determine, but I do not consider it a metaphor for erotic desire (see Exhib. cat. Philadelphia 1984, cat. no. 65).

111. There are several Dutch seventeenth-century group portraits in which husbands present the catches of their hunt to their wives; see, e.g., Bartholomeus van der Helst's *Family Group* in the Wallace Collection in London (reproduced in Cat. London 1968, p. 147, cat. no. P110). However, the presence of hunting equipment and dead game in portraiture is most often intended as a reference to social status; see Sullivan 1984, pp. 33–45. See also Exhib. cat. Haarlem 1986, cat. no. 63.

112. Noteworthy is the presence of a dead rabbit in the painting of the apple peeler, which in this context can only refer to the preparation of a meal. In other words, the rabbit cannot possibly be understood as an erotic metaphor, an association that it often carries in other paintings; see De Jongh 1968–9, pp. 41–3, fig. 13.

113. F. Robinson 1974, p. 25. See also Moiso-Diekamp 1987, pp. 366–7. Gudlaugsson 1968, pp. 25, 31, doubts whether the paintings were considered pendants in the seventeenth century. He also suspects that the one representing the woman peeling apples was painted somewhat later.

114. Renditions of this theme must be carefully examined because a group of them are actually portrayals of marketplaces that existed in the seventeenth century and thus properly belong to the category of cityscapes; see Exhib. cat. Amsterdam 1977, cat. nos. 32, 56, 124, 134. Other paintings of market shopping cannot be included among those representing the theme of the virtuous woman purchasing provisions for her family. A large work by Metsu in the Louvre (see F. Robinson 1974, fig. 94) depicts a woman at a market. A man directly behind this shopper seems to make an obscene gesture at her. In some ways, this scene is reminiscent of ones in which shopping women are robbed; see the drawing by Toorenvliet reproduced in Lugt 1950, pl. LXXVIII, no. 649, and a print of a similar scene in Lagniet (ca. 1657–63), vol. 2, n.p. For socioeconomic aspects of Metsu's painting, see the recent article by Stone-Ferrier 1989. Market shopping was also traditionally associated with the months of the year; see Stone-Ferrier 1989, pp. 435–6. See also the prints by Crispijn van de Passe I of September (Hollstein 1949–, vol. 15, p. 202, no. 585) and C. van Dalen after a painting by Joachim von Sandrart of the month of September, from a series of the twelve months. Joost van den Vondel penned verses in honor of the series; for the Sandrart painting and the print and poem, see Porteman 1987, pp. 120–5. For Sandrart's series, see ibid.; Klemm 1986, cat. nos. 35–46.

115. Cats 1625, chap. 4, sigs. 86v–87v. The housewife's duty to purchase provisions for her family recalls the words of Solomon in Proverbs 31:14: "She [the virtuous woman] is like the merchant's ship; she bringeth her food from afar." The significance of this verse was not lost to contemporaries; Wilkinson 1613, managed to preach an entire wedding sermon about it (6 January 1607, in the presence of James I of England, on the occasion of the marriage of "the Lord Hay, and his Ladie"). See also Sprankhuisen 1658, pp. 143–50. The verse was illustrated in the print series by Coornhert after Heemskerck, previously mentioned (reproduced and discussed in Veldman, 1986, p. 115, fig. 3.) In an anonymous portrait of a woman dated 1602, a ship appears in the background, a clear reference to Proverbs 31:14. For this portrait and the relationship of the ship in its background to Proverbs 31:14, see Exhib. cat. 1986, cat. no. 45.

116. Cats 1625, chap. 4, sig. 87: "Noyt de beste koop, / Leyt in het minste gelt, of inden meesten hoop."

117. For this painting, see Exhib. cat. Dordrecht 1977–8, cat. no. 3. Still earlier are the Netherlandish paintings of markets that usually include a religious scene in the background. These works, whose meanings are currently under debate among art historians, must have influenced the development of market scenes in Dutch seventeenth-century art. However, their subject matter was gradually abandoned by artists during the course of the first half of the seventeenth century.

118. In *The Fishmarket,* the figure in the right background is identified as the artist's self-portrait.

119. De Witte has portrayed the wife and daughter of Joris de Wijs, the man with whom the artist had a contractual arrangement. It provided De Witte with room and board and a stipend in exchange for all the pictures he would paint while living in De Wijs's house. This particular portrait was the subject of lengthy litigation over ownership between De Witte and Adriana van Heusden; see Maclaren 1960, pp. 458–9; Manke 1963, pp. 3–5.

120. See pp. 73–5. See also De Vries 1990a, pp. 55–6, whose reading of this portrait is similar to mine.

121. Perkins 1613, p. 700. For Perkins, see note 18.

122. For example, there are few pictures of women ironing or making beds; see the painting by Jacob Duck of a servant ironing (Utrecht, Centraal Museum), illustrated and discussed in Exhib. cat. Amsterdam 1976, cat. no. 19. See also De Hooch's painting of a woman making a bed, known in three versions; see Sutton 1980, cat. nos. 40A, 40B, 40C. See also De Hooch's painting of two women storing linens (Fig. 88).

123. Foreign travelers to the Netherlands often noted this, with great astonishment. See, e.g., the traveler's descriptions recounted by Sutton 1980, p. 47. See also Schama 1987, p. 375. Though no doubt based at least in some degree on firsthand observations and experiences, the jocular, sarcastic nature of so many of these descriptions warns us that these are not always reliable sources of information about life in the Dutch Republic.

124. For the painting illustrated here, see C. White 1982, cat. no. 45; and Baer 1990, cat. no. 89, who observes that Steen's representation of a woman scouring a kettle actually predates those by Dou.

125. See F. Robinson 1974, p. 79, n. 56. The motif of women scouring pots was sometimes construed as an erotic metaphor; see Becker 1977. However, the examples that Becker discusses have different visual contexts than the paintings examined here.

126. E.g., Wittewrongel 1661, vol. 2, p. 723; Pers 1669, vol. 1, p. 233; Visscher 1669, p. 19, no. 47. De Vries et al. 1882–, vol. 9, cols. 1186–7, interpret the expression "men stak

de handen uit de mouw" as an "zinnebeeld van arbeidzaamheid en ijver."

127. Eddy de Jongh discussed the symbolism of the broom in his lecture "The Interpretation of Genre Paintings: Possibilities and Limits" given at the symposium on Dutch genre painting at the Royal Academy in London in November 1984. My ideas about the significance of the broom are to some extent derived from his lecture.

128. For this painting, see Sutton 1980, cat. no. 74. See also Schama 1987, p. 393, who remarks that, in it, "the overwhelming feeling is that of domestic consecration."

129. The picture depicted over the chimney in the background is no longer legible; perhaps it was a landscape.

130. E.g., Poirters 1659, p. 68. The *pictura* of this emblem is based on an earlier engraving; see Exhib. cat. Cologne 1981, cat. no. 46. Obviously, there is no relationship between the emblem and the motif in the painting. I cite it merely as one example of the widespread association between broom sweeping and moral cleanliness, one that crosses all religious boundaries. This association actually had a long tradition in European culture; Bedaux 1986, pp. 19–20, in discussing the significance of the brush in Jan van Eyck's *Arnolfini Portrait,* notes that, in one late medieval text, a similar object figuratively refers to the cleanliness of the soul (see his fig. 11). See also Bedaux 1990, p. 39.

131. Wittewrongel 1661, vol. 1, frontispiece.

132. Oomius 1661, pp. 211–13.

133. This interpretation cannot be conclusive, despite the widespread contemporary association of brooms with moral and spiritual purity. The problem essentially centers around the lack of internal evidence in the painting – and many others where brooms figure prominently – to support it. Brooms and other utensils for cleaning in Dutch art are also discussed by Schama 1987, pp. 375–97, who interprets them from an anthropological perspective that emphasizes cleanliness as an affirmation of such values as separateness, vigilance, and patriotism.

134. Perkins 1613, p. 700. For Perkins, see note 18.

135. Salter 1579, sig. C8^{v}. Salter's book is actually a close translation, without acknowledgment, of the then-famous work by Bruto 1555; see Kelso 1956, p. 344, no. 161. For the housewife's duty to oversee the servants, see also Vives 1547, sig. 107^{v}; Perkins 1613, p. 700; Gouge 1622, pp. 682–3; Cats 1625, chap. 4, sigs. 101^{v}–107^{v}, esp. sigs. 106–106^{v}.

136. Lasius 1987, pp. 55–6, argues that Quiringh van Brekelenkam played an important role in the development of this theme in Dutch genre painting. Despite the large number of pictures depicting servants who are being sent off to shop, there are no contemporary literary references that discuss marketing as a servant's task.

137. One of the earliest depictions of a housewife inspecting the purchases of her maid is found in a print by Jan Saenredam after Hendrick Goltzius entitled *Midday* from the series *The Four Times of Day;* reproduced in Hollstein 1949–, vol. 23, p. 74, no. 99.

138. This background picture appears in reverse in another painting by Brekelenkam that also shows a housewife inspecting provisions offered for sale by a street vendor. For this painting, now in Leipzig, Museum der bildenden Künste, see Cat. Leipzig 1979, p. 296, fig. 992.

139. This idea can be inferred from several contemporary references that describe parents as shepherds of their families; see Hazart 1678, pp. 243–4. Hazart's book was addressed to Catholics, but many of his ideas about marriage and family life were shared by Protestants. See also Wittewrongel 1661, vol. 1, p. 235, who calls the good ruler of a republic, and by extension, of a family, a shepherd.

140. The subject of housewives and servants – and domestic themes in general – figures prominently in De Hooch's art; see Sutton 1980, p. 45; Franits 1989; Franits 1992, pp. 118–23.

141. For the erotic interpretation of this painting, see Durantini 1983, p. 43; Franits, 1985, p. 698. For Quiringh van Brekelenkam's role in the development of this theme, see Lasius 1987, pp. 58–9.

142. For this painting, see Slatkes 1981, pp. 126–7; Durantini 1983, pp. 215–17.

143. For the history of golf and the older games from which it evolved, see Exhib. cat. Amersfoort 1982.

144. Gouge 1622, p. 670. See also Wittewrongel 1661, vol. 1, p. 210; Teellinck 1626/1975, pp. 9, 14, 20, 38. (Teellinck's short book bitterly attacks "worldly" fashions.) Durantini 1983, p. 354 n. 117, argues that the relationship between the women is unclear. If the plainly dressed woman is the servant, Durantini wonders why the mistress would allow her to put the "valuables" away. In my opinion, the servant is simply helping her mistress. Mistresses were exhorted to work alongside their servants; see the literature cited in note 145.

145. See Gouge 1622, pp. 682–3; Wittewrongel 1661, vol. 2, pp. 723–4.

146. Gouge 1622, p. 682. Curiously, the words "gives a portion" in this verse actually refer to the virtuous housewife who feeds her family and servants: see the print in the series, mentioned previously, by Coornhert after Heemskerck that illustrates this verse, discussed and reproduced in Veldman 1986, pp. 115–16, fig. 4. Proverbs 31 was invoked to justify the mistress's duty to supervise her servants, but authors most frequently cited verse 27: "She looketh well into the ways of her household"; see, e.g., Wittewrongel 1661, vol. 2, p. 724.

147. Durantini 1983, pp. 215–17. Schama 1987, p. 393, seems to follow her interpretation, as he states that De Hooch's painting "anticipated one of Luiken's panegyrics to clean linen and right living." The emblem in question can be found in Luiken 1711, pp. 22–5, no. 7. Slatkes 1981, p. 126, cites the Luiken emblem but does not believe that its meaning can be applied to the painting.

148. Calvin 1960, vol. 1, p. 723. Van Focquenbroch 1682, vol. 1, pp. 80–1 ("Kermis-Gift, aen de jongh-getrouwde Luyden, Monsr. en Juffrouw, N. N."), discusses the need to maintain the goods of the house. From her study of the wording of last wills and testaments, Marshall 1987, p. 1, concluded: "The grace of God was intertwined with the gift of worldly possessions, and there was nothing irreverent about linking the two. The family possessions were a sacred responsibility." See also Weber 1958, p. 162; H. White 1973, pp. 263–5; and, especially, Schama 1987, pp. 289–371.

149. See Durantini 1983, pp. 212–21.

150. Slatkes 1981, p. 126, came to this conclusion.

151. Anon. 1626, no. 5: "Werckt, maer merckt. Ick kan hier oock niet vergeten, / Hoe te slaen de ballen weten / . . . . Hier soo leert u kolf en bal, / Hoe men 'twerck wel spoeyen sal. / Wit, en oochmerck alle menschen / Moeten kiesen van haer wenschen, / Als ghy niet oocht seecker ent / Licht, en twyffelich ghy bent. / Als de bal niet ver moet wycken, / Maer recht nae zyn pael toestrycken, / Op de kolf wel past het leer, / Brengt het spel aen winst en eer." Durantini 1983, p. 217, cites this emblem but confuses the name of the publisher, J. Calom, with that of the anonymous author.

152. See Exhib. cat. Amersfoort 1982, cat. nos. 4, 5, 6, and the illustrations on pp. 18, 25, 51. The precise meaning of this motif in portraiture is unclear.

153. In *The Linen Chest* (Fig. 88), a statue of Mercury is present on a ledge over the doorway. The painting was cleaned in the early 1980s at the Rijksmuseum. I examined it with Dr. P. J. J. van Thiel (who kindly informed me of the cleaning) and agree with his opinion that it is highly probable that the picture on the wall directly behind Mercury was originally painted over the statue by De Hooch himself. Vestiges of the statue only appeared when the painting was cleaned earlier in this century; it was subsequently painted in more fully by the restorer. For a reproduction showing the appearance of the painting before it was cleaned, see Valentiner 1929, p. 69. The subject of the statue in the painting had been identified as Mercury by Keyszelitz 1956, pp. 66–7. Sutton 1980, cat. no. 52, believed that the statue depicted Perseus holding the head of Medusa. Slatkes 1981, p. 126, related the statue to a bronze by Hendrick de Keyser. A similar statue is present in De Hooch's *Woman Drinking with Soldiers* in the Louvre; see Sutton 1980, cat. no. 26; Exhib. cat. Philadelphia 1984, cat. no. 52.

154. Dod and Cleaver 1612, sigs. F5–F5[v]. See also Cats 1625, chap. 4, sig. 106.

155. See, e.g., Gouge 1622, pp. 620, 624; Carter 1627, p. 230; C[olerus] 1663b, p. 9.

156. For this painting, see Exhib. cat. Amsterdam 1976, cat. no. 33; Slatkes 1981, p. 120; Salomon 1984, pp. 191–7; W. Robinson 1987, p. 291.

157. See Exhib. cat. Amsterdam 1976, p. 145; Slatkes 1981, p. 120; Salomon 1984, p. 191; W. Robinson 1987, p. 291.

158. A similar idea is expressed by the objects strewn about the ground around the person-

ification of negligence in the print by Crispijn van der Passe I cited in note 58. Salomon 1984, p. 196, states that the painting "is best understood as a moralistic statement about the consequences of being 'asleep on the job.' "

159. Johan de Brune 1660, vol. 2, p. 386, no. 620: "Een keucken-meyt moet d'eene ooghe, naer de panne, en d'ander naer de katte hebben." This passage is quoted with reference to Maes's painting in Exhib. cat. Amsterdam 1976, p. 146.

160. Gouge 1622, p. 624.

161. E.g., Maes's series of paintings representing eavesdroppers; see Exhib. cat. Amsterdam 1976, cat. no. 34; Slatkes 1981, p. 122; Exhib. cat. Philadelphia 1984, cat. no. 67; W. Robinson 1987; Schama 1987, pp. 460–1. See also *The Idle Servant* by Esaias Boursse, cited by Salomon 1984, p. 192, fig. 170. Sluijter 1991, pp. 52–7, discusses a series of paintings of "lusty maids," many of which involve male temptors.

162. My findings contradict Schama's observation that there are no art works featuring the exemplary servant (Schama 1987, p. 460).

163. See, e.g., Perkins 1613, pp. 696–7; Gouge 1622, p. 646; Carter 1627, p. 205; Wittewrongel 1661, vol. 1, p. 220. See also Groenendijk 1984, pp. 174–5.

164. See, e.g., Perkins 1613, pp. 697–8; Gouge 1622, p. 589; Carter 1627, p. 240; Teellinck 1664, p. 412; Wittewrongel 1661, vol. 1, p. 207. See also Groenendijk 1984, pp. 173–4.

165. For the following argument, I am indebted to Rudolf Dekker, who kindly provided the text of his unpublished lecture "Masters and Servants in the Dutch Republic: An Uneasy Relationship" given at the symposium on Dutch genre painting at the Royal Academy in London in November 1984.

166. Schotel 1867–8, p. 321. Dekker 1984 cites this passage and also discusses the erroneous ideas of other social historians writing during the nineteenth and early twentieth centuries. Their ideas continue to influence our modern-day conceptions about life in Holland during the seventeenth century. For example, Schotel's specious assumption that servants ate together with family members is repeated by Regin 1976, p. 142 and n. 102, and following Regin's hypothesis, by Salomon 1984, p. 193.

167. See Van der Woude 1972, p. 314; Haks 1982, pp. 89–90, 167–74; Van de Pol 1982; 1983; Dekker 1984, who also concludes from his study of contemporary diaries that servants were treated rather roughly. See also Jongejan 1984; Schama 1987, pp. 405–6, 455, 459–60. Naturally, there were exceptions; see Macfarlane 1970, p. 147. Schama 1987, p. 456, remarks that the occasional presence of servants in family portraits provides evidence that they were sometimes well integrated into the family circle. Despite many findings suggesting that master–servant relationships were far from ideal, a book like V., S. de 1682 surely exaggerates the actual vices of servants. Our suspicions as to its credibility are further aroused by a work that appeared shortly after, countering the arguments set forth in *Seven duyvelen:* Anon. 1697. Dekker 1984 cites both works. See also Schama 1987, p. 458; Dresen-Coenders 1989, pp. 39–43. Nineteenth-century social historians mistakenly used De Vries's books as sources to understand master–servant relationships of the seventeenth century; see, e.g., Bake 1899, pp. 395–9. See further, Dekker 1984.

168. Jongejan 1984, p. 216: "De ideale dienstbode was gehoorzaam en diende zijn of haar meester tot in lengte van jaren in 'alle neerstigheyt en getrouwigheyt.' De uitgebreide wetgeving doet vermoeden dat de praktijk niet in overeenstemming was met dit ideaal." See also Haks 1982, pp. 168–70. See also the ordinances published in Purmerend in 1696, reprinted in Fritschy 1980, vol. 2, pp. 75–80. Roodenburg 1990, p. 260, notes several cases, brought before the Amsterdam consistories, of pregnant maids who had allegedly tempted the men of the house to have sex with them. Ibid., p. 260, n. 107, adds, "In 1682 zou zelfs een keur worden uitgevaardigd waarin een straf van zes maanden spinhuis werd gesteld op hoererij van 'kameniers, meyden, minnemoers, naysters of bakermoers' met een mannelijk lid van het huisgezin." For other cases in the records of the Amsterdam consistories of pregnant maids, see ibid., pp. 269, 275. See also Koorn 1987, who examines court cases involving, among others, pregnant maids in Twente during the eighteenth century. Roodenburg 1990, pp. 281, 289, also cites cases of adultery committed by men and their house-

maids. See also Noordam 1987b, p. 136; Schama 1987, pp. 459–60.

CHAPTER 3. "MOEDER"

1. The portrait is discussed by Hofstede de Groot 1919, pp. 114–18, and more recently by Bok and De Meijere 1985–6; Exhib. cat. Haarlem 1986, cat. no. 75; Franits 1986, pp. 42–4. The inscription to which the artist points in the painting includes his family's coat of arms as well as the names and baptismal dates of the family members. The third painting firmly attributed to the artist, a kitchen piece with a portrait of one of his sisters, was recently discovered in France; see Bok 1990.
2. This chapter is titled after the fifth chapter of Cats 1625, one devoted entirely to the subject of parenthood. Cats's advice for prospective parents begins with the marriage bed – where relations must be conducted chastely and moderately to ensure healthy offspring – and continues through pregnancy and the stages of their child's development. For Cats's chapter, see Meertens 1943, pp. 273–6; Carter 1974, pp. 118–21; De Jongh 1974, pp. 176–7; Ten Berge 1979, pp. 87–90. Groenendijk 1984, pp. 82–3, discusses contemporary ideas concerning marital sex.
3. The modern conception of the history of childhood owes much to the 1960 seminal study by the French social historian Philippe Ariès. For my work, I have used the English edition of 1962. Ariès postulates that during the Middle Ages and much of the early modern era, there was no awareness of childhood as a distinct stage in life separate from adulthood. It was only during the course of the seventeenth century that adults gradually began to realize that children were different from them. However, in Ariès's opinion, the increased attention paid to children led to their cruel treatment, as evidenced by the harsh discipline imposed on them. Only in the mid-eighteenth century did a truly modern, enlightened view of childhood emerge, one characterized by heightened parental concern for children, who by then occupied a central place in family life. Ariès's sources and arguments largely relate to French culture, but his findings are applied to Western society as a whole. The authors of other influential studies of the history of childhood and the family have, despite some minor differences, largely concurred with Ariès's views: see, e.g., Shorter 1976; Stone 1977. For critiques of the studies by Ariès, Shorter, and Stone, see Anderson 1980, pp. 39–45, 59–60; Haks 1982, pp. 4–6, 23–5; Pollock 1985, pp. 1–65. See also A. Wilson 1980, pp. 133–5; Stone 1981; S. Wilson 1984; Marshall 1987, pp. 8–29; Schama 1987, p. 496; Peeters 1988, pp. 22–4; Kloek 1989, p. 50. In the wake of these criticisms, a so-called revisionist view of the history of family has surfaced which in essence claims that there has been little change in the structure of the family and affective relationships within it; see, e.g., Wrightson 1982; Houlbrooke 1984; Pollock 1985. Haks 1988 contains an excellent analysis of the revisionist and orthodox schools of thought. See also Spierenburg 1989, pp. 615–16.
4. See, e.g., Dod and Cleaver 1612, sig. R2; Wallenkamp 1661, pp. 94–5; Wittewrongel 1661, vol. 1, p. 197. Catholics also viewed children as divine gifts; see, e.g., Hazart 1678, p. 204. See also Todd 1987, pp. 107–11.
5. Batty 1581, sig. 29; see also sig. 6; Batty's treatise was originally published in Dutch, but unfortunately I have not been able to locate a Dutch edition of this work. See also Dod and Cleaver 1612, sig. Q1; Carter 1627, p. 97; Wittewrongel, 1661, vol. 1, p. 171.
6. See Batty 1581, sig. 54; Dod and Cleaver 1612, sigs. G2^{v}, K4^{v}, Q3–Q3^{v}, R3; De Swaef 1621/1740, pp. 77–91; Gouge 1622, p. 543. See also Groenendijk 1984, pp. 150–2.
7. In some circles, especially those of the Puritans and Pietists, it was believed that Adam's original sin had imputed to all of his descendents inherently corrupt natures that could only be subdued through discipline and intense indoctrination in religion and ethics, commencing at the earliest possible age. Thus, the parental commission to properly rear children had eternal consequences. See De Swaef 1621/1740, pp. 77–156; Gouge 1622, pp. 536–47; Wallenkamp 1661, pp. 93–138; Wittewrongel 1661, vol. 1, pp. 182–98, vol. 2, pp. 741–59. See also Morgan 1966, pp. 92–7; Groenendijk 1980, pp. 10–16; 1984, pp. 146–56. Not all seventeenth-century theorists believed that children had

inherently corrupt natures; see Marvick 1974. See also p. 140.

8. Dod and Cleaver 1612, sig. S3ᵛ. See also Batty 1581, sigs. 18ᵛ–19; Taffin 1640, sig. 207ᵛ.

9. For sixteenth-century attitudes toward education, see Hoffmann 1959, pp. 90, 150–9; Ozment 1983, pp. 132–72; 1984, pp. 48–52; Todd 1987, pp. 30–1, 107–13. For seventeenth-century attitudes, see Groenendijk 1978a, pp. 13–28; 1980; 1984, pp. 144–56.

10. Batty 1581, sig. 31; Wittewrongel 1661, vol. 2, p. 754, describes the benefits of raising children in a godly manner: "Daer de Huysgesinnen soo Godts-dienstigh zijn / daer uyt moeten sulcke plantsoenen voort-komen / die de Politie ende Kercke veel dienst konnen toe-bringen." See also De Swaef 1621/1740, pp. 1, 62, 249.

11. For the family as a microcosm of the state, see Oomius 1661, pp. 266–7; Wittewrongel 1661, vol. 1, pp. 1–5. See also Graafland 1983, pp. 8–10; Groenendijk 1984, p. 105. The view of the family as a microcosm of the state was an essential component of seventeenth-century political theory: see Schochet 1969; 1975. As such it was not exclusively limited to Protestant writings; for this and for its classical and humanist underpinnings, see Todd 1987, pp. 100–102. The number of works and the degree of zealousness is once again what separates Protestant from Catholic writings on the subject. The Pietists endorsed microcosmic theory so enthusiastically that they actually developed comprehensive strategies for transforming society through the cooperative efforts of church, state, and family. The two most important works in this regard were Teellinck 1627 and Koelman 1678. Teellinck's and Koelman's ideas are discussed by Groenendijk 1978b; 1984, pp. 22–3; 1989.

12. See Teellinck 1627, p. 192; Taffin 1640, sig. 215ᵛ; Oomius 1661, preface and pp. 4, 5; Wittewrongel 1661, vol. 1, p. 2. For the ethical outlook of these Pietist theologians, see Stoeffler 1965, pp. 58–68.

13. Groenendijk 1989, an authority on Pietist family literature, has reached the same conclusion: "Ik wijs er nadrukkelijk op dat de genoemde bronnen niet gebruikt moeten worden om er conclusies uit te trekken voor de gezins*praktijk*. . . . Zulke bronnen zijn van belang omdat ze de gezins- en opvoedings*idealen* documenteren die in bepaalde perioden regulatief waren voor bepaalde groeperingen" (p. 645).

14. See further Stone 1981, pp. 81–2; Wrightson 1982, p. 106.

15. For this observation, I am indebted to Greven 1977, who discusses the variety of child-rearing practices in early American culture. See also Haks 1988, p. 52.

16. A theme representing a still earlier stage in the mother–child relationship is the visit to the nursery; see Durantini 1983, pp. 299–311. Vos 1726, vol. 1, p. 388, wrote a poem about a "Schildery van een Kraamvrouw, in de zaal van den E. Heer Scheepen Jan Jakobsen Hinloopen, door G. Moetsu geschildert." Since the poem in honor of the picture was not included in the first edition of Vos's works (1662), it is possible that Gabriel Metsu painted it after that date. It might have represented a father's visit to the nursery, a theme painted by other Dutch artists, especially Jan Steen. The only extant painting of this subject by Metsu is in New York, at the Metropolitan Museum of Art; see F. Robinson 1974, fig. 130. Vos's poem is cited in connection with this painting by Metsu by Schneede 1968, p. 55 n. 35.

17. For a general survey of seventeenth-century attitudes toward breast feeding, see Schnucker 1973–4; Groenendijk 1976. See also Durantini 1983, pp. 18–20. See also Schama 1987, pp. 538–40; Todd 1987, pp. 109–11.

18. See Dod and Cleaver 1612, sigs. P3ᵛ–P4ᵛ; Guillimeau 1612, preface; Erasmus 1664, pp. 276–96.

19. See Dod and Cleaver 1612, sig. P4; Cats 1625, chap. 5, pp. 43–4; Teellinck 1639, vol. 2, p. 85; Wittewrongel 1661, vol. 1, pp. 172–5; Perkins 1613, p. 693. A Dutch edition of Perkins's book was published in 1614.

20. Dod and Cleaver 1612, sig. P4ᵛ. Teellinck 1639, vol. 2, p. 85, states that maternal nursing is "een merck-teecken van een vrome Vrouwe."

21. Gouge 1622, p. 509. Jan de Brune 1681b, p. 301, argues that women's breasts are close to their faces and do not hang from their bellies as they do in other creatures because "de vroede natuur heeft het zo begeert, om

dat zy, hun kinderen de mem gevende, ondertusschen 't genucht mochten hebben van hun te beschouwen, te strooken, en te kussen." See also Van Beverwijck 1639, p. 670; Wittewrongel 1661, vol. 1, p. 174.

22. "Het viel de Moeder zwaar,/ Zo lang haar teed're vrucht wierd inder 't hert gevoed:/ Maar nu verkwikt het haar,/ Schoon dat het kindjen snakt na s'Moeders harte-bloed." Jan de Brune 1681a, p. 83, expresses similar thoughts: "De Bant, die 't harte bint/ Der Moeder aan het Kint,/ Gebaart met wee en smerte,/ Aan hare borst met melk gevoet,/ Zo lang gedragen onder 't herte,/ Verbindt het bloet." See also Vander Minnen 1677, p. 148.

23. See Guillimeau 1612, p. 1; Van Beverwijck 1651, p. 185; Blankaart 1684, pp. 3, 29, where it is suggested that pregnant wet nurses or mothers not breast-feed their children because, in this condition, the quality of the milk (i.e., the blood) changes.

24. See Cats 1625, chap. 5, p. 56; Erasmus 1664, pp. 276–96. Mothers who allowed their offspring to be nourished with animal milk were even more vigorously condemned. Amazingly, medical "experts" believed that these children would develop the behavioral traits of the animals from whom they had received milk; see, e.g., Van Beverwijck 1651, pp. 185–6, who notes that "men schrift van een kindt, dat een teve gesoghen hebbende, 's nachts op stont ende met ander honden gingh bassen."

25. Cats 1625, chap. 5, p. 56: "Hoe menich aerdich kint, gesont en wel geboren, / Heeft door een snoode min sijn eygen aert verloren!." Van Beverwijck 1651, p. 186, states that "also leert ons de dagelijcksche ervarentheyt, dat de Min niet alleen haer quade manieren, maer oock haer ongesontheyt en gebreken de kinderen mede deelt."

26. This supposition was supported by stories from classical history; see Cats 1625, chap. 5, pp. 45–7. See also Gouge 1622, p. 512; Van Beverwijck 1651, p. 186.

27. There is no evidence to support the statement by Durantini 1983, p. 19, that wet nursing was more common in other European countries than in the Netherlands where "Dutch women of all classes nursed their own children." Peeters 1966, pp. 24–5, and several other social historians had previously argued this point; see Groenendijk 1976, p. 583. See also Schama 1987, p. 540.

28. The findings of Pollock 1985, pp. 212–16, and other scholars contradict the argument that the practice of hiring wet nursing constitutes evidence of parental neglect. See also Wrightson 1982, p. 108; S. Wilson 1984, pp. 195–6; Peeters 1988, p. 25.

29. See, e.g., the advice of Guillimaeu 1612, pp. 1–5; Perkins 1613, p. 693; Cats 1625, chap. 5, pp. 57–8; Van Beverwijck 1651, p. 187; Blankaart 1684, pp. 3–11. Pollock 1985, p. 213, quotes several remarks by seventeenth-century diarists concerning their wives' inability to nurse their infants because of medical reasons. Pollock also presents statistical evidence from British diaries, stating that 43% of mothers in the seventeenth century nursed their own children for at least a time versus 67% in the eighteenth century (ibid., pp. 213, 215). However, she adds that "so few texts actually specify how infants were fed that it is impossible to make an adequate comparison."

30. See Peeters 1966, pp. 25–6; Stone 1977, p. 427; Pollock 1985, p. 215.

31. See further Stone 1977, pp. 63–4.

32. The symbolism of other representations of this theme is far more complex, among them the triptych by Willem Joseph Laquy, an eighteenth-century copy of a now-lost work by Gerrit Dou. According to Emmens 1963, this tryptych argued that this complex work actually illustrates the Aristotelian theory that in order to raise children who will be virtuous, *natura* (i.e., natural talent and disposition) must be improved by rules that are taught *(ars)* and practiced *(exercitatio). Ars* is represented by the school scene in the left panel, *exercitatio* by the man sharpening a quill in the right panel, and *natura* by the breast-feeding mother in the center panel. Emmens findings are summarized in Exhib. cat. Amsterdam 1976, cat. no. 17.

33. For the idea of male duties and callings, see Chapter 2, p. 68. Durantini 1983, p. 26, believes that this man's work might illustrate "a Dutch proverb such as: 'Just as the carpenter is, so also are the chips. / The more clever the carpenter, the greater the number of chips.' 'Chips,' in this context of course, refer to children. The sense of the scene would therefore be 'like parent, like child,' a 'chip off the old block.' " There is a general lack of evidence to support this interpretation. However, Wittewrongel 1661, vol. 2, p. 747, does invoke small pieces of wood as a pedagogical metaphor when he calls spoiled children "ongeschaefde houtjes."

34. Gouge 1622, p. 510, defines maternal breast feeding as a calling. For the concept of callings, see Chapter 2, p. 68.
35. See Chapter 2, pp. 88–9.
36. Durantini 1983, p. 26, remarks that "the fact that the cat can sit by a plate of fish and not be tempted to steal any also seems to suggest that the house is well disciplined."
37. The print forms part of a series of the ten ages of man, dated 1675 and entitled *Nützliche Zeitbetrachtung*; see Hollstein 1954–, vol. 27, pp. 117–21, no. 191.
38. See Chapter 2, p. 67.
39. Sumowski 1983–, vol. 3, p. 2015, cat. no. 1345, first observed that the nursing mother in Maes's painting recalls images of the *Madonna lactans*.
40. Schama 1987, p. 541. See also Ariès 1962, p. 347.
41. See, e.g., Cats 1625, chap. 5, p. 58: "Hoort, moeder, hoort u les; tis niet genouch te baren, / Het kint is u beslach tot aende seven jaren." Groenendijk 1984, pp. 139–56, examines the parental charge to care for children in the writings of Wittewrongel and other contemporary authors. For humanist and Catholic thought on this issue, see Todd 1987, pp. 102–13. Schama 1987, p. 541, discusses the striking novelty of the domestication of the *paterfamilias* in the Dutch Republic and his absorption within the family circle. His sensitive reading of the *pictura* of an emblem from Johan de Brune 1624 (see his fig. 272) proves that practice was often far different than theory vis-à-vis a father's participation in the care of young children. See also Hokke 1987, pp. 66–8.
42. Gouge 1622, p. 546; See also Houwaert 1622–3, p. 618; Brathwait 1631, p. 107; Van Beverwijck 1639, p. 305.
43. F. Robinson 1974, p. 16; Slatkes 1981, p. 146; Hedinger 1986, p. 74.
44. Slatkes 1981, p. 146, notes that this *Pietà* reference appears frequently in Italian depictions of the Madonna and Child art as a prefiguration of Christ's death. Thus, in Metsu's painting, the pose might have been meant to prefigure the child's death. The interpretation presented in Exhib. cat. Amsterdam 1976, cat. no. 41, is not entirely convincing. The authors do not mention Metsu's reference to the *Pietà* as they assign undue importance to the woman in their interpretation of the painting as a "modernization" of traditional representations of Caritas: "Interpretatie van het thema is dan ook problematisch, tenzij de nadruk wordt gelegd op de barmhartigheid van de vrouw en deze barmhartigheid mag worden gezien in samenhang met de voorstelling van de kruisiging achter haar. In dat geval is het zinvol Metsu's *Zieke kind* om redenen van vorm, maar vooral van inhoud, te relateren aan het oudere beeldtype van Caritas, de christelijke liefde." One cannot deny that the woman is pivotal to the subject of the painting, but the artist's primary focus is on the sick child who gazes at the viewer. This situation is the opposite of those in representations of Caritas where the female personification is the principal motif. Unconvincing as well, is the argument that the picture of the Crucifixion on the wall in the background might function as the woman's attribute, "gelijk de personificatie van de Caritas in de oudere iconografie voorzien was van een zinnebeeld of prototype van de kruisiging." According to Hedinger 1986, p. 74, the map in the background can be linked to the *caritas* associations conveyed by the mother, and as such proclaims the *Nationaltugenden* of Dutch women. However, there is little evidence to support this hypothesis. Slatkes 1981, p. 146, suggests that the map may indicate a profane concept in contrast to the religious one expressed by the Crucifixion. In this sense, the artist "holds the mother and child between this world and the next." As F. Robinson 1974, p. 62, points out the figures in the picture of the crucifixion in the background are the same as those that appear in a crucifixion by Metsu, now in the Capitoline Museum in Rome (his fig. 144). They appear to be the same but the ones in the background of *The Sick Child* are shown in reverse.
45. De Swaef 1621/1740, p. 39: "Ende sulken vriendelijckheyd der ouders vermaeckt wonderlijck seer de kinderen/ soo datse dencken datse half genesen sijn/ alsse so in des moeders schoot sitten/ tegen haer lichaem lenen/

of haer handt gevoelen." The editor of this edition of De Swaef's treatise, Jacobus Willemsen, adds the following comments to the author's advice: "Tydig is het ook, den kindern, alsze ziek zyn, inteboezemen. 1. dat de ziekte reeds een gevolg hunner zonde zy. 2. daarby, hoe groot een schat de gezondheid zy. 3. Wat dankbaarheid zy deswegen Gode schuldig zyn en 4. hoeze die niet alleen wel bewaaren; maar ook vooral Godvruchtig besteeden moeten, om het groot werk van hunne zaligheid uit te werken." See Groenendijk 1984, pp. 166–7 n. 65. For more practical advice on treating child sicknesses, see Schama 1987, pp. 521–2.

46. Koelman 1679, p. 164, no. 266: "Als zy [children] ziek zijn/ en gy hebt te vooren geen genade in haar gespeurt/ gaat haar dan met grooten ernst/ teerheidt en vriendelijkheidt aan; indien'er iets goedts in haar is/ 't moet en 't zal nu uitkomen; toont haar dat deze roede van Godt is. . . . toont haar, hoe en waar aan, en waar over zy zich hebben te onderzoeken, byzonder over haar bekering, en geloof, en hejligmaking [*sic*]; wat lessen zy nu hebben ter leeren in de ziekte." See also C. Udemans 1659, p. 110, who presents spiritual lessons that are taught by illness. See also Groenendijk 1984, pp. 166–7 n. 65.

47. Groenendijk 1984, pp. 166–7 n. 65, discusses the spiritual biographies of Puritan children who were said to be converted when they were seriously ill or when they were on their deathbeds.

48. E.g., Stone 1977, p. 70. Parents are said to have been apathetic because the high infant mortality rate forced them to remain emotionally distant from their children.

49. See Peeters 1988, p. 24. See Hokke 1986; 1987; also Marshall 1987, p. 1; Noordam 1987a, pp. 96–7, 104; Schama 1987, pp. 517–23.

50. The diaries examined by Pollock 1985, pp. 124–40, contradict this view. Pollock concluded that "almost all parents were extremely concerned whenever any of their offspring were ill, irrespective of the century in which they lived. It seems as if the deep emotional involvement which most parents had with their offspring prevented them from feeling anything but distress and anxiety. . . . Most parents were acutely aware of the frequency of child death, but far from inducing a state of resignation, this only served to heighten their anxiety during any illness of their offspring, and anguish at their death" (ibid. pp. 133, 140). See also Ozment 1983, pp. 166–9, Hokke 1987; Marshall 1987, pp. 13–29; Schama 1987, pp. 517–23. Batty 1581, sigs. 57[v]–59, exhorted parents to bear the grief of their children's death with patience.

51. See the important study by Stearns and Stearns 1985.

52. See ibid., esp. p. 823 and n. 36, where the authors refer to the illuminating article by Roodenburg 1985. Roodenburg's study examines the diary published in 1695 by Isabella de Moerloose, a clergyman's widow. De Moerloose discusses her childhood and especially the seemingly spontaneous beatings that she received from her mother, " 'after she had been petted and caressed for two years' " (Roodenburg 1985, pp. 524–5).

53. A. Wilson 1980, pp. 136, 137–9, 147–8, criticizes the "present-minded" point of view of Ariès with which he searched medieval and early modern sources for present-day ideas about childhood. The inevitable conclusion when these present-day notions were not found was that there was no concept of childhood in earlier times. He has thus recorded an absence of the modern awareness of childhood without investigating how children were actually perceived.

54. For Van Kuijl, see Sluijter 1977.

55. Dead children appear in sixteenth- and seventeenth-century Dutch portraiture in two forms: either as naked souls in a heavenly vision above an earthbound family or as actual dead children in a coffin or on a bier. For the latter, which might strike the modern viewer as macabre, see Exhib. cat. Haarlem 1986, cat. no. 43 and p. 241, fig. 55a. See also Ariès 1962, pp. 40–3.

56. Exhib. cat. Amsterdam 1976, cat. no. 49. See, more recently, Exhib. cat. Amsterdam 1989–90, cat. no. 34.

57. Cats 1632b, pt. 3, p. 148: "Kemt, kemt u menighmael, en niet het hayr alleen,/ Maer oock dat binnen schuylt, tot aen het innigh been:/ Kemt u verwrongen hert, en u verboste sinnen,/ En maeckt doch over al een reynen gront te winnen,/ Want hy, wiens hooft en hert eens wel gereddet zijn,/ Al kemt hy menighmael, hy kemt hem sonder pijn:/ Maer die het sondigh hayr laet wilt daer henen wassen,/ En weet sich nader-hant geen kamme toe te passen,/ Want al wat hy geraeckt, daer is een vuyle nest,/ Ghy, kemt dan alle daegh, dat is de leden best." See also Snoep-Reitsma 1973b, p. 288. See also the poem about a comb maker by Van Nyenborgh 1659, p. 141, which conveys similar associations.

58. I introduce Cats's emblem here with great reluctance. The propensity to regard emblems as magical interpretive keys has become so preponderant that there is a misleading tendency to view Dutch paintings as "painted emblems" and the process of interpreting them as "emblematic interpretation." See Renger 1978, pp. 35–7; Stone-Ferrier 1983, pp. 11–152; Bedaux 1987, pp. 151–4; Bauer 1988; Bedaux 1990, pp. 74–6. Since emblems are essentially literary conceits, it is perhaps more accurate to view them and paintings as analogous cultural expressions that often share sources and convey similar associations. In this regard the emblems of Cats, which reflect popular wisdom that was accessible to an extremely wide audience, will often share common sources with motifs in paintings, versus the more "esoteric" emblems of an author like Visscher. For Visscher 1614, see the interesting discussion by Porteman 1984b, p. 3, who concludes that "de bundel die men 'een door en door Hollandse schepping' heeft genoemd, lijkt meer een directe voortzetting van de impresa, dan een continuering van het humanistenembleem of een bewuste vernieuwing daarvan." See also Praz 1964, vol. 1, pp. 169–70.

59. According to Erasmus 1678, p. 5, "die uyterlijcke betamelijckheit des lichaems voortspruyt uyt een wel geschickt gemoet." This book is a translation of Erasmus's famous *De civilitate morum puerilium* of 1530. See also Hoffmann 1959, pp. 158–9; Veenstra 1968, pp. 125–6; Durantini 1983, p. 112.

60. See Snoep-Reitsma 1973b, pp. 287–8. See also Exhib. cat. Amsterdam 1976, p. 197.

61. See Exhib. cat. Amsterdam 1976, pp. 99, 197–8. See also Durantini 1983, pp. 206–56. The meaning of the motif of the cat playing with a ball is unclear in this context.

62. Visscher 1614, pt. 3, no. 43. Cited by Snoep-Reitsma 1973a, p. 206. See also Exhib. cat. Amsterdam 1976, p. 198; Durantini 1983, pp. 115–16.

63. See Exhib. cat. Amsterdam 1976, p. 198; Exhib. cat. Amsterdam 1989–90, p. 170. See also Snoep-Reitsma 1973a, p. 206.

64. It is important to note that there is some flexibility in the use and interpretation of this motif. For example, a still top and cord lie on the floor before a girl in Jacob Ochtervelt's *Portrait of a Family* (Cambridge, [Mass.], Fogg Art Museum). In this context, the motif can only convey positive pedagogical associations.

65. Cats 1625, preface, sig. I (*) iiij^{v}; cited by Snoep-Reitsma 1973a, p. 206. See also Durantini 1983, p. 114.

66. See, e.g., Revsneri 1591, sig. A3^{v}. See also Raupp 1984, pp. 299, 306–8. Kunzle 1973, p. 246, reproduces a seventeenth-century German broadsheet whose didactic intention is made clear by two figures who hold up a mirror so that the reader can examine his or her behavior. See further Grabes 1982, pp. 48–61, an important study on the use of the mirror as a title metaphor in English and Continental texts of the Middle Ages and Renaissance. This work also contains a useful bibliography of the vast scholarship on the mirror as well as a synoptic listing of mirror titles especially in English literature from the Middle Ages to the late seventeenth century.

67. For this point, see further Raupp 1984, pp. 299, 306–8. According to Wittewrongel 1661, vol. 1, p. 802, self-examination – he quotes the ancient proverb "Kent u selven" (Know thyself) – was especially useful in promoting one's godliness because " 't is de beste wijsheyt na de wereldt, voor hemselven wijs te zijn, sijn eyghen reeckeninghe wel te konnen maecken / 't is een wijsheyt die van boven komt, sijn selven wel te konnen kennen." For the proverb "Kent u selven," see Ripa 1644, p. 295. This proverb is written on the scroll held by the artist Michiel van Comans II in the portrait discussed in Chapter 2, p. 62, Fig. 46. As we have seen, Cats's emblem of the woman combing her hair is symbolic of the need to purify oneself spiritually on a daily basis. This implies that one must examine oneself daily in order to be aware of one's shortcomings and sins. Cats discusses precisely this implication in the explanatory notes to the emblem (after the *subscriptio*), remarking that even the heathen philosphers taught their students to examine themselves for faults; see Cats 1632b, pt. 3, p. 149. See further, Ripa 1644, pp. 295–7.

68. Cats 1632b, n.p. See Smilde 1938, pp. 139–40; Ten Berge 1979, pp. 108–9. The mirror is also an attribute of Veritas in Ripa 1644, p. 590.

69. This point is made in Exhib. cat. Amsterdam 1976, p. 198. Netscher's *A Lady Teaching a Child to Read* (London, National Gallery) also juxtaposes a well-reared child and a poorly trained one; see Exhib. cat. Amsterdam 1989–90, cat. no. 33. (Brown 1984, p. 49, suggests that this painting may be the pendant to my Fig. 103.) In the frontispiece designed by Adriaen van der Werff for F. Junius 1694, a child is introduced to the arts by a personification while two others playing jacks ignore her. (For this print, see Exhib. cat. Amsterdam 1976, p. 198.) Becker 1976, p. 88, cites it in connection with several paintings by Adriaen van der Werff that depict the same contrast between diligent and indolent children as the painting by Netscher. See also Exhib. cat. Amsterdam 1976, cat. no. 74. See also the print introducing a chapter in Van Hoogstraeten 1678, opp. p. 1, which shows a personification of Konst attracting young boys while crushing their toys with her foot. The explanatory poem (p. 1) states: "Dees Print vertoont de Konst, diens lokkende vermogen / De Jonkheid tot zich trekt: een vleyende Sireen, / Die Koot-en Kinderspel met voeten doet vertreên."

70. For this painting, see Gudlaugsson 1959–60, vol. 2, cat. no. 95; Exhib. cat. The Hague 1974, cat. no. 24; Exhib. cat. Amsterdam 1976, p. 42; Slatkes 1981, p. 113.

71. De Vries 1990a, pp. 55–6. Even if one does not accept the hypothesis that these pendants are portraits, it does not substantially alter my reading of them. See also Slatkes 1981, p. 113. The strong genre-painting-like character of Ter Borch's pendants has long been noted; see Gudlaugsson 1959–60, vol. 1, pp. 87–8, vol. 2, cat. nos. 95, 96; Exhib. cat. The Hague 1974, cat. nos. 24, 25; Exhib. cat. Amsterdam 1976, cat. no. 3. Moiso-Diekamp 1987, pp. 481–2, strongly doubts that the paintings are pendants. Elizabeth Honig, writing in Exhib. cat. Leiden 1988, p. 81, points out that there is a precedent for pendants of this type of domestic subject matter in the work of Judith Leyster. Leyster painted pendants of a *Mother Cleaning a Child's Hair* (present location unknown) and a *Mother Sewing with Children by Lamplight and Fire* (Dublin, National Gallery of Ireland); for these pendants, see Hofrichter 1989, cat. nos. 22, 23. For the pendant of Wiesken spinning, see further Chapter 2, pp. 73–6.

72. Cats 1625, chap. 5, p. 58: "Ghy moet het rouwe lant als totte vrucht bereyden,/ Bespitten, open doen, met greppen onderscheyden,/ Het onkruyt roeyen uyt, oock vanden eersten dach,/ Op dat u weerde man daer namaels saeyen mach." See also Plutarch (ca. 1535), sigs. B1–B1[v]; Dod and Cleaver 1612, sig. R3[v]; De Swaef 1621/1740, pp. 88, 92; Wittewrongel 1661, vol. 1, p. 187, vol. 2, pp. 749–50. See also Bedaux 1983, pp. 55–6; Groenendijk 1984, p. 151; Bedaux 1990, pp. 127, 132.

73. See De Swaef 1621/1740, p. 88; Cats 1625, chap. 5, p. 58; Wittewrongel 1661, vol. 2, pp. 749–51. See also Bedaux 1983, pp. 54–5, 58–62; Groenendijk 1984, p. 151; Bedaux 1990, pp. 127, 132. In a detail from a German broadsheet, published 1650, a man and wife are depicted at the dinner table with their children. An illustration on the wall alludes to the children's poor behavior, and the inscription laments the fact that the husband "was not allowed to discipline them, as we should, if they are not to grow up like unpruned trees." For a reproduction of the print and a translation of its inscription, see Kunzle 1973, p. 229.

74. This was first studied by Bedaux 1983, pp. 58–62, figs. 11, 16; see also Bedaux 1990, p. 132. See De Swaef 1621/1740, p. 62; Cats 1625, chap. 5, pp. 58–9; Taffin 1640, sig. 203; Oomius 1661, p. 30; Wittewrongel 1661, vol. 2, p. 751. Dod and Cleaver 1612, sig. R4, state, "Therefore as a good tree is knowne by bringing foorth good fruite: so parents should shew their goodnesse in the good education of their children, which are their fruit." For fruit as a symbol of fertility in Dutch portraiture, see Bedaux 1987; 1990, pp. 69–108.

75. Johan de Brune 1660, vol. 2, p. 319, no. 518: "Een slacke moeder luyzige hoofden"; cited in Exhib. cat. Amsterdam 1976, p. 199.
76. Children, in turn, were obligated to love, honor, respect, and obey their parents; see Groenendijk 1984, pp. 131–9.
77. Dod and Cleaver 1612, sig. D7. See also Chapter 2, p. 68.
78. See further Groenendijk 1984, p. 148.
79. De Swaef 1621/1740, p. 312: "Hier op moet ghelet syn / want het is het mannelyck gheslachte belast alle aensienelycke beroepinghen beyde inde Rebuplycke [*sic*] ende de Gemeente te betrachten / oock soodanige daer hy zyn huysgesin mede kan voorstaen. Daer en tegen den vrouwelycken geslachte is dit generael beroep opgeleydt / van op haer kinderen en huyshouden gade te slaen / dat de kinderen haer ghemack hebben / ende alles in het huyshouden ordentelyck toegae." For De Swaef's treatise, see Groenendijk 1989, pp. 656–7. See also Den Heussen 1657, pp. 87–95, esp. p. 94: "Ende lieve doch / wat kan den jonghe Dochteren / aengaende hare beroepinghe profijtelickers gherecommandeert werden / dan datse haer in de huyshoudelijcke saecken / als naeyen / spinnen / koopen ende besorgen van 't gene noodigh is / alsoo oeffenen / dat / als sy tot den Huwelijcken staet gekomen zijn / alsdan van haer gheseyt mach werden / 't ghene Salomon van een deughdelijcke huys-vrouwe seyt" (in Proverbs 31). Groenendijk 1984, p. 148, believes that the discussion of callings – at least in the writings of Petrus Wittewrongel – appropriate to the sex of the child is actually a discussion of callings for males.
80. Van Nyenborgh 1659, pp. 90–2. See further, Chapter 1, p. 26.
81. Cats 1632b, p. 380.
82. Cats 1625, chap. 5, pp. 61–3.
83. Ibid., preface, sig. I (*) iii–I (**) ii^v.
84. The poem had earlier appeared in Cats 1618, in a shorter form, with a print whose background showed Middelburg; see Ten Berge 1979, pp. 78–9. Durantini 1983, p. 184, fig. 87, reproduces the print from this emblem book. Schama 1987, p. 499, observes that "by situating the games not in some imaginary vacuum of time and space but in topographically meaningful – and sometimes recognizable – settings, nearly always with some public building, a town hall or guildhall, in view, they evoke the civic and public virtues to which the correctly brought-up should be led." See further ibid., pp. 499–503, 507–12.
85. Cats 1625, preface, sig. I (*) iiii: "Siet hoe de mensch sijn eygen aert/ Oock inde kintsheyt openbaert!/ Het meysje speelt met poppe-goet,/ Het knechtje toont een hooger moet;/ Het meysje doet de wiege gaen,/ Het knechtje laet den trommel slaen;/ Het meysje speelt met kleyn beslach/ Dat tot de keucken dienen mach;/ Het knechtje met een swacke lans/ Na wijse van de rouwe mans." For this poem, see also Schama 1987, pp. 511–12. Writing in the eighteenth century, Le Francq van Berkhey 1776, vol. 3, pt. 2, p. 1340, states that doll playing teaches domesticity. Cited by Durantini 1983, p. 250.
86. See Durantini 1983, p. 250, who believes that the girl playing with the doll in Brekelenkam's picture might convey positive associations. Durantini (pp. 249–50) also thinks that it is possible for this motif to have a negative meaning, especially in light of literature condemning doll play. Contemporary attitudes toward play seem to have been ambivalent: it was often condemned but sometimes encouraged. For example, Mulcaster 1581, pp. 22–4, 40–132, contains lengthy discussions in praise of play and exercise for developing the body and spirit of children. Van Beverwijck 1651, p. 188, praises children's play because it exercises their bodies.
87. For this portrait, see also Schama 1987, p. 555.
88. This portrait was discussed in Chapter 1, p. 27.
89. See further Chapter 1, pp. 25–6.
90. Schipper-Van Lottum 1980, p. 52. For French schools, see also Moquette 1915, vol. 1, pp. 61–5; Riemens 1919. [Sweerts] 1698, pt. 1, p. 89, quotes the inscription on a sign advertising a school run by a seamstress. Here, girls were taught only the needle arts. See also ibid., pt. 4, p. 13.
91. See Schipper-Van Lottum 1980, p. 52. See also Noël 1982, pp. 138–40; Hokke 1987, pp. 68–9.
92. See Schipper-Van Lottum 1980, p. 48. For schools, see further ibid., pp. 47–9; De Planque 1926, pp. 8–52; Durantini 1983, pp. 94–130.

93. Otto Naumann, writing in exhib. cat. Philadelphia 1984, p. 159, recognized that this painting did not represent a simple family activity but rather what he termed "a workshop for the instruction of lacemaking." See also Lasius 1987, pp. 126–7.
94. Gouge 1622, p. 553.
95. E.g., Ariès 1962, pp. 261–2; Stone 1977, pp. 167–71. Pollock 1985, pp. 143–56, concludes from her study of contemporary diaries that, during the seventeenth century, there was a wide discrepancy between theory and practice in disciplining children. Pollock also observed that the personality of the parent likely determined the punishment and that parental views on child discipline were not so much shaped by class and religion as by daily involvement with, and intimate knowledge of, their own children.
96. See De Swaef 1621/1740, pp. 227–30; Gouge 1622, p. 556; Cats 1625, chap. 5, pp. 66–7; Wittewrongel 1661, vol. 1, p. 189. See also the influential book by Menno Simons (ca. 1557) that was reprinted in the seventeenth century. See also Groenendijk 1984, p. 155; Todd 1987, pp. 111–13.
97. Valentiner 1924, p. 42, identified the figures as the artist's wife, Adriana Brouwers (whom he married on 31 January 1654); his stepson, Justus (from Adriana's first marriage); and, in the cradle, a son who was born in September 1654 but died in May 1656, or more likely, their daughter Johanna, who died in April 1656. See also Cat. Castagnola 1969, cat. no. 169; Gaskell 1990, cat. no. 53. Maes's painting was probably the source for one by Michiel van Musscher (1683; formerly with Martin Asscher, London) that shows the artist's wife and two children; he has included himself at an easel in a painting on the back wall.
98. The most famous precedent for the representation of an artist in a mirror within a painting is, of course, Jan van Eyck's *Arnolfini Portrait;* see Bedaux 1986; 1990, pp. 21–67. However, in contrast to Van Eyck, Maes depicts himself actively painting.
99. Hazart 1678, p. 189: "Gelijck den doeck van eenen schilder, daer niet met allen opgeteeckent en staet, daerom staet het in den wille des schilders, daer op te schilderen al wat hem belieft: wilt hy? hy kan hem met vuyle kladden besmeuren; wilt hy? hy kan hem met schoone bloemen, landauwen, ofte pasteuren vercieren."
100. Raupp 1984, p. 289 n. 534, cites the classical sources for this theory. [Earle] 1628, p. 21, calls a child "natures fresh picture newly drawn in Oyle, which time and much handling dimmes and defaces." Although Earle believes that the "painting" is already completed at the child's birth – versus Hazart's ideas just cited – he strongly implies that children are morally innocent: "He is purely happy, because he knowes no evill." Earle's popular book was published in several Dutch editions during the seventeenth century under the name W. S. Z. Bóógaart.
101. See note 7.
102. Saavedra 1700, vol. 1, pp. 9–10.
103. The *pictura* reproduced here comes from the Dutch edition: Saavedra 1663, p. 10. For the many editions and translations of this book, see Praz 1964, pp. 483–5. For Saavedra's emblem, see Emmens 1961, p. 58; Raupp 1984, p. 289.
104. For other, to my mind excessively complicated interpretations of the painting, see Durantini 1983, pp. 87–9; Hedinger 1986, pp. 63–70.
105. Perkins 1613, p. 694. See also Batty 1581, sigs. 4^v, 9^v; Dod and Cleaver 1612, sig. $Q2^v$; De Swaef 1621/1740, p. 112; Gouge 1622, p. 536; Wittewrongel 1661, vol. 1, p. 185. See also Groenendijk 1984, pp. 148–56.
106. Batty 1581, sig. 18^v. See also pp. 112–13, this volume.
107. See, e.g., De Swaef 1621/1740, pp. 180–1; Gouge 1622, p. 536; Wittewrongel 1661, vol. 1, p. 185; Koelman 1679, pp. 19, no. 33, 28, no. 59, 123, no. 189. See further Groenendijk 1984, pp. 115–23, 152; Todd 1987, pp. 107–11.
108. See Ozment 1983, p. 140. The following discussion is based on Franits 1986.
109. Still earlier are the scenes of the Holy Family by Netherlandish painters: see, e.g., Gerard David's *Virgin and Child* (Brussels, Musées Royaux des Beaux-Arts de Belgique; reproduced in Friedländer 1967–, vol. 6B, nos. 206–206D), and the *Holy Family* attributed to Jan Mostaert (Cologne, Wallraf-Richartz Museum; reproduced in ibid., vol. 10, no. 20).
110. Ozment 1983, p. 143, provides a complete translation of the inscription.

111. Brunfels 1525; Erasmus 1531. These two books are discussed by Ozment 1983, pp. 136–44. For the book by Erasmus, see also note 59. For other manuals of proper etiquette, see Ariès 1962, pp. 359–60.

112. See further Franits 1986, p. 36 and n. 5. There is also the influence of earlier paintings; see note 109. Ariès 1962, p. 339, observes that, during the sixteenth century, the subject matter of medieval art, for example, the labors of the months, underwent a transformation in which it was "domesticated." In other words, these earlier subjects were replaced by scenes of family life that often retained the same symbolism. Ariès does not offer any explanations for this change. See the criticisms of Vandenbroeck 1983–4, pp. 20–2.

113. See De Jongh 1974, pp. 179, 189–90. Bedaux 1987, pp. 158–61; 1990, pp. 84–9.

114. For this painting, see Exhib. cat. Haarlem 1986, cat. no. 73.

115. Psalm 128:3: "Thy children [shall be] like olive plants round about thy table." The presence of a crucifix in the painting suggests that the family was Catholic; see Exhib. cat. Haarlem 1986, pp. 295–6. This once again demonstrates that the contemporary domestic ideal was pursued not only by Protestants, despite their staggering literary output on the subject. Catholic authors published family literature as well; e.g., David 1607; Hazart 1678. It is also noteworthy that Jan Steen, whose solemn depictions of grace are discussed later (Figs. 126, 129), was a Catholic, as was Gabriel Metsu, the painter of *The Sick Child* (see Fig. 101). For Dutch Catholicism and art during this period, see Van Thiel 1990–1, pp. 53–60.

116. E.g., Baers 1629 (a published version of the sermon that he delivered at a wedding on 23 January 1629); Camphuysen 1644, pp. 330–4; Deutel 1662, pp. 349–50; Brandt 1725–7, vol. 3, p. 44 (wedding poem for Christiaan Hartzoeker and Anna van der My, married on 11 July 1655). See also De Jongh 1974, pp. 189–90.

117. Deutel 1662a, pp. 21–2.

118. See also the prints by P. Serwouters (reproduced in Hollstein 1949–, vol. 26, p. 240, no. 19) and Crispijn van de Passe II. The latter print illustrates the belief, just discussed, that having children is one of the joys of married life. For this print, see Veldman 1985, p. 3; 1986, p. 118, fig. 11.

119. See, e.g., the advice of Koelman 1679, p. 16, no. 23, 19, no. 33. See also Ursinus 1606, sigs. 215–56^{v}; G. Udemans 1658, pp. 69–102; Wittewrongel 1661, vol. 2, pp. 760–806. See also Groenendijk 1984, pp. 119–20.

120. The print is cited in connection with the portrait by De Jongh in Exhib. cat. Haarlem 1986, p. 302.

121. See Dod and Cleaver 1612, sigs. Q2^{v}–Q3; Perkins 1613, p. 669; Gouge 1622, pp. 536–41; Wittewrongel 1661, vol. 2, pp. 729–59; Bayly 1688. Bayly's book, originally published in English in 1613, has been called the most universally read devotional work next to Bunyan's *Pilgrim's Progress;* see Stoeffler 1965, pp. 71–3. For family devotions, see further Groenendijk 1984, pp. 47–8, and Teellinck's eyewitness account of its practice by an English family, quoted on p. 147.

122. In 1985, Marten Jan Bok discovered an inventory in the Utrecht archives of the possessions of the artist's father, Rutger van Bockhoven, drawn up on the occasion of his third marriage in 1636. The family portrait under study here is listed as well as the following: "Een duijtsen bijbel in fol. met kopere sloten anno 1579." The Bible in the painting does indeed have these copper clasps (*kopere sloten*), but the page to which it is held open does not correspond to any that I have seen in Dutch Bibles published in 1579. In fact, it corresponds exactly to the introduction page to the books of the Old Testament prophets as it appears in *Biblia* 1580. The notary might have made a mistake, though it must be added that the page as it now appears in the painting is partly obliterated. My thanks to Marten Jan Bok for generously sharing his discovery.

123. See Perkins 1613, p. 669; Oomius 1661, pp. 20–2.

124. See Perkins 1613, p. 669; De Swaef 1621/1740, pp. 180–3; Taffin 1640, sigs. 215^{v}–216; Oomius 1661, pp. 9–31, 162–211; Wittewrongel 1661, vol. 2, p. 781; Ridderus 1692, preface. See also Teellinck's eyewitness account of an English family's devotions, quoted on p. 147, this volume.

125. It is unlikely that the young women are holding Bibles because those published in smaller formats at this time were thicker than the books shown in the portrait. Moreover, they were usually provided with copper clasps in order to keep them tightly closed and protected from dust and the elements. The inventory discovered by Bok (see note 122) lists "drie duijtsche sallm boecken" (three Dutch psalm books). This might refer to popular reprints of the Book of Psalms or even to songbooks based on the psalms. For the latter, see Scheurleer 1912, pp. 5, 13–15. It is possible that the young women in the painting are indeed holding such psalm books because the reading or singing of psalms was sometimes recommended for family devotions; see Bayly 1688, pp. 244–6, and the account by Teellinck, quoted on p. 147. However, as already suggested, they could also be holding catechism books or works about personal piety; see, e.g., G. Udemans 1658; Bayly 1688. Koelman 1679, p. 158, no. 260, suggests that similar works be read in order to foster spiritual growth.

126. Ridderus 1692. For this work, see Budding 1983, pp. 84–5. De Jongh in Exhib. cat. Haarlem 1986, p. 50, fig. 50, reproduces the frontispiece to the first edition of the book, published in 1657, which is nearly identical to my Fig. 123.

127. Van Bockhoven's father was elected to the post of deacon in 1627, 1628, 1635, 1636, 1640, and 1641. My thanks to Marten Jan Bok for providing this information, which he discovered in the Utrecht archives. This discovery amends and clarifies some of the facts and suggestions set forth in Bok and De Meijere 1985–6, p. 328.

128. See Op 't Hof 1977; 1978; Groenendijk 1984, pp. 23, 34 n. 71, 47–8; 1989, pp. 647–8. Teellinck's stay in England had a decisive impact on his faith, another example of the English influence on Dutch Pietism; see Graafland 1983, p. 3.

129. Whately 1649, preface: "Versamelde het gantsche huysgesin, ende lasen t'samen een capittel vervolgens; alsoo bereyt zijnde door het lesen des woorts, riepen sy eendrachtelijck den naem des Heeren aen, daer na aen tafel, spraken sy van het gene een yder uyt het capittel bemerckt hadde, nae den eten songen sy t'samen een Psalm, dan keerde sich een yder wederom tot syn werck."

130. Gouge 1622, p. 540, states that children can be taught at the "table, by resembling the spirituall food of their soules, to that corporall food, whereby their bodies are nourished." Both Wallenkamp 1661, pp. 719–40, and Ridderus 1692, pp. 293–99, provide detailed instructions on how to promote godliness and civility at the dinner table. See also the literature cited by De Jongh in Exhib. cat. Haarlem 1986, pp. 50, 296, 297.

131. For Fig. 124, see Wäscher 1955, vol. 1, p. 29; Hollstein 1954–, p. 64, no. 41, where it is noted that the print depicts the family of Dietrich Meyer, the artist's father. See also the *Tischzucht* by Abraham Bach, reproduced in Strauss and Alexander 1977, vol. 1, p. 51, no. 19. According to Ariès 1962, p. 361, "Artists were fond of depicting the scene of a child saying grace because they recognized a new significance in this hitherto commonplace prayer. The iconographic theme evoked and associated in a synthesis three emotional forces: piety, the concept of childhood (the smallest child), and the concept of the family (the gathering at table)." Clearly, in his efforts to discover a concept of childhood in the seventeenth century, Ariès has overlooked the pedagogical significance of this theme in art. Ironically, if he had recognized the theme's pedagogical significance, it would have supported his argument.

132. Many of the boys in the prints and the paintings reproduced here have removed their hats, a common gesture of respect at this time. It was performed in the presence of superiors and also during church and other devotional practices. See Batty 1581, sig. 63^v; Koelman 1679, pp. 33–4, no. 72. See also Wittewrongel 1661, frontispiece (Fig. 80), which shows a father instructing his virtuous children at the table. The boy standing at the left has removed his hat.

133. For the theme of grace in genre paintings, see Naumann 1978; Sutton 1982–83, p. 29; Durantini 1983, pp. 47–58; Exhib. cat. Philadelphia 1984, cat. no. 102; Franits 1986, pp. 44–9.

134. See note 148.

135. See Van Veen 1612, pp. 56–7. In the *subscriptio* of this emblem, there is no direct reference to the story of Lycurgus. See also Van Veen 1683, pp. 48–9, no. 25, in which the emblem is inscribed "Gewoonte is de tweede natuur." See also Lebeus-Batillius

1596, no. 36; Anon. 1696, pp. 24–5, no. 12. Bedaux 1983 has made the first important contribution to our understanding of dogs as educational metaphors in Dutch seventeenth-century painting, based in part on his study of Van Veen's emblem and Plutarch's parable discussed next (see note 137). See also Bedaux 1990, pp. 109–69. For Van Veen's emblem book, see Gerards-Nelissen 1971.

136. There are several seventeenth-century Dutch editions of Plutarch's treatise, a work that first appeared in his *Moralia:* Plutarch 1619; R.T. 1634; Anon. 1644, pp. 131–58.

137. Plutarch (ca. 1535), sigs. B1^{v}–B2: "Lycurgus (whiche made and gave lawes to the people called the Spartanes of Lacedemones) for to prove the efficacie of custome, caused ii. [two] whelpes to be taken and brought up in sondrye maners/ thone to be made a ravenour and recheles, thother chaste, suer in lyam, and to hunte truely. That done, on a tyme whan the people were in one place assembled, Lycurgus sayde unto them: O ye Lacedemones, for to gete and attayne unto vertue, custome, discipline, doctryne, and good bryngynge up, be of great effecte and substaunce: Of the whiche I shall unto you anone, make experience. And forthewith, bryngynge before them the whelpes, whiche he kepte: when he hadde sette betwene them a potte with meate and a quicke hare, thone whelpe egerly flewe to the hare, thother with as moche haste or more, thraste his heed in to the potte. And whan the people in no wyse coude comecte what this thinge purported, or wherfore the whelpes were brought forthe: Frendes sayde Lycurgus, both these whelpes havynge one syre and one damme, by custome be trayned in to sondrye disposicions: for the one is become a ravenour, the other a good hunter." Bedaux 1983, p. 50, published the comparable seventeenth-century Dutch text of this passage. See also Bedaux 1990, p. 112.

138. Plutarch's ideas about the power of training to influence behavior reflect his pedagogical theory: "Thre thinges ther be that must concurre & agre in the acconplishing & perfecting of the warke, which I now purpose, that is to say Nature, Reason, and Custome. Reason I take for doctrine, Custome for exercise. The begynninge and entre is to be taken for doctrine, Experience is won by meditacion & exercise. Of all those tygyder is made a perfection: And where any of them do lacke or fayle, nedes must vertue halte" ([ca. 1535], sig. A4^{v}). Plutarch's pedagogical theory is actually based on Aristotle's; see Emmens 1963; Bedaux 1983, pp. 50–1; 1990, p. 112.

139. Batty 1581, sig. 19^{v}. See also Taffin 1640, sig. 207^{v}; Wittewrongel 1661, vol. 1, p. 182: "yemandt (die verstant heeft) door zijn opvoedinge gewent sal worden / Dat wert als sijn natuere." See also Groenendijk 1984, p. 146.

140. Cats 1632b, appendix of proverbs entitled "Kinder-op-voedinghe," after pt. 1, p. 3: "Gewent een winde tot den pot / Een iagt hont wort een keucken-sot."

141. The motif of the well-trained dog in Dutch seventeenth-century painting is likely derived from the story of Lycurgus as well; Bedaux 1983, p. 54, came to the following conclusion: "Waarschijnlijker is echter dat de beeldtraditie rechtstreeks is voortgekomen uit de tekst van Plutarchus, als een vanzelfsprekende vertaling van deze tekst in een compact beeld, dat aansloot bij de praktijk van de zeventiende eeuw, waarbij de anecdotische hond van Lycurgus veranderde in een vast attribuut." See also Bedaux 1990, p. 113; and p. 148, this volume.

142. This was first proposed in Franits 1985, p. 700. It is possible that the ravenous dog in the foreground of the portrait by Geldorp has the same pedagogical meaning; see Fig. 120.

143. The print is part of a series of the ten ages of man, entitled *Nützliche Zeitbetrachtung* (1675); see Hollstein 1954–, pp. 117–21, no. 91.

144. The background illustration to the left depicts a figure bending a young sapling while another, with the aid of a horse, tries to bend a large tree trunk. This represents an educational metaphor that was also popular during the seventeenth century: a young sapling is easier to bend than an old tree trunk, an allusion to the need to mold a child's behavior while he or she is still young. See the emblem by Cats 1632b, pt. 1, pp. 1–3. See also De Swaef 1621/1740, pp. 78–9, 87; Wittewrongel 1661, vol. 1, p. 187. In seventeenth-century literature, child rearing was sometimes likened to the growth of trees;

Dod and Cleaver 1612, sigs. T1–T1[v], remark that, if parents neglect to instruct their children, then like trees, they will be crooked and unfruitful. Conversely, if the parents prune and water their "trees," they will be straight and fruitful. The presence of tall, straight trees, painted on the sides of a baby's high chair in a painting depicting a mother and her children by Dou undoubtedly conveys this association. For this picture, formerly with the E. Speelman Gallery in London, see Sumowski 1983–, vol. 1, p. 582, no. 285. To return to the print by Meyer, the background illustration in the center depicts two men pouring liquid into large casks. Their actions illustrate the Horatian maxim that a vessel always retains the smell of the first liquid that it contained. This refers to Horace's observation that a child will permanently retain whatever he or she has been taught, be it good or evil. See the emblem by Van Veen 1612, pp. 32–3. See also Gouge 1622, p. 545; Wittewrongel 1661, vol. 1, p. 187. For the sapling and vessel metaphors, see also Bedaux 1983, pp. 58–61; 1990, pp. 122, 127, 132; Groenendijk 1984, p. 151.

145. For toys in Dutch paintings as symbols of foolishness and frivolity, see Exhib. cat. Amsterdam 1976, p. 99; Durantini 1983, pp. 206–56. See also p. 126, this volume.

146. See Sutton 1982–3, p. 31 n. 1, who notes that there are numerous copies of the picture. There is also a painting by Carel de Moor (Dunkirk Museum) that seems to have been inspired by Steen's picture; see Exhib cat. Lille 1972, cat. no. 41.

147. E.g., Adriaen van Ostade's print of grace (B. 34), reproduced in Sutton 1982–3, p. 31, fig. 29. See also Steen's *Prayer before the Meal* in the Morrison Collection, with its inscriptions alluding to contentment and simplicity; this painting is illustrated and discussed in Exhib. cat. Philadelphia 1984, cat. no. 102.

148. Koelman 1679, pp. 16, no. 23, 19, no. 33, 20, nos. 37–8, 69, nos. 141–2, 82, no. 161, 84, nos. 165, 169, provides detailed instructions on how to teach a child to pray. Sutton 1982–3, p. 30, correctly interprets the sunflower at the left as a symbol of love for Christ, citing a contemporary emblem with this meaning (his fig. 28). Sutton also notes that the colander in the left background could possibly allude to prudence (ibid.). He cites an emblem in which this utensil symbolizes the need to separate order from disorder in the home. This idea certainly reflects contemporary domestic ideals, but I am nevertheless hesitant to interpret the colander in this manner; Sutton wisely adds that "we may be overreading what is, after all, a common household utensil."

149. Sutton 1982–3, p. 29, identified the first two words – though he has transcribed them as "Pater Nostrum" – of what is now a largely indecipherable inscription. He also notes that, in other paintings by Steen, a *belkroon* is present, clearly inscribed with verses from the Lord's Prayer. The Lord's Prayer was subject to exhaustive analyses in many seventeenth-century catechism books; Ursinus 1606, devotes over one hundred pages to its explanation (sigs. 215–256[v]).

150. See Fiorone 1976, p. 322, no. 267. I wish to thank Han Venema for identifying the type of dog depicted in the painting.

151. Griffons are often included in portraits of wealthy people; see the portrait now attributed to Barent Graat of a well-to-do family in the garden of their country house, reproduced in Edwards 1954, p. 94, fig. 39.

152. It is important to note that Plutarch's parable (see note 137) was recounted with many variations at this time. All of the variations revolve around the two dogs. In some cases, an author will state that the two dogs have the same mother, in others, a different one. Furthermore, some authors will say that the house dog was the glutton and the hunting dog chased the rabbit; others say the exact opposite. Still others fail to introduce the terms "house dog" and "hunting dog." See also Bedaux 1983, p. 69 n. 15, who discusses later variations of the *subscriptio* to Van Veen's emblem that illustrates the parable (see note 137). Curiously, in the *pictura* of this emblem in all the editions, the dogs are two entirely different breeds and therefore could not have come from the same litter. See also Bedaux 1990, p. 169 n. 63.

153. Durantini 1983, pp. 47–52, discusses the print by Saenredam as the earliest example of the theme of "The Schoolboy's Meal." It is no mere coincidence that representations of praying children are shown with their hornbooks because the school was, at least in theory, an important forum for the moral training of children. This explains why a schoolhouse has been depicted in the background of a painting of a schoolboy's meal by De Hooch, now in The J. Paul Getty Museum, Malibu (reproduced in ibid., p. 50, fig. 25).

154. Bedaux 1983, p. 58, discusses the probable pedagogical symbolism of this motif in Saenredam's print.

155. See ibid., where Bedaux also cites other examples of the motif in art that predate the publication of *Houwelyck.* See also Bedaux 1990, pp. 119, 122.

156. See Bedaux 1983, pp. 56–7; 1990, p. 119. See also Chapter 1, p. 20, this volume. A dog squatting on its hind legs also appears on the frontispiece to *Houwelyck* (Fig. 3); see Bedaux 1983, p. 57; 1990, p. 119.

157. Anon. 1640, pp. 304–5. This emblem is cited by Bedaux 1983, pp. 54–5; see also Bedaux 1990, p. 113.

158. See Bedaux 1983, pp. 58–9, 61–4; 1990, pp. 113–22.

159. The following discussion is based on Franits 1990.

160. Plutarch (ca. 1535), sig. B1^{v}. Bedaux 1983, pp. 55–6, cites this very same passage. Bedaux also draws a parallel between this passage and a detail from Pieter Saenredam's *Interior of the Buurkerk at Utrecht* (see pp. 64–5, fig. 27). He calls attention to the pedagogical significance of the detail in question: a graffito on one of the great pillars of the church. The crude drawing depicts an episode derived from the thirteenth-century *chanson de geste* of *Renaud de Montauban* in which the four sons of Aymon of Dordogne escape the scene of a murder on Beyard, the magical horse whom one of the boys has tamed. See also Bedaux 1990, p. 150. Liedtke 1989, 37–47, discusses the rich symbolic associations evoked by equestrian portraits of monarchs and aristocrats.

161. Batty 1581, sig. 87. Another important source for Batty and other pedagogues was found in the Apocrypha, namely in Ecclesiasticus 30:8. See further Franits 1990, p. 217.

162. See, e.g., Zincgref 1624, no. 73.

163. Hofferus 1635, p. 179.

164. Ibid., p. 180: "Juyst even als ghy siet dit peerd seer weeldrigh springhen/ Tot dat de spoor hem streeckt, tot dat de toom hem dwinght,/ Neemt van hem spoor, of toom, dan slaat het, of het springht/ Neemt van de jeughd de tucht ghy sultse niet bedwinghen."

165. Bedaux 1987, pp. 150–4, has rightly called attention to some of the hazards involved with utilizing emblems to interpret Dutch seventeenth-century paintings. See also Renger 1978, p. 36; Bedaux 1990, pp. 74–6. See also note 58.

166. For this portrait, see Cat. Brussels 1984, p. 86, cat. no. 4038. The attribution to Jacob Gerritsz. Cuyp is not entirely convincing; the painting has also been attributed to Jacob van der Merck. It also resembles an anonymous family portrait included in the exhibition on marriage and family portraiture held at Haarlem's Frans Hals Museum; see Exhib. cat. Haarlem 1986, cat. no. 49.

167. The same is true of the boy in the print by Jan Saenredam after Hendrick Goltzius (Fig. 131) and those who doff their hats in portraits of families saying grace; see Figs. 90, 120. See also note 132.

168. Portraits of horses were sometimes commissioned at this time; see, e.g., the painting by Aelbert Cuyp in the Willem van der Vorm Collection of the Museum Boymans-van Beuningen in Rotterdam; Cat. Rotterdam 1972, p. 61, cat. no. vdV 11.

169. Clearly, pedagogical notions are not conveyed by every equestrian portrait depicting children. Often these works refer to hunting and to the wealth and social status associated with it. See, e.g., the portrait by Aelbert Cuyp of two well-dressed youths from the Pompe van Meerdervoort family posed beside their tutor and family servant (New York, The Metropolitan Museum of Art); illustrated in Franits 1990, fig. 4. For the connections between hunting and social status in seventeenth-century Dutch art and culture, see Sullivan 1984, pp. 34–5.

170. For this portrait, which might represent Sieuwert Heynsius, see Ekkart 1990, pp. 198–200, and cat. no. 17. See also Exhib. cat. 's-Hertogenbosch 1980, pp. 23, 121, and cat. no. 308.

171. See, e.g., Exhib. cat. 's-Hertogenbosch 1980, p. 24, figs. 26, 27; Bedaux 1990, p. 132 and fig. 68.

172. Ariès 1962, p. 33, 50–61, 339. See further A. Wilson 1980, pp. 139–40, 144–6; Vanden-

broeck 1983–4, pp. 18–22; Pollock 1985, pp. 22–4, 46–9.

173. The contemporary awareness of childhood as a distinct stage in life also explains why so many pedagogical treatises were published at this time; see, e.g., De Swaef 1621/1740; Koelman 1679. For sixteenth-century pedagogical treatises, see Ozment 1983, pp. 136–44. Kruithof 1982, examines pedagogical literature from the seventeenth to the nineteenth century, concluding that "in opvoedingsadviezen is een patroon te ontwaren dat op zijn minst van de 17e eeuw tot de eerste helft van de 19e eeuw betrekkelijk constant blijft" (p. 170). The large number of prints that illustrate human ages always include childhood, thus providing further proof of the contemporary awareness of this life stage; see Fig. 4. See also Exhib. cat. Kleves 1983–4; Hazelzet 1989. Gouge 1622, p. 526, and Wittewrongel 1661, vol. 1, pp. 175, 186, distinguish between three phases in a child's life beginning at birth and ending with adulthood; see Groenendijk 1984, pp. 139–40. See also Messiae 1607, pp. 163–4.

CHAPTER 4. "WEDUWE"

1. The seventeenth-century term "tronie" is difficult to translate; see De Pauw-De Veen 1969, pp. 190–5; and especially the helpful appendix in Schwartz 1989, pp. 112–14. See also Chapman 1990, p. 38; De Vries 1990b.
2. The elderly were most often censured for being greedy; see Cats 1625, chap. 6, pp. 30–2; Johan de Brune 1636, p. 72. This explains the frequent use in art of elderly women as personifications of Avaritia; see, e.g., the print by Cornelis Bloemaert after Abraham Bloemaert, illustrated and discussed by Bruyn 1988, pp. 70–1, fig. 88. See also Schama 1987, pp. 430–2.
3. For historical views of the elderly, see Minois 1989; Troyansky 1989; and especially Van Kooij 1987, who examines the widespread social problem in the seventeenth century of poverty among the elderly. Particularly helpful is her discussion of *hofjes* (p. 62), little houses or rooms donated by wealthy patrons where aged, poor people could live for free. For charitable institutions for the elderly (including the *hofjes*), see Wolf 1977, pp. 232–44; S. Muller 1985. The former study, intended for the general public, is from the popular pamphlet series "58 miljoen Nederlanders," which in turn was based on a television series.
4. See respectively, Cats 1625, chap. 6, pp. 3–48, 49–76. For this chapter, see Meertens 1943, pp. 276–7; Carter 1974, pp. 122–3; Ten Berge 1979, pp. 90–3.
5. In this chapter, Cats quotes numerous works by classical and humanist authors, including Cicero and Vives. Cicero's *De Senectute* established him as the classical authority on old age. A Dutch translation of this important text appeared in 1624. For Cicero's study on old age and its enormous reputation in early modern Europe, see Minois 1989, pp. 105–11; Troyansky 1989, pp. 89–92.
6. See, e.g., Johan de Brune 1636, p. 253: "Wat is de oudheyd? Niet dan verkoutheid./ De oudheyd zelfs is anders niet,/ Als ziect', en kranckheyd met verdriet." See also ibid., p. 456; 1660, p. 178, no. 263; Jan de Brune 1681a, p. 501. Croon 1665, p. 369, calls old age one of the "dry boden des doodts." Cats 1632b, app. after pt. 3, pp. 12–13, published a series of proverbs about old age, under the title "Ouderdom, sieckte, doot." Laurentius 1599, pp. 176–7, contains a detailed yet poetic description of the physical problems experienced by the elderly. Laurentius, the French physician to King Henri IV, was one of the most respected medical authorities in Europe in the early seventeenth century.
7. Cats 1665, p. 63: "Voorwaer den ouden dagen, die leyt ons tot de reden,/ Of sendt haer boden uyt door ons geheele leden;/ Sy klopt ons aen den arm, of borst, of swacken voet,/ En leert ons dat men haest van hier verhuysen moet." In this book, Cats repeatedly states that those over sixty years old are elderly. Ripa 1644, p. 395, places old age between fifty and sixty years. See further, De Jongh 1981–2, p. 154 n. 31; Gilbert 1967, pp. 7–32.
8. Van de Venne 1623, p. 107. This literary topos is found in numerous works of the period; see, e.g., Johan de Brune 1636, p. 251. See also Joost van den Vondel's poem, quoted on p. 168, this volume. The topos of the elderly already having a foot in the grave

is illustrated in the *pictura* of an emblem by Rollenhagen 1611–13, vol. 1, no. 75.

9. Cats 1625, chap. 6, *voor-reden,* sig. 4 * iiij^v: "De oude vinden duysent lessen in haer eyghen selfs, in hare swackheden, in de kerck-hof-bloemen (ick segge de grijse hayren) die haer op het hooft ende inden baert wassen, elck vande welcke hun voor een predicatie can verstrecken om haer huys te bereyden voor hare erfgenamen, hare lichamen voor den buyck der aerden, ende hare sielen voor het oordeel Gods." See also ibid., chap. 6, p. 24; Pers 1648, pp. 164–6; Brooks 1667, pp. 49–70, esp. p. 52.

10. For an interpretation of this painting that accords with mine, see De Jongh in Exhib. cat. Haarlem 1986, p. 24.

11. For the conviction that the elderly must bridle their passions, see the discussions and literature cited in Bedaux 1975, pp. 20, 22; De Jongh 1981–2, p. 154.

12. See Pers 1648, p. 165 (quoted on p. 184, this volume. Pers also quotes the ancient philosophers Seneca and Cicero, who praise the virtue of the elderly (ibid.). For Cicero, see note 5 this chapter.

13. Brooks 1667, p. 52: "Sy bidden ende betalen gemeenlijck meest/ sy arbeiden meest/ ende verlangen allermeest na de uitgelesenste openbaringen van hem zelf/ ende van sijne genade." See also ibid., pp. 53–5.

14. See, e.g., Pers 1648, p. 165; Johan de Brune 1660, vol. 2, p. 65 no. 84.

15. This print, dated 1675, is part of a series representing the ten ages of man entitled *Nützliche Zeitbetrachtung;* see Hollstein 1954–, vol. 27, pp. 117–21, no. 191.

16. For this print, see De Meyer 1962, p. 408. For the popularity of catchpenny prints at this time, see Chapter 1, note 100.

17. For De Gheyn's print, see Van Regteren Altena 1983, vol. 2, pp. 50–1, cat. no. 199.

18. See, e.g., Poirters 1647, pp. 34–40. In Cramer 1630, p. 1, no. 1, there is an emblem whose *pictura* shows a man, buried up to his knees in earth, pointing to a broken pot that he holds. The emblem is symbolic of *vanitas,* as is clarified by several poems that Cramer included along with his quotation of Genesis 3:19. In this verse, God tells Adam that he has been made from the ground (i.e., the earth) and to the ground he shall return, thereby announcing his inevitable death. Cramer has made a symbolic connection between friable earthenware vessels and the fact that man will return to the very earth whence he came. The same connection was made by other authors of the period; see, e.g., David 1603, pp. 284–5, no. 81.

19. For elderly people as personifications of winter in sixteenth- and seventeenth-century prints, see Veldman 1980, pp. 151–63. See also the print introducing the sixth chapter of Cats 1625, pp. 1–2; it shows an elderly couple standing in a winter landscape and has the following poem: "Siet hier den ouden tijt, de koude winter-dagen, / Verscheyden vande jeucht, en vande somer-vlagen." See also Ripa 1644, p. 396; Cats 1665, p. 62. See further the many examples cited in the excellent study by Van Straten 1977, pp. 35–42. He examines the iconographic history of this link in art and literature.

20. For this painting, see Klemm 1986, pp. 49, 120–2, cat. no. 46; Porteman 1987, pp. 138–41. For the series itself, see Klemm 1986, cat. nos. 35–46; Porteman 1987.

21. Klemm 1986, p. 120, discusses the painting's links with the art of Van Honthorst, suggesting that the latter's *Servant with a Candle* in the collection of the Marquess of Waterford may have been the immediate model; for an illustration of Van Honthorst's painting, see Nicolson 1979, p. 43 and fig. 148.

22. "Hoe treurt de Wintermaent, gelijck een weeuw, in rouwe/ Gedompelt over 't hooft. haar kaars en glas gaan uit./ Het doots-hooft spelt de doot, die 'slevens draeiboom sluit./ d'Onvruchtbre winter slacht een dootsche weduwvrouwe,/ Die noch kastanjen braat: haar almanack rolt af./ Wat is een weeuw? een schim; met eenen voet in 't graf." See Porteman 1987, p. 139. See also Vondel 1927–40, vol. 4, pp. 554–70. For Vondel's friendship with Sandrart, see Porteman 1987, pp. 24–31. The popular series was first engraved by Albert Haelwegh in 1645. It was furnished with inscriptions in Latin by Caspar van Baerle; see Klemm 1986, pp. 103–4; Porteman 1987.

23. Cat. Munich 1983, p. 162, cat. no. 588, offers the following interpretation of the painting: "Frömmigheit, Fleiss, Häuslichkeit, Zufrie-

denheit – Tugenden, die dem holländischen Bürgertum des 17. Jahrhunderts als erstrebenswerte Ideale galten, fanden in diesem Gemälde sinnbildhaften Ausdruck."

24. Among the books specifically addressed to widows are Erasmus 1607; Twisck 1630. Twisck quoted Erasmus's book extensively; see, e.g., note 43 this chapter.

25. It was suggested that those who were widowed at a young age should remarry, though only after a suitable period of mourning, and after careful selection of a new mate. See the lengthy instructions of Cats 1625, chap. 6, pp. 59–71. Not all authors agreed with Cats; Twisck 1630, pp. 43–4, reluctantly advises younger widows to remarry, but he sees widowhood as "die conditien/ tot welcken sy gheroepen waren." See also Vives 1547, sig. 132. Vives's conventional ideas about widowhood are expounded in the last section of his book, which, like Cats's *Houwelyck,* is divided into female life stages. For the influence of this work on Cats, see Friesendorp and Joosse 1983, pp. 245–50. For Vives's prescriptions for widows, see Kelso 1956, p. 121. For the considerable legal rights of widows of the elite in the Netherlands at this time, see Marshall-Wyntjes 1982, pp. 396–405; Marshall 1987, pp. 53–68; Schama 1987, pp. 404–5.

26. These strictures were ideal, but there is evidence that at least some people tried to adhere to them; Roodenburg 1990, pp. 251–2, recounts the case of a widow in Amsterdam who was called before one of the consistories in 1655 for spending too much time outside of her house. She stated that she needed to go out because her children were sick. She added – and this is interesting not only within the context of my discussion here, but also within that of this entire book – that she was diligent "in het aenhooren van Gods Woort ende vlytich in haer werck binnenshuijs" (p. 252).

27. Cats 1625, chap. 6, p. 74: "Siet wat een schamel mensch in druck en sieckte maeckt,/ En latet aende jeucht al wat de kamer raeckt;/ Stil, eensaem, treurich sijn, en, met een soet verlangen,/ Veel tranen evenstaech te rollen opte wangen/ Te storten voor den Heer, dat is reyn gelaet/ Dat is u ten besten vought, en past op uwen staet:/ Veel troosten inder noot, veel bidden, milde deelen,/ Dat sijn voor uwen hals de beste bruyts-juweelen;/ Niet dat de leden ciert, maar dat de siele bout,/ Is dienstigh aen het volck dat niet en is getrout." See also Erasmus 1607; Houwaert 1622–3, pp. 725–835; Twisck 1630; Fuller 1642, pp. 24–6; Sucquet 1649, pp. 60–7. The Pauline Epistles were an important source in molding contemporary attitudes toward the behavior and life-styles deemed most befitting for widows. Paul discussed widowhood at length in two passages, Titus 2:3–5 and I Timothy 5:2–16; see the comments of Pearson 1957, p. 511.

28. The significance of some of the other motifs in this painting is unclear, and there is always the danger of overreading what may simply be household objects devoid of specific associations. However, the broom depicted in the left corner might allude to spiritual purity, a meaning that would certainly be fitting in this context; for the broom as metaphor of spiritual purity, see Chapter 2, pp. 98-100.

29. See, e.g., the metal objects depicted in *vanitas* still lifes by Leonard Bramer and Pieter Claesz, reproduced and discussed in Exhib. cat. Leiden 1970, cat. nos. 4, 6.

30. The portrait is discussed by De Jongh in Exhib. cat. Haarlem 1986, cat. no. 48.

31. See Chapter 2, p. 80, Fig. 62.

32. In this context, the meticulously painted butterfly, which has just alighted on the jamb, refers to *vanitas* as well, a long-standing association of this insect; see Exhib. cat. Leiden 1970, cat. no. 20; Exhib. cat. Amsterdam 1976, pp. 286, 287 n. 12.

33. For this print and the series to which it belongs, see Veldman 1983, pp. 37–46.

34. For the urine flask as a symbol of *vanitas,* see Bedaux 1975, pp. 17–22. See also Snoep-Rietsma 1973a, pp. 289–90. The personification of Conscientia (Conscience) holds a Bible. According to the print, men are often hindered in their last years by their consciences (see Veldman 1983, p. 43). Conscientia probably holds the Bible in order to demonstrate that men can approach death painlessly if they have a thorough knowledge of God and His grace. Cats 1625, chap. 6, preface, sigs. 4 *–4 **iiij, entitled *Aende jonghe lieden,* expounds his conviction that one can approach death without fear through knowledge of God.

35. Maclaren 1960, p. 390. For another interpretation of the painting, see Snoep-Reitsma 1973a, p. 181.
36. See the Introduction, pp. 13-14.
37. The old woman in this print is praying with a rosary and is therefore a Catholic; see Bruyn 1988, p. 71–2.
38. See the wonderful description in Schama 1987, p. 430. See further Hecht in Exhib. cat. Amsterdam 1989–90, pp. 26–7, who downplays the symbolic component of such paintings. For this reason, Hecht's approach has been sharply criticized; see Bruyn 1991; Sluijter 1991. See also Hecht's response – along with Eddy de Jongh's criticisms – in Raben and Vermeij 1990, an article that made use of interviews with the two scholars.
39. For *tronies,* see further, note 1, this chapter.
40. For the painting by Rembrandt, Fig. 153, see Bruyn et al. 1982–, vol. 1, p. 274, cat. no. A27. The authors propose that Rembrandt's picture does not "refer to any specific biblical figure but rather to old age and in particular to pious old age." See also Bruyn 1988, pp. 71–2.
41. See Schwartz 1989, pp. 96–9. See also Chapman 1990, pp. 17–21.
42. I Timothy 5:5. This verse was cited frequently by Protestant and Catholic authors; see, e.g., Erasmus 1607, sig. A8v; Sucquet 1649, p. 63. See also note 27 this chapter. According to Poot 1743–50, vol. 1, p. 412, an old person personifies prayer because "in dien tyt des levens doorgaens meest gebeden wort, vermits het vertrek uit deze werelt de ouden zeer naby is."
43. Twisck 1630, p. 70: "De meeste eere ende prijs der weduwen is/ maticheyt in al haer leven: de maticheydt en is niet alleen ghelegghen in haer spyse/ in de besorghinghe des lichaems/ in haer kleederen/ gangh en ghebare/ maer oock in haer huysghesindt/ gheselschap/ regeringhe ende spelinne daerse mede ommegaet." Twisck quotes this passage, almost verbatim, from Erasmus 1607, sig. C1v.
44. For this print, see Miedema 1977, pp. 217–18.
45. The motif of the devious cat pulling on the tablecloth is difficult to interpret. Is transience, a notion so clearly expressed by other motifs in the painting, implied by the fact that the animal will cause all of the food and dishes to fall off the table? Perhaps the cat's long association with evil is meant to contrast the woman's piety in order to illustrate the pervasive power of sin. For this creature's association with evil, see Bax 1949, pp. 175–6; Durantini 1983, p. 275.
46. Cats 1625, chap. 6, p. 55: "Een hert, dat sich verquickt in Godes bouck te lesen,/ Een oogh, dat sich vermaeckt met tranen nat te wesen,/ Een siel van stillen aert, die sich der werelt schaemt."
47. See Exhib. cat. Philadelphia 1984, cat. no. 32. There is another version of this painting in Schwerin; see Sumowski 1983–, vol. 1, p. 529, no. 264. Some scholars do not believe that the painting in Schwerin is by Dou; see Naumann 1981b, pp. 617–18. See also Baer 1990, cat. no. 10.
48. There is also a broom present, resting against the wine cask in the right foreground. In this context, this cleaning implement might allude to spiritual purity, a meaning that would certainly be appropriate in this context; for the broom as metaphor of purity, see Chapter 2, pp. 98–100.
49. Cats 1625, chap. 6, p. 53. Held 1965, p. 113, calls attention to a portrait of a widow by an anonymous Flemish artist (The Hague, Mauritshuis; ca. 1615) in which the tulip that she holds is said to pay homage to her deceased husband; reproduced in Cat. The Hague 1977, p. 89, no. 695. De Jongh in Exhib. cat. Haarlem 1986, pp. 84, 86 n. 8, also mentions it and suggests that the flower is meant as a metaphor of widowhood just as it is in *Houwelyck.* However, the identification of the young woman in this painting as a widow is not entirely convincing. Furthermore, the painting predates the first edition of *Houwelyck* by about ten years. Therefore, the tulip in this picture likely retains its long-standing association with vanity, as does the skull – inscribed "Sum quod eris" – that the woman touches with her other hand. In a portrait of Madeleine de Cuyper by Jacob Jordaens (private collection), a tulip in a vase on the window ledge could very well be a metaphor of the state of widowhood in the Catsian sense; see Held 1965, p. 113, who thought that the motif was also meant to pay homage to the woman's deceased husband. See also De Jongh 1986, pp. 84, 86 n. 8. The portrait by Jordaens is

reproduced in D'Hulst, 1982, p. 274, fig. 238.

50. Cats 1625, chap. 6, p. 54: "Stelt u een bloemjen voor, dat vande steel gesneden/ Heeft door het vinnich mes sijn eerste doot geleden,/ Dat even metter daet, na dat het is gevelt,/ Wort in een enge fles, wort in het nat gestelt;/ Daer staet het teer gewas, daer staet het in gesloten,/ Daer staet het in en queelt met tranen overgoten,/ Daer staet het treurich heen, daer staet het in gebocht,/ Sijn troost, ja leven selfs, dat is een droevich vocht. . . . Siet daer, o sedich volck, siet daer een eygen wapen,/ Voor die onthylickt sijn, en sonder hoeder slapen,/ Voor die van haren man sijn haestich afgeruckt,/ Gelijckmen vande steel een aerdich bloemje pluckt."
51. Houwaert 1622–3, p. 751: "Een weduwe moet met eerlijcke protectie/ modereren haren druck met occupatie."
52. See Erasmus 1607, sig. B6.
53. According to Cat. Berlin 1978, p. 249, cat. no. 819 C, the apples, which are symbolically linked to the Fall of Man, caution one to resist the temptations of the world and abide by God's commandments. This interpretation is questionable as is the identification of the objects in the wall niche as metaphors of the woman's purity and chastity.
54. This garment and the woman herself symbolize *vanitas.* The concept of transience is even more forcefully communicated in a picture of an old woman plucking a dead bird (perhaps a rooster) by Abraham de Pape (The Hague, Mauritshuis) where a young boy points to the fowl. In Anon. 1667, n.p., the annual slaughtering of domesticated animals is construed as a reminder that man must face death and the Last Judgement; cited by De Jongh 1971, pp. 169–70. For De Pape's picture, which also includes a gleaming metal pot, see Exhib. cat. Leiden 1988, cat. no. 62.
55. According to Cat. Berlin 1978, pp. 138–9, cat. no. 2031, "Jesus' statement which underlies this scene presumably refers also to the old woman's preparations for a meal: 'But whosoever drinketh of the water that I shall give him shall never thirst' (John 4, 14)." Sutton 1980, p. 49, follows this interpretation.
56. Fig. 163 by Gerard Dou has long been considered the pendant of the artist's *Old Woman Reading* in the same museum; Moiso-Diekamp 1987, p. 319, rejects this idea. See also Baer 1990, cat. no. 96.
57. The cross-reel rarely appears in literature; Huygens did write a short poem about it: "Siet eens hoe den haspel pocht/ Met den arbeit van goe handen;/ Sulcken ydelen gedrocht/ Vindtmen meest in alle Landen:/ Veel in 't Hof veel inde Kerck/ Poncktmen met een anders werck" (1672, vol. 2, p. 40, no. 74). Exhib. cat. Leiden 1988, p. 105 n. 6, discusses the obscene connotations of the device in proverbial literature in connection with a painting by Dou in the Rijksmuseum of an old woman holding a cross-reel.
58. The following description of the process of winding thread is based on Groves 1973, p. 30.
59. See, e.g., the allegory of temperance, holding various tools of measure and restraint, in Rollenhagen 1611–13, vol. 2, no. 35.
60. Pers 1648, p. 165: "Verkrijgen sy andere gaven des gemoedts, als wijsheyt, matigheyt en andere deughden, die den oude Luyden betamelijck zijn." In this passage, Pers is quoting Cicero; see note 5 this chapter. According to Messiae 1607, p. 165, in old age (ages 56–68, which he distinguishes from the "last age," ages 68–88), men do "alle goede wercken / beminnende de maticheyt ende liefde / begeerende deere meetten lof: sy zijn eerbaer / vreesende schanden ende oneere."
61. See the passage from contemporary literature, quoted on p. 176.
62. Maclaren 1960, p. 291, states that the couple probably represent Tobit and Anna. In my opinion, there is really no visual evidence to support this interpretation.
63. See also a print in Cats 1625, chap. 6, p. 39, which shows an old man, seated by a fireplace, who discusses his approaching death and trust in God (pp. 39–43). See also Van Dorp 1679, pp. 130–8. Van Straten 1977, pp. 35–8; Van Gelderblom 1981, pp. 28–31, discuss the iconographic history of this theme in art and literature.
64. This association was grounded in the ancient humoral theory of physiology, one widely accepted in the seventeenth century. See, e.g., Laurentius 1599, pp. 170–1, 174; Messiae 1607, p. 165; and C[olerus] 1663a, p. 348, who states, "In summa de Winter is kout en droogh / gelijck de melanckolie en

de ouderdom des menschen." See also Minois 1989, pp. 103–5; Troyansky 1989, pp. 109–11.

65. Johan de Brune 1624, pp. 318–22, no. 54.

66. Ibid., p. 318: "Hoe kost'lick is't, voor God, hoe zoet, voor ons, t'aenschouwen!/ Dat man en vrouw te zaem haer zelven onderhouwen,/ Van haerer handen werck, en wachten, van de Heer,/ Niet wat de wereld geeft, veel onrust, goed en eer,/ Maer met een vrolick hert, gevest op rotsche gronden / Van Godes trouw en eed, en aen haer plicht verbonden, / Des hemels rust en lust; vertrouwend' dat de man, / Die Godes rijcke zoeckt, noyt yet ontbreken kan."

67. Several scholars have cited this emblem but not all have noted that its meaning hinges on the presence of an elderly couple in the *pictura.* See, e.g., Exhib. cat. Amsterdam 1976, p. 49; Stone-Ferrier 1985, p. 85.

68. Johan De Brune 1624, p. 320: "haere burgerschap is in den hemel, van waer zy den Zaligh-maecker verwachten."

69. See pp. 163–4, this volume.

70. Pers 1648, p. 165: "Dies hy gebruyckt verstant en reeden/ en bescheyt/ Wijsheyt en deughd/ en goede zeeden/ matigheyt/ Om bequaem/ aengenaem/ Voor God den Heer te zijn/ in daed en schijn. Schoon hem de leden heel verstijven/ 't hert is gau/ Hy weet dat niemandt hier sal blijven/ dies hy nau/ Stelt sijn perck/ en sijn merck/ Op Godes pad en Woort/ nae 's Levens poort."

71. Erasmus 1607, sig. A4^{v}: "De authoriteyt ende bestieringhe over de Maechden ende ghehoude Vrouwen/ by de Weduwen is. Want het comt den Weduwen toe de ghene die houwen sullen/ ende die onlancx gehouwet zijn/ te leeren hoe sy haer draghen sullen teghens haer Mannen/ teghens haer kinderen ende Huysghesinne/ teghens haer Vrienden ende Maghen. Den selfden Weduwen comt toe/ de Maechden in tucht te houden: haer te onderwijsen/ hoe sy haer sonder opsprake sullen dragen/ haren naem ende faem sullen gade slaen." See also Brathwait 1631, p. 112; Griffith 1633, pp. 139–40; Anon. 1642, p. 15; G. Udemans 1658, p. 227. Many of these passages directly quote Titus 2:4; see note 27 this chapter.

72. The subject depicted here, a young widow peeling apples in the presence of a girl (who could be her daughter), is virtually unique in Dutch seventeenth-century painting. Slatkes 1981, p. 114, was the first to recognize that the woman wears a mourning veil. He also pointed out that the basic theme of a figure occupied with peeling fruit can be traced to the work of Caravaggio. For the painting by Ter Borch, see also Gudlaugsson 1959–60, vol. 2, cat. no. 167; Exhib. cat. The Hague 1974, cat. no. 46; Exhib. cat. Philadelphia 1984, cat. no. 14.

73. Visscher 1614, p. 27, no. 27. Slatkes 1981, p. 114, cites this emblem in connection with the motif of the fruit bowl in the painting. See also Exhib. cat. Philadelphia 1984, p. 152.

74. See Chapter 3, pp. 124–6. The pedagogical significance of the motif in Van Brekelenkam's painting was first pointed out in Otto Nauman's entry in Exhib. cat. Philadelphia 1984, cat. no. 17. See also Lasius 1987, pp. 153–4; Exhib. cat. Leiden 1988, cat. no. 1, p. 81, where this is doubted. According to Elizabeth Honig, the author of the catalogue entry, the old woman's action "kan het beste gekoppeld worden aan andere huiselijke taken; daarbij lijken associates met vroomheid te worden opgewekt. . . . In plaats van een didactische aansporing moet de voorstelling in zijn geheel gezien worden als een weergave van prijzenswaardige netheid en vroomheid van het gewone volk."

75. Exhib. cat. Philadelphia 1984, p. 158; Lasius 1987, p. 153.

76. It is difficult to determine the subject of the triptych because the painting is now known only from photographs. In Van Brekelenkam's painting, the striving for moral and spiritual purity is possibly underscored by the engraved portrait of the Leiden theologian Lodovicus de Dieu (1590–1642) on the wall in the right background. This identification was made in Cat. Leiden 1983, pp. 83–4, cat. no. 47. See also Exhib cat. Philadelphia 1984, p. 158; Exhib. cat. Leiden 1988, p. 83 n. 9.

77. The contrast between youth and old age here, which poignantly underscores the concept of vanity, was one made in many contemporary paintings; see, e.g., Abraham de Pape's painting of an old woman plucking a rooster beside a young boy (The Hague, Mauritshuis) illustrated and discussed in Exhib. cat. Leiden 1988, cat. no. 62. See also a work by

Dou (present location unknown) where an old woman combs a boy's hair; reproduced in Martin 1913, pl. 94. Behind him, is another boy inflating an animal's bladder, a long-standing symbol of *vanitas.* See cat. Amsterdam 1976, pp. 117–19. The boy having his hair combed in the painting by Dou holds up a tiny object. Perhaps it is a pin with which to burst the bladder, but this cannot be unequivocally determined. Honig, writing in Exhib. cat. Leiden 1988, identifies it as a louse; even though the boy is having his hair deloused, it is unlikely that he is holding a louse because this insect is approximately the same size as the head of a pin and therefore would not be visible from such a distance.

78. The elderly are presented to the reader in precisely this manner in Cats 1625, chap. 6, preface, sigs. 4 *–4 ** iiij, entitled *Aende jonghe lieden.*

BIBLIOGRAPHY

PRIMARY REFERENCES

Angel, Philips. *Lof der schilder-konst.* Leiden, 1642.

Anon. *Afbeeldinghe van d'eerste eeuwe der Societeyt Iesu....* Antwerp, 1640.

Anon. *Christelijcke huyshoudinghe.* Hoorn, 1642.

Anon. *De seven engelen der dienst-maagden, zijnde een rare en beknopte wederlegginge tegen een nu-onlangs uitgegeven boekje genaamd 7. duivelen der dienst-maagden.* Leiden, 1697.

Anon. *Den bloem-hof van de Nederlantsche ieucht.* Amsterdam, 1610.

Anon. *Den nieuwen verbeterden lust-hof.* Amsterdam, 1607.

Anon. *Der ionghe dochters tijt-cortinghe.* N.p., 1591.

Anon. *Groote comptoir almanach*... Amsterdam, 1667.

Anon. *Handt-boecxken van Epicetus.* Amsterdam, 1644.

Anon. *Kinder-werck, ofte sinne-beelden van de spelen der kinderen.* Amsterdam 1626.

Anon. *Nieuwen ieucht spiegel*... N.p., n.d. (ca. 1620).

Anon. *Versameling van uytgeleesene sinnebeelden.* Leiden, 1696.

Baardt, Petri. *Deugden-spoor; in de on-deughden des werelts aff-gebeeldt*... Leeuwarden, 1645.

Baers, Joann. *Een bruylofts-predicatie/ ofte een corte verclaringhe over den 128. Psalm Davids* ... N.p., 1629.

Batty, Bartholomew. *The Christian Mans Closet.* Trans. W. Lowth. London, 1581.

Bayly, Ludovicus. *De practycke ofte oeffeninge der godtsaligheydt.* 17th ed. Trans. E. Schuttenium. (First published in English in 1620.) Amsterdam, 1688.

Berkhey, J. le Francq van. *Natuurlyke historie van Holland.* 9 vols. Amsterdam, 1769–1811.

Beverwijck, Johan van. *Van de wtnementheyt des vrouwelicken geslachts.* Dordrecht, 1639.

Schat der gesontheyd. In *Alle de wercken,* vol. 1. Utrecht, 1651.

Biblia: dat is de gantsche Heylighe Schrift... Dordrecht, 1580.

Biens, C. P. *Handt-boecxken der Christelijcke gedichten.* 2d ed. Hoorn, 1635.

Blankaart, Steph. *Verhandelinge van de opvoedinge en ziekten der kinderen.* Amsterdam, 1684.

Blasius, Joan. *Fidamants kusjes, minne-wysen en by-rymen aan Celestyne.* Amsterdam, 1663.

[Bosc, Jacques du]. *De deugdelyke vrou.* Trans. I. H. Glazemaker. Amsterdam, 1643.

Brandt, G. *Poëzy.* 2d ed. 3 vols. (First published in 1688.) Amsterdam, 1725–7.

Brathwait, Richard. *The English Gentlewoman.* London, 1631.

Bredero, G. A. *Boertigh, amoreus, en aendachtigh groot lied-boeck*... Amsterdam, 1622; reprint ed., Ed. A. A. van Rijnbach. Rotterdam, 1971.

Brooks, Thomas. *Gouden' appelen voor ionghmans ende iongh-dochters, als ook eene kroone der heerlykheyt voor oude-mannen ende oude-vrouwen.* Trans. D. Montanus. (First published in English in 1657.) Utrecht, 1667.

Brune, Jan de. *Jok en ernst*... In *Alle volgeestige werken*, 4th ed., vol. 2. (First published in 1665.) Amsterdam, 1681a.

Wetsteen der vernuften... In *Alle volgeestige werken*, 4th ed., vol. 1. (First published in 1665.) Amsterdam, 1681b.

Brune, Johan de. *Emblemata of zinne-werck*. Amsterdam, 1624.

Nieuwe wyn in oude le'er-zacken. Middelburg, 1636.

Bankket-werk van goede gedagten. 2d ed. 2 vols. (First published in 1658.) Middelburg, 1660.

Brunfels, Otto. *Von der Zucht und Underweisung der Kinder*. (First published in Latin in 1519.) Strasbourg, 1525.

Bruto, G. M. *La institutione di una fanciualla nota nobilmente*. Antwerp, 1555.

Bullinger, H. *The Christen State of Matrimonye*. Trans. M. Coverdale. (First published in German in 1540.) N.p., 1541.

Huysboec. Trans. J. Haller. (First published in Latin in 1549.) Emden, 1563.

Calvin, John. *Institutes of the Christian Religion*. 2 vols. Ed. J. T. McNeill. Philadelphia, 1960.

Camphuysen, Dirck Rafaelsz. *Stichtelycke rymen*. 5th ed. (First published in 1624.) Rotterdam, 1644.

Carter, Thomas. *Carters Christian Commonwealth; or Domesticall Dutyes Deciphered*. London, 1627.

Cato. *Catoos koppel-dichten van de seden*. Trans. and rhymed by S. Ampzing. Haarlem, 1632.

Cats, Jacob. *Maechden-plicht ofte ampt der ionckvrouwen in eerbaer liefde, aen-ghewesen door sinne-beelden*. Middleburg, 1618.

Silenus Alcibiadis, sive Proteus... Middelburg, 1618.

Houwelyck. Dat is de gansche gelegentheyt des echten staets. Middelburg, 1625.

Proteus ofte minne-beelden verandert in sinnebeelden. Rotterdam, 1627.

Houwelyck. Dat is de gansche gelegentheyt des echten staets. 4th ed. The Hague, 1632a.

Spiegel vanden ouden ende nieuwen tijdt. 3 pts. The Hague, 1632b.

's Werelts begin, midden, eynde, besloten in den trou-ringh met den proef-steen van den selven. Dordrecht, 1637.

Ouderdom, buyten-leven, en hof-gedachten, op Sorgh-Vliet. In *Alle de wercken*, 3d ed., pt. 8. Amsterdam, 1665.

Cicero.... *van het ouderdom*... In *M. T. Ciceronis guldene philosophische boecken*... pp. 1–83. Amsterdam, 1624.

C[olerus], J[ohannes]. *De vermeerderde wyse jaer-beschryver*... Amsterdam, 1663a.

De verstandige huys-houder... 2d enlarged ed. Amsterdam, 1663b.

Colse, Peter. *Penelopes Complaint: Or, a Mirrour of Wanton Minions*. London, 1596.

Coornhert, D. V. *Recht ghebruyck ende misbruyck van tydlicke have*. 2d ed. (First published in 1585.) Amsterdam, 1610.

Zedekunst, dat is, wellevenskunste... N.p., 1586; reprint ed., ed. B. Becker., Leiden, 1942.

Cramer, Daniel. *Octoginta emblemata moralia nova*. Frankfort, 1630.

Croon, P. *Almanach voor heden en morgen... voor een nieuw-iaer*. Antwerp, 1665.

Cuffe, Henry. *The Differences of the Ages of Mans Life: Together with the Original Causes, Progresse, and End Thereof*. London, 1607.

David, Johannes. *Christeliicken waerseggher*... Antwerp, 1603.

Christeliicke huys-houder. Antwerp, 1607.

Deutel, J. J. *Huwelijckx weegh-schael*. 2d ed. (First published in 1641.) Hoorn, 1662a.

Stichtelyck vermaeck der deught-lievende jonckheydt. 2d ed. Hoorn, 1662b.

Dod, John, and Cleaver, Robert. *A Godly Forme of Houshold Government*... 5th ed. (First published in 1598.) London, 1612.

D[oes], I[ohan] v[an der]. *Den lof der vrouwen*. Gorinchem, 1622.

Dorp, Frederick van. *Stichtelycke gedichten*... The Hague, 1679.

[Earle, John]. *Micro-Cosmographie*. London, 1628.

De roe op de schoorsteen... 2d ed. [Trans. W. Sz. Bóógaart.] 2 vols. Wormer-Veer, 1647–8.

Erasmus. *Christiani matrimonii institutio*. Basel, 1526.

Züchtiger Sitten zierlichen Wandels und höflicher Geberden der Jugent. (First published in Latin in 1530.) Strasbourg, 1531.

De kersten weduwe... Amsterdam, 1607.

Colloquia familiaria. Dat is: gemeensame tsamenspreeckingen. Utrecht, 1664.

Het boeckje... aengaende de beleeftheidt der kinderlijcke zeden. (First published in Latin in 1519.) Amsterdam, 1678.

Eyb, Albrecht von. *Ehebüchlein.* Nuremberg, 1472.

Focquenbroch, W. C. G. van. *Alle de wercken* . . . 4 vols. Amsterdam, 1682.

Fuller, Thomas. *The Holy State and the Profane State.* Cambridge, 1642.

Gataker, Thomas. *A Good Wife Gods Gift and a Wife Indeed: Two Marriage Sermons.* In *Certaine Sermons, First Preached, and after Published at Severall Times,* vol. 2, pp. 130–80. London, 1637.

Godewycx, Pieter. *Witte-broots kinderen / of bedorve jongelingen.* Dordrecht 1641.

Gouge, William. *Of Domesticall Duties* . . . London, 1622.

Griffith, Matthew. *Bethel: Or a Forme of Families.* London, 1633.

Guillimeau, Jean. *The Nursing of Children.* (First published in French in 1609.) London, 1612.

Hannay, Patrick. *A Happy Husband: Or, Directions for a Maid to Choose her Mate.* London, 1619.

Hazart, Cornelis. *Het gheluckich ende deughdelyck houwelyck* . . . Antwerp, 1678.

Heemskerck, Johan van. *Pub. Ovidii Nasonis minne-kunst, gepast op d'Amsterdamsche vryagien.* Amsterdam, 1622.

Heinsius, Daniel. *Nederduytsche poemata.* Amsterdam, 1616.

Heussen, Frans Esausz. den. *Den Christelijken jongeling* . . . 5th ed. Amsterdam, 1657.

Heyns, Zacharias. *Deuchden-schole ofte spiegel der jonghe-dochteren.* Rotterdam, 1625a.

Emblemata. 4 pts. Rotterdam, 1625b.

Heywood, Thomas. *The Rape of Lucrece.* London, 1608.

Hofferus, Adrianus. *Nederduytsche poemata* . . . Amsterdam, 1635.

Hooft, Peter Cornelisz. *Emblemata amatoria* . . . *(Amsterdam, 1611).* Intro. K. Porteman. Leiden, 1983.

Hoogstraten, Samuel van. *Inleyding tot de hooge schoole der schilderkunst* . . . Rotterdam, 1678.

Houwaert, Johan Baptist. *Pegasides pleyn. Ofte den lust-hof der maechden.* 5th ed. (First published in 1583.) Rotterdam, 1622–3.

Huygens, Constantin. *Koren-bloemen.* 2d ed. 2 vols. (First published in 1654.) Amsterdam, 1672.

Junius, Franciscus. *De pictura veterum* . . . Rotterdam, 1694.

Junius, Hadrianus. *Emblemata* . . . Antwerp, 1562.

Koelman, Jacobus. *De pointen van de nodige reformatie.* Vlissingen, 1678.

De pligten der ouders. Amsterdam, 1679.

Krul, Jan Hermansz. *Eerlycke tytkorting.* 10 pts. Amsterdam, 1634.

Pampiere wereld . . . 4 pts. Amsterdam, 1644.

Lagniet, Jacques. *Recueil des plus illustres proverbes.* 4 vols. Paris, n.d. (ca. 1657–63).

Laurentius, Andreas. *A Discourse of the Preservation of the Sight: of Melancholike Diseases; of Rheumes, and of Old Age.* Trans. R. Surphlet. London, 1599.

Lebeus-Batillius, Dionysius. *Regii mediomatricum praesidis emblemata.* Frankfort, 1596.

Luiken, Jan. *Het leerzaam huisraad.* Amsterdam, 1711.

Luther, Martin. *Vom ehelichen Leben.* N.p., 1522.

Mander, Karel van. *Het schilder-boeck* . . . 6 bks. Haarlem, 1604.

Marcon-velle, Jan van. *Van het geluck en ongeluck des houwelicks* . . . *hier achter is noch by-ghevoeght, 49. gheboden of wetten des houwelicks door Plutarchus.* Wormer-Veer, 1647.

Markham, Gervase. *The English House-Wife: Containing the Inward and Outward Vertues Which Ought to be in the Compleate Woman.* 5th ed. (First published in 1615.) London, 1637.

May-Vogel, Jacob Coenraeds. *Vermakelycke bruylofts-kroon* . . . Amsterdam, 1680.

Menius, Justus. *Oeconomia christiana.* Nuremberg, 1529.

Menno Simons. *Kindertucht.* N.p., n.d. (ca. 1557).

Messiae, Petrus. *De verscheyden lessen* . . . Leiden, 1607.

Minnen, Joncker Livinus van der [pseud.]. *Den eerelycken pluck-voghel.* 4th ed. Brussels, 1684.

Moerman, Jan. *De cleyn werelt* . . . 2d ed. (First published in 1584.) Amsterdam, 1608.

Moryson, F. *An Itinerary.* (First published in 1617.) 3 pts. Amsterdam, 1971.

Mulcaster, Richard. . . . *the Training up of Children* . . . London, 1581.

Niccoles, Alexander. *A Discourse of Marriage and Wiving.* London, 1615.

Nyenborgh, Johan van. *De weeck-wercken* . . . Groningen, 1657.

Toonneel [sic] der ambachten: of den winckel der handt-wercken en konsten. 2d ed. Groningen, 1659.

Oomius, Simon. *Ecclesiola, dat is kleyne kercke.* Amsterdam, 1661.

Oraeum, Henricum. *Aeroplastes theo-sophicus sive eicones mysticae.* Frankfort, 1620.

Overbury, Thomas. *A Wife.* London, 1614.

Overstege, C. van, *Poezy.* Dordrecht, 1661.

Perkins, William. *A Treatise of the Vocations...* In *The Workes...* vol. 1, pp. 728–56. London, 1609a.

The Whole Treatise of the Cases of the Conscience. In *The Workes...* vol. 2, pp. 1–176. London, 1609b.

Christian Oeconomie. In *The Workes...* vol. 3, pp. 668–700. London, 1613.

The Work of William Perkins. Ed. I. Breward. Appleford, 1970.

Pers, D. P. *Lucretia ofte het beeld der eerbaerheyt ...* Amsterdam, 1624.

Gezangh der zeeden... Amsterdam, 1648.

Bellerophon, of lust tot wysheyt. 9th ed. 3 vols. (First published in 1614.) Amsterdam, 1669.

Suyp-Stad of dronckaerts leven (Amsterdam, 1628). Intro. J. E. Verlaan and E. K. Grootes. Culemborg, 1978.

Plutarch. *The Education or Bringinge Up of Children.* Trans. T. Eliot. London, n.d. (ca. 1535).

Den spieghel des houwelicks... N.p. 1575.

Tractaet vande op-voedinghe der kinderen. Trans. S. de Swaef. Middelburg, 1619.

Poirters, A. *Den alderheijlichsten naem voor een nieu-jaer-gift...* Antwerp, 1647.

Het heyligh herte... Antwerp, 1659.

Poot, Hubert Korneliszoon. *Het groot natuur- en zedekundigh wereltoneel.* 3 vols. Delft, 1743–50.

Renesse, Lodewyck G. van. *Vier boecken vande voorsienigheyt Godts in het beleydt der houwelycken...* Amsterdam, 1639.

Revsneri, Nicolai. *Aureolorum emblematum.* 2d ed. Argentorati, 1591.

Ridderus, Franciscus. *Historisch a, b, c.* Rotterdam, 1664.

Dagelijckse huys-catechisatie. 10th ed. (First published in 1657.) Amsterdam, 1692.

Ripa, Cesare. *Iconologia, of uytbeeldingen des verstands.* Trans. D. P. Pers. Amsterdam, 1644.

Rollenhagen, Gabriel. *Nucleus emblematum selectissimorum.* 2 vols. Arnhem/Utrecht, 1611–13.

Royen, Jacob van. *'s Menschen leven van de wieg tot het graf...* Amsterdam, n.d. (before 1730).

Saavedra, D. *Christelyke staets-vorst...* Amsterdam, 1663.

The Royal Politician... Trans. J. A. Astray. 2 vols. London, 1700.

Salter, Thomas. *A Mirrhor Mete for all Mothers, Matrones, and Maidens, Intituled the Mirrhor of Modestie...* London, 1579.

Schaep, Jan Claesz. *Bloem-tuyntje...* 2d ed. Amsterdam, 1671.

Sibmacher, Johan. *Newes Modelbüch in Küpffer gemacht.* 2d ed. Nuremberg, 1604.

Soet, Jan. *Maagden-baak...* Amsterdam, 1641.

Sprankhuisen, Dionysius. *Lof en plicht des houwelyx...* In *Opuscula practica ofte alle de stichtelijke werken...* pt. 1, pp. 135–52. Amsterdam, 1658.

Stam, W. I. *Cupido's lusthof.* Amsterdam, 1613.

Sucquet, A. *Den wech des eeuwich levens...* Trans. G. Zoes. Antwerp, 1649.

Swaef, Joannes de. *De geestelycke queeckerye van de jonge planten des Heeren...* 2d ed. Intro. and ed. J. Willemsen. (First published in 1621.) Middelburg, 1740.

[Sweerts, Hieronymous]. *Koddige en ernstige opschriften, op luyssens, wagens, glazen, uithangborden, en andere taferelen.* 4 pts. Amsterdam, 1698.

R.T. *Eenighe morale of zedige wercken van Plutarchus...* Amsterdam, 1634.

Taffin, Jean. *De boetveerdicheyt des levens...* 12th ed. Trans. J. Crucius. (First published in 1594.) Amsterdam, 1640.

Taylor, John. *The Needles Excellency.* 10th ed. (First published in 1631.) London, 1634.

Teellinck, Willem. *Noodwendigh vertoogh, aengaende den tegenwoordigen bedroefden staet van Gods volck.* Middelburg, 1627.

Huys-boeck. 2 vols. Middelburg, 1639.

Sleutel der devotie ons opende de deure des hemels. 2 pts. In *Alle de wercken,* vol. 3. Amsterdam, 1664.

De spiegel der zedigheid. 1626; reprint ed., Ede, 1975.

Twisck, Pieter Ianszoon. *Troost-brief der weduwen...* Hoorn, 1630.

Udemans, Cornelis. *Het geestelyck gebouw, met sinne-beelden verciert...* Middelburg, 1659.

Udemans, Godefridum. *Practijcke, dat is werckelijcke oeffeninge van de Christelijcke hooftdeugden...* 5th ed. (First published in 1612.) Amsterdam, 1658.

Ursinus, Zacharias. *Het schat-boeck der Christelycke leere.* 2d ed. Leiden, 1606.

V., S. de [Simon de Vries?]. *Seven duyvelen, regeerende en vervoerende de hedendaeghsche dienst-maegdfn [sic].* Amsterdam, 1682.

Veen, Otto van. *Amorum emblemata.* Antwerp, 1608.

Quinti Horatii Flacci emblemata. 2d ed. Antwerp, 1612.

Zinnebeelden, getrokken uit Horatius Flaccus ... Amsterdam, 1683.

Venne, Adriaen van de. *Tafereel van sinne-mal.* Middelburg, 1623.

Visscher, Roemer. *Sinne-poppen.* Amsterdam, 1614

Brabbelingh. 3d. ed. (First published in 1614.) Amsterdam, 1669.

Vives, Juan Ludovicus. *Institutio feminae christianae.* Antwerp, 1524.

... the Instruction of a Christen Woman... Trans. R. Hyrde. London, 1547.

The Office and Duetie of an Husband. Trans. T. Paynell. London, 1553.

Vondel, Joost van den. *Den gulden winckel.* Amsterdam, 1613.

De werken van Vondel. 11 vols. Ed. J. F. M. Sterck et al. Amsterdam, 1927–40.

Vos, Jan. *Alle de gedichten...* 2d ed. 2 vols. (First published in 1662.) Amsterdam, 1726.

Wallenkamp, Bernhardum. *Inleydinghe in Zions-schole.* Utrecht, 1661.

Westerbaen, J. *Den avond-school voor vryers en vrysters...* The Hague, 1665.

Westermannus, Adamus. *Christelijcke zee-vaert ende wandel-wech/ hoe een schipper/ coopman ende reysende man in de vreese Godes in zijn uyt ende in reyse... hem houden ende draghen sal.* 5th ed. (First published in 1613.) Amsterdam, 1631.

Whately, William. *A Bride-Bush or a Wedding Sermon: Compendiously Describing the Duties of Married Persons...* London, 1617.

Korte verhandelinge van de voornaemste Christelijcke oeffeningen. 2d ed. Trans. W. Teellinck. (First published in English in 1609.) Dordrecht, 1649.

Whitney, Geoffrey. *A Choice of Emblemes.* 2 pts. Leiden, 1586.

Wilkinson, Robert. *The Merchant Royall...* London, 1613.

Wits, C. J. *Stigtelyke [sic] bedenkinge.* 10th ed. (First published in 1639.) Amsterdam, 1706.

Wittewrongel, Petrus. *Oeconomia Christiana ofte Christelicke huys-houdinghe.* 3d enlarged ed. 2 vols. (First published in 1655.) Amsterdam, 1661.

Wormerveer, Oom Jacob Dircksz. van. *Den Christelyken huys-vader...* Amsterdam, 1677.

Xenophon. *Xenophons Treatise of Housholde.* Trans. G. Hervet. London, 1557.

Zincgref, J. W. *Sapienta picta. Das ist/ künstliche sinnreiche Bildnissen und figuren...* Frankfurt, 1624.

GENERAL BIBLIOGRAPHY

Ackerman, James S. "A Theory of Style." *Journal of Aesthetics and Art Criticism* 20 (1961–2): 227–37.

Alpers, Svetlana. "Realism as a Comic Mode: Low-Life Painting Seen through Bredero's Eyes." *Simiolus* 8 (1975–6): 115–44.

The Art of Describing: Dutch Art in the Seventeenth Century. Chicago, 1983.

Anderson, Michael. *Approaches to the History of the Western Family.* London, 1980.

Andrews, Keith. *Adam Elsheimer.* New York, 1977.

Ariès, Philippe. *L'enfant et la vie familiale sous l'Ancien Règime.* Paris, 1960.

Centuries of Childhood: A Social History of Family Life. Trans. R. Baldick. New York, 1962.

Baer, Rhonda. *The Paintings of Gerrit Dou (1613–1675).* Ph.D. dissertation, Institute of Fine Arts, New York University, New York, 1990.

Baines, Patricia. *Spinning Wheels, Spinners and Spinning.* London, 1977.

Bake, C. "Dienstboden en meesters in den goeden ouden tijd." *De Tijdspiegel* 56 (1899): 329–426.

Banks, Oliver T. *Watteau and the North: Studies in the Dutch and Flemish Baroque Influence on French Rococo Painting.* New York, 1977.

Bauch, Kurt. *Studien zur Kunstgeschichte.* Berlin, 1967.

Bauer, Linda Freeman. "Seventeenth-Century Naturalism and the Emblematic Interpretation of Paintings." *Emblematica: An Interdisciplinary Journal for Emblem Studies* 3 (1988): 209–27.

Bax, D. *Ontcijfering van Jeroen Bosch.* The Hague, 1949.

Becker, Jochen. " 'Dieses emblematische Stück stellet die Erzeihung der Jugend vor': zu Adriaen van der Werff. München, Alte Pinakothek, inv. nr. 250." *Oud Holland* 90 (1976): 77–107.

"Over oude deksels, jonge potten en dat schuren niet noodzakelijk netjes hoeft te zijn-bij Jan Miense Molenaers *Keukenscène* (Kopenhagen, Statensmuseum for Kunst, inv. no. 3024)." *Institutblad K. H. I. Utrecht* 4 (1977): 7–11.

Bedaux, Jan Baptist. "Minnekoorts-, zwangerschaps- en doodsverschijnselen op zeventiende-eeuwse schilderijen." *Antiek* 10 (1975): 17–42.

"Beelden van 'leersucht' en tucht. Opvoedingsmetaforen in de Nederlandse schilderkunst van de zeventiende eeuw." *Nederlands Kunsthistorisch Jaarboek* 33 (1983): 49–74.

"The Reality of Symbols: The Question of Disguised Symbolism in Jan van Eyck's *Arnolfini Portrait.*" *Simiolus* 16 (1986): 5–28.

"Fruit and Fertility: Fruit Symbolism in Netherlandish Portraiture of the Sixteenth and Seventeenth Centuries." *Simiolus* 17 (1987): 150–68.

The Reality of Symbols: Studies in the Iconology of Netherlandish Art, 1400–1800. The Hague, 1990.

Bedaux, Jan Baptist, and Hecht, Peter. "Ter Borch 2." *Hollands Maandblad* 136 (1974): 38–41.

Benjamin, Lloyd. "Disguised Symbolism Exposed and the History of Early Netherlandish Painting." *Studies in Iconography* 2 (1976): 11–24.

Berge, Domien ten. *De hooggeleerde en zoetvloeiende dichter Jacob Cats.* The Hague, 1979.

Bergström, Ingvar. "Disguised Symbolism in 'Madonna' Pictures and Still-Life." *Burlington Magazine* 97 (1955): 303–8, 342–9.

Bialostocki, Jan. "Einfache Nachahmung der Natur oder symbolische Weltschau; zu den Deutungsproblemen der holländischen Malerei des 17. Jhdt." *Zeitschrift für Kunstgeschichte* 44 (1984): 421–38.

"Review of Svetlana Alpers, *The Art of Describing: Dutch Art in the Seventeenth Century.*" *Art Bulletin* 67 (1985): 520–6.

Biéler, André. *L'homme et la femme dans la morale calviniste.* Geneva, 1963.

Blankert, Albert. *Vermeer of Delft.* New York, 1978.

"General Introduction." In Exhib. cat. Washington, D.C., *Gods, Saints & Heroes: Dutch Painting in the Age of Rembrandt,* pp. 15–33. National Gallery of Art, 1980–1.

"What is Dutch Seventeenth-Century Genre Painting? A Definition and Its Limitations." In *Holländische Genremalerei im 17. Jahrhundert. Symposium Berlin, 1984,* ed. H. Bock and T. W. Gaehtgens, pp. 9–32. Berlin, 1987.

Bock, Eug. de. *Johan Baptist Houwaert.* Antwerp, 1950.

Bodt, Saskia de. . . . *op de Raempte off mette Brodse . . . Nederlands borduurwerk uit de zeventiende eeuw.* Bloemendaal, 1987.

Boheemen, Petra van " 'Hoe men een lief vinden en krygen zal'; Ovidus als leermeester." In Exhib. cat. Apeldoorn, *Kent, en versint, eer datje mint; vrijen en trouwen, 1500–1800,* pp. 53–63. Historisch Museum Marialust, 1989.

Bok, Marten Jan. " 'Het troigne van Hilleken'." *Kunstschrift* no. 2 (1990): 5–6.

Bok, Marten Jan, and Meijere, J. A. L. de. "Een familieportret door de Utrechtse schilder Andries van Bockhoven (1609–1634)." *Antiek* 20 (1985–6): 323–9.

Boot, Marjan. " 'Huislykheid is 't vrouwen kroon cieraad'; de positie van vrouwen sinds de middeleeuwen." *Openbaar Kunstbezit* 22 (1978): 168–75.

Brom, Gerard. *Schilderkunst & letteratuur in de 16e en 17e eeuw.* Utrecht, 1957.

Broos, B. P. J. "De caers uit de schaemschoe uit, een vergeten erotisch symbool." *Vrij Nederland,* April 24, 1971, 25.

Meesterwerken in het Mauritshuis. The Hague, 1987.

Brown, Christopher. *Images of a Golden Past: Dutch Genre Painting of the 17th Century.* New York, 1984.

Bruyn, J. "Vroege portretten van Maerten van Heemskerck." *Bulletin van het Rijksmuseum* 3 (1955): 27–35.

Over het voortleven der middeleeuwen (Rede uitgesproken bij de aanvaarding van het ambt van gewoon hoogleraar in de algemene kunstgeschiedenis . . . aan de Universiteit van Amsterdam). Amsterdam, 1961.

Geschiedschrijving als parabel (Rede uitgesproken ter gelegenheid van de 349ste dies natalis van de Universiteit van Amsterdam). Amsterdam, 1981.

"Review of Svetlana Alpers, *The Art of Describing: Dutch Art in the Seventeenth Century.*" *Oud Holland* 99 (1985): 155–60.

"Mittelalterliche 'doctrina exemplaris' und Allegorie als Komponente des sog. Genrebildes." In *Holländische Genremalerei im 17. Jahrhundert. Symposium Berlin 1984,* ed. H. Bock and T. W. Gaehtgens, pp. 33–59. Berlin, 1987.

"Jung und Alt-ikonographische Bemerkungen zur *tronie.*" In *Hendrick ter Brugghen und die Nachfolger Caravaggios in Holland,* ed. R. Klessmann, pp. 67–76. Brunswick, 1988.

"Review of Peter Hecht, *De Hollandse fijnschilders. Van Gerard Dou tot Adriaen van der Werff.*" *Oud Holland* 105 (1991): 64–9.

Bruyn, J., et al. *Historisch perspectief van het zeventiende eeuwse "genre" geillustreerd aan enkele thema's* (Grote Werkgroep Nieuwere Tijd, 1977–8; Kunsthistorisch Instituut Universiteit van Amsterdam). Amsterdam, 1978.

Bruyn, J., et al. *A Corpus of Rembrandt Paintings.* vols. 1–. Trans. D. Cook-Radmore. The Hague, 1982–.

Bryson, Norman. "Introduction." In *Calligram: Essays in New Art History from France,* ed. N. Bryson, pp. xiii–xxix. Cambridge, 1988.

"Semiology and Visual Interpretation." In *Visual Theory: Painting and Interpretation,* ed. M. A. Holly, N. Bryson, and K. Moxey, pp. 61–73. New York, 1991.

Budding, D. J. "Franciscus Ridderus, zijn leven en werken en zijn opvattingen aangaande het Heilige Avondmaal." *Documentatieblad Nadere Reformatie* 7 (1983): pp. 73–108.

Carter, Alice Clare. "Marriage Counselling in the Early Seventeenth Century: England and The Netherlands Compared." In *Ten Studies in Anglo-Dutch Relations,* ed. J. van Dorsten, pp. 94–127. London, 1974.

Cat. Amsterdam. *All the Paintings of the Rijksmuseum in Amsterdam,* 1976.

Cat. Berlin (Staatliche Museen Preussischer Kulturbesitz). *Catalogue of Paintings, 13th–18th Century.* 2d ed. Trans. L. B. Parshall, 1978.

Cat. Brussels. *Koninklijke Musea voor Schone Kunsten van België; inventariscatalogus van de oude schilderkunst,* 1984.

Cat. Castagnola (Villa Favorita). *The Thyssen-Bornemisza Collection,* 1969.

Cat. Leiden (Stedelijk Museum De Lakenhal). *Catalogus van de schilderijen en tekeningen,* 1983.

Cat. Leipzig (Museum der bildenden Künste). *Katalog der Gemälde,* 1979.

Cat. London. *Wallace Collection Catalogues: Pictures and Drawings.* 16th ed., 1968.

Cat. Munich. *Alte Pinakothek München; Erläuterungen zu den ausgestellten Gemälden,* 1983.

Cat. Rotterdam. *Catalogue Museum Boymans-van Beuningen, Old Paintings, 1400–1900,* 1972.

Cat. Schwerin (Staatliches Museum). *Holländische Maler,* 1962.

Cat. The Hague (Mauritshuis). *Illustrated General Catalogue,* 1977.

Chapman, H. Perry. *Rembrandt's Self-Portraits: A Study in Seventeenth-Century Identity.* Princeton, 1990.

Cheney, Liana de Girolami. "The Oyster in Dutch Genre Paintings: Moral or Erotic Symbolism." *Artibus et Historiae* 15 (1987): 135–58.

Chew, Samuel C. *The Pilgrimage of Life.* New Haven, 1962.

Clark, Alice. *Working Life of Women in the Seventeenth Century.* London, 1919.

Cock, A. de. *Spreekwoorden en zegswijzen over de vrouwen de liefde en het huwelijk.* Ghent, 1911.

Collinson, Patrick. *The Birthpangs of Protestant England: Religious and Cultural Change in the Sixteenth and Seventeenth Centuries.* London, 1988.

Coupe, William. *The German Illustrated Broadsheet in the Seventeenth Century: Historical and Iconographical Studies.* 2 vols. Baden-Baden, 1966.

Cropper, Elizabeth, and Dempsey, Charles. "The State of Research in Italian Painting of the Seventeenth Century." *Art Bulletin* 69 (1987): 494–509.

Daalder, D. L. *Wormcruyt met suycker. Historisch-critisch overzicht van de Nederlandse kinderliteratuur.* Amsterdam, 1950.

Davies, Kathaleen M. "The Sacred Condition of Equality – How Original were Puritan Doctrines of Marriage?" *Social History* 5 (1977): 563–80.

"Continuity and Change in Literary Advice on Marriage." In *Marriage and Society: Studies in the Social History of Marriage,* ed. R. B. Outhwaite, pp. 58–80. New York, 1981.

Davis, Natalie Zemon. *Society and Culture in Early Modern France.* Stanford, Calif., 1975.

Dekker, Rudolf. "Masters and Servants in the Dutch Republic: An Uneasy Relationship." Unpublished lecture given at the symposium, *Images of the World: Dutch Genre Painting in Its Historical Context.* London, Royal Academy, 1984.

"Review of Simon Schama, *The Embarrassment of Riches.*" *Parool,* April 2, 1988, 31.

"Een bedorven mens? Problemen rond opvoeding en onderwijs in de 17e eeuw in het dagboek van Constantijn Huygens jr." *Jeugd en Samenleving* 19 (1989): 708–17.

Demetz, Peter. "Defenses of Dutch Painting and the Theory of Realism." *Comparative Literature* 15 (1963): 97–115.

Deursen, A. Th. van. *Het kopergeld van de gouden eeuw.* 4 vols. Assen, 1978–81.

Plain Lives in a Golden Age: Popular Culture, Religion and Society in Seventeenth-Century Holland. Trans. M. Ultee. Cambridge, 1991.

Dresen-Coenders, Lène. "Huis en haard." In Exhib. cat. Apeldoorn, *Kent, en versint, eer datje mint; vrijen en trouwen, 1500–1800,* pp. 8–19. Historisch Museum Marialust, 1989a.

" 'Wegh-wyser ten houwelick.' " In Exhib. cat. Apeldoorn, *Kent, en versint, eer datje mint; vrijen en trouwen, 1500–1800,* pp. 20–52. Historisch Museum Marialust, 1989b.

Dresen-Coenders, Lène, and Haaren, Jan van. "Ontmoetingsplaatsen van vrijers en vrijsters." In Exhib. cat. Apeldoorn, *Kent, en versint, eer datje mint; vrijen en trouwen, 1500–1800,* pp. 64–84. Historisch Museum Marialust, 1989.

Duncan, Carol. "Happy Mothers and Other New Ideas in French Art." *Art Bulletin* 55 (1973): 570–83.

Durantini, Mary Frances. *The Child in Seventeenth-Century Dutch Painting.* Ann Arbor, 1983.

Edwards, Ralph. *Early Conversation Pictures from the Middle Ages to about 1730.* London, 1954.

Eggermont, P. L. "De werken van Jean Taffin Sr. (1529–1602) in de Nederlandse taal." *Documentatieblad Nadere Reformatie* 1 (1977): 1–20.

Ekkart, Rudolf E. O. "De Enkhuizer schilder Jan Claesz." *Oud Holland* 104 (1990): 180–218.

Elliott, J. H. "From Bogs to Riches: Review of Simon Schama, *The Embarrassment of Riches.*" *New Republic,* August 24, 1987, 28–31.

Elshtain, Jean Bethke. *Public Man, Private Woman: Women in Social and Political Thought.* Princeton, N.J., 1981.

Emmens, Jan. "Les Ménines de Velasquez, miroir des princes pour Philippe IV." *Nederlands Kunsthistorisch Jaarboek* 12 (1961): 51–79.

"Natuur, onderwijzing en oefening; bij een drieluik van Gerrit Dou." In *Album discipulorum aangeboden aan Professor Dr J. G. van Gelder,* pp. 125–63. Utrecht, 1963.

Rembrandt en de regels van de kunst. Utrecht, 1968.

"Apelles en Apollo; Nederlandse gedichten op schilderijen in de 17de eeuw" (Doctoraelscripte, 1955). In *J. A. Emmens. Kunsthistorische Opstellen,* vol. 1, pp. 5–60. Amsterdam, 1981.

Englert, Anton. "Die menschlichen Alterstufen in Wort und Bild I." *Zeitschrift des Vereins für Volkskunde* 15 (1905): 399–412.

"Die menschlichen Alterstufen in Wort und Bild II." *Zeitschrift des Vereins für Volkskunde* 17 (1907): 16–42.

Exhib. cat. Amersfoort. *Colf. kolf. golf; van middeleeuws volkspel tot moderne sport.* Museum Flehite, 1982.

Exhib. cat. Amsterdam. *Tot lering en vermaak; betekenissen van Hollandse genrevoorstellingen uit de zeventiende eeuw.* Rijksmuseum, 1976.

Opkomst en bloei van het Noordnederlandse stadsgezicht in de 17de eeuw. Historisch Museum, 1977.

Prijst de lijst; de Hollandse schilderlijst in de zeventiende eeuw. Rijksmuseum, 1984.

De Hollandse fijnschilders; van Gerard Dou tot Adriaen van der Werff. Rijksmuseum, 1989–90.

Exhib. cat. Apeldoorn. *Kent, en versint, eer datje mint; vrijen en trouwen, 1500–1800.* Historisch Museum Marialust, 1989.

Exhib. cat. Auckland. *Still-life in the Age of Rembrandt.* Auckland City Art Gallery, 1982.

Exhib. cat. Basel. *Im Lichte Hollands; hollän-*

dische Malerei des 17. Jahrhunderts aus den Sammlungen des Fürsten von Liechtenstein und aus Schweizer Besitz. Kunstmuseum, 1987.

Exhib. cat. Brunswick. *Die Sprache der Bilder.* Herzog Anton Ulrich-Museum, 1978.

Exhib. cat. Brussels. *Rembrandt en zijn tijd.* Paleis voor Schone Kunsten, 1971.

Het kind in onze kunst van 1800 tot heden. Galerij ASLK, 1983–4.

Exhib. cat. Cologne. *Wort und Bild; Buchkunst und Druckgraphik in den Niederlanden im 16. und 17. Jahrhundert.* Belgisches Haus, 1981.

Exhib. cat. Dordrecht. *Aelbert Cuyp en zijn familie; schilders te Dordrecht.* Dordrechts Museum, 1977–8.

Exhib. cat. Haarlem. *Portretten van echt en trouw; huwelijk en gezin in de Nederlandse kunst van de zeventiende eeuw* (catalogue by E. de Jongh). Frans Hals Museum, 1986.

Exhib. cat. Kleves. *Die Lebenstreppe. Bilder der menschlichen Lebensalter.* Städisches Museum Haus Koekoek, 1983–4.

Exhib. cat. Lawrence. *Dutch Prints of Daily Life.* Spencer Museum of Art, 1983.

Exhib. cat. Leiden. *Ijdelheid der ijdelheden; Hollandse vanitas-voorstellingen uit de zeventiende eeuw.* Stedelijk Museum De Lakenhal, 1970.

Leidse Fijnschilders; van Gerrit Dou tot Frans van Mieris de Jonge, 1630–1760. Stedelijk Museum De Lakenhal, 1988.

Exhib. cat. Lille. *Trésors des musées du nord de la France, peinture hollandaise.* Musée des Beaux-Arts, 1972.

Exhib. cat. Nijmegen. *Tussen heks & heilige; het vrouwenbeeld op de drempel van de moderne tijd, 15de/16de eeuw.* Nijmeegs Museum "Commanderie van Sint-Jan," 1985.

Exhib. cat. Paris. *Reflets du siècle d'or; tableaux hollandais du dix-septieme siecle.* Institut Néerlandais, 1983.

Exhib. cat. Philadelphia. *Masters of Seventeenth-Century Dutch Genre Painting.* Philadelphia Museum of Art, 1984.

Exhib. cat. Pittsburgh. *Gardens of Earthly Delight: Sixteenth and Seventeenth-Century Netherlandish Love Gardens.* Frick Art Museum, 1986.

Exhib. cat. 's-Hertogenbosch. *In het zadel; het Nederlands ruiterportret van 1550 tot 1900.* Noordbrabants Museum, 1980.

Exhib. cat. The Hague. *Gerard ter Borch.* Mauritshuis, 1974.

Paintings from England: William III and the Royal Collections. Mauritshuis, 1988–9.

Alba Amicorum: vijf eeuwen vriendschap op papier gezet: het album amicorum en het poëziealbum in De Nederlanden. Rijksmuseum Meermanno-Westereenianum/Museum van Het Boek, 1990.

Great Dutch Paintings from America. Mauritshuis, 1990–1.

Exhib. cat. Washington, D.C. *The William Clark Collection.* Corcoran Gallery of Art, 1978.

Gods, Saints & Heroes: Dutch Painting in the Age of Rembrandt. National Gallery of Art, 1980–1.

Still Lifes of the Golden Age: Northern European Paintings from the Heinz Family Collection. National Gallery of Art, 1989.

Falkenburg, Reindert L. *Joachim Patinir: Landscape as an Image of the Pilgrimage of Life.* Trans. M. Hoyle. Amsterdam, 1988.

Ferguson, Margaret W.; Quilligan, M.; and Vickers, N. "Introduction." In *Rewriting the Renaissance: The Discourses of Sexual Difference in Early Modern Europe,* ed. M. W. Ferguson et al., pp. xv–xxxi. Chicago/London, 1986.

Fiorone, F. *Elseviers groot rashonden boek.* Amsterdam, 1976.

Fischer, Peter. *Music in Paintings of the Low Countries in the 16th and 17th Centuries.* Amsterdam, 1975.

Forster, Leonard. *The Icy Fire: Five Studies in European Petrarchism.* Cambridge, 1969.

Fox, Vivian C. "Is Adolescence a Phenomenon of Modern Times?" *Journal of Psychohistory* 5 (1977): 271–90.

Franits, Wayne. "Review of Mary Frances Durantini, *The Child in Seventeenth-Century Dutch Painting.*" *Art Bulletin* 67 (1985): 695–700.

"The Family at Grace: A Theme in Dutch Art of the Seventeenth Century." *Simiolus* 16 (1986): 36–49.

"Review of Eddy de Jongh, *Portretten van echt en trouw; huwelijk en gezin in de Nederlandse kunst van de zeventiende eeuw.*" *Oud Holland* 102 (1988): 249–56.

"The Depiction of Servants in Some Paintings by Pieter de Hooch." *Zeitschrift für Kunstgeschichte* 52 (1989): 559–66.

" 'Betemt de jeughd, Soo doet sy deughd': A Pedagogical Metaphor in Seventeenth-

Century Dutch Art." In *Nederlandse portretten; bijdragen over de portretkunst in de Nederlanden uit de zestiende, zeventiende en achttiende eeuw (Leids Kunsthistorisch Jaarboek* 8), ed. E. J. Sluijter et al., pp. 217–26. The Hague, 1990.

"Housewives and Their Maids in Seventeenth-Century Dutch Art." In *Politics, Gender, and the Arts; Women, the Arts, and Society (Susquehanna University Studies)*, eds. R. Dotterer and S. Bowers, pp. 112–29. Selinsgrove, 1992.

Friedländer, Max J. *Early Netherlandish Painting.* 14 vols. Leiden, 1967–76.

Friesendorp, Marijke, and Joosse, Astrid. "Cats, Vivies en acht wijze maagden." *De Nieuwe Taalgids* 76 (1983): 245–50.

Fritschy, Wantje, ed. *Fragmenten vrouwengeschiedenis.* 2 vols. The Hague, 1980.

Garrard, Mary D. *Artemisia Gentileschi: The Image of the Female Hero in Italian Baroque Art.* Princeton, 1989.

Gaskell, Ivan. "Review of Svetlana Alpers, *The Art of Describing: Dutch Art in the Seventeenth-Century.*" *Oxford Art Journal* 7 (1984): 57–60.

The Thyssen-Bornemisza Collection: Seventeenth-Century Dutch and Flemish Painting. London, 1990.

Geertz, Clifford. "Art as a Cultural System." *Modern Language Notes* 91 (1976): 1473–99.

Gelder, J. G. van. "Van blompot tot blomglas." *Elsevier's Geillustreerd Maandschrift* 91 (1938): 73–82, 155–66.

Gelderblom, Arie-Jan van. "De identiteit van een grijze dutter; naar aanleiding van Huygens' *Voorhout* r. 33–40." *Tijdschrift voor Nederlandse Taal- en Letterkunde* 97 (1981): 27–34.

Gent, Lucy. *Picture and Poetry, 1560–1620: Relations Between Literature and the Visual Arts in the English Renaissance.* Leamington Spa, 1981.

Gerards-Nelissen, Inemie. "Otto van Veen's Emblemata Horatiana." *Simiolus* 5 (1971):20–63.

Gilbert, Creighton. "When Did a Man in the Renaissance Grow Old?" *Studies in the Renaissance* 14 (1967): 7–32.

Glynne, Jonathan. "So to Speak" (review of Svetlana Alpers, *The Art of Describing: Dutch Art in the Seventeenth Century). Art History* 7 (1984): 247–52.

Goedde, Lawrence O. "Convention, Realism, and the Interpretation of Dutch and Flemish Tempest Painting." *Simiolus* 16 (1986): 139–49.

"A Little World Made Cunningly: Dutch Still Life and Ekphrasis." In Exhib. cat. Washington, D.C. *Still Lifes of the Golden Age: Northern European Paintings from the Heinz Family Collection,* pp. 35–44. National Gallery of Art, 1989a.

Tempest and Shipwreck in Dutch and Flemish Art: Convention, Rhetoric, and Interpretation. University Park, 1989b.

Gombrich, E. H. "Mysteries of Dutch Painting" (review of Svetlana Alpers, *The Art of Describing: Dutch Art in the Seventeenth Century). New York Review of Books,* November 10, 1983, pp. 13–17.

Goode, William J. "The Theoretical Importance of Love." *American Sociological Review* 24 (1959): 38–47.

Goodman, Elise. "Rubens' *Conversatie à la Mode:* Garden of Leisure, Fashion and Gallantry." *Art Bulletin* 64 (1982): 247–59.

"Petrarchism in Titian's *The Lady and the Musician.*" *Storia del arte* (1983): 179–86.

"The Landscape on the Wall in Vermeer." *Konsthistorisk Tidskrift* 58 (1989): 76–88.

Goossens, Korneel. *David Vinckboons.* Reprint ed. (First published in 1954.) Soest, 1977.

Graafland, C. "De invloed van het Puritanisme op het ontstaan van het gereformeerd Piëtisme in Nederland." *Documentatieblad Nadere Reformatie* 7 (1983): 1–24.

Grabes, Herbert. *The Mutable Glass: Mirror-Imagery in Titles and Texts of the Middle Ages and English Renaissance.* Trans. G. Collier. Cambridge, 1982.

Grafton, Anthony, and Kaufmann, Thomas DaCosta. "Holland without Huizinga: Dutch Visual Culture in the Seventeenth Century" (review of Svetlana Alpers, *The Art of Describing: Dutch Art in the Seventeenth Century). Journal of Interdisciplinary History* 16 (1985): 255–65.

Greven, Philip. *The Protestant Temperament: Patterns of Child-Rearing, Religious Experience and the Self in Early America.* New York, 1977.

Groenendijk, L. F. "Piëtisten en borstvoeding." *Pedagogisch Tijdschrift / Forum voor Opvoedkunde* 1 (1976): 583–90.

"Inhoud en oorsprong van de opvoedingsleer van Petrus Wittewrongel." *Documentatieblad Nadere Reformatie* 2 (1978a): 13–28.

"Jacobus Koelman's actieplan voor de nadere

reformatie." *Documentatieblad Nadere Reformatie* 2 (1978b): 121–6.

"Opvoeding en kind-zijn bij Puriteinen en Piëtisten." *Documentatieblad Nadere Reformatie* 4 (1980): 10–16.

De nadere reformatie van het gezin; de visie van Petrus Wittewrongel op de Christelijke huishouding. Dordrecht, 1984.

" 'Tot Gods eere, het gemeene beste ende der kinderen heyl'; het gezinspedagogische ideaal van gereformeerde protestanten in de Republiek." *Jeugd en samenleving* 19 (1989): 644–61.

Grootes, E. K. "Literatuur-historie en Cats' visie op de jeugd." *Spektator; Tijdschrift voor Neerlandistiek* 9 (1979–80): 477–93.

"Het jeugdige publiek van de 'nieuwe liedboeken' in het eerste kwart van de zeventiende eeuw.," In *Het woord aan de lezer; zeven literatuurhistorische verkenningen,* ed. W. van den Berg and J. Stouten, pp. 72–88. Groningen, 1987.

Grosshans, Rainald. *Maerten van Heemskerck; Die Gemälde.* Berlin, 1980.

Groves, Sylvia. *The History of Needlework Tools and Accessories.* New York, 1973.

Gudlaugsson, S. J. *Gerard ter Borch.* 2 vols. The Hague, 1959–60.

"Kanttekeningen bij de ontwikkeling van Metsu." *Oud Holland* 83 (1968): 13–44.

Haar, J. van der. *From Abbadie to Young: A Bibliography of English, Most Puritian [sic] Works, Translated i/t Dutch Language.* Veenendaal, 1980.

Hagstrum, Jean H. *The Sister Arts: The Tradition of Literary Pictorialism and English Poetry from Dryden to Gray.* Chicago, 1958.

Haks, Donald. *Huwelijk en gezin in Holland in de 17de en 18de eeuw.* Assen, 1982.

"Continuïteit en verandering in het gezin van de vroeg-moderne tijd." In *Vijf eeuwen gezinsleven; liefde, huwelijk en opvoeding in Nederland,* ed. H. Peeters, L. Dresen-Coenders, and T. Brandenbarg, pp. 31–56. Nijmegen, 1988.

Haller, William. "Hail Wedded Love." *ELH: A Journal of English Literary History* 13 (1946): 79–97.

Hamilton, Roberta. *The Liberation of Women: A Study of Patriarchy and Capitalism.* London, 1978.

Harkness, Georgia. *John Calvin: The Man and His Ethics.* New York, 1931.

Haverkamp-Begemann, Egbert. "The State of Research in Northern Baroque Art." *Art Bulletin* 69 (1987): 510–19.

Hazelzet, Korine. "De levenstrap als les voor jong en oud." *Jeugd en samenleving* 19 (1989): 680–96.

Hedinger, Bärbel. *Karten in Bildern; zur Ikonographie der Wandkarte in holländischen Interieurgemälden des 17. Jahrhunderts.* Hildesheim, 1986.

Hekma, Gert, and Roodenburg, Herman. "Proloog." In *Soete minne en helsche boosheit; seksuele voorstellingen in Nederland, 1300–1850,* ed. G. Hekma and H. Roodenburg, pp. 7–22. Nijmegen, 1988.

Held, Julius S. "Notes on Jacob Jordaens." *Oud Holland* 80 (1965): 112–22.

"Some Studies of Heads by Flemish and Dutch Seventeenth-Century Artists." *Master Drawings* 23, no. 4 (1985–6): 46–53.

Hill, Christopher. *Society and Puritanism in Pre-Revolutionary England.* New York, 1964.

Hobson, Marian. *The Object of Art: The Theory of Illusion in Eighteenth-Century France.* Cambridge, 1982.

Hof, W. J. op 't. "Willem Teellinck in het licht van zijner schriften (4)." *Documentatieblad Nadere Reformatie* 1 (1977): 105–14.

"Willem Teellinck in het licht van zijner schriften (8)." *Documentatieblad Nadere Reformatie* 2 (1978): 97–105.

Engelse pietistische geschriften in Het Nederlands, 1598–1622. Rotterdam, 1987.

Hoffmann, Julius. *Die 'Hausväterliteratur' und die 'Predigten über den christlichen Hausstand.' Lehre vom Hause und Bildung für das häusliche Leben im 16. 17. und 18. Jahrhundert.* Weinheim, 1959.

Hofrichter, Frima Fox. *Judith Leyster: A Woman Painter in Holland's Golden Age.* Doornspijk, 1989.

Hofstede de Groot, Cornelis. "Eenige schilderijen van weinig bekende Utrechtse schilders." *Oud Holland* 37 (1919): 111–19.

Hokke, Judith. "Affect Was Low, and Hard to Find." *Proceedings Congres balans en perspectief over aard en functie van kennis van het verleden,* vol. 2, pp. 675–87. Utrecht, 1986.

" 'Mijn alderliefste Jantielief'; Vrouw en gezin in de Republiek: regentenvrouwen en hun relaties." *Jaarboek voor vrouwengeschiedenis* 8 (1987): 45–73.

Hollstein, F. W. H. *Dutch and Flemish Etchings, Engravings and Woodcuts ca. 1450–1700*, vols. 1–. Amsterdam, 1949–.

German Engravings, Etchings and Woodcuts ca. 1400–1700, vols. 1–. Amsterdam, 1954–.

Honig, Elizabeth Alice. "An Enterprise of Describing? Svetlana Alpers' Art Historical Strategies." *Theoretische geschiedenis* 17 (1990): 33–44.

Houlbrooke, Ralph A. *The English Family, 1450–1700*. London, 1984.

Howell, Martha C. *Women, Production, and Patriarchy in Late Medieval Cities*. Chicago, 1986.

Hull, Suzanne W. *Chaste Silent & Obedient: English Books for Women, 1475–1640*. San Marino, 1982.

Hulst, R.-A. d'. *Jacob Jordaens*. Trans. P. S. Falla. Ithaca, N.Y., 1982.

Israel, Jonathan I. *Dutch Primacy in World Trade, 1585–1740*. Oxford, 1989.

Johnson, James Turner. *A Society Ordained by God: English Puritan Marriage Doctrine in the First Half of the Seventeenth Century*. Nashville, 1970.

Jongejan, Marlies. "Dienstboden in de Zeeuwse steden, 1650–1800." *Spiegel Historiael* 19 (1984): 214–21.

Jongh, Eddy de. *Zinne- en minnebeelden in de schilderkunst van de zeventiende eeuw*. N.p. (Amsterdam), 1967.

"Erotica in vogelperspectief; de dubbelzinnigheid van een reeks 17de eeuwse genrevoorstellingen." *Simiolus* 3 (1968–9): 22–74.

"Realisme en schijnrealisme in de Hollandse schilderkunst van de zeventiende eeuw." In Exhib. cat. Brussels, *Rembrandt en zijn tijd*, pp. 143–94. Paleis voor Schone Kunsten, 1971.

"Grape Symbolism in Paintings of the 16th and 17th Centuries." *Simiolus* 7 (1974): 166–91.

"Pearls of Virtue and Pearls of Vice." *Simiolus* 8 (1975–6): 69–97.

"Inleiding." In Exhib. cat. *Tot lering en vermaak; betekenissen van Hollandse genrevoorstellingen uit de zeventiende eeuw*, pp. 14–28. Amsterdam (Rijksmuseum), 1976.

"Bol vincet amorum." *Simiolus* 12 (1981–2): 147–61.

"The Interpretation of Still-Life Paintings: Possibilities and Limits." In exhib. cat. *Still-life in the Age of Rembrandt*, pp. 27–37. Auckland (Auckland City Art Gallery), 1982.

"Review of Svetlana Alpers, *The Art of Describing: Dutch Art in the Seventeenth Century*." *Simiolus* 14 (1984): 51–9.

"The Interpretation of Genre Paintings: Possibilities and Limits." Unpublished lecture given at the symposium *Images of the World: Dutch Genre Painting in its Historical Context*. London, Royal Academy, 1984.

"De bijl en de wortels (Review of Jan Baptist Bedaux, *The Reality of Symbols: Studies in the Iconology of Netherlandish Art, 1400–1800*)." *N. R. C. Handelsblad (Culturele Supplement)*, September 7, 1990, 6.

Jongh, E. de, and Vinken, P. J. "Frans Hals als voortzetter van een emblematische traditie." *Oud Holland* 76 (1961): 117–52.

Judson, J. R. *Dirck Barendsz, 1534–1592*. Amsterdam, 1970.

Kauffman, Hans. "Die Fünf Sinne in der niederländischen Malerei des 17. Jahrhunderts." In *Kunstgeschichtliche Studien. Festschrift für Dagobert Frey*, pp. 133–57. Breslau, 1943.

Kaufman, Gloria. "Juan Luis Vives on the Education of Women." *Signs: A Journal of Women in Culture and Society* 3 (1977–8): 891–6.

Keersmaekers, A. A. "Drie Amsterdamse liedboeken, 1602–1615. Doorbraak van de renaissance." *Nieuwe Taalgids* 74 (1981): 121–33.

Wandelend in den nieuwen lust-hof; studie over een Amsterdams liedboek 1602–(1604)–1607–(1610). Nijmegen, 1985.

Kelly-Gadol, Joan. "The Social Relation of the Sexes: Methodological Implications of Women's History." *Signs: A Journal of Women in Culture and Society* 1 (1976): 809–23.

Kelso, Ruth. *Doctrine for the Lady of the Renaissance*. Urbana, Ill., 1956.

Kettering, Alison McNeil. *The Dutch Arcadia: Pastoral Art and Its Audience during the Golden Age*. Montclair N.J., 1983.

Drawings from the Ter Borch Studio Estate. The Hague, 1988.

"Gerard ter Borch's Ladies in Satin." *Art History* 16 (1993): 95–124.

Keyes, George. S. *Esaias van den Velde, 1587–1630*. Doornspijk, 1984.

Keyszelitz, Robert. *Der "clavis interpretandi" in der holländischen Malerei des 17. Jahrhunderts*. Ph.D. dissertation, Ludwig-Maximilians-Universität, Munich, 1956.

Klemm, Christian. *Joachim von Sandrart; Kunst-Werke u. Lebens-Lauf*. Berlin, 1986.

Klibansky, Raymond; Panofsky, Erwin; and Saxl, Fritz. *Saturn and Melancholy: Studies in the History of Natural Philosophy, Religion, and Art.* London, 1964.

Kloek, Els. "De Reformatie als thema van vrouwengeschiedenis." *Jaarboek voor Vrouwengeschiedenis* 4 (1983): 106–49.

Gezinshistorici over vrouwen; een overzicht van het werk van gezinshistorici en de betekenis daarvan voor de vrouwen geschiedenis. 4th ed. Amsterdam, 1989.

Koerner, Joseph Leo. "Review of Keith Moxey, *Peasants, Warriors, and Wives: Popular Imagery in the Reformation.*" *Art Bulletin* 73 (1991): 144–9.

Kooij, Cora van. *Van de oude mensen vroeger en nu; over de geschiedenis van de ouderdom en de zorg voor oude mensen.* Deventer, 1987.

Koorn, Florence. "Illegitimiteit en eergevoel; Ongehuwde moeders in Twente in de achttiende eeuw." *Jaarboek voor vrouwensgeschiedenis* 8 (1987): 74–98.

Kruithof, B. "Opvoedingsadviezen van Cats tot Beets; continuïteit en verscheidenheid." In *Textes du colloque, Enseignement & éducation dans les Pays-Bas au dix-huitième siècle,* pp. 169–78. Doesburg, 1982.

Kubler, George. "Towards a Reductive Theory of Visual Style." In *Ars Auro Prior; Studia Ioanni Bialostocki Sexagenario Dicata,* pp. 21–6. Warsaw, 1981.

Kunzle, David. *The Early Comic Strip: Narrative Strips and Picture Stories in the European Broadsheet from ca. 1450 to 1825.* Berkeley, 1973.

Kuretsky, Susan Donahue. *The Paintings of Jacob Ochtervelt (1634–1682).* Montclair N.J., 1979.

Land, Norman E. "Titian's *Martyrdom of St Peter Martyr* and the 'Limitations' of Ekphrastic Art Criticism." *Art History* 13 (1990): 293–317.

Larsen, Erik. *Calvinistic Economy and 17th-Century Dutch Art.* Lawrence, Kans., 1979.

Lasius, Angelika. *Quiringh Gerritsz. van Brekelenkam.* Ph.D. dissertation, Georg-August-Universität, Göttingen, 1987.

Laslett, Peter, and Wall, Richard, eds. *Household and Family in Past Time.* Cambridge, 1972.

Lee, Rensselaer. *Ut Pictura Poesis: The Humanistic Theory of Painting.* (First published in 1940.) New York, 1967.

Leites, Edmund. "The Duty to Desire: Love, Friendship, and Sexuality in Some Puritan Theories of Marriage." *Journal of Social History* 15 (1982): 383–408.

Leuker, Maria-Theresia, and Roodenburg, Herman. " 'Die dan hare wyven laten afweyen'; overspel, eer en schande in de zeventiende eeuw." In *Soete minne en helsche boosheit; seksuele voorstellingen in Nederland, 1300–1850,* ed. G. Hekma and H. Roodenburg, pp. 61–84. Nijmegen, 1988.

Levey, Santina. *Lace: A History.* London, 1983.

Liedtke, Walter. *The Royal Horse and Rider: Painting, Sculpture and Horsemanship, 1500–1800.* New York, 1989.

Linde, S. van der. *Jean Taffin.* Amsterdam 1982.

Logan, A. M. *The Cabinet of the Brothers Gerard and Jan Reyst,* Amsterdam, 1979.

Lowenthal, Anne Walter. *Joachim Wtewael and Dutch Mannerism.* Doornspijk, 1986a.

"Response to Peter Hecht." *Simiolus* 16 (1986b): 188–90.

Lugt, Frits. *École nationale supérieure des beaux-arts. Inventaire général des écoles du Nord.* vol. 1. Paris, 1950.

Luijten, H. " 'Swiren vol leer, amblemsche wijs geduijt'; een opmerkelijk zeventiende-eeuws poëzie-album van Gesina ter Borch." *Bulletin van het Rijksmuseum* 36 (1988): 315–42.

Mace, D. T. " '*Ut pictura poesis*': Dryden, Poussin and the Parallel of Poetry and Painting in the Seventeenth Century." In *Encounters: Essays on Literature and the Visual Arts,* ed. J. D. Hunt, pp. 58–81. London, 1971.

Macfarlane, Alan. *The Family Life of Ralph Josselin: A Seventeenth-Century Clergyman.* Cambridge, 1970.

Maclaren, Neil. *The National Gallery Catalogues: The Dutch School.* London, 1960.

Maclean, Ian. *The Renaissance Notion of Women.* Cambridge, 1980.

Mahon, Dennis. "Notes on the 'Dutch Gift' to Charles II: I." *Burlington Magazine* 91 (1949a): 303–5.

"Notes on the 'Dutch Gift' to Charles II: II." *Burlington Magazine* 91 (1949b): 349–50.

Manke, Ilse. *Emanuel de Witte, 1617–1692.* Amsterdam, 1963.

Marrow, James H. "Symbol and Meaning in Northern European Art of the Late Middle Ages and Early Renaissance." *Simiolus* 16 (1986): 150–69.

Marshall-Wyntjes, Sherrin. "Survivors and Status: Widowhood and Family in the Early Modern

Netherlands." *Journal of Family History* 7 (1982): 396–405.

Marshall, Sherrin. *The Dutch Gentry, 1500–1650: Family, Faith and Fortune.* Westport, 1987.

Martin, W. *Gerard Dou.* Trans. C. Bell. London, 1902.

Gerard Dou (*Klassiker der Kunst.* vol. 24). Stuttgart, 1913.

Marvick, Elizabeth Wirth. "Nature Versus Nature: Patterns and Trends in Seventeenth-Century French Child-Rearing." In *The History of Childhood,* ed. L. de Mause, pp. 259–301. New York, 1974.

McGrath, Elizabeth. "Rubens's 'Susanna and the Elders' and Moralizing Inscriptions on Prints." In *Wort und Bild in der niederländischen Kunst und Literatur des 16. und 17. Jahrhunderts,* ed. J. Vekeman and J. Müller Hofstede, pp. 73–90. Erfstadt, 1984.

Meertens, Pieter Jacobus. *Letterkundig leven in Zeeland in de zestiende en de eerste helft der zeventiende eeuw.* Amsterdam, 1943.

Merrill, T. F., ed. *William Perkins, 1558–1602: English Puritanist.* Nieuwkoop, 1966.

Meyer, Maurits de. *De volks- en kinderprent in de Nederlanden van de 15e tot de 20e eeuw.* Amsterdam, 1962.

Miedema, Hessel. "Over het realisme in de Nederlandse schilderkunst van de zeventiende eeuw." *Oud Holland* 89 (1975): 2–18.

"Realism and Comic Mode: The Peasant." *Simiolus* 9 (1977): 205–19.

"Feestende boeren – lachende dorpers." *Bulletin van het Rijksmuseum* 29 (1981a): 191–213.

Kunst, kunstenaar en kunstwerk bij Karel van Mander; een analyse van zijn levensbeschrijvingen. Alphen aan den Rijn, 1981b.

"Tekst en afbeelding als bronnen bij historisch onderzoek." In *Wort und Bild in der niederländischen Kunst und Literatur des 16. und 17. Jahrhunderts,* ed. J. Vekeman and J. Müller-Hofstede, pp. 7–16. Erfstadt, 1984.

"Philips Angels *Lof der schilderkunst.*" *Oud Holland* 103 (1989): 181–222.

"Review of Jan Baptist Bedaux, *The Reality of Symbols: Studies in the Iconology of Netherlandish Art, 1400–1800.*" *Oud Holland* 105 (1991): 69–74.

Minois, Georges. *History of Old Age: From Antiquity to the Renaissance.* Trans. S. H. Tenison. Chicago, 1989.

Mirimonde, A. P. de. "Les sujets musicaux chez Vermeer de Delft." *Gazette des Beaux-Arts* 57 (1961): 29–52.

Möbius, Helga. "Die Moralisierung des Körpers; Frauenbilder und Männerwünsche im frühneuzeitlichen Holland." In *Frauen. Bilder. Männer. Mythen,* ed. I. Barta et al., pp. 69–83. Berlin, 1987.

Moiso-Diekamp, Cornelia. *Das Pendant in der holländischen Malerei des 17. Jahrhunderts.* Frankfurt am Main, 1987.

Mol, Hans de. " 'Het huwelyck is goddelyck van aart, wanneer men tsaam uyt reine liefde paart'; kerkelijke opvattingen over vrijen en trouwen." In Exhib. cat. Apeldoorn, *Kent, en versint, eer datje mint; vrijen en trouwen 1500–1800,* pp. 85–120. Historisch Museum Marialust, 1989.

Mook, Bertha. *The Dutch Family in the 17th & 18th Centuries.* Ottawa, 1977.

Moquette, H. C. H. *De vrouw.* 2 vols. Amsterdam, 1915.

Morgan, Edmund S. *The Puritan Family: Religion and Domestic Relations in Seventeenth-Century New England.* 3d revised ed. New York, 1966.

Mortier, Bianca M. "De handschoen in de huwelijkssymboliek van de zeventiende eeuw." *Bulletin van het Rijksmuseum* 32 (1984): 189–201.

Moxey, Keith. "Interpreting Pieter Aertsen: The Problem of 'Hidden Symbolism.' " *Nederlands Kunsthistorisch Jaarboek* 40 (1989a): 29–39.

Peasants, Warriors, and Wives: Popular Imagery in the Reformation. Chicago, 1989b.

Mukarovsky, Jan. "Art as Semiological Fact" (1934). In *Calligram: Essays in New Art History from France,* ed. N. Bryson, pp. 1–7. Cambridge, 1988.

Muller, F. *De Nederlandsche geschiedenis in platen.* 4 vols. Amsterdam, 1863–82.

Muller, Sheila D. *Charity in the Dutch Republic: Pictures of Rich and Poor for Charitable Institutions.* Ann Arbor, Mich., 1985.

Müller-Hofstede, Justus. " 'Wort und Bild': Fragen zu Signifikanz und Realität in der holländischen Malerei des 17. Jahrhunderts." In *Wort und Bild in der niederländischen Kunst und Literatur des 16. und 17. Jahrhunderts,* ed. J. Vekeman and J. Müller-Hofstede, pp. ix–xxiii. Erfstadt, 1984.

Naumann, Otto. "The Lesson (Reattributed)." In

Exhib. cat. Washington, D.C., *The William Clark Collection*, pp. 68–71. Corcoran Gallery of Art, 1978.

Frans van Mieris the Elder (1635–1681). 2 vols. Doornspijk, 1981a.

"Gerard Dou and Van Tol." *Burlington Magazine* 123 (1981b): 617–18.

Nauwelaerts, M.A. "Opvoeding van meisjes in de 16de eeuw." *Spiegel Historiael* 10 (1975): 130–7.

"De meisjesopvoeding volgens Juan Luis Vives." In *Liber amicorum Professor Dr Victor d'Espallier*, pp. 117–42. Louvain, 1976.

Nicolson, Benedict. *The International Caravaggesque Movement: Lists of Pictures by Caravaggio and His Followers Throughout Europe from 1590–1630*. Oxford, 1979.

Nochlin, Linda. *The Politics of Vision: Essays on Nineteenth-Century Art and Society*. New York, 1989.

"Women, Art, and Power." In *Visual Theory; Painting and Interpretation*, ed. M. A. Holly, N. Bryson, and K. Moxey, pp. 13–46. New York, 1991.

Noël, J. M. J. L. "L'école des filles et la philosophie du mariage dans les Pays-Bas du XVIe et du XVIIe siècles." In *Enseignement & éducation dans les Pays-Bas au dix-huitième siècle. Textes du colloque, Doesburg 1982*, pp. 137–54. Amsterdam, 1983.

"Education morale des filles et des garçons dans les Pays Bas au 16e siècle: deux manuels pédagogiques." In *Women and Men in Spiritual Culture, XIV–XVII Centuries: A Meeting of South and North*, ed. E. Schulte van Kessel, pp. 93–109. The Hague, 1986.

Noordam, D.J. "Volmaakt geluk? Vier eeuwen huwelijk en gezin in Nederland." In *Een kind onder het hart; verloskunde, volksgeloof, gezin, seksualiteit en moraal vroeger en nu*, ed. R. Kistemaker, pp. 85–126. Amsterdam, 1987a.

"Lust, last en plezier: vier eeuwen seksualiteit in Nederland." In *Een kind onder het hart; verloskunde, volksgeloof, gezin, seksualiteit en moraal vroeger en nu*, ed. R. Kistemaker, pp. 127–70. Amsterdam, 1987b.

Olyslager, Hanneke. "Wellust en deugd; het thema Hercules op de tweesprong in twee 17de eeuwse allegoriën van Theodoor van Thulden." *Kunstlicht* 16 (1985): 20–5.

Ozment, Steven. *When Fathers Ruled: Family Life in Reformation Europe*. Cambridge, Mass., 1983.

"Luther and the Family." *Harvard Library Bulletin* 32 (1984): 36–53.

Pace, Claire. "Virtuoso to Connoisseur: Some Seventeenth-Century English Responses to the Visual Arts." *Seventeenth Century* 2 (1987): 167–88.

Pächt, Otto. "Panofsky's 'Early Netherlandish Painting'-II." *Burlington Magazine* 98 (1956): 267–79.

Panofsky, Erwin. " 'Imago Pietatis.' Ein Beitrag zur Typengeschichte des 'Schmerzensmanns' und der 'Maria Mediatrix'." In *Festschrift für Max J. Friedländer zum 60. Geburstage*, pp. 261–308. Leipzig, 1927.

"Jan van Eyck's *Arnolfini* Portrait." *Burlington Magazine* 64 (1934): 117–27.

Pauw-De Veen, Lydia de. *De begrippen "schilder," "schilderij," en "schilderen" in de zeventiende eeuw*. Brussels, 1969.

Pearson, Lu Emily. *Elizabethans at Home*. Stanford, Calif., 1957.

Peeters, H. F. M. *Kind en jeugdige in het begin van de moderne tijd (ca. 1500–ca. 1650)*. Antwerp, 1966.

"Vijf eeuwen gezin in West-Europa." In *Vijf eeuwn gezinsleven; liefde, huwelijk en opvoeding in Nederland*, ed. H. Peeters, L. Dresden-Coenders, and T. Brandenbarg, pp. 11–30. Nijmegen, 1988.

Planque, P. A. de. *Valcooch's regel der duytsche schoolmeesters; bijdrage tot de kennis van het schoolwezen in de zestiende eeuw*. Groningen, 1926.

Pluym, Willem van der. *Vijf eeuwen binnenhuis en meubels in Nederland, 1450–1950*. Amsterdam, 1954.

Pol, Lotte C. van de. "Op zoek naar vrouwen in de 17[e] eeuw." In *Een tipje van de sluier; vrouwengeschiedenis in Nederland*, pp. 61–3. Amsterdam, 1978.

"Vrouwencriminaliteit in de Gouden Eeuw." *Ons Amsterdam* 34 (1982): 266–8.

Vrouwencriminaliteit en prostitutie in de tweede helft der 17e eeuw in Amsterdam. The Hague, 1983.

"Seksualiteit tussen middleeuwen en moderne tijd." In *Vijf eeuwen gezinsleven; liefde, huwelijk en opvoeding in Nederland*, ed. H. Peeters, L. Dresden-Coenders, and T. Brandenbarg, pp. 163–93. Nijmegen, 1988a.

"Beeld en werkelijkheid van de prostitutie in de zeventiende eeuw." In *Soete minne en helsche boosheit; seksuele voorstellingen in Nederland, 1300–1850*, ed. G. Hekma and H. Roodenburg, pp. 109–44. Nijmegen, 1988b.

Pollock, Linda A. *Forgotten Children: Parent–Child Relations from 1500–1900*. 2d ed. Cambridge, 1985.

Porteman, Karel. *Inleiding tot de Nederlandse emblemataliteratuur*. Groningen, 1977.

"Vondel en de schilderkunst." *Vlaanderen* 172 (1979): 299–305.

"Iets over het literaire realisme in de zeventiende eeuw." *Neerlandica Wratislaviensia* 1 (1983): 99–114.

"Geschreven met de linkerhand? Letteren tegenover schilderkunst in de Gouden Eeuw." In *Historische letterkunde*, ed. M. Spies, pp. 93–113. Groningen, 1984a.

"Nederlandse embleemtheorie; van Marcus Antonius Gillis (1566) tot Jacob Cats (1618)." In *Wort und Bild in der niederländischen Kunst und Literatur des 16. und 17. Jahrhunderts*, eds. J. Vekeman and J. Müller-Hofstede, pp. 1–6. Erfstadt, 1984b.

Joachim von Sandrart; Joost van den Vondel; Caspar Barlaeus; de maanden van het jaar. Wommelgen, 1987.

Porteman, Karel, and Brems, Hugo. *Poëzie en beeldende kunst; een thematische bloemlezing uit de Nederlandse poëzie vanaf de 16e eeuw tot heden*. Louvain, 1979.

Posthumus, N. N. *De geschiedenis van de Leidsche lakenindustrie*. 6 vols. The Hague, 1910–22.

Powell, Chilton L. *English Domestic Relations, 1487–1653*. 3d ed. (First published in 1917.) New York, 1972.

Praz, Mario. *Studies in Seventeenth-Century Imagery*. 2d ed. Rome, 1964.

Raben, Remco, and Vermeij, Roos. "Wortelloof en cultuurhistorie; Kunstopvattingen van Peter Hecht en Eddy de Jongh." *Leidschrift* 6, no. 3 (1990): 41–58.

Raupp, Hans-Joachim. "Ansätze zu einer Theorie der Genremalerei in den Niederlanden im 17. Jahrhundert." *Zeitschrift für Kunstgeschichte* 46 (1983): 401–18.

Untersuchungen zu Künstlerbildnis und Künstlerdarstellung in den Niederlanden im 17. Jahrhundert. Hildesheim, 1984.

Regin, Deric. *Traders, Artists, Burghers: A Cultural History of Amsterdam in the 17th Century*. Assen, 1976.

Regteren Altena, I. Q. van. *Jacques de Gheyn: Three Generations*. 3 vols. The Hague, 1983.

Renger, Konrad. "Zur Forschungsgeschichte der Bilddeutung in der holländischen Malerei." In Exhib. cat. Brunswick, *Die Sprache der Bilder*, pp. 34–8. Herzog Anton Ulrich-Museum, 1978.

"Verhältnis von Text und Bild in der Graphik (Beobachtungen zu Missverhältnissen)." In *Wort und Bild in der niederländischen Kunst und Literatur des 16. und 17. Jahrhunderts*, ed. J. Vekeman and J. Müller-Hofstede, pp. 151–61. Erfstadt, 1984.

Riemens, K. J. *Esquisse historique de l'enseignment du Francais en Hollande de XVI siècle au XIXe siècle*. Leiden, 1919.

Ringbom, Sixten. *Icon to Narrative: The Rise of the Dramatic Close-Up in Fifteenth-Century Devotional Painting*. Abo, 1965.

Robinson, Franklin. *Gabriel Metsu (1629–1667): A Study of His Place in Dutch Genre Painting of the Golden Age*. New York, 1974.

Robinson, William W. "The *Eavesdroppers* and Related Paintings by Nicolaes Maes." In *Höllandische Genremalerei im 17. Jahrhundert. Symposium Berlin 1984*, ed. H. Bock and T. W. Gaehtgens, pp. 283–313. Berlin, 1987.

Roever, N. de. *Van vrijen en trouwen*. Haarlem, 1891.

Roodenburg, Herman. "The Autobiography of Isabella de Moerloose: Sex, Childrearing and Popular Belief in Seventeenth Century Holland." *Journal of Social History* 18 (1985): 517–40.

Onder censuur; de kerkelijke tucht in de gereformeerde gemeente van Amsterdam, 1578–1700 (proefschrift, Vrije Universiteit te Amsterdam). Hilversum, 1990.

Roose, Lode. *"En is 't de liefde niet," Het Nederlandse sonnet in de zestiende en zeventiende eeuw*. Leiden, 1971.

Rose, Peter G., ed. and trans. *The Sensible Cook: Dutch Foodways in the Old and New World*. Syracuse, N.Y., 1989.

Rudolph, Hermann. " 'Vanitas.' Die Bedeutung mittelalterlicher und humanistischer Bildinhalte in der niederländischen Malerei des 17. Jahrhunderts." *Festschrift Wilhelm Pinder zum sechzigsten Geburtstage*, pp. 405–31. Leipzig, 1938.

Salomon, Nanette. *Dreamers, Idlers, and Other Dozers: Aspects of Sleep in Dutch Art.* Ph.D. dissertation, Institute of Fine Arts, New York University, New York, 1984.

Schama, Simon. "Wives and Wantons: Versions of Womanhood in 17th Century Dutch Art." *Oxford Art Journal* 3 (1980): 5–13.

"The Dutch Masters' Revenge" (Review of Svetlana Alpers, *The Art of Describing: Dutch Art in the Seventeenth Century*). *New Republic*, May 14, 1984, 25–31.

The Embarrassment of Riches: An Interpretation of Dutch Culture in the Golden Age. New York, 1987.

Schapiro, Meyer. "Style" (1953). In *Aesthetics Today*, ed. M. Philipson, pp. 81–128. Cleveland, 1961.

Scheltema, Jacobus. *Volksgebruiken der Nederlanders, bij het vrijen en trouwen.* Utrecht, 1832.

Scheurleer, D. F. *Nederlandsche liedboeken.* The Hague, 1912.

Schipper-Van Lottum, M. G. A. "Een naijmantgen met een naijcussen." *Antiek* 10 (1975): 137–63.

Over merklappen gesproken . . . de geschiedenis van de Nederlandse merklop, vooral belicht vanuit Noord- Holland. Amsterdam, 1980.

Schneede, Uwe. "Gabriel Metsu und der holländische Realismus." *Oud Holland* 83 (1968): 44–61.

Schnucker, R. W. "The English Puritans and Pregnancy, Delivery and Breast Feeding." *History of Childhood Quarterly* 1 (1973–4): 637–58.

Schochet, Gordon J. "Patriarchalism, Politics and Mass Attitudes in Stuart England." *Historical Journal* 12 (1969): 413–41.

Patriarchalism in Political Thought. New York, 1975.

Schoneveld, Cornelis W. *Intertraffic of the Mind: Studies in Seventeenth-Century Anglo-Dutch Translations with a Check List of Books Translated from English into Dutch, 1600–1700.* Leiden, 1983.

Schotel, G. D. J. *Het Oud-Hollandsch huisgezin der zeventiende eeuw.* Haarlem, 1867–8.

Schwartz, Frederic. " 'The Motions of the Countenance': Rembrandt's Early Portraits and the *Tronie*." *RES* 17–18 (1989): 94–116.

Scott, Mary Ann. *Dutch, Flemish, and German Paintings in the Cincinnati Art Museum.* Cincinnati, 1987.

Shorter, Edward. *The Making of the Modern Family.* London, 1976.

Siegel, Paul N. "Milton and the Humanist Attitude Toward Women." *Journal of the History of Ideas* 11 (1950): 42–53.

Silver, Larry. "Step-Sister of the Muses: Painting as a Liberal Art and Sister Art." In *Articulate Images: The Sister Arts from Hogarth to Tennyson*, ed. R. Wendorf, pp. 36–69. Minneapolis, 1983.

Simons, Patricia. "Women in Frames: The Eye, the Gaze, the Profile in Renaissance Portraiture." *History Workshop* 25 (1988): 4–30.

Slatkes, Leonard J. *Vermeer and His Contemporaries.* New York, 1981.

Sluijter, Eric Jan. "Niet Gysbert van der Kuyl uit Gouda, maar Gerard van Kuijl uit Gorinchem; Een identiteitsverwisseling sinds Houbraken." *Oud Holland* 91 (1977): 166–95.

De 'heydensche fabulen' in de Noordnederlandse schilderkunst circa 1590–1670 (proefschrift, Rijksuniversiteit te Leiden). Enschede, 1986.

"Belering en verhulling? Enkele 17de-eeuwse teksten over de schilderkunst en de iconologische benadering van Noordnederlandse schilderijen uit deze periode." *De zeventiende eeuw* 4 (1988a): 3–28.

"Schilders van 'cleyne, subtile ende curieuse dingen'; Leidse 'fijnschilders' in contemporaine bronnen." In Exhib. cat. Leiden, *Leidse Fijnschilders; van Gerrit Dou tot Frans van Mieris de Jonge, 1630–1760*, pp. 15–55. Stedelijk Museum De Lakenhal, 1988b.

"Hoe realistisch is de Noordnederlandse schilderkunst van de zeventiende eeuw? De problemen van een vraagstelling." *Leidschrift* 6, no. 3 (1990): 5–39.

"Over fijnschilders en 'betekenis'; Naar aanleiding van Peter Hecht, *De Hollandse fijnschilders*." *Oud Holland* 105 (1991): 50–63.

Smilde, H. *Jacob Cats in Dordrecht: leven en werken gedurende de jaren, 1623–1636.* Groningen, 1938.

Smith, David R. *Masks of Wedlock: Seventeenth-Century Dutch Marriage Portraiture.* Ann Arbor, Mich., 1982.

"Irony and Civility: Notes on the Convergence of Genre and Portraiture in Seventeenth-Century Dutch Painting." *Art Bulletin* 69 (1987): 407–30.

Smith, Steven R. "Religion and the Conception of Youth in Seventeenth-Century England." *History of Childhood Quarterly* 2 (1974–5): 493–516.

Snoep, D. P. "Een 17de eeuws liedboek met tekeningen van Gerard ter Borch de Oude en Pieter en Roeland van Laer." *Simiolus* 3 (1968–9): 77–134.

Snoep-Reitsma, Ella. "Chardin and the Bourgeois Ideals of His Time." *Nederlands Kunsthistorisch Jaarboek* 24 (1973a): 147–243.

"De waterzuchtige vrouw van Gerard Dou en de betekenis van de lampetkan." In *Album amicorum J. G. van Gelder,* pp. 285–92. Utrecht, 1973b.

Spierenburg, Pieter. "Verkering, huwelijk en gezin in historisch perspectief; thema's en discussies uit het onderzoeksgebied, met de nadruk op de periode, 1500–1850." *Jeugd en samenleving* 19 (1989): 614–27.

Spies, Marijke. "Charlotte de Huybert en het gelijk; de geleerde en de werkende vrouw in de zeventiende eeuw." *Literatuur: Tijdschrift over Nederlandse Letterkunde* 3 (1986): 339–50.

"Zoals de ouden zongen, lazen de jongen; over de overgang van zang- naar leescultuur in de eerste helft van de zeventiende eeuw." In *Het woord aan de lezer; zeven literatuurhistorische verkenningen,* ed. W. van den Berg and J. Stouten, pp. 89–109. Groningen, 1987.

Stallybrass, Peter. "Patriarchal Territories: The Body Enclosed." In *Rewriting the Renaissance: The Discourses of Sexual Difference in Early Modern Europe,* ed. M. W. Ferguson et al., pp. 123–42. Chicago, 1986.

Stearns, Peter N., and Stearns, Carol Z. "Emotionology: Clarifying the History of Emotions and Emotional Standards." *American Historical Review* 90 (1985): 813–29.

Stechow, Wolfgang. "Lusus Laetititaeque Modus." *Art Quarterly* 35 (1972): 165–75.

Stechow, Wolfgang, and Comer, Christopher. "The History of the Term *Genre.*" *Allen Memorial Art Museum Bulletin* 33 (1975–6): 89–94.

Stighelen, Katlijne van der. *Anna Maria van Schurman (1607–1678) of "Hoe hooge dat een maeght kan in de konsten stijgen."* Louvain, 1987.

Stoeffler, F. Ernst. *The Rise of Evangelical Pietism.* Leiden, 1965.

Stone, Lawrence. *The Family, Sex and Marriage in England, 1500–1800.* New York, 1977.

"Family History in the 1980s: Past Achievements and Future Trends." *Journal of Interdisciplinary History* 12 (1981): 51–87.

Stone-Ferrier, Linda A. "Petty Ornaments and Clever Images: Interpretations of Dutch Art." In Exhib. cat. Lawrence, *Dutch Prints of Daily Life,* pp. 3–35. Spencer Museum of Art, 1983.

Images of Textiles: The Weave of Seventeenth-Century Dutch Art and Society. Ann Arbor, Mich., 1985.

"Gabriel Metsu's *Vegetable Market in Amsterdam:* Seventeenth-Century Dutch Market Paintings and Horticulture." *Art Bulletin* 71 (1989): 428–52.

Straten, Evert van. *Koud tot op het bot; de verbeelding van de winter in de zestiende en zeventiende eeuw in Nederlanden.* The Hague, 1977.

Strauss, Walter. *Hendrick Goltzius, 1558–1617: The Complete Engravings and Woodcuts.* 2 vols. New York, 1977.

Strauss, Walter, general ed. *The Illustrated Bartsch.* vols. 1–. New York, 1973–.

Strauss, Walter L., and Alexander, Dorothy. *The German Single-Leaf Woodcut, 1600–1700.* 2 vols. New York, 1977.

Stumpel, Jeroen. "Review of Svetlana Alpers, *The Art of Describing: Dutch Art in the Seventeenth Century.*" *Burlington Magazine* 126 (1984): 580–1.

Sullivan, Scott A. *The Dutch Gamepiece.* Totowa, 1984.

Sumowski, Werner. *Gemälde der Rembrandt-Schüler.* vols. 1–. Lindau, 1983–.

Sutton, Peter C. *Pieter de Hooch.* Ithaca, 1980.

"Jan Steen." *Bulletin of the Philadelphia Museum of Art* 78, nos. 337–8 (Winter 1982–Spring 1983): 1–64.

"Masters of Dutch Genre Painting." In Exhib. cat. Philadelphia, *Masters of Seventeenth-Century Dutch Genre Painting,* pp. xiii–lxvi. Philadelphia Museum of Art, 1984.

Northern European Paintings in the Philadelphia Museum of Art. Philadelphia, 1990.

Tawney, R. H. *Religion and the Rise of Capi-*

talism. 3d ed. (First published in 1926.) Gloucester, 1962.
Telle, Emile V. *Érasme de Rotterdam et le septième sacrement.* Geneva, 1954.
Thiel, P. J. J. van. "Michael van Musscher's vroegste werk naar aanleiding van zijn portret van het echtpaar Comans." *Bulletin van het Rijksmuseum* 17 (1969): 3–35.
"*Poor Parents, Rich Children* and *Family Saying Grace:* Two Related Aspects of the Iconography of Late Sixteenth and Seventeenth-Century Dutch Domestic Morality." *Simiolus* 17 (1987): 90–149.
"Catholic Elements in Seventeenth-Century Dutch Painting, Apropos of a Children's Portrait by Thomas de Keyser." *Simiolus* 20 (1990–1): 39–62.
Thomas, Keith. "Women and the Civil War Sects." *Past and Present* 13 (1958): 42–62.
Thornton, Peter. *Seventeenth-Century Interior Decoration in England, France and Holland.* 4th ed. New Haven, 1983.
Todd, Margo. *Christian Humanism and the Puritan Social Order.* Cambridge, 1987.
Troyansky, David G. *Old Age in the Old Regime: Image and Experience in Eighteenth-Century France.* Ithaca, 1989.
Valentiner, W. R. *Nicolaes Maes.* Stuttgart, 1924.
Pieter de Hooch; des Meisters Gemälde (Klassiker der Kunst, vol. 35). Stuttgart, 1929.
Vandenbroeck, Paul. "Aspekten van de kinderikonografie in de oude Nederlanden (voornamelijk 16e–17e eeuw)." In Exhib. cat. Brussels, *Het kind in onze kunst van 1800 tot heden,* pp. 17–63. Galerij ASLK, 1983–4.
Vann, Richard T. "Toward a New Lifestyle: Women in Preindustrial Capitalism." In *Becoming Visible: Women in European History,* ed. R. Bridenthal and C. Koonz, pp. 192–216. Boston, 1977.
Veenstra, Fokke. *Ethiek en moraal bij P. C. Hooft.* Zwolle, 1968.
Veldman, Ilja M. "Seasons, Planets and Temperaments in the Work of Maarten van Heemskerck: Cosmo-Astrological Allegory in Sixteenth-Century Netherlandish Prints." *Simiolus* 11 (1980): 149–76.
"De macht van de planeten over het mensdom in prenten naar Maarten de Vos." *Bulletin van het Rijksmuseum* 31 (1983): 21–53.
"Lessen voor vrouwen; thema's uit de oudheid in de 16de en 17de eeuwse propaganda voor de Christelijke huwelijksmoraal." *Kunstlicht* 15 (1985): 2–9.
"Lessons for Ladies: A Selection of Sixteenth and Seventeenth-Century Dutch Prints." *Simiolus* 16 (1986): 113–27.
Veltman, Kim H. "Review of Svetlana Alpers, *The Art of Describing: Dutch Art in the Seventeenth Century.*" *Kunstchronik* 37 (1984): 262–7.
Vis, Dirck. *Een jonge vrouw geschildert door Govaert Flinck, 1655.* Amsterdam, 1986.
Vries, Lyckle de. *Jan Steen "de kluchtschilder"* (proefschrift, Rijksuniversiteit te Groningen). Groningen, 1977.
"Portraits of People at Work." In *Opstellen voor Hans Locher,* ed. J. de Jong et al., pp. 52–9. Groningen, 1990a.
"Tronies and Other Single Figured Netherlandish Paintings." In *Nederlandse portretten; bijdragen over de portretkunst in de Nederlanden uit de zestiende, zeventiende en achtiende eeuw* (Leids Kunsthistorisch Jaarboek 8, 1989), ed. E. J. Sluijter et al., pp. 185–202. The Hague, 1990b.
Vries, M. de, et al. eds. *Woordenboek der Nederlandsche taal.* vols. 1–. Leiden, 1882–.
Wäscher, Herman. *Das deutsche illustrierte Flugblatt.* 2 vols. N.p., 1955.
Wallace, Ronald S. *Calvin's Doctrine of the Christian Life.* 2d ed. Tyler, 1982.
Warners, J. D. P. "Gewoon, hoog en diep lezen." *Spiegel der Letteren* 11 (1968–9): 191–201.
"Al sietmen de luy men kentse daarom niet." *Spiegel der Letteren* 14 (1972): 113–31.
Weber, Max. *The Protestant Ethic and the Spirit of Capitalism.* Trans. T. Parsons. New York, 1958.
White, Christopher. *The Dutch Pictures in the Collection of Her Majesty the Queen.* Cambridge/New York, 1982.
White, Helen C. *Social Criticism in Popular Religious Literature of the Sixteenth Century.* 3d ed. New York, 1973.
Wiesner, Merry E. "Spinsters and Seamstresses: Women in Cloth and Clothing Production." In *Rewriting the Renaissance: The Discourses of Sexual Difference in Early Modern Europe,* ed. M. W. Ferguson, M. Quilligan, and N. Vickers, pp. 191–205. Chicago, 1986.
Wikman, K. R. V. "Die Einleitung der Ehe. Eine vergleichend ethno-soziologische Untersu-

chung über die Vorstufe der Ehe in den Sitten des Schwedischen Volkstums." *Humaniora* 11 (1937): 1–395.
Wilson, Adrian. "The Infancy of the History of Childhood: An Appraisal of Philippe Ariès." *History and Theory* 19 (1980): 132–53.
Wilson, Stephen. "The Myth of Motherhood a Myth: The Historical View of European Child-Rearing." *Social History* 9 (1984): 181–98.
Wolf, H. C. de. *58 miljoen Nederlanders en hun bejaarden,* vol. 9 in the series *58 miljoen Nederlanders,* pp. 225–52. Amsterdam, 1977.
Wolff, Janet. *The Social Production of Art.* New York, 1981.
Woude, A. M. van der. "Variations in the Size and Structure of the Household in the United Provinces of The Netherlands in the Seventeenth and Eighteenth Centuries." In *Household and Family in Past Time,* ed. P. Laslett and R. Wall, pp. 299–318. Cambridge, 1972.
Wright, Louis B. "William Perkins: Elizabethan Apostle of Practical Divinity." *Huntington Library Quarterly* 3 (1939–40): 171–96.
Middle-Class Culture in Elizabethan England. 3d ed. (First published in 1935.) New York, 1980.
Wrightson, Keith. *English Society, 1580–1680.* New Brunswick, 1982.
Würtenburger, F. *Das holländische Gesellschaftsbild.* Schramberg im Schwarzwald, 1937.
Ypes, C. *Petrarca in de Nederlandse letterkunde.* Amsterdam, 1934.
Zaretsky, Eli. *Capitalism, the Family, and Personal Life.* London, 1973.
Zaunschirm, Thomas. "Affe und Papagei – Mimensis und Sprache in der Kunst." *Kunsthistoriker* 2 (1985): 14–17.
Zimmermann, Elisabeth. "Der schlesische Garn- und Leinenhandel mit Holland im 16. und 17. Jahrhundert." *Economische-Historisch Jaarboek; Bijdragen tot de Economische Geschiedenis van Nederland* 26 (1956): 193–254.

INDEX

(Works of art are listed under the name of the artist.)